ISBN 978-1-331-28058-3
PIBN 10168416

The Itinerary
of
Fynes Moryson

In Four Volumes

Volume II

GLASGOW

PRINTED AT THE UNIVERSITY PRESS BY
ROBERT MACLEHOSE & COMPANY LTD. FOR
JAMES MACLEHOSE AND SONS, PUBLISHERS
TO THE UNIVERSITY OF GLASGOW

MACMILLAN AND CO. LTD.	LONDON
THE MACMILLAN CO.	NEW YORK
THE MACMILLAN CO. OF CANADA	TORONTO
SIMPKIN, HAMILTON AND CO.	LONDON
MACMILLAN AND BOWES	CAMBRIDGE
DOUGLAS AND FOULIS	EDINBURGH

MCMVII

Containing His Ten Yeeres Travell through the Twelve Dominions of Germany, Bohmerland, Sweitzerland, Netherland, Denmarke, Poland, Italy, Turky, France, England, Scotland & Ireland

Written by

VOLUME II

Glasgow
James MacLehose and Sons
Publishers to the University
MCMVII

THE TABLE

PAGE

The Contents of the severall Chapters contained in the Third Booke of the First Part (*Continued*).

THE TABLE

The Contents of the severall Chapters—*Continued.* PAGE

The Contents of the severall Chapters contained in the First Booke of the Second Part.

The Contents of the severall Chapters contained in the Second Booke of the Second Part.

ILLUSTRATIONS

The Second Volume

OF

The Itinerary of Fynes Moryson

Chap. II.

The description of the City of Jerusalem, and the territory thereof.

Am unskilfull in Geography, and much more in the making of Mappes: but according to the faithfull view of my eyes, I will first draw the situation of Jerusalem, and after explaine it, aswell as I can. And first I thinke good to professe that by my journy to this City, I had no thought to expiate any least sinne of mine; much lesse did I hope to merit any grace from God; but when I had once begun to visite forraigne parts, I was so stirred up by emulation and curiosity, as I did never behold any without a kind of sweete envy, who in this kind had dared more then my selfe. Thus affected, I thought no place more worthy to be viewed in the whole world, then this City, where howsoever I gave all divine worship to God, and thought none to be given to the places, yet I confesse that (through the grace of God) the very places strucke me with a religious horrour, and filled my mind prepared to devotion, with holy motions. In like sort I professe, that I will faithfully relate the situation of the City, and the description of the monuments made to me by the Friars, making conscience not to adde or detract, but as neere as I can to use their owne words. Yet doe I not my selfe beleeve all the particulars I write upon their report, neither doe I perswade any man to beleeve them. But for many monuments, the scripture

Jerusalem.

gives credit to them, and it is not probable in so great difference and emulation, (whereof I shall after speake) of Sects of Christians there abiding, and being most apt
[I iii. 218.] to note errours one in another, that any apparant fictions could be admitted: as on the contrary, it is most certaine, that some superstitious inventions (wherewith all the sectes are more or lesse infected) have in time obtained, to be reputed true, and religiously to be beleeved. Howsoever he that conferres the situation of the City and of the monuments, with the holy Scriptures, and with the old ruines of Rome, and other Cities, shall easily discerne what things are necessarily true or false, and what are more or lesse probable.

Jerusalem seated in the same place.

And it will notoriously appeare, that the Citie is now seated in the same place, in which it flourished when our Saviour lived there in the flesh. Neither let any man object to me the prophecies of the fatall and irreparable ruine thereof, which all Divines understand of the Temple to be utterly demolished; and for my part, I would rather admit (if necessitie require) any figurative speech, then I would bee so wicked or so blockish, as not to beleeve the holy Scriptures, or that which I did see with these eyes. Upon the West side, the Citie could never have been more enlarged then now it is, since Mount Calverie (without all doubt) was of old without the walles, which now is inclosed within them, so as rather it appeares the Citie hath been so much inlarged on that side. In like sort on the East side, the Citie is so compassed with the Valley of Jehosephat, and the famous Mount Olivet, as it appeares the City could not that way have been larger then now it is. On the North side I did never reade nor heare any, that described this Citie to have been larger then now it is, yet in respect of huge ruines still remaining there, upon a large Plaine of the highest part of the Citie, if any should confidently affirme that they belonged to the old Citie, for my part I could not gainesay it. From the Plaine of this highest part of the Citie it

Jerusalem now enlarged.

declines by little and little (if you except some little Hilles within the walles) from the North to the East (where the Temple of Salomon is seated upon the lowest part of Mount Moriah) and likewise it declines from the North to the South Gates, whereof the one is called Sterquilinea, of the filth there carried out, the other Præsentationis, because the Virgin Mary entered there, when she presented Christ to the Priest in the Temple, which gates (as the whole Citie) are seated upon Mountaines, yet lower then any other part of the Citie. Upon the higher part of Mount Sion, on the same South side towards the West, lie many ruines of houses, and it is most certaine, that the Tower of David, and other famous houses there, which are now without the walles, were of old inclosed within them, and that the City extended somewhat further towards the South, then now it doth. Yet the Hill of Sion is so compassed with knowne Vallies, and those Vallies with high Mountaines, as this extent could not be great.

The Tower of David.

Jerusalem was of old called Moria (where they write that Adam was created of red earth), & is seated upon Mount Moriah, upon the top wherof towards the North-west is Mount Calvery (where they say that Abraham was ready to sacrifice his sonne Isaac, and where without doubt our Saviour Christ suffered), and in the lowest part of this Mountaine, the Temple of Salomon was seated. The Citie was after called Salem, and thirdly, Jebus, and fourthly Jerusalem, and at this day the Turkes have named it Chutz. It is compassed with stately walles (the like whereof I did never see) of red and blacke stone more then an Elle long, and about halfe an Elle broad. I call them stately, for the antiquitie, wherein for the most part they much excell the Roman walles. I numbred seven Gates. The first of Damasco, (of old called the Gate of Ephraim) on the North side. The second of Saint Stephen on the East side (which of old had the name of the beasts for sacrifice brought in that way.) The third the golden Gate, also on the East side (which

Jerusalem seated upon Mount Moriah.

The Seven gates.

at this day is shut and bricked up.) The fourth the Gate of presentation on the South-side, leading into the Temple of Salomon, but at this day shut up. The fifth Sterquilinea also on the South side, so called of the filth there carried out. The sixth, the Gate of Syon also on the South side, neare that part of Mount Syon, which at this day is without the walles, but this Gate hath been newly built. The seventh of Joppa towards the West also newly built. In generall, the Gates are nothing lesse then fortified, only as it were to terrifie the Christians, who enter at the Gate of Joppa, they have braggingly fortified the same, and planted great Ordinance upon it. And howsoever the Citie seemes strong enough against sudden tumults, yet it is no way able to hold out against a Christian Army well furnished, neither doe the Turkes trust to their Forts, but to their forces in field.

Christians enter at the gate of Joppa.

[I. iii. 219.]

The houses here, and in all parts of Asia that I have seene, are built of Flint stone, very low, onely one storie high, the top whereof is plaine, and plastered, and hath battlements almost a yard high, and in the day time they hide themselves within the chamber under this plastered floare from the Sunne, and after Sunne-set, walke, eate, and sleepe, upon the said plastred floare, where as they walke, each one may see their neighbours sleeping in bed, or eating at table. But as in the beate of the day, they can scarce indure to weare linnen hose, so when the Syren or dew falls at night, they keepe themselves within dores till it be dried up, or else fling some garment over their heads. And with this dew of the night all the fields are moistened, the falling of raine being very rare in these parts towards the Equinoctiall line, and in this place particularly happening onely about the month of October, about which time it falles sometimes with great force by whole pales full. The houses neare the Temple of Salomon, are built with arches into the streete, under which they walke drie, and covered from the Sunne, as likewise the houses are built in that sort, in that part of the Citie, where they shew the house of Herod, in both

The houses built of flint stone.

The Dew falls instead of raine.

which places the way on both sides the streete is raised for those that walke on foote, lying low in the middest for the passage of laded Asses. In other parts the Citie lies uninhabited, there being onely Monasteries of divers Christian Sects, with their Gardens. And by reason of these waste places, and heapes of Flint lying at the dores of the houses, and the low building of them, some streetes seeme rather ruines then dwelling houses, to him that lookes on them neere hand. But to them who behold the Citie from eminent places, and especially from the most pleasant Mount Olivet (abounding with Olives, and the highest of all the Mountaines), the prospect of the Citie, and more specially of the Churches and Monasteries (which are built with elevated Globes covered with brasse, or such glistering mettall) promiseth much more beauty of the whole Citie to the beholders eyes, then indeed it hath. The circuit of the walles containeth some two or three Italian miles.

Parts of the Citie uninhabited.

All the Citizens are either Tailors, Shoomakers, Cookes, or Smiths (which Smiths make their keyes and lockes not of Iron, but of wood), and in generall poore rascall people, mingled of the scumme of divers Nations, partly Arabians, partly Moores, partly the basest inhabitants of neighbour Countries, by which kind of people all the adjoyning Territorie is likewise inhabited. The Jewes in Turky are distinguished from others by red hats, and being practicall, doe live for the most part upon the sea-coasts, and few or none of them come to this Citie, inhabited by Christians that hate them, and which should have no traffique, if the Christian Monasteries were taken away. Finally, the Inhabitants of Jerusalem at this day are as wicked as they were when they crucified our Lord, gladly taking all occasions to use Christians despitefully. They esteemed us Princes, because wee wore gloves, and brought with us shirts, and like necessaries, though otherwise we were most poorely appareled, yet when we went to see the monuments, they sent out their boyes to scorne us, who leaped upon our backes from the higher parts of

The Citizens poore rascall people.

Jewes in Turky weare red hats.

Rude Boyes. the streete, we passing in the lower part, and snatched from us our hats and other things, while their fathers were no lesse ready to doe us all injuries, which we were forced to beare silently and with incredible patience. Hence it was that Robert Duke of Normandy, being sicke, and carried into Jerusalem upon the backs of like rascalls, when he met by the way a friend, who then was returning into Europe, desiring to know what hee would command him to his friends, hee earnestly intreated him to tell them, that he saw Duke Robert caried into heaven upon the backs of Divels.

[I. iii. 220.] The description of the Citie and the Territorie.

The explication of the Citie. Now followes the explication of the Citie described: and first the small Line drawne within the present walles on the West side of the Citie, shewes the old walles thereof, before Mount Calvery was inclosed within the walles by the Christian Kings, for now there remaine no ruines of the old walles, this line being onely imaginarie.

(1) Mount Sion without the walles, for part of it is yet inclosed with them.

The Castle. (2) The faire Castle, which was built by the Pisans of Italy, while yet they were a free State, and the building is not unlike to the Italian Castles. It was now kept by a Turkish Agha and Garrison, having great store of short Iron Ordinance of a huge boare, lying at the Gate for terrour of the people. I remember that when wee walked (after Sunne-set) upon the top of the Latine Monastery (as those of Asia walke upon their houses), this Agha sent a souldier to us, commanding us to goe from beholding the Castle, or else he would shoote at us, whom we presently obeyed. Thus they suspect Christians, and suffer them not to enter this Citie with Armes, but narrowly search their baggage.

(3) The Gate of Joppa (Zaffa, or Griaffa) in some sort fortified, where for terrour to the Christians, they have planted some Ordinance, for the other Gates have none,

neither are fortified at all, and all the Christians enter at this Gate.

(4) The Gate of Mount Sion, no whit fortified, and newly built (as it seemes) by the Turkes, as also that of Joppa is.

The ruines of the High Priest's Pallace.

(5) The ruines of the house or Pallace of the High Priest Caiphas, where they shew a place with a pillar, upon which the Cock crowed when Peter denied Christ; and a placē where the fire was made, at which Peter warmed himselfe; and a tree in the place where he denied Christ; finally, a narrow prison, in which Christ was shut up till the day brake, and so he was led to Pilate. And the Sect of the Armenian Christians keepes this monument.

The old Monasterie of the Latine Christians.

(6) The old Monasterie of the Latine Christians, called il Santo Cenacolo, which the Turkes have taken from the Christians, and turned to a Mahumetan Mosche or Church, and no Christian may enter this place, kept by the Santons or Turkish Priests, except he will give an unreasonable reward, which given, yet he is not free from danger, if other Turkes see him enter. Here Christ [I. iii. 221.] did wash his Apostles feete, did eate his last Supper with them, did appeare to them after his Resurrection, the doores being shut, and againe after eight dayes appeared to Thomas doubting. Here the holy Ghost descended upon the Apostles, and the Apostle Matthew was chosen by lot. The Italian Monastery (noted with the figure (33) hath all these representations painted, and to these pictures the Pope hath given as large indulgences for Papists, as if they had seene the other places, from which the Turkes keepe them as unwashed dogges. The Sepulcher of David is not farre from this place, kept by the Turkes, forbidding entrie to the Christians. And here they shew the ruines of the Tower of David, or of his Pallace, on the South side of the Church-yard given to Christians of Europe for buriall, in the same place where David of old drove out the Jebuzites. In like sort on the South side of this old Monastery, is the place

where they say the Virgin Mary died. (7) Here they shew a place where the Jewes strove in vaine to take the body of the Virgin Mary from the hands of the Apostles, as they carried it to be buried in the Valley of Jehosophat.

(8) The Cave wherein they say Peter used to bewaile the denying of Christ.

(9) Here they say the Apostles hid themselves, whilst Christ suffered on the Crosse.

The field Acheldamus.

(10) Here they shew the field Acheldamus, bought by the Jewes for a buriall place, with the thirtie pence Judas brought back to them. And here looking into a huge cave of the Mountaine, we did see infinite whole bodies imbalmed of dead men, and standing upright. And this place is given for buriall to the Christians of Asia.

(11) the Gate Sterquilinea, at which the filth of the Citie is carried out, and cast into the Brooke Cedron. And Christ betraied by Judas, was brought into the Citie by this Gate (as they say), which Gate is old, and nothing lesse then fortified.

(12) The Gate by which the Virgin Marie entring into the outer Temple, is said to have offered Christ then an Infant to the hands of Simion, which Gate they say, in honour of our Redeemer, was shut up by the Christian Kings, and so remaines to this day. (13) The outer Temple where they say Christ was exhibited to Simion, and the Italians call it the Temple of the Presentation.

The Temple of Salomon.

(14) In this large circuit compassed all with walles, of old the Temple of Salomon stood. At this day it was over-growne with grasse, and in the middest thereof the Turkes had a Mosche for their wicked worship of Mahomet, neither may any Christian come within this circuit, much lesse into the Mosche, either being a capitall offence, which they say some curious Christians had tried with losse of life, after they had been drawne to enter into it by some Turkes vaine promises.

The golden Gate.

(15) The golden Gate at which Christ entered on Pàlme-Sunday, shut up by the Christian Kings, and so remaining.

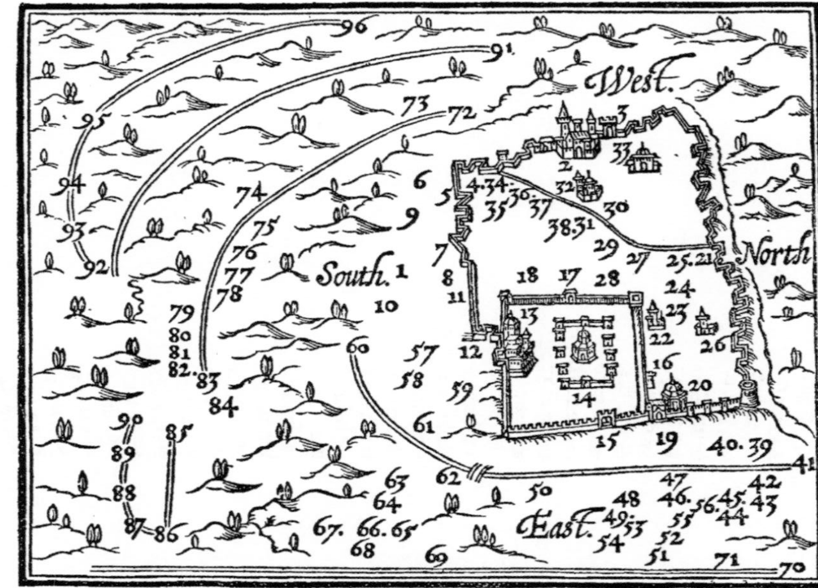

The description of the Citie of Jerusalem and the Territorie

(16) *Probatica P*
where the *Angel*
man that entred the
dried up.

(17) *The beautiful*
the man walke, who

(18) *Salomons*
into the *Temple*, and
Cady, who hath an
pleasant Fountaines
circuit where the Tem
when the said Magis
remember we were
entred in to him, we
upon the ground, wi
and his shooes of

(19) This Gate of
of cattell brought
called the Gate of
out that Procession

(20) Heere they sa
shee bare the Virgin M

(21) The Gate of D
Ephraim.

(22) The house of P
Sangiaco (who is the
Province) did then
into the house with
say that in this house
sighes, nightly to this
superstitious he is,
thereof. They say
ascended, when he was
carried to Rome, and
the Romans call Hol
worship with great
but for my part let ev
they were brought fr

(16) Probatica Piscina without the Gate of the Temple, where the Angell troubling the waters, the first diseased man that entred them was healed. It was at this time dried up.

(17) The beautifull Gate where Peter and John made the man walke, who was lame from his mothers wombe.

(18) Salomons house, of old having a Gate leading into the Temple, and it is now inhabited by the Turkish Cady, who hath an Episcopall office. Here I did see pleasant Fountaines of waters, and did looke into the circuit where the Temple stood, through an Iron grate, when the said Magistrate called us before him. And I remember we were bidden put off our shooes before we entred in to him, where hee sat upon a Carpet spread upon the ground, with his legges crossed like a Tailor, and his shooes of (as the Turkes use.)

Salomons House.

(19) This Gate of old had the name of the Droves of cattell brought in for sacrifices: but at this day is called the Gate of Saint Stephen, because the Jewes drew out that Protomartyr by this Gate, and so stoned him.

The gate of Saint Stephen.

(20) Heere they say was the house of Anna, wherein shee bare the Virgin Marie.

(21) The Gate of Damasco, of old called the Gate of Ephraim.

(22) The house of Pontius Pilate, in which the Turkish Sangiaco (who is the military Governour of the City and Province) did then dwell, so as no Christian might come into the house without giving a reward. The Fryars say that in this house are heard noises, whippings, and sighes, nightly to this very time, and each man the more superstitious he is, the more incredible things he tels thereof. They say that the staires upon which Christ ascended, when he was brought to Pilate, were long since carried to Rome, and these be the staires which I said the Romans call Holy (vulgarly Scale Sante), and doe worship with great superstition. They be of marble, but for my part let every man beleeve as he list, whither they were brought from thence, and be the same staires

[I. iii. 222.] *The House of Pontius Pilate.* *Fryars Superstitions.*

that Christ ascended or not. Onely I am sure that here they shew the place void in the very streete, where staires have beene of old; yet must I needs say, that marble staires ill befit the poore building of this house. Here the Souldiers spoiled our Redeemer of his garments, and in scorne attired him with purple.

The Arch of Pilate.

(23) The Arch of Pilate, which is a gallery of bricke, built over the street, from one wall to another, whence Pilate shewed Christ to the people, saying; behold the man, doe with him what you will.

(24) Here they say the Virgin Mary fell downe fainting, when Christ was led to Mount Calvary.

(25) Here they say that Christ fainting, the Jewes tooke his Crosse, and laied it upon Symon of Cyren. (26) The Pallace of King Herod.

(27) Here they say Christ uttered these words; Daughters of Syon weepe not for me, weepe for your selves, &c.

(28) Here they say the rich glutton dwelt, and not farre hence they shew the house where Mary Magdalen washed Christs feete with her teares, and dried them with the haires of her head.

Veronica's dwelling place.

(29) Here they say Veronica dwelt, and that this woman gave her white hand-kercher to Christ when he did sweat blood, who wiping his face therewith, left the lively print of it therein: about which hand-kercher the Romans and the Spaniards contend, both saying that they have it, and shewing it for an holy relike to the people.

The gate of the dolorous way.

(30) The Gate of old called Judiciall, now not extant, by which Christ was led to Mount Calvary to be crucified, for this mountaine now inclosed within the wals, was then without the wals. And the way from the house of Pontius Pilate (noted with the figures 22) to this gate, is called the dolorous way by the Italian Christians, because Christ was led by it to his passion. (31) The prison from whence the Angell brought Peter, breaking his chaines, and opening the iron doore, and it is seated under the

ruines of the Pallace, which since that time belonged to the Knights of Jerusalem.

(32) The Church which the Christians built over the Sepulcher of Christ, of which I will after write more largely, making a rude Mappe thereof, as I have done of the City.

The Monastery of the Franciscan Friars.

(33) The Monastery of the Franciscan Friars, in which we did lodge, being seated on the highest part of Mount Calvary, which since hath beene called the Mount of our holy Saviour. And this is called the new Monastery, in respect of the old (noted with the figure 6) and onely hath the monuments of the old painted, to the visiting whereof the Pope hath given large indulgences. The Franciscan Friars conducting us, shewed us some other monuments within the wals. And not farre from the gate of Syon, (noted with the figure 4) they shewed us (34) the house of the High Priest Anna, where Christ was examined by the Pharises, and there they shewed us an Olive tree, (which must needs be old), to which they say Christ was bound. (35) The Church of the Apostle Saint James, whom the Spaniards call Saint James of Gallicia, and worship for their protecting Saint, who was called James the greater, and they say was here beheaded. This Church is stately built, for the poverty of the Armenians, who built it, and maintained there an Archbishoppe, to keepe it, and to performe there the rites of their religion.

The Church of the Apostle Saint James.

The place where Christ appeared to the three Maries.

(36) The place where they say Christ appeared to the three Maries dwelling together, upon the very day of his resurrection, where the Christians built three Churches, which the Turks have converted to 3 Moschees, yet bearing no reverence to the place, because they beleeve not that Christ died, and much lesse beleeve that he rose againe.

[I. iii. 223.]

(37) The house of the Evangelist Saint Marke, mentioned in the twelfth Chapter of the Acts. This is the house of Mary the Mother of John, surnamed Marke, whither Peter came when the Angell delivered him out

of prison, into which Herod had cast him, (noted with the figure 31). At this day there was an obscure Church, kept by the Syrian Priests.

(38) Here they shew the Iron gate, which Peter found miraculously opened, and by the same entring into the other City, came to the house of Saint Marke.

We going out at Saint Stevens Gate towards the East, descended into the vally of Jehosaphat, and here they say (39) the bridge stood, by which the Queene of Saba passed over the Brooke Cedron, and that the Crosse of Christ was made of the wood of this bridge.

The brook Cedron.

(40) In this place they say the Protomartyre Saint Steven was stoned. (41) This smal line without the Easterne gates, shewes the bed of the brook Cedron, (or Kidron) which is very narrow, having not at this time one drop of water, so as we passed over the stony bed with drie feet. But of old when Jerusalem flourished, and had many conduits of water drawne to it, then it is probable that it was filled with water. And at this day, when any raine fals, the water runnes swiftly from the mountaines on the North side, according to this blacke line, through the most pleasant vally of Jehosaphat.

The vally of Jehosaphat.

This vally extendeth it selfe on both sides of this brooke, some two Italian miles in length, but is very narrow, and it hath on the West side the wals of the City, where Salomons Temple stood upon the lower part of the Mount Moriah, and it hath upon the East side the most high Mount Olivet, and it hath on the North side mountaines somewhat (but not farre) distant from the City, and upon the South-side mountaines a little more distant. Many interpret the Prophet Joell, in his third Chapter and second verse, as if Gods Tribunall at the day of judgement should stand in this vally, and thereupon the Jewes when they die in remote parts, will be brought to be buried in this vally, for the expedition of their triall. But the best Divines doe teach, that the word Jehosaphat signifies the Judgement of the Lord, and that the Prophet may be interpreted figuratively, namely, that as the Lord often defeated with great slaughters the enemies of his Church in this valley, so in the day of judgement he will strike the wicked with like confusion.

The Sepulcher of Joseph.

(42) Beyond the Brooke is a stately Sepulcher for the most part under the earth, into which we descended by some fiftie staires, and about the middle descent, on the left hand towards the City, under an Altar, lie the bodies of Joseph, and Joachimus, and on the right hand the body of Anna (namely, of the Husband, Father, and Mother of the Virgin Marie.) In the bottome is a Church, in the middle whereof, under a stone raised some few feete from the ground, they say the Apostles buried the Virgin Mary. This Church (so they call all places where they have Altars to sing Masses) is very darke, having no light but by one window or vent, made through the earth, and upon this monument lies part of the bed of the Brook Cedron. On the right hand the Turks (who greately reverence the monuments of Christ while he lived), have made themselves an Oratory. But for the monument it selfe, the Franciscan Friers of the Latin Church have alone the priviledge to keepe the same, and the Altar thereof, for their singing of Masses.

The Virgin's burying place.

(43) Here is a Cave, at the foote of Mount Olivet, in which they say Christ used to pray, and did sweat bloud.

The place where the Virgin appeared to S. Thomas.

(44) Here they shew a place where they say (beleeve it who list), that S. Thomas after the Virgines buriall, did see her both in body and soule assumed into heaven, and that she casting her girdle to him, gave it for testimony thereof, that all others might beleeve it. In my opinion they did well to make Saint Thomas see it, for otherwise hee would never have beleeved it.

(45) The place where they say the Virgin was wont to rest, when she visited the places frequented by her Sonne in the time hee lived heere, and where she beheld the stoning of Saint Stephen, and prayed for [I. iii. 224.] him.

(46) The stone where Christ, leaving Peter, James,

and John, said, that his soule was heavy unto death, and went aside to pray, warning them to watch.

The Garden where Christ was betrayed.

(47) Here is a little circuit inclosed with a low wall, where they report the Garden to be, at the foot of Mount Olivet, where Christ used to pray, and was betrayed by Judas with a kisse.

(48) The place where they say, the Village of Getsemany was of old seated. Round about this place the Turks doe bury their dead (as they do also in a field on the North side without the walles); for they never burie within Cities, excepting onely the monuments of their Emperours.

(49) Here they say Saint James the lesse did lye hidden, till hee heard that Christ was risen againe the third day after his Passion.

Two old sepulchers.

(50) Here be two old Sepulchers, almost of a round forme, built of Free-stone, or rather cut out of the living stone, wherof the one is called the Sepulcher of Absolon, the sonne of David, the other of King Manasses (or as others say, of the King Ezekias.) And considering the antiquitie, they seeme no Plebean Sepulchers, but stately and fit for Princes, being foure Elles from the ground in height.

The top of Mount Olivet.

(51) Here is the top of Mount Olivet, the highest of all the Mountaines that compasse Jerusalem, and here, in a Chappell, they shew in stone the print of Christs feete when he ascended into Heaven. And this Chappell is kept by a Turkish Zanton, that is a kinde of their Priests, and the Turkes give such reverence to the monuments of Christ living on earth, as they are much offended with Christians, if they creepe not on their knees, and with their shooes off to this and like monuments. To the keeper hereof we gave a few meidines for reward.

(52) Here they say Christ did weepe over the Citie and rich Temple of Salomon, and in this place is the fullest prospect to view the Citie and Temple.

(53) Here they shew the ruines of the house, wherein the Apostles assembled did write the Creede.

(54) Here they say Christ taught his Disciples to pray in the forme ever since received, and here was a Church built by the Christians of old.

(55) Here they say Christ foretold the signes of the day of Judgement.

(56) Here they say the Angell foretold the Virgin shee should die at three dayes ende.

The way to Bethania.

Upon Thursday the sixth of June, we being to goe to Bethania, hired each of us an Asse for foure meidines, that place being scarse two Italian miles from the citie. Of our company we were foure Lay-men, and because the Friers our consorts pleaded themselves to be free from such expences, we were content to yeeld to them, and gave jointly into the hands of the Fryer our guide two zechines, wherewith he was to give small rewards, and to pay the Muccaro, who furnished us with Asses: for we meant not to eate till our returne, the place being no further distant, and there being no dwellings, but onely the ruines of houses. What our guide spent I know not; for he never offered to give us account, and because he was a Frier, wee would not trouble him in demaunding it. We went out by the Gate Sterquilinea (noted with the figure (11) on the South side).

The Fountaine Siloe.

(57) First, we came to the Fountaine Siloe, to which Christ sent the blind man to wash his eyes, and there we found Turkish women washing, who beate us away with stones.

(58) Here they shew a monument of the Prophet Elia, but what it was I remember not.

(59) Here they shew a Fountaine, where they say, the Virgin washed Christs clothes when he was an infant.

The Mount of Offence.

(60) The Mount of Offence, opposite to Mount Sion, which Mount lies beyond the Brooke Cedron, and extendeth Eastward towards Bethania, and upon the top thereof they shew the ruines of the Pallace which Salomon built for his Concubines, and of the Altar, upon which hee sacrificed to Idols. Betweene this Mount and that of Mount Sion, they shew the Valley of the sonnes of [I. iii. 225.]

Hinnon towards the West, and there they shew a place, wherein the Jewes offered their children to the Idoll Molech, (that is, Saturne); yet we reade, that this Valley lies by the entry of the East-Gate, Jeremiah, chap. 19. vers. 2.

The Prophet Isaiah's death.

(61) Here they say, the Prophet Isaiah was cut in pieces with a Sawe, at the commaund of King Manasses.

(62) Here is a bridge over the Brook Kedron, or Cedron of one Arch, & built of stone, whereby they passe when the bed of the Brooke is filled with water, which now wee passed drie footed. And here they shew a place, where they say Christ fell upon the stones of the bed where the brook should runne, when he being betraied by Judas, was drawne into the Citie in a great presse of the Jewes. And upon these stones are the prints of hands and feete (as they say, his.)

(63) The way leading to Bethania over Mount Olivet.

The place where Judas hanged himself.

(64) The place where they say Judas hanged himselfe, and burst; after he had betraied his Lord. Not farre hence they shew a figge tree, which they say Christ cursed, because it had leaves without fruit.

(65) Here descending from Mount Olivet towards the East, we did see farre off the valley Jordan, to which the Mountaines decline by little and little. And now we were come to Bethania, where we did see the House of Simon the Leaper, not yet ruined, and inhabited by a Moore, to whom we gave a few meidines.

The Pallace of Lazarus.

(66) Here they shew stately ruines of a Pallace, which they say belonged to Lazarus. And not farre thence is a Chappell, built over the stately sepulcher of Lazarus, the key whereof the Friars our guides had with them. For the Turkes putting great religion in reverencing this place, have an Oratory neere it, and enter into the Sepulcher by another way. Here they say Christ raised Lazarus out of his grave. At our going forth, wee were forced to give some few meidines to certaine Turkes and Arabians, (I know not whether they had the Place in keeping, or no).

(67) The House of Mary. (68) The House of Martha her sister.

(69) The stone upon which they say Christ did sit, before he did see the sisters of Lazarus bewailing his death, and it is some halfe mile from Bethania.

The bed of the River Jordan.

(70) This small line sheweth the bed of the River Jordan, running through a most pleasant valley, which River we did see some ten Italian miles distant. On the North-side of Jerusalem, (I cannot say whether beyond Jordan or no), we did see many Towers, having globes of glistering mettall, and that very distinctly, the day being cleere; also we did see the wals of a City neere the River Jordan, and they said, that it was Jericho. Further towards the North they shewed us from farre off a place, where they say our Saviour was baptized by John. And they affirme upon experience had, that the water of Jordan taken in a pitcher, will very long keepe sweet, and that it corrupted not, though they carried it into forraigne parts. This water seemed very cleere, till it fell into a Lake, where they say Sodome with the other Cities stood of old, before they were burnt by fier from Heaven. And the day being cleere, we did plainely see, and much marvell that the cleere and silver streame of Jordan, flowing from the North to the South, when in the end it fell into the said Lake, became as blacke as pitch.

The water of Jordan doth not corrupt.

The Lake of Sodom.

The Friers our guides seriously protested, that if any living thing were cast into this Lake of Sodom, it could not be made to sinke, whereas any heavy dead thing went presently to the bottome. Also that a candle lighted cannot be thrust under the water by any force, nor be extinguished by the water, but that a candle unlighted will presently sinke. I omit for brevities sake, many wondrous things they told us, of the putrifaction of the aire, and other strange things with such confidence, as if they would extort beliefe from us. We had a great desire to see these places, but were discouraged from that attempt, by the feare of the Arabians and Moores: for they inhabite all these Territories. And I said before, that the Arabians, howsoever subject to the Turk, yet exercise continuall robberies with all libertie and impunitie, the Turkes being not able to restraine them, because they are barbarous, and live farre from their chiefe power, where they can easily flye into desart places. Yet these Barbarians doe strictly observe their faith to those that are under their protection. And all the Merchants chuse one or other of the Arabian Captaines, and for a small pension procure themselves to be received into their protection, which done, these Captaines proclaime their names through all their Cities and Tents (in which for the most part they live), and ever after will severely revenge any wrong done to them, so as they passe most safely with their goods. All other men they spoile, and make excursions with their leaders, and sometime with their King, to the sea side, as farre as Joppa, and much further within Land, spoyling, and many times killing all they meet.

The Turkes cannot restrain the Arabians.

[I. iii. 226.]

The ruines of Bethphage.

When we returned from Bethania, we declined to the North side of Mount Olivet, and came to the ruines of (71) Bethphage, where Christ sent for the Colt of an Asse, and riding thereupon, while the people cried Hosanna to the Highest, and laid branches and leaves under his feet, did enter into Jerusalem. Upon Friday the seventh of June towards the evening, we tooke our journey to Bethlehem Juda, and we foure lay consorts, (the Friars by our consent still having the priviledge to be free from these expences) delivered jointly foure zechines to the Friars ours guides, for our charges, whereof they gave us no other account, then they did formerly, yet they onely disbursed some small rewards, since we went on foot, and were otherwise tied to satisfie the Friars of the Monastery, under the name of gift or almes, for our diet there: but since they used us friendly, we would not displease them for so small a matter.

We went out of the City by the gate of Joppa, on the West side, and so along (72) this line passed by a paved causey beyond Mount Sion, and then ascended another Mountaine to Bethlehem.

The Garden of Uria.

(73) Here they shew the Garden of Uria, and the Fountaine wherein Bersheba washed her selfe, which at that time was drie. And from the place where the Tower of David was seated upon Mount Sion, (noted with the figure 6), is an easie prospect into this garden.

(74) Here they show the Tower of Saint Simion.

A Tree of Terebinth.

(75) Here is a Tree of Terebinth, which beares a fruit of a blacke colour, like unto an Olive, yeelding oyle; and under this tree they say the Virgine did rest, when shee carried Christ to be presented in the Temple. For which cause the Papists make their beades of this tree, and esteeming them holy, especially when they have touched the rest of the monuments, they carry them into Europe, and give them to their friends, for great presents and holy relikes.

(76) Here they shew a fountaine called of the Wise-men of the East, and they say that the starre did here againe appeare to them, after they came from Herod.

(77) Here they shew the ruines of a house, wherein they say that the Prophet Habakcuk dwelt, and was thence carried by the haires of the head to feede Daniel in the Lions Den at Babylon.

The Fountaine of the Prophet Elias.

(78) Here they shew the Fountaine of the Prophet Elias, and the stone upon which he used to sleepe, upon which they shew the print of his head, shoulders, and other members, which prints have some similitude, but no just proportion of those members. From a rock neere this place we did see at once both Jerusalem & Bethlehem.

(79) Here they shew a Tower and ruines, where the Patriarck Jacob dwelt, and here againe we did see both Cities.

The Sepulcher of Rachel.

(80) Here is an old stately Sepulcher, in which they say Rachel, Jacobs wife was buried. It is almost of a round forme, built of stone and lime foure foote high, having the like cover above it, borne up by foure pillars.

There be two other Sepulchers, but nothing so faire, and all three are inclosed within one wall of stone.

(81) Here they shew the Fountaine, for the water whereof David thirsted, yet would not drinke it, when it was brought with the hazard of blood.

(82) Here the City Bethlehem is seated, which then was but a Village, having no beauty but the Monastery.

The Monastery of Bethlehem.

(83) Here the Monastery is seated, large in circuit, and built rather after the manner of Europe, then Asia, which the Italian Franciscan Friars, (called Latines, and more commonly Franckes) doe possesse: but other [I. iii. 227.] Christian sects have their Altars in the Church by speciall priviledge, and the Turkes themselves comming hither in Pilgrimage, doe lie within the Church: for the Turkes have a peculiar way by a doore of Iron, (made of old, and kept by them) to enter into the Chappell, where they say Christ was borne. This Monastery seemes strong enough against the sudden attempts of the Turkes or Arabians, yet the Friars in that case dare not resist them, living onely in safety by the reverence which that people beares to this place, and by the opinion of their owne poverty. The greater Church is large, and high, in which I numbred twenty foure pillars, but my consorts being more curious, observed that the pillars were set in foure rankes, every ranke having eleven pillars seven foote distant one from the other, whereof many were of porphery, and had beautifull spots. The highest roofe of the Church on the inside, is painted with Histories of the Scripture, with a rich painting that shineth with gold and glasse as if it were enameled, (called in Italian Alla Mosaica), and the pavement is rich, with stones of marble, porphery, and Jaspar.

The greater Church.

The lesse Church.

From the lesse Church called of Saint Katherine, we entred a Cave under the earth, where the Friars gave every one of us a lighted waxe candle in his hand. Let them place what religion they will therein, I am sure the Cave was so darke, as we could not have passed it without a light. In this Cave wee did first see the bones of the Infants killed by Herod, then the Sepulchers of Eusebius, and of Saint Jerome in his Chappell, for they hold that he long dwelt there. Then they did lead us into a more darke place, where they say he did live an austere life fifty yeeres space, and translated the Bible out of Hebrew into Latine, and wrote many volumes. But the place seemed to me more fit to dull the braine, then to yeeld such fruites of wit, by reason it was darke, and digged deepe under ground.

The bones of the Infants killed by Herod.

From this Cave we ascended by ten marble staires into a Chappell, all covered with marble, and lying in length from the West (at which end we entered) to the East. And from this West end, as well Turkes as Christians of all sects, goe upon their knees to the Easterne end, and there kisse a marked stone in the pavement, in which verie place they say the Redeemer of the World was borne. By this stone on the South-side lieth a little Chappell, having two doores onely divided with a pillar. In which Chappell at the right hand or West-side, is a manger, raised from the ground, and all of marble, in which they say Christ was laid after his birth: and in the wall they shew a stone having (as they say) the lively picture of Saint Hierome. In the said little Chappell on the left hand or East side, they shew a place, where they say Christ was circumcised, and shed the first drops of his precious blood for the saving of mankind: And there they shewed another place, where they say the Wise-men of the East adored Christ, and offered to him their gifts. The wals of both Chappels, the pavements, and all things, are covered with marble. The roofe on the inside, is painted with the foresaid rich pictures, glistering like enamelled worke. To conclude, all things are stately and rich, and remain so under the Turkish tiranny, yet more rich in the Chappell of Christs birth, then in the greater Church, where all things then began to fall to ruine, because the Turkes beleeve not that Christ died. The Turkes doe so reverence this monument of Christs birth, as they creepe groveling upon hands & knees to

Christs birth.

kisse the said stone; yet in the meane time they despise the monuments of his death, because they beleeve not that he died.

A foolish Superstition. From hence going backe the same way we entered, they shew upon the right hand, a hole in the highest roofe of the Church, by which they say the starre that conducted the Wise-men, fell from above into the bowels of the earth. Can he forbeare laughter who considers the bignes of the starres, yea, even of Comets, as some write that was, specially finding no mention of this falling of the starre to be made in the holy scriptures. The City or Village of Bethlehem, is distant from Jerusalem some five miles, (in Turky I alwaies understand Italian miles), and we came hither from the Westerne gate of Jerusalem, through a faire way, and mountaines planted with Vines, Olives, and fruitfull Trees. Bethlehem is seated upon Mountaines, and hath pleasant hils on the East and South-sides, a pleasant plaine on the North-side, ending in great mountaines towards Jerusalem.

[I. iii. 228.] (84) As wee went out of Bethlehem to visit the Monuments, here they shewed us the field, in which the Angell made knowne the birth of Christ to the Shepheards, and the Cave wherein they did lie by day, to shun the beate of the Sunne.

The first Vine. (85) Here they say the Patriarch Lot planted the first Vine.

(86) Here beyond pleasant Hilles, wee did distinctly see the Plaine of Jordan, and the dead Sea, with the situation of Sodom and Gomorra.

(87) Here they say Bethalia was seated of old.

(88) Here we did see the ruines of a house, in which, they say, Joseph the Virgins Husband did dwell.

(89) Here they say the Virgin hid her selfe from the tyranny of Herod.

King Salomon's garden. (90) Here they say that King Salomon had his Garden. The Franciscan Friers sent out of Italy each third yeere into these parts, did courteously intertaine us at Bethlehem, and at our first comming, in imitation of

Christ, they washed our feete. It happened that my brother fell sicke here of an Ague, and so when our consorts upon Saterday in the evening returned to Jerusalem, wee were forced to stay here that night. But the next day in the evening we came to them at the Monastery of Jerusalem. And because they made haste to returne homeward, wee went forth the next day, being Munday the tenth of June earely in the morning, to see the Mountaines of Judea. And that day it happened, that I was troubled with loosenesse of body, whereof I made good use, as I shall hereafter shew, which makes me name it.

We went out of the Citie at the Gate of Joppa on the West side, and upon our right hand they shewed us (91) this place, where they say that Salomon was anointed King.

(92) Thence we went right forward to a Fountaine in the Desart, where they say, Phillip the Apostle did interpret the Scriptures to the Eunuch of Candace, Queene of Ethiopia, and baptized him.

The Desart in which John Baptist preached.

(93) Here they say is the Desart, in which John Baptist preached, and they shewed us his Cave cut out of a Rocke, and a long stone therein, upon which he used to lye, and a pleasant spring issuing out of the Rocke, where hee used to drinke, and another stone upon which he used to sit.

(94) Here we came to the Mountaines (or Mountanous places) of Judea, and here they say the Prophet Zacharias dwelt, where a woman of the Moores kept the Church of old built there.

The house of Zacharias.

(95) From hence a Musket shot, or little more, is another house, which, they say, belonged to Zacharias, and in one of these houses, he pronounced the Song, Blessed bee the Lord God of Israel, &c. And when the Virgin visited Elizabeth, the Babe here sprang in her wombe; and the Virgin here pronounced the Song, My soule doth magnifie, &c. And John Baptist was borne here.

The Crosse of Christ.

(96) From this place, they say, the Tree was taken, upon which the Crosse of Christ was made, and Greeke Friers keepe the Church that was here built. This place is two miles distant from Jerusalem, whether we returned the same way we came out, and entered the Citie by the West Gate of Joppa.

The Church built upon Christs Sepulcher.

The Church built upon Christs Sepulcher of old by the Christians at Jerusalem, is formerly noted by the figure (32); and wee entered the same upon Tuesday the eleventh of June towards the evening, at which time the Turkish Cady sent us his Officer to open the dore of it, to whom we payed for tribute after the dore was opened each of us nine zechines, and besides gave the Officer or Janizare a small reward for himselfe. But it is the custome, that he that hath once payed this tribute, may any time after enter this Church, without paying any thing, if he can watch the opportunity of other Christians entering the same.

[I. iii. 229.]

The rude, but true figure in plaine of Christs Sepulcher and the Church built over it at Jerusalem.

The description of Christ's Sepulcher and the Church built over it.

(α) By this one and only dore being of brasse, and on the South side of the Church, entrance is given into the said Church. They say there was of old another dore not farre from this towards the East, but now it was not extant.

(β) This marke shewes where the Belfrey stands, which is of ancient building, and now in great part was ruined, while the Turkes admit no use of any Belles.

(A) A Marble stone called the stone of Unction, where they say the body of Christ was imbalmed, before it was buried. And it is compassed with grates of Iron, having above it nine Lampes continually burning, maintained by the nine Sects of Christians.

(B) The Sepulcher of Godfrey King of Jerusalem, to which other lesse Sepulchers are adjoyning, erected to

ree was taken,
le, and Greeke
lt. This place
ter we returned
d the Citie by

cher of old by
noted by the
upon Tuesday
, at which time
open the dore
er the dore was
esides gave the
mselfe. But it
ved this tribute,
without paying
munity of other

ine of Christs
ilt over it at

of brasse, and on
is given into the
old another dore
t now it was not

ey stands, which
part was ruined,
Belles.
Unction, where
d, before it was
of Iron, having
ing, maintained

f Jerusalem, to
ng, erected to

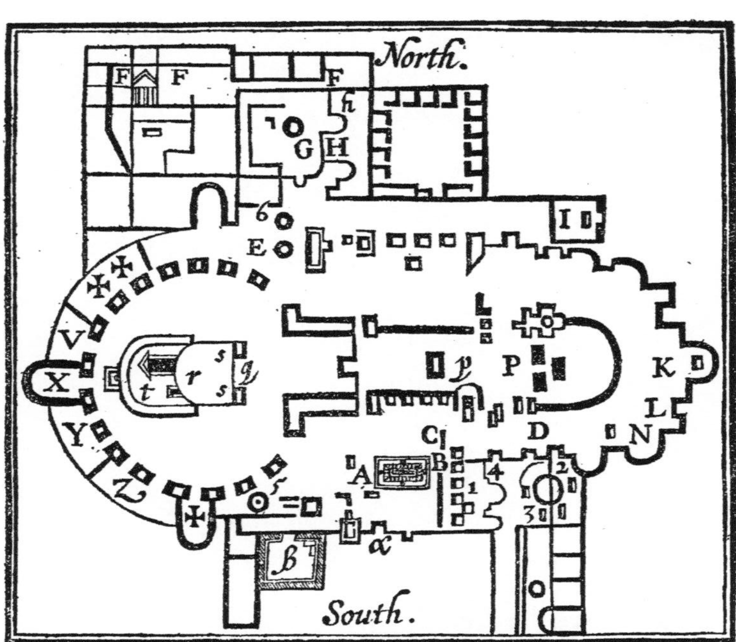

The figure of Christs Sepulcher and the Church built over it at Jerusalem

Kings and Queenes of his Family. And this Sepulcher hath this Epitaph in Latin:

The description of Christ's Sepulcher.

Here lyes worthy Godfrey of Bullon, who conquered all this Land to the worship of Christ, whose soule may it rest in peace. Amen.

(C) The Sepulcher of Baldwine his brother, and successor in the Kingdome, with this Epitaph in Latin:

King Balduinus another Judas Machabeus, the Hope of his Countrey, the Life of the Church, the strength of both.

These verses added:

Quem formidabant, cui Dona, Tributa ferebant,
Ægipti Cæsar, Dan, ac homicida Damascus.

Whom Egypt, Dan, Damascus homicide,
With gifts and Tributes gladly pacifide.

Mount Calvary.

(D) Here is Mount Calvary, and the staires to ascend thereunto, the walles of al the building upon it, the Altars, and the pavements, all shine with Marble; the roofe on the inside glisters with the foresaid rich painting, which [I. iii. 230.] seemes to be enameled. And divers Altars are proper to divers Nations or Sects, for their Rites of Religion. To these Altars upon the Mountaine, we ascended by some twenty staires; and there they shewed us three holes, wherein the three Crosses of Christ and the two theeves were erected. And at the figure (1) (where they say the Crosse of Christ stood) they shewed us stones rent, or the rending of the Mountaine, when Christ died. Under this Mountaine in the corner towards the dore of the Church, they bade us looke in at a little window, and there they shewed us a scull, which they say was the scull of Adam, of which they say the Mountaine was called Golgotha. (2) Without the doore of the Church we ascended to a Chappell above this Mount, where they shewed us an Altar, upon which they say Melchisedeck offered sacrifices. (3) Also a Chappell, where they say

The description of Christ's Sepulcher.

Abraham would have offered Isaac. (4) The Altars of Mount Calvary. (5) A place in the way to the Sepulcher, where they say, that Christ laid downe his Crosse, and where the Virgin Marie and John the Evangelist stood while he was crucified.

(E) Here they shew a stone, which they call Noli me tangere, that is, Touch me not; because Christ appearing here to Marie Magdalen, used those words. (6) And in this place they say Marie Magdalen stood.

(FFF) Here is a retreat of certaine Chambers and Chappels, under the keeping of the Latin or European Friers. For they continually send two or three of their Friers to bee locked weekely within this Church for the performance of the Rites of their Religion, whom they recall at the weekes end to their Monasterie in the Citie, sending new in their place to attend that service. And this retreat hath onely a doore to passe into the Church, but none into the streete.

(G) The Chappell of Apparition, so called, because they say Christ there appeared to the Virgin Marie after his Resurrection.

(H) The pillar of whipping, so called, because they say, Christ was bound to it, when he was beaten with rods.

(*h*) This Altar they call the Altar of the holy Crosse.

(I) A most narrow prison, in which they say Christ was shut up for a little time.

(K) The Chappell where they say, that the Souldiers divided Christs garments.

(L) Here we descended some fiftie staires into a cave under the earth, which they have made a Chappell, and here they say, the Empresse Helena found the Crosse of Christ, and thereupon built this Chappell, in which they say, foure pillars many times make a sound of groaning and sighing, and they shew the very place where the Crosse of Christ, and where the Crosses of the two theeves were found.

(N) After Christ was beaten, they say he was forced to sit here, till they crowned his head with Thornes.

The description of Christ's Sepulcher.

(P) The Chauncell of the Church.

(*p*) A hole in the pavement of this Chauncell, which the Greekes (having the Chauncell to keepe) hold to be the middest of the World.

(*q*) This place lies open over head, having the Sepulcher on the West side, and two little Marble walles raised some two foote on the North and South sides, within which wals the place is paved with Marble. The walles are so high, as a man cannot conveniently sit upon them. And in this place they use to pray, before they enter the Sepulcher.

(*r*) The outward Chappell or Porch of the Sepulcher, (as I may so terme it) where the Angell is said to have appeared to the women. And therein lies a foure-square stone, fitted to the little dore of the Sepulcher, upon which stone roled from the dore, they say the Angell did sit, after Christ was risen.

The Sepulcher.

(*ss*) These be seats on both sides of this outward Chappell, in which seates they use to pray. (*t*) In this Chappell (so they call the Sepulcher it selfe), and under the stone noted with blacke, they say the body of Christ was laied. And this stone is raised as high as an Altar, and covered with Marble, as all the walles bee. The little dore by which they enter this Chappell or Sepulcher,
is scarce 3 foote high, and 2 broad, so as they enter it [I. iii. 231.]
with difficulty, bending downe their bodies, as if they crept into a cave. The very stone covering the Sepulcher (or place where Christs body did lie) is somewhat raised from the ground, and hath seven foote in length, and some sixe in bredth. This Sepulcher lyes under the first Globe of the Church, as the Chauncell lies under the second, and it lyes under the middle of that Globe; neither hath the Church any window, but the Globe hanging over the Sepulcher, is open in the roofe, and so giveth light to all the Church. And in the very Sepulcher, the burning Lampes give light, besides that the dores lye open. And because raine must needes fall from the open Globe, the Sepulcher hath a cover borne

The description of Christ's Sepulcher.

up with pillars of Marble, and laid over with Lead to receive the raine. The Sepulcher within and without is beautified with marble, and was cut out of a Rocke before the Church was built. The Franciscan Friers are for the most part Italians, but are vulgarly called Francks, of the French who are in league with the Turkish Ottoman, and they have the priviledge of singing their Masses in the Sepulcher (not of free grant, but because they are best able to pay for their priviledges); yet it is free for any of the Christian Sects to come into the Sepulcher. They say, that from the situation of this Sepulcher, the custome came among Christians, to be buried with their feet & face towards the East, as expecting the resurrection.

(V) A Chappell kept by the Sect of the Gofti.

(X) The Sepulchers of Joseph of Arimathea, and of Nicodemus.

(Y) The Chappell of the Jacobites.

(Z) The Chappell of the Abissines.

(⋈) The Chappell of the Armenians.

(⋈ ⋈) The Chappell of the Georgians.

The Church hath the forme of a Crosse.

Some write, that this Church hath the forme of a Crosse, and if the retreat or chambers of the Italian Friers with the Chappell of Aparition on the North side, and the two Towers of the Belfrey on the South side, be joyntly considered with the Church, (which seeme rather fastned thereunto then of the same building), a superstitious man may faigne to himselfe the figure of a Crosse, but shall never plainely demonstrate it to others. Above the roofe of the Church on the outside, are two faire Globes, whereof the greater covered with leade, lies over the Sepulcher, and the lesse, all made of stone, is over the Chauncell. And this greater Globe, on the inside of the Church is beautified with engraven Cedar trees, and borne up with pillars of Marble, and the lesse hath faire pictures of the foresaid rich painting, shining like enameled worke. The breadth of the Church under both Globes, containes seventie paces, and the length 140 paces and in generall

The description of Christ's Sepulcher.

as well within as without, it retaines only the shaddow of the old magnificence.

We entred the Church on Tuesday in the afternoone, and were locked there in all the night following, and almost all the next day, to fulfill our devotions. But I formerly said, that the Italian Friers have chambers of retreat within the Church, in which we did eate and rest at our pleasure. Yet these chambers and the like retreats (wherein the Priests of other Sects with their wives, children and family doe lodge, and eate, and performe the rites of their Religion), have not any one dore into the streete, but all enter the Church, and goe forth by the foresaid onely dore of the Church towards the South, and the key of this dore is kept by the Turkes, who open it at set times, to admit strangers, and once every weeke, to let the Friers returne to their Monasteries, and to receive new Friers into the Church, which are sent from thence, to performe the severall rites of Religion. And this dore hath a grate or little window, at which the inclosed Friers may talke with their friends without, and receive meate sent them from their Monasteries.

Nine Sects of Christians.

Nine sundry Sects of Christians have their Monasteries within this City, by whom the great Turke and his officers have great profit, and the Turkes themselves repute all the monuments and places holy, which Christ in his life frequented: but this monument of his death, and other like they despise, and keepe them onely for their profit. From the said Monasteries, Friers are weekely sent to performe their severall rites, and at the weekes end they are recalled to the Monasteries, and new sent in their place; which custome I thinke they take from the Jewes. [I. iii. 232.] For when David divided the twentie foure Families of the sonnes of Aaron into twentie foure courses, that each of them might one after the other in due order performe the holy offices in the Temple, Josephus writes, that these courses, or Families in order one after the other lived in the Temple from Sabbath to Sabbath, to performe those duties.

Of these nine Christian Sects, each hath priviledges to keepe this or that monument within the Citie, and in the field, in which places they performe the rites of their Religion. And according to the number of the Sects, they maintaine nine Lampes continually burning in the foresaid common Church upon the stone of Unction, as many upon the Sepulcher, and as many upon Mount Calvarie. The nine Sects are thus called; Franks (namely, the Italians), Georgians, Greekes, Sorians, Costi, Abissines, Armenians, Nestorians, and Maronites.

1. The Frankes. The Religion of the Frankes (namely, Papists) is so well knowne, as I will omit it here, and referre it to his due place. I will onely say, that they have the keeping of the Sepulcher, the Chappell of Aparition (and therein of the pillar of whipping) and of one Altar upon Mount Calvarie, for the performance of their rites.

2. The Georgians. The Georgians are a warlike Nation, inhabiting Media, and the Caspian Mountaines, and have their name of Saint George, whom they have chosen their protecting Saint. They have a King, and making warre valiantly sometimes upon the Turkes, sometimes upon the Persians, could never bee conquered by either. Yea, if they bee oppressed by either, they easily finde helpe from the other, out of their mutuall hatred. Therfore they pay no tribute to the Turkes, but by singular priviledge freely enter into Jerusalem armed, and with banner displaied. Neither dare the Turkes offer them the least injurie, lest when they returne home, they should revenge it upon the Turkes lying neare them. Their very women are warlike, like the Amazons, and carrying bowes, shew valour both in countenance and behaviour. The men weare long haire on their heads and beards, save that they all are shaven like Clerkes upon the Crowne of the head, the Lay-men in a foure-square, the Priests in a round forme. They expresly follow the Religion, Rites, and Ceremonies of the Greekes, and in their Divine service use the Greeke tongue, otherwise speaking their owne language (as I thinke Caldean.) These in the Church of Jerusalem have the keeping of Mount Calvary, and the Altar there built over the place, where they say the Crosse of Christ stood, and in the Citie they keepe the house of the High Priest Annas.

3. The Greekes.

Of the Greekes Religion I must speake at large in his due place. Now I will onely say, that in the Church they keepe the Chauncell, and therein shew a hole in the pavement compassed with Marble, which they say is the very middle point of the world. Against which opinion I argued with them, and objected, that the earth is round, and that in a Globe the center is in the middest, all centers in the outside being but imaginarie, and to be placed wheresoever the measurer will. Also that in measuring (after their manner) the outside of the earth, Palestina was farre distant from the Equinoctiall line, which divideth the World into equall parts. And if Palestina were just under that line, yet that all the countries having the same Meridian, should be the middest of the World, aswell as Palestina. They answered, that David saith in his Psalmes; In the middest of the World I will worke their salvation. To which I replied, that the middest of the World was there taken for the face, and in the sight of the World, so as none should be able to denie it. Whereupon they grew angry, and said, that the Scripture must be beleeved, in spite of all Cosmographers and Philosophers. It had been vaine to dispute further with them, there being not one learned man among these Greekes at Jerusalem. And to say truth, (if you except the Greeke Ilands under the Venetians), they have few or no learned men. For my part, I never found in all the vast Empire of Ottoman any learned Greeke, but onely one, called Milesius, who was after made Patriarke of Constantinople. And these Greekes, as in this point, so in all other, follow the literall sense of the Scriptures. For which cause they also beleeve the corporall presence of Christ in the Sacrament. And whereas Saint Paul saith, Let the Bishop be the husband [I. iii. 233.]
of one wife, &c. they so interpret it, as if the Priests wife

die within few dayes after his mariage, yet he may never marry againe.

4. *The Sorians.* The Sorians are so called of Syria, in which Province they live, having their owne Patriarke, neither could they ever bee brought to consent to the Roman faith: for whatsoever the Romanes challenge due to the Seat of S. Peter, that they say rather belongeth to them, in respect Saint Peter was Bishop of Antioch. They agreed with the Greekes in many things, they denie Purgatorie, they fast foure Lents in the yeere, they permit their Priests to marrie, they use the Greeke tongue in their Divine service, and otherwise speake their owne language (which I take to be the Arabian tongue.) In Jerusalem Church they keepe the Sepulchers of Joseph of Aramathia, and of Nicodemus, and in the Citie they keepe the house of Saint Marke, noted with the figure (37.)

5. *The Costi.* The Costi are Egyptians, dwelling about Numidia. They retaine the heresie of Arrius, and follow the Ceremonies of the Abissines. This I write upon the report of the Italian Friers, who are to be blamed if it be not true. These in the Church keepe the Chappell, wherein Godfrey and his Regall Family lye buried, and the Cave under Mount Calverie, where they say the scull of Adam lies, and have also their proper Altar upon Mount Calvarie.

6. *The Abisines.* The Abissines inhabit the South parts of Africk, and they are subject to their King Preti-Giani. They received the Christian faith of the Eunuch baptized by Phillip, and themselves are baptized not onely with water, but with the signe of the Crosse printed in their flesh with hot Iron, gathering that fire is as necessary to Baptisme as water, out of those words of S. John Baptist; I baptise you with water, but he shall baptise you with the Spirit and fire. Also they use the Jewes and Mahometans circumcision, like wary Notaries, who fearing to faile in their assurance, never think they have used words enough; yet doe they greatly hate the Jewes, and thinke their Altars defiled, if they doe but looke upon them. They

give the Sacrament of our Lords Supper to very children, and they (as all the rest excepting the Franks, that is, Papists), give it in both kindes. When they sing Masse or Psalmes, they leape and clap their hands, and like the Jewes use Stage-Players actions. They use their owne, that is, the Egyptian tongue, in Divine service, and observing a Lent of fiftie dayes at one time, do greatly macerate their bodies. In the Church they keepe the Chappell adjoyning to the Sepulcher, and the pillar where they say Christ was crowned with Thornes.

7. *The Armenians.*

The Armenians are so called of the Province Armenia, which they inhabite, and they call their chiefe Bishop Catholicon, whom they reverence as another Pope. They disagree with the Greekes, and rather apply themselves to the Franks; yet they keepe not the Feast of Christs birth, but fast that day. They keepe the Roman Lent, but more strictly, abstaining from Fish, and very Oyle (which they use for butter), but upon some Holy-dayes in that time, they eate flesh. They mingle no water with the Wine of the Sacrament, as the Papists doe, but with them, they lift up the bread, (yea and the Cup also) to be worshipped. Of old, with reservation of customes, they joyned themselves to the Roman Church; but finding the Pope to give them no helpe against their enemies, they quickly fell from him. The very Lay men are shaved like Clerkes upon their heads, but in the forme of a Crosse, and their Priests keepe the haire of their heads long, in two tufts, placing therein great Religion. In the Church they keepe the pillar, where they say the garments of Christ were parted, and lots cast upon his Coate, and in the Citie, the place where they say Saint James was beheaded, and the house of the High Priest Cayphas, upon Mount Sion.

8. *The Nestorians.*

The Nestorians are so called of the Monke Nestorius, who infected the Persians, Tartars, and Jewes, with his heresie. They give the Sacrament of the Lords Supper in both kindes, and that to children as well as men. They use the Caldean tongue in divine service, and otherwise the Arabian. In the Church they keepe the prison, wherein they say Christ was shut up.

9. *The Maronites.* [I. iii. 234.] The Maronites inhabite Phænicia, and the Mount of Libanus, and they use the Syrian tongue in their divine service, namely, (as I thinke) the Arabian. And they said, that these men for poverty were lately fled from Jerusalem. Some make mention of a tenth sect, namely, the Jacobites, (named of Jacob, Disciple to the Patriarke of Alexandria), who live mingled among Turkes & Tartares, inhabiting partly Nubia in Afrike, partly the Provinces of India. I remember not to have seene any such at my being there, neither yet to have heard any mention of them; yet others write that they admit circumcision as well as baptisme, and besides print the signe of the Crosse by an hot Iron, in some conspicuous part of their body, that they confesse their sinnes onely to God, not to their Priests, that they acknowledge but one nature in Christ, that in token of their faith they make the signe of the Crosse with one finger, and give the Sacrament of our Lords Supper in both kinds, yea, to Infants, as well as to those who are of full age.

I cannot omit an old Spanish woman, who had for many yeeres lived there, locked up in the Temple, lodging every night at the doore of the sepulcher, and having her diet by the Friars almes. Shee said that shee came to Jerusalem to expiate her sinnes by that holy pilgrimage, that shee had then beene there seven yeeres; and in that time had alwaies lived in the Church, and that shee would not refuse any opportunity to goe backe into Spaine, but otherwise would die there, & thereby thought to merit much of God. Neither doe I thinke shee lost the hope of this vaine merit, since it was not easie to find a man who would carry an old woman, and beare her charges so long a journey.

The stone of unction in the Church, is common to all the nine Christian sects, neither doe the Keepers of any other monuments refuse any Christian to enter into them, but onely by priviledge keepe their Altars private to themselves. Most of the sects have their Monasteries in the City, and (as I formerly said) each of them hath the priviledge to keepe some monuments, as well within as without the wals. But some of the sects only come to Jerusalem at solemne feasts, and dwelling neere the City, easily maintaine a Friar or two, to keepe their monuments, and so are freed from the necessity of building a monastery in the City.

Gifts to the Turkes.

Upon Wednesday the twelfth of June towards evening, the Turkes did open the Church to let us out, and each of us Lay-men gave the chiefe Turke thirty meidines, and the Doore-keeper twenty of free gift; and for the waxe candles burnt the night before in the Church, each gave sixty meidines to one of our Italian Friars. This done, we returned to the Monastery, where we lodged, with great joy that we were presently to goe backe to Joppa.

The Franciscan Friars.

I formerly said that the Franciscan Friars with whom we lodged, were of Europe, whether at three yeeres end they were to be recalled, and some fifty new Friars to be sent hither in their place, which still each third yeere use to be changed. And these Friars are called the Family of Frankes, for the great Turke permits them as French to live there, and forbids the comming of any Spanish or Roman Friars: yet are they for the most part of Sicily, Naples, or Rome; but denying their Countrey, affirme that they are Venetians, and if they were knowne to be subjects to Spaine or Rome, they should incurre great danger. Of them some few are indeed Venetians, and at this time some two were Frenchmen. All these live of the almes of the Merchants in the East of their Religion, who for the most part are Italians, and especially Venetians: yet hath the Monastery also some rents of Lands given to it of old in Sicily and in Spaine; and from thence they bring with them every third yeere at their first arrivall, a present of great value to the Turkish Ottoman. I said formerly, that of old the Venetians yeerly sent a gally to carry Pilgrimes to the Holy Land,

The Venetians sent a gally yeerly to the Holy Land.

till the Christians were so oppressed by exactions of the Turkes, as they rarely undertooke that journey, and so the Venetians also left that custome. From that time this Family of Frankes, (so these Friars are called) useth to passe in a Venetian ship to Cyprus, and from thence to Joppa, in the Holy Land, hiring there a Græcian barke to that purpose; and in like sort the old Family upon the arrivall of the new, returnes into Italy. And as soone as this family arriveth, they disperce themselves, the [I. iii. 235.] greater part abiding at Jerusalem and Bethlehem, and some single men or couples being sent to doe the office of Priests at Cayro (or Babylon) in Ægypt, at Haleppo in Asia, (where most part of their Merchants reside) and at Scanderona, (of old by all, and still by Christians called Alexandretta). These Friars thus dispersed, are not onely maintained by the Merchants to whom they are sent, but they also send from them large almes to the rest at Jerusalem, and they often change places, that all may equally beare these burthens.

The Friars dispersed.

Toies of no worth.

We being now to take our journey from Jerusalem, many Christians and Jewes brought us divers toies, to buy and carry with us, being of no worth, save onely that they were far fetcht, namely, beades for Papists to number their praiers, and also crosses, both made of the earth whereof they say Adam was formed, or of the Olive trees of Mount Olivet, or of Terebinth, (under one of which trees they say the Virgin Mary rested, when shee carried Christ an Infant to be presented in the Temple), and round stones called Cornioli, of yellow colour, and others of white, called the Sea-water of India. Also girdles of the Virgin Mary, & glistering stones of litle price (as all the rest are.) Among which they attribute to the stone of Judea, the vertue to provoke urine, to the Eagles stone called Aquilina, the virtue to expell poyson, to facilitate the birth of children, to heale the falling sickenesse, to restore weomens milke, and so to divers stones, divers and incredible virtues. Besides, our Franciscan Friars gave each to his friend and the Guardian

Vertues attributed to stones.

to us all, Agnos Dei, Dust and little stones taken from the fore said monuments, for a great treasure to be carried to our friends at home. Moreover they gave to each of us freely and unasked (as it seemes of custome) as well to us Lay-men as to the Friars, a testimony under the seale of the Monastery, that we had beene at Jerusalem, and for better credit, they expressed therein some markable signes of our faces and bodies.

Testimony under the seal of the Monastery.

Now there remained nothing but the Epilogue of the Comedy, that we should make some fit present to the Guardian of the Monastery, in satisfaction for our diet, and the curtesie of the Friars towards us, which my selfe and my brother thought very fit to be done: but two of the Friars our consorts, either wanting money, or used to eate of free cost, did not onely refuse to give any thing, but perswaded the French Lay-men to joine with them in deniall thereof. The third Friar our consort, and for his experience used by the other as a Conducter, hearing this, did vehemently reprove them, using these words in French; Que voules vous doncques payer en blanche? (that is, what will you then pay them in white?) which phrase they use when a man requites a curtesie in words, or faire written promises, not really. They on the other side, no lesse angry, answered that it was unfit and irreligious for Friars to extort gifts from Christian Pilgrimes. My selfe and my brother laughed to our selves hearing this difference, for we found now, and had often heard, that these Friars were most deare Hosts, and that as they in England, who referre their payment to pleasure, are alwaies over-paid, so these Friars asking nothing for diet, yet under the title of gift or almes, expect more then any the most greedy Host could demand: yet lest we should provoke them, either to hinder our departure, or to doe us any shrewd turne, as they most easily might doe: yea, lest they should surmise my selfe and my brother to be authours or partners of this conspiracy, I perswaded the French Lay-men our consorts, that howsoever the Friars still remained

Presents to the guardian of the Monastery.

Greedy Friars.

obstinate to give nothing, yet we foure should present the Guardian some sixe zechines. This effected, the Guardian dismissed us for good sons, yet in truth we were wel contented with this faire occasion to restraine our gift, which howsoever it were farre from bounty, yet was it free from base sparing, since we gave at Bethlehem for our diet another present to those Friars, and while we visited the monuments of Jerusalem, being daily abroad, and commonly dining in Villages, we were onely beholding to these Friars for some ten suppers, besides that we had alwaies professed poverty (most safe to strangers). To which may be added, that in this Province, (whether for aboundance of all things, or want of mony) all things were sold at cheap rate: for when we went out to see the mountaines or hill Countrey of Judea, and dined in a Village, I remember we bought twenty egges for a meidine, and a pound of mutton for five meidines, foure cakes for one, and a hen for two meidines and a halfe. In the Monastery they gave us enough of mutton, hennes, and sallets, and of good wine, but somwhat sharpe; and the Friars our consorts did eate continually with the Friars, and we Lay-men by our selves, the Friars onely once inviting us to eate with them in the publike Refectory.

All things cheap in the Holy Land.

[I. iii. 236.]

If this discourse makes any surmise that we did some things against our conscience while wee lived in this Monastery, let him reade the foure and twentie Precept of Dissimulation in the Chapter of Precepts, the third Part, and the first booke, wherein I have explaned my opinion of the outward reverence of the body shewed in time of the Papists Divine service. And for the rest, let him know, that I now confesse (as I did formerly) that we therein erred, that we did not first goe to Constantinople or Haleppo, from whence having a Janizare to guide us, chosen by our Ambassador or Merchants, we might have escaped many of those troubles, which now we indured being alone, and that with no greater charge then now we were at, since these troubles

An error in judgment.

increased our charge; and might also easily have obtained any courtesie at these Friers hands, or at least have seene Jerusalem safely, though they were ill affected to us. But since many things diverted us from this course, and now we were fallen into these Italian Friers hands, we thought best to bring our selves out of this danger by discretion and moderation in our deeds and words. Also I confesse, that in those dayes my conscience was not so tender, as since (by the grace of God) I have found it, yet was it never so unsensible, as it could have passed over the worshipping of an Idoll, or the denying of my faith. If I had here gone to Masse, it would seeme no wonder to our English Gentlemen, who have lived any time in Italy; and I am confidently of opinion, that no man returnes home with more detestation of the Papists Religion, then he who well instructed in the truth, hath taken the libertie to behold with his eyes their strange superstitions, which one of experience may well see, without any great participation of their folly. For my part, as I had alwaies been unwilling to bee present at their Masse, so I abhorred from the receiving of the Lords Supper with them. And this was the highest mischiefe, which we could be forced to incurre at Jerusalem. Now for the Communion of our Lords Supper, except it be in great sicknesse and danger of death, they never impose it so earnestly on any man, as hee may not with discreete answeres put it off till another time, without all suspition of contrarietie in Religion. For their Masses, they never sing or mumble them, but in the mornings, and that fasting. Now we came the fourth of June in the afternoone to Jerusalem, and the fifth and sixth dayes we went abroad before full day, to see the monuments, and returned not to the Monasterie till night, at which time the greatest offence to our conscience that could happen, was to heare them sing Psalmes in their Chappell. Upon Friday the seventh of June we tooke our journey to Bethlehem, where my brother falling sick, we had scarse leasure to satisfie our

Detestation of the Papists religion.

The Communion of our Lords Supper.

curiositie, much lesse to bee present at any unpleasing rites of their Religion. Upon Saturday, the eight of June, our consorts returning to Jerusalem, we tooke occasion by my brothers sicknesse to stay at Bethlehem, and came not to Jerusalem till Sunday at night. On Munday the ninth of June we visited the Mountaines or Hill Countrey of Judea, at which time my brother was so ill disposed, as our Consorts themselves doubted his death, and for my part I was all the day troubled with a loosenesse of body. And because the greatest danger of our participating with them in their Rites, was like to be, when we should be locked with them in the Church of the Sepulcher, which onely remained to be seene by us, I made such use of this my brothers and my owne weakenesse, as increasing their opinion of his danger, and my selfe lighting from my Asse oftner then I had cause, to make them thinke my sicknesse the greater, it happened that in the evening our consorts burning with desire of returning homeward, appointed the next day for the visiting of the Sepulcher: but I in respect of my owne and my brothers weakenesse, desired to have it deferred some few dayes, till the very Friers our consorts, impatient of delay, and yet unwilling to incurre the blame of leaving us behind them, made free offer to us of that which wee most desired, saying, that in their chambers within the Church, they had beds for us to rest upon, and that they would provide us meate, and all necessaries, which we could have staying in the Monastery. We gladly took this condition, and so being locked up in the Church of the Sepulcher upon Tuesday the eleventh of June in the afternoone, after we had satisfied our curiositie, we laid us downe upon the beds, and onely forbearing meate for avoiding of suspition, we rested there till Wednesday the twelfth of June in the afternoone, when we came forth, and returned to the Monastery. The thirteenth day we had no thought but of making us ready for our returne, and the next day early in the morning, wee departed from Jerusalem. So as in all this

The mountaines of Judea.

The masse avoided by pretence of great sicknesse.

[I. iii. 237.]

time, the Friers themselves our consorts, had no leasure to bee at a Masse, but onely the Sunday when we were at Bethlehem, and in the Church of the Sepulcher, when upon pretence of sicknesse we rested on our beds. Otherwise we professed our selves Catholiques, as the Papists will be called, yet enemies to the King of Spaine, as the enemie of our Queene and Country. And when our superstitious consorts, being now to leave Jerusalem, had gathered great heapes of stones from the monuments, to carrie into their Country, and had received of the Guardians gift, for great treasure, holy beades, Agnus Dei, and like trash, wee so refused to take any such burthen, as still we bewailed our misfortune, that we being not to returne the right way home, as they did, but to passe to Constantinople, could not carrie such reliques with us, lest they should fall into some Turks hands, who might abuse them. And when our consorts at Bethlehem printed the signe of the Crosse with inke and a pen-knife upon their armes, so as the print was never to bee taken out, wee would not follow them in this small matter, but excused our selves, that being to passe home through many Kingdomes, we durst not beare any such marke upon our bodies, whereby wee might bee knowne. Besides, it was some advantage to us, that the Frenchmen our consorts were of their Kings partie, and professed no lesse hate against Spaine then our selves.

Good excuses for not bearing treasures or markes.

Frenchmens hatred against Spaine.

To conclude, the Friers of our consorts told me and my brother, that the Guardian would make us Knights of the Sepulcher, so we would crave that honour, which was never granted to any but them that craved it, in which case they offered to be intercessors for us. I well knew that they had offered this honour (as they termed it) to a Plebean Frenchman our consort, and had heard, that the Friers used this art to get money from Pilgrimes, making no difference to whom they gave this title. And for my part, I never affected titles, thinking better to be of an inferiour condition with plenty, then of high degree with want. Therefore I so answered them, as giving due thanks for their courtesie, yet I professed, that if I were worthy of that title, I might not crave it, nor receive it offered, in respect of the oath imposing militarie duties upon me, and the profession of service to the King of Spaine, the publique enemy of our Country; besides that, I should be tied thereby, to hate and prosecute all of the reformed Religion, which many of my friends and kinsmen professed. It is true that if wee had had a Janizare to guide and protect us, wee might have lodged in Jerusalem with some Christian, who would have shewed us the monuments, without troubling the Italian Friers. And it is well knowne, that the great Turke gives libertie to all Religions. But the other Sects of Christians being poore, and these Friers being full of money, aswell the Christians as Turkes depend greatly upon them, so as if they would, they might easily have brought us into danger, neither could wee have had such convenient diet and lodging with any other, as with them. And howsoever by our Merchants helpe, we might have obtained letters from the Italian Merchants at Haleppo, for our entertainement and good usage in this Monastery, yet since for the foresaid reasons we had at Cyprus committed our selves to the protection of the Friers our consorts, we had now no meanes but honest dissembling to free our selves from danger: For it had been easie for these Friers secretly to have drawne us into danger of life, and we knew that Papists make no conscience, or rather thinke it meritorious to use like practises against those of our Religion. And if they would not practise against our lives, yet we knew that they might have cast us into many dangers, both here and in our returne through Italy, if wee should have provoked them to wish us ill. Therefore this our foresaid dissembling may well bee excused, especially since thereby wee did not in any sort wound our consciences to my best remembrance.

The Friers full of money but the other Sects poore.

Honest dissembling.

[I. iii. 238.] Now that this dissembling might prove more profitable and honest, it behooved us thorowly to know our consorts, and so to apply our selves to them. Of which the two

French Lay-men were yong, and of no experience in the World; and one of the Friars was more simple then simplicity it selfe, so as small art was required to deceive these. The second Friar had beene a Souldier in the warre of France, and had made himselfe Friar after the peace, onely to escape the privat revenge of some, whose friends he had killed, for they never seeke revenge of those that put on a religious habite, and to gaine this mans love, it was sufficient to use good fellowship towards him. The third Friar had a sharpe wit, joined with the wisdome of experience, so as all the rest chose him for their guide, and to governe their expences. And because he might easily incense our consorts, and the Friars at Jerusalem against us, we thought good to gaine his good will, by all good respects to him; so as howsoever we were not ignorant to manage our owne affaires, yet joining our selves to the rest, we made him also governour of our expences, to witnesse our confidence in his love, and cared not to beare some losse, so we might bind him to us under the title of friendship, which we easily effected with him, being of a curteous disposition. To conclude, I did often experience his good will, and howsoever I found him lovingly and courteously to make us respected, as well of our consorts as the Friars at Jerusalem, yet I perceived by many and cleere arguments, that he thought us to differ from him in religion. For in particular when I refused (for the foresaid reasons, and with due modesty) the Friars offer to make me Knight of the Sepulcher, he smiling, said to me, (alluding to my name) in the French tongue; En verité vous estes fin, &c. That is, in truth you are crafty as your name imports, but I will endeavour to make the Guardian interpret your excuse to the best. Besides his friendship, it was no small advantage to us, that our stay at Jerusalem was so short, as the time permitted them not to inquire after our religion. By the aforesaid art wee freed our selves from all danger, yet would I not advise any by imitating us to incurre the like, who can have the foresaid better commodities of

A Souldier made Friar to escape privat revenge.

A curteous fellow-traveler.

performing this journey, since it would bee hard for any so to disguise their condition, who have not first had good practice and acquaintance with Friars in Italy, as my selfe had. Besides that, all our skill was sharpened to greater warinesse, by a late Tragicall example of others, the memory whereof was daily and hourely before our eies.

A Tragicall example of Englishmen and Flemmings.

For we beheld upon the wall in the chamber where we lodged, the names written of Henry Bacon, and Andrew Verseline, (two English Gentlemen), of Abraham Serwenterb Frederichson, and Henry Vonwildt Peterson Van Narden, (two Flemmings), whose names were written there upon the foureteenth of August, 1595, and lay before us, both sleeping and waking, warning us like so many prodigies or visions to take wary heed to our steps. These foure comming in company to Jerusalem, had beene received into this Monastery, and when they had seene the monuments within and neere Jerusalem, they went to Bethlehem, where it happened that upon a health drunke by the Flemmings to the King of Spaine, which the English refused to pledge, they fell from words to blowes, so as two of them returned wounded to the Monastery of Jerusalem. Then these Italian Friars, (according to the Papists manner, who first make the sicke confesse their sinnes, and receive the Lords Supper, before they suffer Physitian or Apothecary to come to them, or any kitchin physicke to be given them): I say the Friars pressed them to confesse their sinnes, and so to receive the Lords Supper, which when they refused to doe, it was apparant to the Friars, that they were of the reformed Religion, (whom they terme heretikes). Whereupon the Friars beganne to neglect them (I will not say to hate them): and while the two which were wounded staied for recovery of their health, and so detained the other two with them, it happened that the third fell sicke. So as none had their health now, but Master Verseline, who lovingly and like a servant more then a friend, provided all necessaries for his companion Master Bacon, till at last himselfe also fell sicke, and was the first of them that died. Then within eight daies space, all the rest died, either for that they were neglected by the Friers, (which I thinke sufficient in that Countrey to cast away any in their case), or by their too much care, namely by poison (as some suspect): for the Friars have one of their order, [I. iii. 239.] who is skilfull in physicke, and hath a chamber furnished with cooling waters, sirops, and other medicines most fit for that Countrey. When they were dead, the Friars gave into the Turkes hands, the bodies of the two Flemmings and Master Verseline, (who had little store of crownes, which belonged to the great Turke, as heire to all strangers), and the Turkes permitted them to be buried upon Mount Syon without the wals, in the Church yard proper to the Christians of Europe: But Master Bacon, overliving the rest, and now seeing his life to depend upon the Friars care of him, shewed a Novice Friar long bracelets of peeces of gold twined about his arme, and promising to give them all to him, and greater rewards if he would goe with him into England, so as he would take care of him in his sickenesse, he had perswaded the young Friar to goe with him into England, and to promise him faithfull service there: yet when this Novice at his confession made this knowne, and after verified as much to the Guardian and chiefe Friars, I know not whether the hope of this booty made him die sooner, but I am sure he lived very few daies after. And give me leave to tell the truth, these Friars either to gaine his money, (which was due to the Great Turke), or for feare that inquisition should be made by the Turkes after the cause of his death, appearing by manifest signes upon his body (as others suspected and reported), I say these Friers buried this Gentleman in a yard of their Monastery secretly, which if the Great Turke or any of his Magistrates had knowne, no doubt they would gladly have taken this occasion to extort much money from the Frires, since by the like forged accusations, they use sometimes to oppresse them; the very Turkes having at other times themselves buried dead bodies within the

A Friar skilfull in physicke.

Master Bacon secretly buried.

circuit of the Monastery, and after caused them to be digged up, as if they had beene casually found; and then crying that their Ottoman was deceived, put the Friars to pay large ransomes for redeeming of their lives. And let no man wonder that these hungry Governours of Cities and Provinces in Turkey, should use like frauds to intrap Christians, (as they doe very frequently,) since they buy their Offices, and many times are recalled, before they be warme in their seats, if any man at Constantinople offer larger summes for their imployment.

Turkes frauds.

So as this one Province of Palestine, and one City of Jerusalem, (though having small or no trafficke), hath had in one yeeres space foure Zaniacci, the old being recalled to Constantinople, assoone as his successour had outbribed him there. And this is one of the greatest mischiefes in this Empire, since starveling flies sucke much more, then those that are fully gorged. The foresaid Zaniacco is chiefe Governour for military and civill affaires of all Pallestine, and lies at Jerusalem in the house of Pontius Pilate. His Substitute or Liefetenant is called Caiake, who cast one of our consorts for a time into prison, because he complained of the Turkish exactions, and his owne poverty. The third Magistrate is called Cady, who governes Ecclesiastiall matters, and dwelt in Salomons house (as they call it) at Jerusalem, neere the yard of the old Temple of the Jewes, (in which now a Turkish Mosche was built); and of this man we had our leave to enter the City, and to see the sepulcher, and being called before him, we were commanded to put off our shooes, he sitting crosse leg'd (like a Tailor) on the ground upon a Turkey Carpet. The fourth Magistrate was called Agha, who kept the Castle of Jerusalem, and when we walked one evening on that part of the roofe of our Monastery, whence we had the fairest prospect into the City, he sent a messenger to command us to retire from beholding the Castle, or otherwise he would discharge a peece of Ordinance at us.

Jerusalem had foure Governours in one yeeres space.

The Turkish officers at Jerusalem.

Chap. III.

[I. iii 240.]

Of our journey from Jerusalem, by land to Joppa, by Sea to Tripoli in Syria, by land to Haleppo and Scanderona, and of our passage by Sea to the Iland Candia.

June 14. Ann. 1596.

Pon Friday the fourteenth of June, in the yeere 1596 we went out of Jerusalem, and by the same way, and in the same manner as wee came, rode backe to Ramma, delivering to our guide as many zechines as before, to pay for the Turkish exactions, and to our Muccari for their Asses which we had hired. Neither did any memorable thing happen to us by the way, save that when we came neere to Ramma, and by chance rode over the place of buriall for the Turks, where some women were then mourning for their dead friends, they thinking it a reproch that we should ride over their graves, did with inraged countenances fling stones at us, till wee appeased them by dismounting from our Asses. The fifteenth of June we came backe to Joppa, where our guide gave three meidines to a Janizare, that hee would beate with a cudgell certaine Arabians, who had offered us wrong by the way, which hee did readily and roundly. Then without delay we went aboard our little Greeke Barke, which (according to our bargaine at Cyprus) staied here for our returne. For the Master thereof was further tied to transport us from hence to Tripoli in Syria, neither had he yet received full paiment for transporting us hither, the money being left in Cyprus with an Italian Merchant, who was to pay it him at his returne, if hee brought a testimony under our hands, that he had performed his bargaine to us. This condition we made providently, and by advice of experienced men, for otherwise the Master of our Barke, upon any profitable occasion, would have left this port

Inraged women.

Provident advice.

before our returne from Jerusalem, and wee should hardly have found another Barke here, in a place not much frequented with ships. Besides that the restraint of the money, not to be payed but upon a testimony brought under our hands, was a good caution, that he should not use us ill, nor any way betray us. The sixteenth of June upon Sunday by twilight of the morning, we set sayle from Joppa, and coasting the shoare of Asia, had the land so neere us every day, as wee might easily distinguish the situation of the Cities and Territories. And first we passed by the Citie called Cæsaria Philippi, seated in a Plaine, and twentie five miles distant from Joppa, which of old was a famous Citie, but now for the most part ruined, and become an infamous nest of Turkes, Moores and Arabians. Here Christ raised to life the daughter of Jairus, and healed the woman, which for twelve yeeres had a flux of bloud. And here Saint Peter did baptize the Centurion Cornelius, and Saint Paul in the presence of Fœlix disputed with Tertullus. Here Titus the sonne of Vespasian landing, when hee came to destroy Jerusalem, cast great multitudes of Jewes to wilde beasts to be devoured. In the right way to Tripoli, Antipatris was not farre distant, which Herod did rebuild, and thither the souldiers did leade Saint Paul, by the command of the Tribune Lysias, but we could not see this Village. Next, we did see the Pilgrims Castle, now called Tortora. Then we sailed by the Promontory (hanging farre over the Sea) of the Mountaine Carmelus, made famous by the aboade of the Prophet Elias. Then we passed within sight of the old Citie Ptolemais, after called Achon and Acri, seated in a faire playne within a Creeke of the sea of the same name, and compassing the Citie. And such a faire plaine lyes all along the Coast from Joppa to Tripoli. This Citie was famous by the armies of Europe, passing to conquer these parts, and at this day it hath a large circuit, compassed with walls, and a commodious Haven, and is thirtie five miles distant from Cæsaria. From hence sailing twentie miles, we

Caesaria. *Antipatris.* *Carmel.* *Achon.*

passed by the Citie Tyrus, then called Sur, the ruines whereof witnesse the old magnificence. *Tyre.* The seate thereof seemed most pleasant, being built upon a low Rocke, in the forme of a Peninsule, which Rocke was part of a high Promontory hanging over the sea. And it may [I. iii. 241.] appeare how strongly it was fortified of old by Quintus Curtius, relating the difficulties with which Alexander the Great took and subdued the same. When we had sailed some ten miles further, we did see the ruines of Sarepta, where the Prophet Elias lodged with a widdow, *Sarepta.* in the time of a great famine. After we had sayled some twenty miles further, we did see and passed by the City Sydon, now called Saetta, seated on the North side of a *Sydon.* Promontory, and lying towards the West and South, to the very sea side. These most pleasant Territories are inhabited by wicked people, but God sent us a faire wind, by which we escaped from them, into whose Ports if we had beene driven, they would have taken all just and unjust occasions to extort money from us, if they did us no worse harme. Mention is often made in the Holy Scriptures of Sydon, Tire, and these Territories, as well in the old as new Testament, the particulars whereof I omit. Here first we did gladly see the hils and high tops of Mount Lybanus, being a very pleasant *Lybanus.* and fruitful mountaine, the wines whereof are carried as farre as Haleppo. The Castle Barutti is some two miles *Barutti.* distant from the Promontory of Saetta, and it is seated upon the North-side of a hil, hanging over the sea. Here they say that Saint George delivered the Kings daughter, by killing a Dragon: And to this place, as also to Tyre and Sydon, there is great concourse of Merchants, who have their chiefe trafficke at Damascus, and especially at Haleppo. From hence we passed ten miles to Biblis; *Biblis.* then after ten miles saile, we passed by Petrona, and againe after ten miles saile by a Promontory, which the Italians call Capo Peso.

Lastly we passed ten miles sailing by a most pleasant plaine, and so upon Thursday the seventeenth of June

Tripoli. landed at Tripoli of Syria, (so called for difference from Tripoli in Africke), The Haven is compassed with a wall, and lies upon the west-side of the City, wherein were many little Barkes, and some Shippes of Marsiles in France. The Haven is fortified with seven Towers, whereof the fourth is called the Tower of Love, because it was built by an Italian Merchant, who was found in bed with a Turkish woman, which offence is capitall as well to the Turke as Christian, if he had not thus redeemed his life. Upon the Haven are built many store-houses for Merchants goods, and shops wherein they are set to sayle. The City of Tripoli is some halfe mile distant from the Haven, to which the way is sandy, having many gardens on both sides. In this way they shew a pillar fastned upon a hill of sand, by which they say the sand is inchanted, lest it should grow to overwhelme the City. Likewise they shew other pillars, under which they say great multitudes of Scorpions were in like sort inchanted, which of old wasted all that Territory; and they thinke that if these pillars were taken away, the City would be destroied by the sand and Scorpions. *The scituation of the City.* The length of the City somewhat passeth the bredth, and lieth from the South to the North, seated upon the side of an hill, so cut by nature as it conveyes a brooke into the streetes. Upon the West side of the City, towards the South corner, is a Castle upon a high hill, which the French men built of old to keepe the Citizens in subjection, and therein the Great Turke to the same end keepes a garrison of Souldiers, under his Agha or Governour of the City. Upon the East side are two bridges over the foresaid brooke, whence many pleasant fountains spring, which running from the South to the North, passe through the streetes of the City, and then water the gardens. Beyond this brooke are fruitfull hils, and beyond the hils Mount Lybanus lies, so high as it hinders all further prospect, which mountaine is very pleasant, abounding with fruitfull trees, and with grapes yeelding a rich wine. Upon the North side without the

A.D. 1596.

gates, are many most pleasant gardens, in which they keepe great store of silke-wormes: for the Turks sell their raw silke to the Italians, and buy of them the stuffes woven thereof. The building of Tripoli and of these parts, is like to that of Cyprus and Jerusalem. The streete that leades to the way of Haleppo, is broad, the rest narrow, and the aire and waters are unhealthfull. Mount Lybanus (as I formerly said) is incredibly fruitfull, and the plaine of Tripoli reaching ten miles, is more fruitfull then can easily be expressed, bearing great store of pleasant fruites, whereof one among the rest is called Amazza-Franchi, that is, kill Frankes (or French), because the men of Europe died in great numbers by eating immoderately thereof. The plaine of Tripoli did of old yeeld two hundred thousand crownes yeerely to the Count thereof, as Historians write. And howsoever the old trafficke of Tripoli, is for the most part removed to Damascus and Haleppo, yet the City of Tripoli still yeelds foure hundred thousand crownes yeerely to the Great Turke.

Silke-wormes.

[I. iii. 242.]

It may seeme incredible, but it is most certaine, that here and throughout Syria, they have sheepe of such bignes, as the very tailes of them, hanging in many wreathes to the ground, doe weigh twenty five pounds, and many times thirty three pounds.

Great sheepe of Syria.

A Christian who useth to entertaine the French, did very well intreat us here: and when I did see a bed made for me and my brother, with cleane sheetes, I could scarcely containe my selfe from going to bed before supper, because I had never lien in naked bed since I came from Venice to this day, having alwaies slept by sea and land in my doublet, with linnen breeches and stockings, upon a mattresse, and betweene coverlets or quilts, with my breeches under my head. But after supper all this joy vanished by an event least expected: For in this part of Asia great store of cotten growes (as it were) upon stalkes like Cabbage, (as I formerly said in my journey from Joppa to Jerusalem);

A good Christian.

and these sheetes being made thereof, did so increase the perpetuall heat of this Countrey, now most unsupportable in the summer time, as I was forced to leape out of my bed, and sleepe as I had formerly done.

My Host told me a strange thing, namely that in Alexandria of Ægypt, seated upon one of the mouthes of the River Nilus, there was a Dove-cote, & that also at Cairo (or Babylon,) farre within the Land of Ægypt, there was another Dove-cote; and because it much concernes the Merchants, to have speedy newes of any commodity arriving, he assured mee that they used to tie letters about the neckes of the Doves at Alexandria, and so to let them loose, which Doves having formerly bred in the Dove-cote at Cayro, did flie thither most swiftly, and the Keeper of them there taking the Letters they brought, used to deliver them to the Merchants. This I beleeved not, till I came to Haleppo, and telling it for a fable to the English Merchants there, they seriously affirmed the same to be true: Moreover the Host of Tripoli told me newes from Constantinople, namely, that the Greekes had burnt great part of the City, (which he thought to be false, and onely invented to oppresse them in other parts); and that the Janizaries had raised a great tumult against the Subasha of the City, who used great severity towards them, by restraining them from drinking wine, and from keeping harlots; and that some one hundred of these seditious Janizaries were drowned in the Haven, and the rest were daily sought out to be punished. Moreover that Halil Basha the Admirall of Turkey, was parted from Constantinople with sixty Gallies, having taken many Greeke and Armenian Christians by force, to row in his Gallies; besides that, for want of Marriners, he had left there twenty Gallies, which were prepared to keepe that narrow sea. Finally, that the Great Turke was presently to goe with his Army into Hungary, but was not yet departed from the City.

Letters carried on the neckes of Doves.

Newes from Constantinople.

Now the French-men our consorts went aboard a ship of Marsiles to returne into France. But my selfe and my

A.D. 1596.

brother being to goe by Land to Haleppo, agreed to give our Muccaro nine piastri, for two Asses to ride upon, and their meate; and for three tributes (called cafarri) which he was to pay for us by the way, (comming to some twenty meidines). They call him Muccaro, who lets out Mules, Asses, or Horses; and they call him Malem, who conducts the Merchants goods. Moreover we were forced to give a suger-loafe to the value of a Zechine, to the Governour of the City, and a Piastro to the Scribe or Clerke of the City, for the priviledge to goe without a Janizare to conduct us, (so they pretended, omitting no occasions to extort from Christians). But we covenanted not to pay the nine piastri to our Muccaro, till our journey was ended, onely giving one piastro into his hands for earnest, and pretending that we would pay the rest at Haleppo, where we were to receive money; lest they thinking that we had store of crowns with us, should practise any treason or oppression against us. This Piastro we gave him in hand, to buy meat for his beasts, and the other eight we paid after at Haleppo, and besides gave him of free gift a zechine for his faithfull service to us by the way. We were to take our journey with the Caravan going from Tripoli to Haleppo. The Turkes call a Caravan the company of Merchants, passengers, and drivers of loaded Camels, keeping together, for safety against Theeves, and using to lodge in the open field. For in Turkey they make journeies in great troopes, neither did I ever see any ride alone, but onely a horseman of the Armie, and that very rarely.

Charges for Aleppo.

[I. iii. 243.]

A caravan.

Upon Saturday the two and twentie of June, we went out of Tripoli at the North Gate, and passed over a Bridge of the foresaid Brooke, and from eight of the clocke till Noone, we passed along the Sea-shoare, and over high Mountaines, then over an untilled Plaine, seeing not one Village, nor so much as the least house by the way. Then at last comming to a little shade of Fig-trees, we rested there the heate of the day, and fed upon such victuals as we had, while our Muccaro and the rest gave meate to their beasts. At three of the clock in the after-noone we went forward in the like way, and late in the evening we came to a Village, neere which we lodged in the open field, in a pleasant plot of grasse, neere the banke of a River, planted with some trees. Upon Sunday wee rose early, and for two howers space passed a Promontory of the Sea; then turning towards the Land, wee passed through wilde and untilled Hilles and plaine fields, and at Noone we rested under the shaddow of some Brambles, refreshing our selves with meate and sleepe, and giving meate to our Asses. At three in the afternoone wee went forward, and passed by the Castle Huss, in which some say Job dwelt, and which they say was possessed by the French, while they had the Kingdome of Jerusalem. Also we passed by a Monastery of Saint George, then possessed by Christian Friers, and seated in a pleasant Valley, yeelding trees of Figs and Olives. And towards evening, we incamped (as I may terme it) in the open field at the foot of a high Mountaine. They say Job did of old possesse this Territorie, and that not farre hence in the way leading to Damascus, there is a Citie now called Hemps, and of old called Huss, which the Christian Inhabitants to this day call the Citie of Job, and the Valley not far distant the Valley of Huss, and the Turkes have built a Mosche or Church in this Citie, which they thinke to be built upon the very ruines of the house wherein Job dwelt, and that his body was carried from hence to Constantinople. Others object, that according to the Scriptures, Job could not dwell here, because they write, that hee dwelt among the Idumeans, and was robbed by the Sabeans. I dare not affirme that he dwelt here, but I dare boldly say, that I know more then Socretes did, even two things, whereas he knew but one: first, that the Arabians to this day make excursions into these parts, robbing the Caravans that goe from Haleppo to Tripoli, so as if Job were alive, and had an hundred thousand head of cattell, they were as like to rob him here, as in any other place.

A monastery of Saint George.

Huss.

Job's House.

Secondly, I know that we passed a sad night in this place, and never had more need of Job his patience then here.

For it happened that one of the women (which the leaders of the Caravan use to have for their attendance) lighting a fire to make ready their supper, by chance some sparke or flame brake out of the stones wherewith it was compassed, and set the drie hearbs of the field on fire, which being neglected at the first, did spread it selfe for a great compasse. Whereupon the Governour of the Province dwelling upon the Mountaine, and beholding the fields on fier, sent to us one Janizary, armed onely with a cudgell, who fell upon the men of our Caravan, being some hundred in number, beating them with his cudgell, till they fell upon the fier with the upper long garments they use to weare, and so extinguished it. In the meane time my selfe and my brother went aside, lying out of his sight, by the advantage of a high ground betweene him and us, where wee were astonished to see one man armed onely with a cudgell to beate a hundred men (and the very Zantons or Priests) armed with swords and many Callivers. The fire being put out, we thinking all safe, joyned our selves to the company againe, but soone espied our errour: for the Janizare drove us all before him like so many Calves, to appeare before the Governour, and satisfie him for this damage. And if at any time we went slowly, hee wheeled his cudgell about his head, and crying Wohowe Rooe, presently struck them that were next him. My brother and my selfe treated with him by the way, to give him a reward that he would dismisse us: but when he gave this warning, we were the first to run from him, with laughter to see our men thus driven like beasts, and commending to our selves the honesty of the man, who first gave warning before he struck. Then presently assoone as wee did see the Gentleman pacified, we returned againe to him, with our Muccaro to interpret our words, and told him, that we were the servants of a Christian Merchant, and had no goods in the Caravan, nor any thing to doe with them,

The fields set on fire by chance.

One man beates a hundred.

[I. iii. 244.]

and offering him a reward, so he would let us returne. For we knew that the Turks would take any occasion to oppresse us as Christians, and that the Governor would have dealt worse with the Caravan, if he perceived that Christians were with them. Thus we often fled from him when he gave the said signe of anger, (for howsoever wee offered him a gift, yet wee could not otherwise escape his blowes), and often we returned to him being pacified offering him a gift to dismisse us, which at last wee obtained, giving him a zechine. When we were dismissed, wee were in no lesse feare of some violence, while wee returned alone and unarmed, to the place where our baggage lay: but going forward betweene hope and feare, at last we came safe thither, and there hid our selves til our consorts should returne, who after an howers space returning, told us, that the chiefe of the Caravan, being the cause of the fire making, had paid ten piastri for the damage: and the Governour swore, that if the fire had gone over the Mountaine into the plaine field of Corne, hee would have hanged us all upon the highest trees, on the top of the Mountaine. This Tragedy ended, wee refreshed our selves with meate and sleepe.

The Janizare appeased by a gift.

Upon Monday early in the morning, we set forward, and spent eight howers in ascending the Mountaine, which was very high, but the way easie, with many turnings about the Mountaine, which of it selfe without manuring yeelded many wilde, but pleasant fruits, seeming to passe in pleasantnesse the best manured Orchards. Upon the top of the Mountaine we met some horsemen of the Army, not without feare of some violence to be offered us, till we understood that they were sent out to purge the high waies of theeves. They were armed with Launces, Shields, and short broad Swords, so as a man would have said, they had been the Knights of Amades de Gaule. Neither is it unprobable, that those fictions came from the horsemen of Asia, since wee did see some mile from Tripoli, a Bridge called the Bridge of Rodomont, and a Fountaine neere Scandarona, called the

Horsemen of the Army.

Amazons Fountaine, and many like monuments in these parts. When wee had passed the foresaid high Mountaine, wee came into a very large and fruitfull Plaine of Corne, which was yet uncut-downe. Here we refreshed our selves and our beasts with meate, resting neere a Fountaine (for the Turkes require no better Inne for their beasts and themselves, then a Fountaine of cleere water.) After dinner we went forward in this Plaine, and did see some Villages, which in this vast Empire are very rare, and neere one of these Villages wee did sit downe at night, supping and resting in the open field. Upon Tuesday earely in the morning, we tooke our journy, and for sixe howers passed in the same Plaine, having not so much as the shaddow of one tree, and came to the City Aman (which in the Scripture the second of the Kings, the seventeenth Chapter, is called Hamath) being some three dayes journey from Damasco. This Citie is of large circuit, and pleasantly seated upon two Hilles, (for the third Hill of the Castle hath nothing but ruines), having a River running by it, and abounding with Orchards of Palmes and fruitfull trees, and neere the same were sixe Villages in sight. Here we rested part of this day, and the next night, the Master of our Caravan having businesse in the City, neither imported it where we lodged; for they have no publike Innes, nor beds in any house, nor Cookes, but every man buyes his meate, and can dresse it. But to the end wee might be ready to goe early with the Caravan in the morning, most of us lodged in poore houses of the Suburbs. My selfe and my brother being to sleepe in the yard upon our owne quilts, and the yard declining from the house to the bottome, where our beasts were tied, wee laid our selves downe upon the top of the Hill, but in the morning found our selves tumbled downe between the feet of the Asses & Camels, when I could not remember the English Innes without sighing. This Citie hath great traffique, [I. iii. 245.] and aboundeth with necessaries to sustaine life, and here our Muccaro bought for us, sower Curds (vulgarly caled

The Turkes Innes.

Hamath.

No publike Innes.

Charges for food. Mish Mash) for two meidines, a cheese for sixe, three hennes for three meidines, twenty eggs for foure meidines, Cucumers for three, milke for five, Aqua vitæ (which they call Harach, and drinke as largely as Wine) for ten meidines, foure pounds of wine for one zechine, Bisket (for the Turkes have no other bread but cakes baked on the harth) for thirty meidines, which things we provided for our Supper, and to carry with us by the way, yet might we have bought, and did buy most things by the way, excepting Wine and Bread, which are hardly found, and must be carried by those that will have them. The guide of our Caravan was detained here by his businesse most part of the next day, being Wednesday, and in the meane time it fortunately happened, that a Turkish Basha, returning with his traine from his Governement, and being to goe our way, rested here, so as his company freed us the rest of our journey from feare of theeves.

Upon Wednesday in the afternoone we set forward, in the company of this Basha, and journied all night in this Plaine, wherein there was not the shadow of one tree, and at eight of the clock the next morning, we did sit downe in the open field, resting under the ruines of old walles. *Inquiries by the Janizaries.* Here the Janizaries of the Basha inquired curiously after the condition of me and my brother, so as our Muccaro advised us to give them halfe a piastro, which they receiving, promised to defend us from all injury, but in the meane time they did so swallow our wine, as when it was spent, we were forced to drinke water, to which we were not used. Upon Thursday at three of the clock in the afternoone, we set forward, and *Marrha.* about midnight we came to the Citie Marrha, where our Muccaro and divers others payed each of them ten meidines for cafar or tribute, and at the Citie Gate a man was hanged in chaines (also the next day we did see another impalled, that is sitting and rotting upon a stake fastned in the ground, and thrust into his fundament and bowels.) Upon Friday before day wee set forward, and passing a stony barren way, but full of Walnut trees, upon which many birds did sit and sing, wee came in foure houers space to an Hospitall, which they call Caon, and it was stately built of stone, in a round forme, with arches round about the Court-yard, under which arches each severall company chose their place to eate and rest, both which they must doe upon the ground, except they bring Tables and beds with them. Neither were any victuals there to be sold or dressed, but every man bought his victuals in the Village adjoyning, and dressed it after his manner. The same Friday at foure in the afternoone, wee went forward, and riding all night, did upon Saturday early in the morning sleepe an hower in the open field, while meate was given to our beasts.

An Hospitall called Caon.

Then going forward, we came by Noone, the same day being the nine and twentie of June, (after the Popes new stile, which I have followed hitherto, being in company of Italians and Friers), to the famous Citie of Haleppo, where the English Merchants living in three houses, as it were in Colledges, entertained my brother and mee very curteously. And George Dorington the Consul of the English there, led us to the house, wherein he lived with other Merchants, and there most courteously entertained us, with plentifull diet, good lodging, and most friendly conversation, refusing to take any money for this our entertainement. And howsoever wee brought him onely a bill of exchange for one hundred Crownes, yet when we complained to him, that we now perceived the same would not serve our turnes, hee freely lent us as much more upon our owne credit. Yea, when after my brothers death my selfe fell dangerously sicke, and was forced to goe from those parts before I could recover my health, so as all men doubted of my returne into England, yet he lent me a farre greater summe upon my bare word, which howsoever I duly repayed after my comming into England, yet I confesse, that I cannot sufficiently acknowledge his love to mee, and his noble consideration of poore and afflicted strangers.

June 29.

Haleppo.

George Dorington's curtesy.

The Citie Haleppo is said to have the name of Halep, which signifies milke, because the Province is most fruitfull, or of the word Aleph, as the chiefe Citie of Syria, and to have been called of old Aram Sobab
[I. iii. 246.] (mentioned the second of Samuel, the eight Chapter and third verse), or at least to be built not farre from the ruines thereof. *The Trafficke in Haleppo.* The Trafficke in this place is exceeding great, so as the goods of all Asia and the Easterne Ilands are brought hither, or to Cayro in Egypt. And before the Portugals found the way into East India, these commodities were all brought from these two Cities. And the Venetians and some free Cities of Italy solly enjoyed all this trafficke of old. But after that time, the Portugals trading in East India, served all Europe with these commodities, selling them, yea and many adulterate Druggs, at what price they listed, cutting off most part of this trafficke from the Italians. At last the French King making league with the great Turke, the Merchants of Marsiles were made partners of this trafficke, and in our age the English, under the Raigne of Queene Elizabeth, obtained like priviledge, though great opposition was made against them by the Venetians & French Merchants. And the Turkey company in London was at this time the richest of all other, silently enjoying the safety and profit of this trafficke, (understand that when I wrote this, the trafficke into the East Indies was nothing at all or very little knowne to the English or Flemmings).

The description of Haleppo. This City lies within Land, the Port whereof (called Alexandretta by the Christians, and Scanderona by the Turkes) I shall hereafter describe. The building of this City (as of all houses in Syria) is like to that of Jerusalem, but one roofe high, with a plaine top plaistered to walke upon, and with Arches before the houses, under which they walke dry, and keepe shops of wares. The City is nothing lesse then well fortified, but most pleasantly seated, having many sweet gardens. The aire was so hot, as me thought I supped hot broth, when I drew it in; but it is very subtile, so as the Christians comming hither from Scanderona, (a most unhealthfull place, having the aire choaked with Fens), continually fall sicke, and often die. And this is the cause, that the English Factors imployed here, seldome returne into England, the twentieth man scarcely living till his prentiship being out, he may trade here for himselfe. The Christians here, and the Turkes at the Christians cost, drinke excellent wines, whereof the white wines grow in that territory, but the red wines are brought from Mount Libanus. Moreover all things for diet are sold at cheape rates, and indeed the Turkes want not good meat, but only good Cookes to dresse it. The English Merchants can beare me witnes, that these parts yeeld sheepe, whereof the taile of one wreathed to the ground, doth weigh some thirty or more pounds, in fat and wooll. In one of the City gates, they shew the Sepulcher of Saint George, where the Turkes maintaine Lampes continually burning: for among all the Christian Saints, they onely reverence Saint George. In a garden of the suburbes I did see a Serpent of wonderfull bignes, and they report, that the male Serpent and young ones, being killed by certaine boyes, this shee Serpent observing the water where the boyes used to drinke, did poyson the same, so as many of the boyes died thereof; and that the Citizens thereupon came out to kill her, but seeing her lie with her face upward, as complaining to the Heavens that her revenge was just, that they touched with a superstitious conceit, let her alone: finally that this Serpent had lived here many ages, and was of incredible yeeres. Moreover they shew a well neere to the City, in which they report, that a chest of treasure was of old cast, so as it might be seene by passengers, and that some attempting to take it out, were assaulted and affrighted with Divels.

Diet cheape.

A Serpent of wonderfull bignes.

In this City my selfe and my brother Henry lay sicke some few daies, but by the helpe of a Jew Physician, we soone recovered our health, and for feare of wanting money, and especially out of our desire to returne home,

A Jew Physician.

wee made too great haste to beginne our journey for Constantinople. If we would have expected eight daies, *The Cassenda.* the Cassenda, (so they call a troope of Horsemen, guarding the great Turkes treasure), was in that time to goe for Constantinople, in whose company wee might safely and swiftly have performed this journey, namely in sixeteene daies, whereas those who followed the slow pace of Cammels, scarcely arrive there in thirty daies. But this Province being extreamely hot in this time of summer, and wee being scanted of money for our long journey, all mention of longer staying was most unpleasing to us. Moreover Master George Dorington, (never to be [I. iii. 247.] named by me without mention of love and respect), did at this time send a Caravan, (that is, Camels loaded with goods) of his own to Constantinople, and being to make a present to a Cady, returning from his governement to Constantinople, that he would take his Caravan into his protection, and to passe in his company, and lovingly making offer to us, to recommend us in like sort with his goods to the same Cady, we were easily perswaded to take this journey presently, in the company of his servants, and of a curteous English Merchant, called *Master Jasper Tyant.* Master Jasper Tyant, being then to goe for Constantinople. This our conclusion proved greatly to the losse of Sir John Spencer, Merchant of London, whose goods these were which Master Dorington sent with us. For my brother dying by the way, and the great Turke being heire to all Christians and strangers, dying in his Empire, the Turkes either thought, or fradulently pretended that these goods belonged to my brother, and so tooke them into the great Turkes store-houses, and kept them there, till they had unjustly extorted good summes of money from Master Dorington, besides the great losse which was sustained by the servants and Camels hired in vaine.

Camell hire. Being now to enter this journey, we hired for seventy one piastri, a Camell to carry our victuals, an ambling Mule for my brother, and a horse for my selfe, and so much we presently gave into the hands of our Muccaro, with covenant that he should pay for the meat of the beasts. Moreover we presently laid out one hundred and twenty piastri for divers necessaries, namely, two long chaires, like cradles covered with red cloth, to hang on the two sides of our Camell, (which chaires the Turkes use to ride in, and to sleepe upon Camels backes, but we bought them to carry victuals), for bisket, and a tent wherein we might sleepe, and for like provisions. But behold, when all this mony was laid out, and the very evening before the day in which we were to begin our journey, my brother Henry fell sicke of a flux. Being amased with this sudden chance, we stood doubtfull for a time what to do, til the consideration of the great summes of money we had laied out, and of the difficulty to get more, made us resolve to take this fatall journey, yet with this purpose, when we came to Scanderona, some foure daies journy distant, to goe no further, except in that time he recovered his health, propounding this comfort to our miserable estate, that there we might have commodity of convenient lodging with an Englishman, there abiding factor for our Merchants.

Necessaries for the journey.

Upon Thursday the last of June, (that I may now follow the old stile, taken here from the English, and generally used in Turkey, among the very Christians, howsoever hitherto I have followed the new stile, taking it from the Venetian shippe in which I came, and from the Friers at my abode in Jerusalem); I say the last of June we went out of Haleppo, passing over stony hils, and by the Village Havaden, where the Jewes say the Prophet Jeremy was buried. Then riding forward all that night, at last we sate downe at eight of the clocke in the morning, and pitched our Tents neere a Village, where I did see a pillar erected to Pompey, and here we rested and refreshed our selves the heat of the day. This kind of journying was strange to us, and contrary to our health: for we beganne our journey at foure in the afternoone, to shun the heat of the day past, and rode all night, so as we not used to this watching, were so sleepy

The last of June.

Strange journying.

towards the Sunne rise, as we could not abstaine from nodding, and were many times like to fall from our horses. To which mischiefe we could find no other remedy, then to ride swiftly to the head of the Caravan, and there dismounting, to lie downe and slumber, with our horses bridle tied to our legges, one of us by course walking by us, to keepe us from injuries, and to awaken us when the last Camel passed by, lest we should there be left a pray to theeves. And we having some two hundred Camels in our Caravan, did in this sort passe the sleepy houres in the morning, till seven or eight of the clocke, at which time we used to pitch our tents, and rest. Moreover this greatly afflicted us, that spending the morning till ten or eleven of the clocke in pitching our Tent, preparing meat, and eating, we had no time to rest, but the extreme heat of the noone day, which so pierced our tents, that we could no more sleepe, then if in England upon a Summers day we had lien neere a hot sea-cole fire. And howsoever wee lessened this heate, by flinging our gownes over our Tent, betweene the sunne and us, yet for my part I was so afflicted with want of sleepe, and with this immoderate heate, as I feared to fall into a Lunacy, what then should a man think would become of my sickly brother in this case?

A remedy to obtaine sleepe.

[I. iii. 248.]

Upon Friday the first of July, towards evening, wee tooke up our Tents, supping while our Muccaro loaded our beasts, then we rode over Mountaines all night, and the next morning againe pitched our Tents neere a poore Village. And our Muccaro bought us some fresh victuals in the Village, according to the manner of Turky, where the very Cities yeeld no Innes. Upon Saturday towards evening, wee set forward, and rode that night over a large Plaine, and next day after Sunne-rise wee came to Antioch, a citie of Asia, famous for the Patriarchate, and by Histories sacred and prophane. Upon the east-side, and upon the top of a high Mountaine, lye great ruines of the old walles and houses, whence the seat of the citie declineth to the Plaine on the West side. In

Antioch.

which Plaine our Caravan rested the heat of this day, neere the pleasant and large Fountaine of water, wherin the Scriptures record so many to have been baptized together, as first in this place the faithfull had the name of Christians. This Fountaine hath faire building, and seemes of old to have been very stately, and here wee pitched our Tents in the middest of the Gardens of this Plaine within the walles. For howsoever the ruines of the walles shew, that of old the circuit of the citie was very large, yet scarce the hundreth part thereof was now filled with houses. Upon the West side without the walles, the citie is all compassed with a River, and a great Fen, and upon the East-side with Mountaines, which situation makes it naturally strong. Here first wretched I perceived the imminent danger of my most deare brothers death, which I never suspected til this day, much lesse had any just cause to feare it. A Turke in this Caravan troubled with the same disease of a Flux, went to the ground more then twentie times each nights journey, and yet lived; whereas my brother only three or foure times descended from his Mule to that purpose, which filled us with good hope. But here first I learned by miserable experience, that nothing is worse for one troubled with the Flux, then to stop or much restraine the course therof. For my brother stopping this naturall purge, by taking Red wine and Marmelat, experienced men did attribute (all too late) his death to no other thing. I could not hire a horse-litter by any endevour of our Muccaro, nor for any price, though I offered an incredible summe for that, or like commoditie to carrie him, and we thought it very dangerous to stay here among the Turkes, after our Caravan departed, especially since Scanderona was but five and twenty miles distant, where wee should have the commoditie to lodge with an Englishman, and so to get all necessaries for his recoverie. Therefore upon Sunday in the evening, wee put all our provisions in one of the foresaid covered chaires or cradles, caried by the Camell, and made my brother a bed in the

My brother sicke of the Flux.

A Camell-bed.

other cradle, where (as we thought) he might commodiously rest. And I promised the Muccaro halfe a piastro for every time my brother should descend from the Camell to ease himselfe, for wee were to ride before with the horsemen, and hee was now to come behind with the Camels. So we set forward, and my selfe twice in the night, and once towards morning, left the horsemen, and rode back to my brother, to know how he fared, and when hee gave mee no answere, I returned to the horsemen, thinking that he slept. Then towards morning I was so afflicted with my wonted desire of sleepe, as I thought an howers rest worth a Kings ransome. Therefore my selfe and Master Jasper Tyant our loving consort, rode a good pace to the Village Byland, where we were to pitch our Tents, that we might make all things ready to receive him.

Byland.

But within short space our Muccaro running to our Tent, and telling me, that hee had left my brother ready to give up his last breth in the first house of the Village, seemed to say to me, Goe quickly and hang thy selfe. With all possible speede I ran to this house, imbraced my dying brother, and confounded with sorrow, understood from his mouth, how farre the events of our nights journey had been contrary to our hope. For whereas my selfe advised him to leave his Mule, and lie in the chaire upon the Camels backe, he told me that he was
[I. iii. 249.] shaken in pieces with the hard pace of the Camell. And whereas I had offered the Muccaro halfe a piastro, for each time hee should light to ease himselfe, he told mee that he had often asked this favour of the Muccaro, but could never obtaine it, he excusing himselfe by feare to be left behind the Caravan, for a prey to theeves. And whereas the Camels hinder parts being higher then the fore parts, I had laied my brothers head towards the hinder parts, and raised it as high as I could with pillowes and clothes, for his better ease, it happened (which I being ignorant of the way could not foresee) that we all the night ascending mountaines, his feet were farre higher

A faithless Muccaro.

then his head; whereupon he told me, that most part of the night he had lien in a trance, which was the cause that he could not answer me, at such times as I came to inquire of his health. Thus mischiefe lighted upon mischiefe, to make my wretched state most miserable: Why should I use many words in a case, from the remembrance whereof my mind abhorreth. Therefore I will say in a word; My most deere brother Henry upon Munday the fourth of July, (after the old stile), the yeere of our Lord 1596, and of his age the seven and twentieth, died in my armes, after many loving speeches, and the expressing of great comfort in his Divine meditations.

July 4. Anno 1596.

The Turkes presently snatched all things that were his, as belonging to the Great Turke; yea, my selfe cast his shirts, with many other things of good value, and whatsoever I could see that was his, out of the Tent into the Turkes hands, and as a man halfe out of my wits, could indure to see nothing that might renew the bitter remembrance of him. The Turkish Officers in the Great Turkes name seazed upon all the goods of Sir John Spencer, which Master Dorington sent with us, as if they had belonged to my brother, neither could they be released, without great bribes, after the contrary was proved. Presently I sent for the English Factor lying at Scanderona, who scarcely obtained with the paying of five zechines, to have my brothers body buried in the open fields: besides, the Janizares, Turkes, and Moores, came in severall swarmes to me in this miserable case, threatning to hinder his buriall, or to dig him up after hee was buried, except I would satisfie their insatiable extortions. And had not the foresaid English Factor taken upon him to satisfie these people, and taken up my purse full of zechines, which I cast among them in a rage, surely for my part I had willingly given my selfe and all that I had with me, to them for a prey. One thing above measure afflicted me, (which I thinke Job himselfe could not have suffered), namely, that while my selfe and my brother were in our last imbraces, and mournefull

Covetousnesse of the Turkes.

speeches, the rascall multitude of Turkes and Moores, ceased not to girne & laugh at our sighes and teares; neither know I why my heart-strings brake not in these desperate afflictions: but I am sure from that day to this I never enjoied my former health, and that this houre was the first of my old age.

Towards the evening the same fourth day of July, we descended with the said English Factor, (taking care to have our baggage carried) from the mountaines towards *Scanderona.* Scanderona, little distant from this place, in the furthest Northerne part of the vally upon the seashore. From hence Jasper Tyant our loving consort in this misery, returned back to Haleppo; but my selfe not knowing what to resolve, nor having power to thinke of disposing my selfe, remained at Scanderona in the English Factors house. The next night while I lay waking, I heard multitudes of Woolves, (as I thought) howling upon the mountaines of Byland, and in the morning I understood by the English Merchant, that a kind of beast little bigger then a Foxe, and ingendered betweene Foxes *Jagales.* and Wolves, vulgarly called Jagale, used to range upon these mountaines in troopes, and many times to scratch the bodies of the dead out of their graves; whereupon I hired an Asse to carry me, and a Janizare to accompany me, and went to see the place of my brothers buriall, from which part I thought to heare those howlings: And there beyond my expectation, I found that they had scratched up the earth almost to his body, and the Turkes made no doubt, but that these beasts hiding themselves from day light, would according to their manner, returne the next night to devoure his body. Therefore I hired many poore people to bring stones, whereof I made such a pile round about his body, as I preserved that prey from their cursed jaws, which done, I returned to [I. iii. 250.] Scanderona (so called by the Turkes), which the Christians call Alexandretta.

This is a poore Village, built all of straw and durt, excepting the houses of some Christian Factors, built of timber and clay in some convenient sort, and it lies along the sea-shoare. For the famous Citie of Haleppo having no other Haven, the Merchants doe here unloade their goods, but themselves make haste to Haleppo, staying as little here as possibly they can, and committing the care of carrying their goods thither upon Camels to the Factors of their Nation, continually abiding here. The pestilent aire of this place is the cause that they dare not make any stay here: for this Village seated in Cilicia (now called Caramania), is compassed on three sides with a Fenny Plaine, and the fourth side lies upon the Sea. In the way to Haleppo (as I remember) towards the East, there is in this Plaine a Fountaine of cleare water, some mile distant from this Village; and howsoever all other waters falling out of the Fen are most unwholsome, yet the goodnes of this Fountaine is so much prized, as the Merchants use to carrie their meate thither, and eate there under a pleasant shade. Not farre from this Fountaine, there stands an old Castle at the foote of the mountaines, which they call the Castle of Penthesilea, Queene of the Amazons. On the same side, beyond the Fen, is a most high mountaine, which keepes the sight of the Sunne from Scandarona, and being full of bogges, infects the Fenny Plaine with ill vapours, and beyond this mountaine, my dearest brother lies buried. On the other side towards the North (as I remember) in the way leading to Constantinople, the like Fenny Plaine lies, and the mountaines, though more remote, doe barre the sight of the Sunne, and the boggy earth yeelding ill vapours, makes Scanderona infamous for the death of Christians.

Scanderoon very unwholsome.

The Castle of Penthesilea.

On the same side, Asia the lesse stretcheth it selfe into the sea towards the West, and in the next shoare thereof, is a pleasant Village, now called Bias, which of old was called Tarsus, where Saint Paul was borne, being sixe miles from Scanderona, and seated in the same Province of Cilicia, and abounding with fruits, silke-wormes, and al things necessarie to sustaine life.

Tarsus.

Scanderona on the South side towards Palestina is also

Scanderona.

compassed with the like fenny Plaine, but farre more large then on the other sides. Finally, on the West side, towards the Sea and Italy, is a safe Haven in the furthest part of the Mediteranean Sea, towards the East. And into this Sea the Prophet Jonas was cast, and preserved miraculously by a Whale, was in this part cast upon the shoare, they say, that the Owes of the Sea doe here much increase the malignitie of the aire, yet the Sea men use to sleep in their ships, and seldome to come on land, till the Sunne be risen above the mountains hiding it, and hath drawne up the ill vapours. The foresaid mountaines of Cilicia are held for part of Mount Taurus, which in Scythia is called Caucasus, and in these parts Amanus. I have formerly said, that these parts neere the Equinoctiall Line have seldome any raine, but the earth is commonly moistned with the dew falling after Sunne-set. But while I staied here, a great tempest fell of thunder, haile, and raine upon the seventh of August, and the raine did not fall by drops, but by pailefuls, as wee reade it falles, but much more violently, towards West India, and neere the Equinoctiall Line, and as no violent thing is perpetuall, so this tempest soone passed.

Cause of the malignitie of the aire.

Shortly after I came to this unhappy Village Scanderona, the griefe of my mind cast me into a great sicknesse, so as I, who in perfect health had passed so many Kingdomes of Europe, at this time in the very flower of my age, first began to wax old. This sicknesse brought the first weakenesse to my body, and the second, proceeding of another griefe after my returne into England, tooke from mee all thought of youthfull pleasures, and demonstratively taught me, that the Poet most truly said, Cura facit canos, that is, Care maketh gray-headed.

A great sicknesse caused by grief of my mind.

While I languished here in a lasting sicknes, it hapned that upon occasion, I looked upon the two testimonies, given to my brother and my self at Jerusalem, of our having been there, and I was not a little astonished, to see that they being both at the same time cut out of the same skin of parchment, and written with the same hand

and inck, yet that of my brother was in all parts eaten with wormes, when mine was altogether untouched. And [I. iii. 251.] after I did more wonder, that to this day the same Testimonie given to my brother is no more eaten with wormes, then at that time it was, and mine still remaines unperished.

My foresaid sicknesse was so vehement and so long, that all men doubted I would never recover, so as my friends in England, after they had heard of my brothers death, were advertised within few weekes that my selfe also was dead. But for my part, though my nightly dreames, that I was walking in the caves and sepulchers of Italy, might have somewhat discouraged me, and though I had no other Phisitian, then the Barber-Surgean of a ship, yet could I never doubt of recovering my health, but my minde still presaged that I should returne home. Yet when divers times I began to recover, and presently by the beate of the clime, and ill aire of the place, had been cast downe againe, I resolved to follow their counsell, who perswaded me to trie if the aire of the sea would strengthen me. Therefore my deare friend Master George Dorington having sent me one hundred zechines for my expences, the great summes of money which I had being all spent, by the accidents of my brothers death, and my sicknesse (the particulars of which expence I omit, because in this griefe and weakenesse I had no minde to note them, onely for a taste remembring, that I paid a piastro each day to a poore man, who continually cooled my heate with a fan.)

My death advertised in England.

Master George Dorington's kindnesse.

Master Dorington, I say, having sent me money, and I having provided all necessaries for my journey, at last upon Thursday, the tenth of October (after the new stile) and in the yeere 1596, I was carried aboard a French Ship of Marsiles, partly by the helpe of Porters, partly in a boate, being so weake as I could not stand. This ship was called John Baptist, and the Christian name of the Master was Simon, with whom I had covenanted, that I paying him thirtie piastri (or duckets) for my selfe

Octo. 19. An. 1596.

and my servant, he should set us on land in some good Haven of the Iland Candia, and if it were possible, in the chiefe Citie thereof, called Candia, and lying on the North side of the Iland, whence I was now resolved to take my journey to Constantinople, leaving all thought of going by land. Upon Friday the eleventh of October, we sayled prosperously: but after, the windes grew so contrary, as we were driven to the South of Candia. Therfore the French Marriners murmuring against us, as hereticks causing their ill passage, and there being no hope left with those windes to set us on land at Candia the chiefe Citie, the Master of our ship sent us in his boat with some few Marriners which hee least esteemed, that we might sayle to land, being fiftie miles distant.

French marriners murmur.

The Island of Candia.

Thus upon Thursday the three and twentieth of October, having sayled eight howers in great danger, towards the evening we landed under a Promontory of Candia, where there was neither citie, village, house, nor cottage, so as plenty of raine falling that night, yet we were forced to lie in an open boat, where my companion (or servant) not knowing our danger slept soundly, but my selfe durst never close mine eyes, fearing lest these Marriners (being Marsilians, who at that time little loved the English), should offer us violence to gaine our goods. This consort (or servant of mine was an English man, and by profession a Cooke, and was come into these parts to serve Master Sandy, who being sent from London to be the English Consull at Haleppo, as he passed from Constantinople thither, died in Asia Minor, of the same disease whereof my brother died, and in the same moneth. This servant being (after his Masters death) to returne into England, I tooke to attend mee, that I might by his company avoide solitude, and mittigate some part of my sorrow. He was no sooner entered into the French ship, but he presently fell sicke, and not able to serve himselfe, could not give me the expected comforts, much lesse doe me any service, but greatly increased my charge, spending all upon my purse, & much troubled me, having

Master Sandy sent to be English Consul at Haleppo.

not himselfe the least skil in any forraine language, so as he recovering not till we came to Venice (where being among Christians, I had small use of his helpe), hee was rather a burthen then a comfort to me. When I was to enter the French ship, I laid in provisions of Hennes, Egges, Damaske Prunes, and other things: but my languishing stomack not desiring nor being able to digest any other then salt meate, these provisions fell to the share of my sicke servant, and my self being nothing but skin and bone, as one that languished in a Con- [I. iii. 252.] sumption, my bloud and humours renued with these salt meates, could not but weaken my future health, so as I having been alwaies very leane, after (by decay of naturall heate) became very fat, and having lost the retentive faculty of my stomack, so as I continually cast all that lay upon it, so soone as in the morning I came into the aire, I had no remedie against this weakenesse, but the taking of Tobacco.

The French Marriners, who brought us to the shoare of Candia, parted from us on Friday the twenty five of *The Iland of Candia.* July (after the new stile) early in the morning, and when I had well rewarded them for their paines; then first they shewed me above the wilde Rockes, called Calisminiones, a Monastery of the Greeks, some three miles distant, *A Greeke monastery.* and called Santa Maria Ogidietra. We being left alone, and staying there fasting till noone, at last espied, and called to us two men passing by upon the Mountaines, but they thinking us to bee Pirats, fled away as fast as they could. Presently behold, my man comming out of the Wood, and bringing with him an Asse, which hee had found there, who perswaded me to lay my baggage on that beast, and so to walke softly towards the Monastery. I willingly tried my strength, and leaning upon our two swords for want of a staffe, and yet often falling, went forward like a snaile, till despairing of going further, I fell upon the ground. After an howers space, a Shepheard passing by, and I shewing him gold, and naming Monastery, which word he understood, he swiftly ran to the Monastery, and telling the Monkes (called by the Greekes Caloiri) our state and condition, they presently sent a servant to us, who in the Italian tongue telling us the great danger wherein we should be, if we staied upon those Mountaines till night, advised us to make haste to the Monastery. Thus driven with feare, and incouraged by his company, I tried againe to goe forward, and with great trouble passed one mile over the Mountaines. For leaning, as I said on two swords, and upon the passage of any steepe Mountaine, by reason of the lightnesse of my head, creeping upon hands and feete, with great difficulty I went so farre. And now being not able to goe any further, no not to save my life, behold a boy, who came to water his Asse at a Fountaine adjoyning, to whom the servant of the Monkes gave a piastro, and so whether he would or no tooke his Asse, and set me upon it, and so at last wee passed the other two miles (longer then three English miles) and came to the Monastery. The Caloiri or Monkes received us curteously, and gave us such victuals as they had, namely, Pomegranates, Olives, Bread, and sharpe Wine, which were no good meates for sicke men, having fasted almost two dayes. Also they conferred lovingly with us, but still desiring us to keepe aloofe from them. At bed time they gave us a straw mat, to lay upon a plastred floare for our bed; but we were better provided of Matterasses and quilts of our owne, and though lying upon the ground, yet slept soundly, because we were in safety.

Danger in the mountaines.

Curteous monkes.

The Italians in regard of their clime, are very curious to receive strangers in a time of plague, and appoint chiefe men to the office of providing for the publike health, calling the place where they meete, the Office of Health. Also without their Cities (especially in the State of Venice) they have publike houses, called Lazaretti, and for the most part pleasantly seated, whether passengers and Merchants with their goods, must at their first arrivall retire, till the Providers for Health have curiously inquired, if they come from any suspected place, or have

The Italian office of Health.

any infectious sicknesse. And here they have all things necessary in abundance, but may not converse or talke with any man, till they obtaine the grant of free conversation (called la prattica), or if any man speake with them, he must be inclosed in the same house, and because they stay fortie dayes there, for the triall of their health, this triall is called far' la Quarantana. Moreover, they that goe by land in Italy, must bring a Testimonie of Health called Boletino, before they can passe or converse. The Venetians are more curious in this, then any other using this triall when there is no Plague, I know not for what reason, except it bee that the Citie of Constantinople is seldome or never free of the Plague, whence many of their ships come, or for that some mysterie, for the good of traffick, or of the Common-wealth, lyes hidden under the pretence of this custome. For no man dares enter the Citie, and converse there, till he have gotten license of these Provisors, neither dare any Merchant dispose of his goods, till they are brought to this house, and there searched by the Officers, if they see cause. This Preface I make, because the Iland of Candia is subject to the Venetians, and the Prior of this Monastery would in no sort give us free conversation, till by Letters wee had signified our state to the Provisors of health, residing at the chiefe City Candia, and til they should send some answere backe unto us. In the meane time they shut us up in a garden house, where we had plesant walkes, and store of Oranges and like fruites, and the Country people bringing us Partridges and many good things to eate, and my man having skill to dresse them, and the Monkes furnishing us with such necessaries as wee could not otherwise buy, we wanted here no convenience, to make the time of our abode seeme shorter, but onely good beds. Thus I was forced to write this following Letter in the Italian tongue, and to send a messenger with it to Candia the Chiefe City.

The Testimonie of Health.

[I. iii. 253.]

The monkes shut us up in a garden house.

[All' Illustrmo.

All' Illustrmo. & Excellmo. Sigr. il Sigr. Nicolao Donati, Proveditore & Inquisitore Generale nel regno di Candia.

mio osservmo.:

Letter to the Signor Nicholas Donati.

SA Sigria. Illustrma. se degna intendere, ch' io Fynes Morysoni Inghlese, con un' mio huomo, ci siamo partiti a li tre di questo mese, d' Alessandretta, per venir' a la volta di Candia: Et che in quel' paese tutti i contorni sono sani, come porta la mia Patente netta, sigillata col' solito sigillo di San' Marco. Il Patron' della Nave Francese, in chi di la c' imbarcammo, non mantenendoci la suoa parola di metterci in terra in qualche buona villa di questa Isola, ci mandò con la suoa fregata a Calisminiones, doveci lascio' soletti. Di la con gran' disagio (domandando la strada da i villani) arrivammo a i vinti cinque del presente, a San' Maria Ogidietra: dove i Frati, fin' che conoscano la volontà di vostra Eccellenza, non ci vogliono dar' prattica in modo nessuno; Et in quel' mentre c' hanno rinchiuso in una casa a parte. Il viaggio mio' e di passar' piu inanzi fin' a Constantinopoli, per i fatti dell' Illustmo. Ambasciatore d' Inghilterra. Il perche humilmente suplico che suoa Eccellza. se degna d' haver rispetto d' un' povero forestiero, anche nativo d' una Natione molto affectionata a la suoa: et che (per suoa gratia) mi manda libera prattica, accio che io passa seguitar' il mio viaggio, che di qua, oltre il rincrescimento della solitudine, anche ogni cosu mi da noia. Con questo assicurando mi che vostra Eccellza. haurà compassione d' un' suo servitore, con disagi grandissimi per mar' & per terra battuto, priegho Iddio per l' accrescimento del suo honore. Et le bascio humilmente le mani. Da San' Maria Ogidietra, a i vinti cinque d' Ottobre (all uso nuovo) l' An. 1596.

Di vos. Sigria. Illustma. Humilmo. servire.

Fynes Morysoni.

Of these Letters I received the following answere.

Al molto magco. Sigr. il Sigre. Fy: Morysoni, suo come fratello.

Letter from Signor Nicholas Donati.

MOlto magco. Sigr. come fratello. Per le vostre lettre scritte alli 25, del presente (al uso nuovo) all Illmo. Sigr. Generale, et da ss. ss. Eccellma. mandate qui all' officio nostro, habbiamo veduto il suo bisogno, & desiderando favorir' et agiutarla in questa occasione, con il riguardo anco della salute pubca., Mandiamo duoi stradiotti per accompagnarla con il suo huomo, et condurla di qua, dove sar a ben' trattata, & li si darà commodità, di poter, con l' occasione di qualche vassello, seguitar' il suo viazzo, usate prima le debite cautele, per assicuration' delle cose di questa offo. Però, S.S. senza pratticar' altrte., seguitara' questa guida che le mandiamo, & vegnerà di qua con animo consolato di trovar' Christiani & amici, obedendo per adesso, & esseguendo l' ordine da noi dato a detti stradiotti, come cirendiamo certi che farà. Et. a. V.S. c' offeriamo. Di Candia. Alli 20. d' Ottobre (all' uso vecchio) 1596.

Porterà con essa, la suoa fede, sive patente.

Di V. S. come fratlli.:
li proveditori alla Sanita.

These Letters follow translated into English. [I. iii. 254.]

The Letters in English.

To the most Illustrious and most excellent Lord, the Lord Nicholas Donati Generall Provisor and Inquisitor in the Kingdome of Candia.

my most respected.

MOst Illustrious, &c. Your Excellency may please to understand, that I Fynes Morison an Englishman, with my servant, the third of this moneth set saile from Alexandretta, to sayle into Candia, and that those parts are free from all infectious sickenesse, as appeares by my testimoniall sealed with the wonted seale of Saint

The Letters in English. Marke. The Master of the French Shippe in which I passed, broke his covenant with me, in that he did not land us in the Haven of Candia, the chiefe City of this Kingdome; but sent us in his boate to the wild Promontory Calisminiones, landing and leaving us there, in a place altogether disinhabited. From thence we asking the way of the Countrey people, did with much trouble at last come to the Monastery Saint Maria Ogidietra, upon the five and twenty of this present (after the new stile), where the Friers, till they may know the pleasure of your Excellency, wil in no sort give us liberty to converse; but in the meane time have shut us up in a solitary garden house. My journey lies further to Constantinople, for the affaires of the Lord Ambassadour of England there abiding: Wherefore I humbly pray that your excellency will vouchsafe to have favourable respect of a poore stranger, borne of a Nation well affected to that of your Excellency, and that by your favour licence may bee sent me freely to converse, and to take my journey to the City of Candia, since my solitary living here, all delay, and many other things in this place, are irksome unto me. Thus assuring my selfe that your Excellency will have compassion of his servant, tired with many misfortunes by Sea and Land, I beseech God for the increase of your honor, and so humbly kisse your hands. From San' Maria Ogidietra this five and twenty of October (after the new stile) in the yeere 1596.

Your Excellencies humble Servant,

Fynes Moryson.

The Letters sent me in answere thus follow;

To the noble Gentleman Master Fynes Moryson, deare to us as a brother.

NOble Sir, deare to us in place of a Brother. By your Letters dated the five and twenty of this moneth (after the new stile) and directed to the Illustrious Lord

Generall, and by his Excellency sent to our Office; we have understood your request, and desirous to favour you in this occasion, with due respect to the publike health, we have sent you two Horsemen, who shall guide you and your servant hither, where you shall be curteously received, and shall not want the opportunity of a Barke, to finish your journey, after we have taken due order (according to our Office) for the preserving of the publike health. Therefore without conversing with any man, follow these guides wee have sent you, and come hither with a cheerefull heart, as to Christians and friends. But faile not to follow the order which we have given to these guides, whereof we doubt not and so tender our selves to you. From Candia the twenty of October (after the old stile) in the yeere 1596.

The Letters in English.

Bring with you the testimony
of your health.

Yours in place of brethren,
the Provisors for health.

This testimoniall above mentioned, I tooke from the Venetian Consull (who knew my disease free from all infection) when I parted from Alexandretta, foreknowing the necessity thereof. The foresaid two horsemen being arrived, which with great curtesie were sent to conduct me, I parted from the Monastery to goe in their company to the City of Candia, eight & thirty miles distant, being to passe almost the whole bredth of this Kingdome in the very middle part thereof. The bredth of the Iland containes five and forty miles, the length two hundred and thirty miles, and the circuit (as Ortelius writes) five hundred & twenty, (others say six hundred or seven hundred miles) the ancient and moderne writers reckoning diversly. This Iland is distànt from the Cape of Otranto in Italy, five hundred miles, (others write five hundred and thirty): From Alexandria in Ægypt foure hundred and fifty miles (others write five hundred), from the next shoare of Affricke two hundred and fifty miles, from Joppa in Palestine six hundred and sixty miles, (others write six

[I. iii. 255.]

The circuit of the Island.

hundred and forty): from Tripoli in Syria seven hundred miles, from the Iland Cyprus foure hundred miles, from Venice 1500 miles, and from Constantinople seven hundred and twenty miles.

The Labe-rinth.

We beganne our journey in the afternoone, and as we rode, our guide shewed us not farre out of the high way, the Monument famous for the love of the Kings daughter Ariadne to Thesius, called the Laberinth of Crete, (for so Candia was called of old, and Saturne the first King thereof, begat Radamanthus, Minos, and Sarpedon, of Europa the daughter of Agenor, as they write). Also our guides told us that not far out of the way to the city Candia, there was a monument of the cave of Minos, which the Candians call the sepulcher of Jupiter: but my former adversities had taken from me my wonted desire to see antiquities, so as we kept the high way, and passing that day by a City of the Jewes, lodged that night at a Village, not in any Inne, but in the very Church, upon straw and our owne bedding, being content with such victuals as our guides brought us, namely, cheese, fruites, and good wine. It is probable, that if we had had free conversation, we might perhaps have found good lodging in the Village, yet did we justly doubt thereof, because we could buy no better meate, nor get any provender for our beasts. The next day in the morning we set forward, and came to a pleasant village, where we dined in a faire Church, but could get no meat for our horses, except they would have eaten pomegranates or like fruits.

The City of Candia.

The same day in the afternoone, we came to the City of Candia, where we staied at the gate, till we knew the pleasure of the Provisors for health. They could not be ignorant that our sickenesse was free from all infection, yet imagining (as after I perceived) that we should be Merchants, & have some rich Jewels, they sent us to the Lazaretto, where in a weekes space, when their spies (according to their manner) had inquired after our state, and found that there was no hope of gaine by our imaginary Jewels, and it then falling out, that other Merchants being landed with goods, were to be lodged in our chamber; at last the Generall Sigr. Nicolao Donato (called Generall for his commanding in the warre, and Provisor of health by the said Office, and chiefe inquisitor for Religion, which Office is sparingly executed in the State of Venice, yet being not the chiefe Commander of the Iland; for Il Sigr. Marc' Antonio Venerio, was then Liefetenant to the Duke of Venice in this Iland, with limited authority as the Duke himselfe hath). I say this generall Provisour for the health, sent unto us a Gentleman of that office, Il Sigr. Vicenzo Cornaro (who used us nobly and curteously) and the Scrivano, (that is, Clerke or Secretary) of that office, called Il Sigr. Giovanni Papadapolo with authority to give us free conversation. These Gentlemen (according to the custome, such as the state of no passenger can be hidden from them) caused ropes to be hanged acrosse our chamber, and all things we had, yea, our very shirts, to be severally taken out, and hanged thereupon, and so perfumed them with brimstone, to our great anoyance, though they well knew we had no infectious sicknesse, which done, they gave us freedome to goe into the City, and wheresoever we would. To the Scrivano I gave a zechine, desiring him to take it in good part, as the guift of a poore gentleman, and nothing lesse then an Indian Merchant, as they suspected. This house called Lazaretto, was built of free stone, with Cellers for the laying up of goods, and had pleasant walks both in the yard and garden, and the Keeper of this house had furnished me with a bed and all necessaries, and for the seven daies past, had bought us our meat in the City, which he would likewise have dressed, but that my servant was a Cooke, and for this service he had done, I gave him also a zechine.

Things perfumed with brimstone.

The Lazaretto.

Then we went into the Citie, & lodged with an Italian, who had often brought us meat and necessaries to the Lazaretto, and with him my selfe and my servant had convenient beds, and plentifull diet, for which I paid sixe [I. iii. 256.]

lyres each day. But the horsemen who conducted us to Candia came often to me, and for that service I gave to each of them a zechine, and by them I understood the prices of the Market for diet. So as all the Candians speaking Italian, aswell as their naturall Greeke tongue, and I finding the rate of our expences to bee excessive, I determined to hier a chamber, and to buy my owne meate in the Market. But it happened, that at the same time an English Merchant landed, who was a Factor to buy Muskedines of Candia (whereof, and especially of red Muskedine, there is great plenty in this Iland), and this Merchant called Richard Darson, being wel acquainted with the best courses of living in Candia, had hired a little house, and a woman to dresse his meate, and at my intreaty he was content to give us a chamber in his house, and to hier us two beds, that so we might dyet together, where he used us very curteously, and our dyet was as plentifull as before, at a far lower rate, dividing our expences into three parts, whereof he paied one, and my selfe two, for my owne and my servants diet. There was at that time great dearth of Corne, so as white bread was hardly to be got, though the Italians, making their meales for the most part of bread, use to have it very white and good. Here we bought a Bocale of rich Wine, containing two English quarts and a halfe for a lire of Venice; a Pigion for 7 soldi; a Partridge for a lire, or 16 soldi; a pound of veale for 7 soldi, of mutton for some 5 soldi, & we had plentie of fruits for a small price. The Beefe in Italy useth to be leane, and is seldome eaten, and such beefe they had here; for by the Law, called Foscherini, it is commaunded, that no man shall kill a beefe, till it be unfit to draw in the Plough, and to doe like service. Here I paid foure lires for a paire of shooes, the rest of my expences I omit for brevitie sake, those sufficing, to give a passenger some guesse at what rate he may live. Onely I will adde, that the worke of Porters and labouring men, as well in Italy as here, is had for small wages, because there is great number of poore people, and they

Richard Darson an English Merchant.

Charges in Candia.

abhorre from begging, so as one soldo contents a Porter for bringing your victuals from the Market.

When I went to Jerusalem and sailed by the Iland of Candia, I made some mention thereof, and I have now formerly set downe the length, breadth, and circuit, and the distance thereof from other Provinces, and have shewed that Candia is subject to the Venetians, and have also named the chiefe Governours thereof for that time. I will now briefely adde, that this Iland is defended by a Venetian Garrison against the Great Turke, to whom all the adjacent Countries are subject. That it hath great plentie, of red Muskedines, wherewith England for the most part is served. That it hath great plentie of all kinds of Corne, of all manner of Pulse, of Oyle, of all kinds of flesh, of Canes of sugar, of Hony, of Cedar trees, of all coloured Dyings of Cypres trees, (whereof many sweete smelling Chests are made, and carried into forraine parts), and of all necessaries for human life. Neither is any venemous beast found in this Iland, but it hath store of medicinable hearbs, especially upon the famous Mountaine Ida.

The great plentie of Candia.

The Cities of this Iland were of old one hundred, and in the time of Pliny fortie; but at this day there bee onely three, namely, Canea at the West ende of the Iland, neere which lies the Fort Souda, with a Haven capable of a thousand Gallies. The second called Rethino by the Italians, seated on the South-side of the Iland, (upon which side the Italians adde a fourth Citie called Settia), and the third called Candia, the Metropolitan Citie of the Iland, which is faire and large, built of stone, with a low roofe, after the manner of Italy, and the streets thereof are faire and large. It is strongly fortified (as need requires) by the Venetians against the Turkes, and to that purpose hath a strong Castle. From this Citie a large and pleasant Plaine leades to the foresaid cave of Minos, (which the Candians call the Sepulcher of Jupiter), neere which is the most famous Mountaine Ida, which they hold to bee seated in the middest of the Iland,

The Cities of the Iland.

The City Candia.

being higher then any of the other Mountaines thereof, and it aboundeth with Cypres trees. Finally, I remember, that when I lodged in the Monastery San' Maria Ogidietra, the Caloiri (or Monkes, who for the most part are unlearned, and till the ground, and labour like laimen), assured me that each measure of corne sowed in their fields the yeere past, had yeelded ninetie five measures.

Ninetie five measures of corne from one measure.

[I. iii. 257.]

Chap. IIII.

Of my journey from Candia (partly by land, partly by Sea) by the sea shoares, and by the Ilands of the Ægean Sea, Pontus, and Propontis, to the Citie of Constantinople. And of my journey thence by Sea to Venice, and by Land to Augsburg, Nurnberg and Stode (in Germany.) And of my passage over Sea into England. And of my journey through many severall Shires, of England, Scotland and Ireland.

December 20.

Pon Monday the twentie of December (after the old stile) at three of the clock in the afternoone, we went aboard a little Greeke Barke loaded with Muskedines, and with tunnes of Lemons Juyce (which the Turks drinke like Nectar), and with Onions, and ready to saile for Constantinople, where I payed for my passage five zechines, and as much for my servant. The night following was very bright with Moone-shine, yet we staied all the night in the Haven (compassed with walles), either because the Governour of the Castle would not let the Barke go forth, till the Master had satisfied him, or because the Master pretending that cause of stay, had some businesse to dispatch. The next morning early, being the one and twentie of December, we set saile, and the same day

A.D. 1596.

we sailed close by the Iland Zantorini, more then one hundred miles distant from Candia. They report, that this Iland, and another of the same name (both of little circuit) were in our age cast up in the middest of the Sea, with an eruption of flames and of Brimstone, and that they are not inhabited, but are commonly called the Divels Ilands, because many ships casting anchor there, and fastning their Cables upon land, have had their Cables loosed by spirits in the night, and so suffered shipwrack, or hardly escaped the same. The night following we sailed in the middest of many Ilands which made that Channell very dangerous, and for my part I was more affraid of the danger, because our Candian Merchant growing acquainted with an harlot in the ship, was not ashamed to have the use of her body in the sight of the Marriners that watched, and much blamed him for the same. Upon Wednesday the two and twentie of December, we sailed by the Iland Paros, celebrated by Poets for the fine Marble growing there, and so we came to the Iland Naxos, two hundred miles distant from Candia. Naxos and the adjacent Ilands had their owne Duke of old, but now are subject to the Turke, as the other Ilands bee for the most part. And our Marriners dwelling in this Iland, and landing to see their wives, we also landed with them, where I did see upon a Hill like a Peninsul neere this chiefe Village, two Marble images erected to Thesius and Ariadne. Here I observed, that when any stranger or Inhabitant lands, the beggers flock to the dores of the houses or Innes where they eate, and having formerly observed in the Greeke Church at Venice, that when they gave their Almes to beggers, they not onely suffered them to touch their garments with their lousie rags, but also tooke them familiarly by the hands, I knew not whether I should attribute this fashion to their charitable affection in time of their bondage, or to their seldom feasting, and the multitude of beggars.

Zantorini. *Paros.* *Naxos.*

In the evening we loosed from Naxos, and sailing over a channell no lesse dangerous then the former, for the multitude of Ilands, upon the three and twentie of December we passed close by the shoare of the Iland Zio, called Chios of old. It is inhabited by Greekes (as the other Ilands are), and is famous for the pleasantnesse and fertiltie of the situation and soyle. It yeeldeth great store of Mastick, and the country people keepe flocks of tame Partridges, as of Hens other where. They brag, that Homer lyes buried upon the Mountaine Helias, and this Iland hath Saint George for their protecting Saint, and beares his Crosse in their Flags, as England doth. Here we might distinctly see the shoare of Asia, in that part, where of old the seven Churches stood not farre distant, to which Saint John writes his Revelation. And the Iland Pathmos is not farre distant, where Saint John lived in exile. Towards the evening we cast anchor neere the Iland Metelene, which is seated (as Zio) in the Egean Sea, and is no lesse pleasant and fertile. Of old it was called Lesbos, then Issa, and after Pelasgia, and therein were borne, Pythagoras, the Poet Alceus, Antimenides, Theophrastus, Phanius, Arton, and Tersandrus, and the famous woman Poet Sapho. Zio is distant one hundred and forty miles from Naxos and Meteline, ninety miles from Zio.

Zio. *Seven Churches.* *Pathmos.* [I. iii. 258.] *Metelene.*

The foure and twenty of December, (being Christmas even, after the old stile used among the Greekes, and in all Turkey), early in the morning we weighed anchor, and with a faire but gentle wind, sayled close by the shoare where the City of Troy stood of old, seated in a plaine, and upon pleasant hils neere the Sea, and at this day the ruines of Illium the Castle of Priamus are seene upon a hill, and the ruines of the wals in the plaine, yet shew the circuit of the City. The Poets said truly;

Troy.

Hic seges est ubi Troia fuit,

Corne growes now where Troy once stood.

Yet the plowed fields have very many ruines of buildings. On the North side of these Trojan ruines, a necke of Land lies towards the Sea, where they say the

Greekes encamped, and left their fatall Trojan Horse. Right over against this Land lies the Iland Tenedos, scarce ten miles distant, in the Haven whereof we cast anchor for an hower, under a little Castle, and this Tenedos is sixty miles distant from Metelene. From hence sailing some eighteene miles, we passed by two necks of Land, one of Greece on the West-side, the other of Asia the lesse, (now called Natolia) on the East-side, and after twelve miles saile, we entered the streight of Hellespont, now called the two Castles, the description whereof I will defer till my returne this way.

Tenedos.

Sestos & Abydos.

The Greek Marriners have a custome here to demand a gift of all Merchants & passengers in their ship, for joy of their happy voyage, and they say, (which I beleeve not) that if any refuse, they tie a rope to his feete, and draw him up to the top of the maste, till he yeeld to this custome: but howsoever, we all obeyed this ridiculous custome, not to offend them who had used us well.

This channell running from the blacke sea, called Euxinus, into Propontis, and so by Constantinople to these said two Castles, and from hence into the Ægean sea, from the North towards the South, is alwaies contrary to those that sayle from the mediteranian sea to Constantinople, especially after they enter this streight of the two Castles, and neere Constantinople it runnes with such force towards the South, as they that saile to the City, (whereof we had experience) with the best winds, yet sayle very slowly. This violence of the Channell is attributed to great Rivers violently falling into the blacke Sea.

The foresaid Christmas even we landed at Gallipolis a Greeke City, seated in Thrace, having the name (as it seemes) from the French, and eight and twenty miles distant from the two Castles. On Saturday the five and twenty of December, being Christmas day, after the old stile, we set saile; but the winds drove us backe to the Haven of Gallipolis, where being detained some few daies, though I staied in the ship for feare of some fraud from

Gallipolis.

the Turkes, yet once I went on Land with our Marriners. The City lieth in length upon the shoare of Propontis, from the South to the North, and it hath without the wals towards the West, great number of Wind-mils, the buildings are of flint or little unpolished stones, one or two stories high, and the roofe is low and tiled, (not plaine and plastered to walke upon, as they be in Syria and Cyprus); and this roofe is so low as it hath no windowes, so as the buildings of these parts are very like those of Italy. The Haven is on the East side, and upon the opposite shoare of Asia towards the East, are the ruines not farre distant of Nice, a City of Bithinia, famous for the holy Councell held there of old. Upon Saterday the first of January, we sailed sixty miles in this
Marmora. straight of Propontis, to the Iland Marmora, not without feare of Turkish Pirats, the Haven of Camera being neere us, where the great Turkes Gallies lie. By the way they shewed me a Castle towards the East, upon the shore of Asia the lesse, which they say stands upon the confines of the Trojan Dominion, and thereof hath the name to this day. The Iland Marmora is so called (as I think) of the marble wherewith it aboundeth. The second of January we set sayle from Marmora, and being by contrary winds driven backe (as I think, or little advanced) we
[I. iii. 259.] came to the Iland Aloni some ten miles distant from
Aloni. Marmora (and so called of the forme of a yard, in which Oxen used to grinde Corne, or beate it small.) After the beginning of the new yeere (which the Greekes, as
Janua. 1. most of Europe, begin the first of Januarie) the first
Anno 1597. Wednesday (being the fourth of that month), the Grecian Marriners have a custom retained from old times, to baptize the Sea, (as they terme it), which done, they thinke the Flouds and Windes to grow more calme then formerly. The Iland Aloni hath a Port on all sides compassed with Ilands, and that very large and safe, where while we passed some stormy daies, wee heard of many Barkes and Gallies cast away. While I walked here upon the shoare, a wild-headed Turke tooke my hat from my

head (being of the fashion of Europe not used there), and having turned it, and long beheld it, he said (to use his rude words) Lend me this vessell to ease my belly therein; and so girning flung it on the dyrtie ground, which I with patience tooke up. These and like wrongs of speech, even threatnings of blowes I sometimes indured in Turkey, but never had the disaster to have any blow given me by any of them, which many good Christians notwithstanding have suffered and daily suffer, and my selfe if they had fallen to my share, must have suffered with patience, except I would by resistance have incurred shamefull and cruell death: On Thursday the thirteenth of January, at last wee set sayle with a faire winde, and after twentie miles sayling we passed by the Citie Palormo seated upon the shoare of Asia the lesse, and famous for the white Wine it yeeldeth (the best that ever I tasted), and having sayled ten miles further, we sailed by the Citie Heraclea, seated on the shore of Greece (whereof in my returne this way I shall have cause to speake more at large.)

Palormo.

Heraclea.

Towards evening we thought we were come to one of the corners of Constantinople, called the seven Towers, yet by reason of the foresaid swift channell running from the black Sea full against us, with a most faire wind we could not land in the Haven of Constantinople till midnight, having that day sayled one hundred and twentie miles in all from the said Ile Aloni. This voyage was more tedious to us, in that howsoever landing we had somtimes good dyet, yet while we were at Sea, we had no good victuals in the ship. For the Greeke Marriners feede of Onions, Garlike, and dried fishes, (one kinde whereof they call Palamides, and the Italians call Palamito) and in stead of a banket, they will give you a head of Garlick rosted in the ashes, and pleasantly call it a pigeon. With this and Bisket they content themselves, and these we were forced to eate, having omitted to provide any dried or salt meates at Candia, because wee hoped to find those in our Barke, and knowing that

Greeke Marriners Diet.

it was in vaine to provide any fresh meates, because they would not suffer a fier to be made in so small a Barke, wherewith we might dresse them. But after we had eaten Bisket and dried fishes, we had an unknowne comfort or helpe to disgest them. For in our privat cabbin, we had the head of a tun of Muskedine lying under our heads when we slept, in stead of a bolster, and our ship being bound on the upper part of the sides with bundles of Reedes, to beate off the force of the waves, we taking one of the long Reedes, found meanes to pierce the vessell, and get good Wine to our ill fare, and drunke so merrily, that before wee came to our journies end, our former Reede became too short, so as we were faine to piece it with another.

Constantinople. Having cast anchor (as I said) in the Port of Constantinople, behold, as soone as day began to breake, many companies of Turkes rushing into our Barke, who like so many starved flies fell to sucke the sweete Wines, each rascall among them beating with cudgels and ropes the best of our Marriners, if he durst but repine against it, till within short space the Candian Merchant having advertised the Venetian Ambassadour of their arrivall, he sent a Janizare to protect the Barke, and the goods; and assoone as he came, it seemed to me no lesse strange, that this one man should beate all those Turkes, and drive them out of the Barke like so many dogs, the common Turkes daring no more resist a souldier, or especially a Janizare, then Christians dare resist them. And the Serjant of the Magistrate having taken some of our Greeke Marriners (though subject to the State of Venice) to worke for their Ottoman in gathering stones, and like base imployments, this Janizary caused them presently to be released, and to be sent againe into their Barke, such is the tyranny of the Turkes against all Christians [I. iii. 260.] aswel their subjects as others, so as no man sayleth into these parts, but under the Banner of England, France, or Venice, who being in league with the great Turke, have their Ambassadours in this Citie, and their Consuls in other Havens, to protect those that come under their Banner, in this sort sending them a Janizare to keepe them from wrongs, so soone as they are advertised of their arrivall.

My selfe lodged in the house of Master Edward Barton, the English Ambassadour, who gave me a Janizare to guide and protect me, while I went to view the City, round about the whole circuit whereof I went on foot and by boat in foure houres space, the forme of the Citie being triangular, and containing nine miles by Sea towards the North and East, and five miles by land towards the West. I professe my selfe to have small skill in the art of Geography, yet will I adventure (though rudely) to set downe the forme and situation of this City, so plainely, as I doubt not but the Reader may easily understand it, howsoever in the same (as in other cities formerly described) I acknowledge that I use not the rule of the scale, in the distance of places, nor other exquisite rules of that Art, having no other end, but to make the Reader more easily understand my description.

Master Edward Barton, the English Ambassadour.

The description of the City of Constantinople, and the adjacent Territories and Seas.

The great lines or walles shew the forme of the City, and the single small lines describe the Teritory adjoyning. (A) In this Tower they hang out a light of pitch and like burning matter, to direct the Saylers by night, comming to the City, or sayling along the coast out of the Sea Euxinus (which they say is called the Black Sea of many shipwracks therein happening.) And this Tower [I. iii. 261.] is sixteene miles distant from the Citie.

The description of Constantinople.

(B) Here is a marble pillar erected upon a Rocke compassed with the sea, which they call the pillar of Pompey, and therein many passengers (for their memory) use to ingrave their names. And here are innumerable flocks of Sea foule and of many kindes, wherewith hee that is skilfull to shoote in his Peece, may abundantly furnish himselfe.

(C) Here is the Euxine or black Sea.

Two strong Castles.

(D E) Here lie two strong Castles, one in Europe, the other in Asia, some eight miles distant from the Citie, built to defend the Haven from the assault of the enemies by Sea on that side, and the Garrison there kept, searcheth the ships comming from the Citie, that no slaves or prohibited goods be carried therein, neither can any ship passe unsearched, except they will hazard to be sunck. Finally, the great Turke sends his chiefe prisoners to be kept in these strong Castles.

(F) Here great ships use to cast anchor at their first arrivall, till they bee unloaded, and here againe they ride at anchor to expect windes, when they are loaded and ready to depart.

(G) All along this banke and the opposite side for a large circuit, the greatest ships use to lie when they are unloaded, and they lie most safely and close by the shore, fastaned by cables on land.

Gallata and Perah.

(H) Here lyes the old Citie built by the Genoesi of Italy, called Gallata by the Turks, and Perah by the Greekes (of the situation beyond the Channell.) It is now accounted a Suburbe of Constantinople, and is seated upon a most pleasant hill, wherein for the most part live Christians, as well subjects as others, and the Ambassadours of England, France, and Venice, only the Emperours Ambassadour must lye within the Citie, more like a pledge of peace, then a free Ambassadour, and very few Turkes live here mingled with the Christians. The situation of Gallata (as I said) is most pleasant. Formerly the Ambassadours of England were wont to dwell upon the Sea-shore in the Plaine, and their Pallace is not farre distant from this note (K); but Master Edward Barton the English Ambassadour at this time dwelt upon the top of the hill, in a faire house within a large field, and pleasant gardens compassed with a wall. And all Gallata is full of very pleasant gardens, and compassed with pleasant fields, whereof some towards the land furthest from the Sea, are used for the buriall of Turkes.

Master Edward Barton's house.

(I) Here a little Creeke of the Sea is compassed with walles and buildings, within which the Gallies of the great Turke lie in safety, and there be fit places to build Gallies, and store-houses for all things thereunto belonging.

(K) Here is the chiefe passage over the water called Tapano, where a man may passe for two aspers. All along this Sea banke lye very many great Gunnes (as upon the Tower Wharfe at London), and here the fishers land, and sell their fish.

(L) Here the Megarenses of old built Chalcedon, a Citie of Bethinia, famous for a Councell held there, by the ruine of which Citie, Constantinople increased. At this day there is onely a Village, or rather some scattered houses, and it is commonly called Scuteri, or Scudretta. *Chalcedon.*

(M) Here the Great Turks mother then living, had her private Garden.

(N) Hither the Heyre of the Empire is sent, as it were into banishment, under pretence to governe the Province Bursia, assoone as he is circumcised, and so being made a Musulman (that is, a circumcised Turke) first begins to draw the eyes of the Army and Janizares towards him.

(O) Here is the Pallace or Court of the great Turke, called by the Italians Seraglio, and vulgarly Saray, and it was of old the Monastery of Saint Sophia. Mahomet the second first compassed it with walls, and the buildings together with the large and pleasant gardens are some three or foure miles in circuit. I entered the outward Court thereof by a stately Gate kept by many Janizares called Capigi of that office. The court yard was large, all compassed with building of free stone two stories high, with a low and almost plaine roofe tyled, and without windowes, after the maner of the building of Italy, and round about the inside, it was cast out with arches like the building of Cloisters, under which they walked drie in the greatest raine. And in this Court is a large *The Pallace of the great Turke.* [I. iii. 262.]

pulpit or open roome, where the great Turke useth to shew himselfe to the Janizares to satisfie them when they make any mutiny.

(P) Here is a banqueting house, vulgarly called Chuske, the prospect whereof is more pleasant then can be expressed, beholding foure Seats at once, and the land on all sides beyond them.

The Church of Saint Sophia.

(Q) Here is the Church of Saint Sophia, opposite to the Court Gate, of old built by the Christians after the forme of Salomons Temple, and indowed with the annuall rent of three hundred thousand Zechines, now made a Mosche or Mahometan Church. And howsoever the Turks cannot indure that unwashed Christians (so called by them, because they use not Baths so continually as they doe) should enter their Mosches, or passe over their Sepulchers, yet my self entered this Church with the Janizare my guid, trusting to his power to defend me, yet he willed me first to put of my shooes, and according to the Turkes custome to leave them in the porch, where they were safe till we returned. The Church is of a round forme, and built of bricke, and supported with faire pillars, and paved with Marble (over which the Turks layed Mats to kneele, and prostrate themselves more commodiously upon them.) The roofe is beautified with pictures of that rich painting, which the Italians call alla Mosaica, shining like enameled work, which now by antiquity were much decaied, and in some parts defaced. Round about the Church hung many Lampes, which they use to burne in the time of their Lent (called Beyram), and every weeke upon Thursday in the evening, and Friday all day, which they keepe holy after their fashion for their Sabbath day. Round about the upper part of the Church are large and most faire Galleries. And here I did see two Nuts of Marble of huge bignesse and great beauty. Moreover I did see the great Turke when he entered this Church, and howsoever it lie close to the Gate of his Pallace, yet he came riding upon a horse richly trapped, with many troopes of his chiefe horsemen,

Alla Mosaica.

standing in ranke within the Courts of his Pallace, and from the Court Gate to the Church dore, betweene which troopes on both sides, he passed as betweene walles of brasse, with great pompe. And when a Chaus (or Pensioner) being on horseback did see mee close by the Emperours side, hee rushed upon me to strike me with his mace, saying, What doth this Christian dog so neere the person of our great Lord? But the Janizare, whom our Ambassadour had given me for a Guide and Protector, repelled him from doing mee any wrong, and many Janizares (according to their manner) comming to helpe him, the Chaus was glad to let mee alone, and they bade me be bold to stand still, though I were the second or third person from the Emperour. Neere this Church is the stately Sepulcher of Selymus the second, and another Sepulcher no lesse stately, and newly built for Amurath lately deceased, where he lay with those male children round about him, who according to the manner were strangled by his Successour after hee was dead. Not farre thence is the Market place having some one hundred marble pillars about it, and adorned with a Pyramis or pinacle, erected upon foure Globes, and with a pleasant Fountaine of water, together with other ornaments left (as it seemes) by Christian Emperours.

The Sepulcher of Selymus the second.

(R) The wonderfull Mosche and Sepulcher of Solyman, numbred among the miracles of the World.

(S) Two houses for the same use, as the Exchange of London, where the Merchants meete, namely, for the selling of fine wares, but no way to be compared to the same for the building. They are called the great and the lesse Bezestan, and use to bee opened onely certaine daies of the weeke, and for some sixe howers, at which times small and more pretious wares are there to be sold, as Jewels, Semiters (or Swords), set with Jewels, but commonly counterfet, pieces of Velvet, Satten, and Damaske, and the like. And the Market place is not farre distant, where Captives of both sexes are weekely sold, and the buyers if they will, may take them into a

Two houses for Exchange.

house, and there see them naked, and handle them (as wee handle beasts to know their fatnesse and strength.)

[I. iii. 263.] *Fort Jadicule.* (T) Here is a Fort that is fortified with seven Towers, called by the Turkes Jadicule, and by Christians the seven Towers, where a garrison of Souldiers is kept, because the Emperors treasure is there laied up, and cheefe Prisoners use to be kept there. The treasure is vulgarly said to bee laied up there, but the great Turke seldome goes thither; and since it is true, that where the treasure is, there is the mind, I thinke it probable (which I have heard of experienced men) that most of the treasure lies in the Seraglio, where the great Turke holds his Court.

(V) Here be the ruines of a Pallace upon the very wals of the City, called the Pallace of Constantine, wherein I did see an Elephant, called Philo by the Turkes, and another beast newly brought out of Affricke, (the Mother of Monsters) which beast is altogether unknowne in our parts, and is called Surnapa by the people of Asia, *Description of a Giraffa.* Astanapa by others, and Giraffa by the Italians, the picture whereof I remember to have seene in the Mappes of Mercator; and because the beast is very rare, I will describe his forme as well as I can. His haire is red coloured, with many blacke and white spots; I could scarce reach with the points of my fingers to the hinder part of his backe, which grew higher and higher towards his foreshoulder, and his necke was thinne and some three els long, so as hee easily turned his head in a moment to any part or corner of the roome wherein he stood, putting it over the beames thereof, being built like a Barne, and high (for the Turkish building, not unlike the building of Italy, both which I have formerly described) by reason whereof he many times put his nose in my necke, when I thought my selfe furthest distant from him, which familiarity of his I liked not; and howsoever the Keepers assured me he would not hurt me, yet I avoided these his familiar kisses as much as I could. His body was slender, not greater, but much higher then the body of a stagge or Hart, and his head and face was like to that

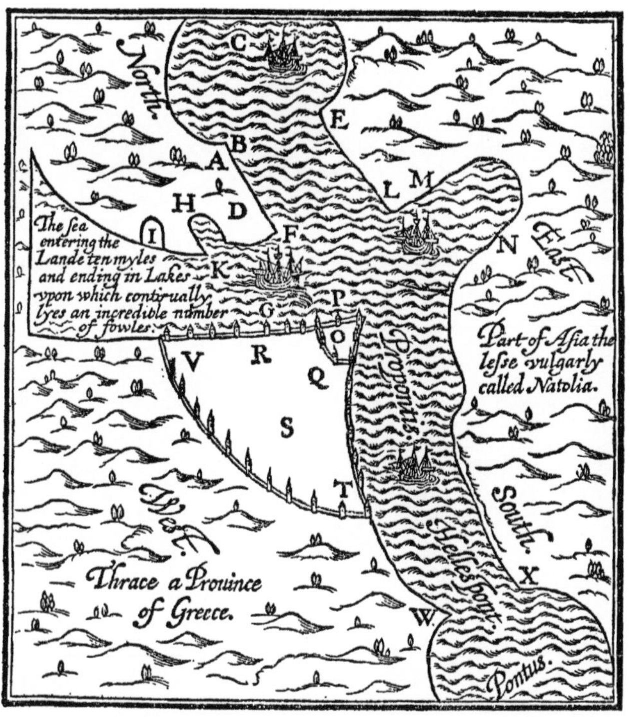

The description of the *City* of *C*onstantinople, and the adjacent Territories and Seas

of a stagge, but the head was lesse and the face more beautifull: He had two hornes, but short and scarce halfe a foote long; and in the forehead he had two bunches of flesh, his eares and feete like an Oxe, and his legges like a stagge. The Janizare my guide did in my name and for me give twenty Aspers to the Keeper of this Beast.

Castles divided by the Hellespont.

(WX) Here be two Castles or Forts, divided by the Hellespont, one seated in Europe, the other in Asia, whereof I made mention in my sayling to Constantinople, and of which I shall speake more largely at my going from this City.

The situation of Constantinople.

Constantinople built (sixe hundred sixty three yeeres before Christ was borne), by Pausanius a Lacedemonian, was first called Bizantium, till Constantine the Great in the yeere of the Lord 315, did rebuild it, after it had beene destroied by the Emperour Severus, and called it by his name. The Turkes under Mahomet the second, first tooke this City, in the yeere 1453, from the Christians, with destruction of great multitudes of them, and at this day it is called (of the great circuit) Stimboli by the Græcians, and Stambolda by the Turkes. It is seated in Thrace (also called Romania) and is built in forme of a Triangle, whereof two sides towards the North and East, lie upon two seas, and the third side towards the West, lies upon the continent of Greece. For many causes this City is famous, and in two respects may be justly preferred to any other in the World knowne to us, namely for the pleasantnesse of the situation, and the largenesse and safety of the Haven. The forme thereof formerly set downe, doth in part shew the pleasantnes of the situation, but the fruitfulnesse of the fields, the sweetnes and beauty of the flowers, and the variety and goodnesse of the fruits cannot sufficiently be praised. The fishes in the winter season flying from the cold of the Euxine or black Sea, fall downe in great numbers into the Sea Propontis, passing close by the wals of the City; and againe in Summer time, not induring the heat of the Mediterranean sea, returne backe in like numbers the same way. This City hath a thousand pleasant creekes of the Sea within sight. To conclude, the Countrey is no lesse pleasant then the Inhabitants are wicked.

The Haven. The Haven will receive an huge number of shippes, and upon both the bankes of the City and Gallata, shippes of 500. tunnes or greater once unloaded, may so lie with their cables fastened on the Land, as they can passe from the shippes to Land without any boates, and for the excellency of the Port, the City it selfe is called the Port [I. iii. 264.] by the Turkes, and Ovid cals it the Port of two Seas, for the two channels of Propontis, and the Euxine Sea. Of old the City had eleven gates called, Aurea, Pargea, Romana, Carthasea, Regia, Caligaria, Kilma, Harmagona, Phara, Theodosia, and Spilica. At this day the slender wall of bricke towards the Sea, hath thirteene gates not worth *The Walls.* the naming. The wall towards the Land is of bricke, and is said to have beene much ruined in the yeere 1509, by an Earth-quake, yet still on that side are three wals which are broad enough for a cart to passe, of which the outmost towards land is little higher then the foundation of the second, nor that much higher then the foundation of the third, the fields on that side being plaine, yet in like sort rising higher and higher as they be neerer to the wals of the City, save that neere the foresaid Pallace of Constantine, some hils lie without the wals.

The Seven Hills. This City (as Rome) is said to containe seven Hils or mounts within the wals, wherof some to me seemed imaginary, but I will reckon them as they doe, and first beginne with the hill, upon which stand the ruines of Constantines Pallace. The second hath the stately Mosche (or Turkish Church) built upon the Pallace, which of old belonged to the Græcian Patriarke. Upon the third stands the stately Mosche and most richly built Sepulcher of Mahomet the second, with an Hospitall built by the same Emperour, where all Turkish Pilgrimes have their lodging and diet freely for three daies, and it hath one hundred and fifty chambers built for the poore of the

City, and the yeerely rents thereof are valued at two hundred thousand zechines, yea the Court or Seraglio of the Great Turke paies each day an hundred Aspers to this Hospitall. The Sepulcher of Selimus takes up the fourth hill, and the sepulcher of Baiazet, the fifth hill. Betweene the fifth and the sixth hill, is the old Pallace of the Great Turke, (which the Italians call Seraglio vecchio), where the Concubines of the deceased Emperour, and the present Emperours sisters and a great number of his concubines, (for the fairest and dearest to him are taken to live in his Court), are kept by Eunuches within this old Seraglio, which is of great circuit, containing many houses and gardens compassed within one wall. Upon the sixth hill stands the foresaid wonderfull Mosche and Sepulcher of Solyman, noted with the letter (R). Lastly, the seventh hill containes the chiefe Pallace of the Great Turke, and the Church Saint Sophia, now made a Mosche, noted with the Letters O.Q.

The old Pallace.

The tops of the Sepulchers and Mosches, being of a round forme and covered with brasse, and the spacious gardens of Cypresse and Firre trees, make shew of more beauty and magnificence to the beholder from any high place, or without the wals, then in deed the City hath. The Sepulchers are no doubt very stately built, having upon the top one two or more round globes covered with leade or brasse. On the inside they seeme like lightsome Chappels with many windowes, and they being built in a round forme, the dead Emperour is laied in the middest or center of the Sepulcher, in a chest or coffin raised some three foot from the ground, having the Tulbent which hee wore upon his head in his life time laied upon his Tombe, being set forth with the Jewels he most esteemed, (which Tulbent is made of some twenty or more yards of pure and fine white linnen, foulded in many foulds, in the forme of a halfe globe). Next the Emperour lies the Sultana or Empresse, in her Coffin, (so they call his Concubine, Mother of his Heire and Successour), provided alwaies that shee have had a letter of dowry by

The Sepulchers of the Emperours.

which shee is made his wife; for otherwise shee is not buried with him. And round about the Emperour and Empresse in Coffins lower then theirs, lie the bodies of his male children, which (according to their manner) are strangled by his Successour assoone as he was dead, and upon their Coffins likewise their Tulbents are laied severally. These children are laied in little Coffins of Cypresse, and this middle part wherein the dead bodies lie, is compassed with a grate, so as betweene the bodies and the windowes there is a gallery round about, which is spred with Turkey carpets, and upon them the Priests that keepe the Sepulcher, doe lie by night, and sit crosse legged by day, neither is the roome at any time without some of these Keepers, so as the Emperours are attended even after death.

The Emperours male children strangled.

The buildings of the City have no magnificence, being partly of a matter like bricke, but white, and (as it seemes) unhardned by fire, partly of timber and clay, excepting some few pallaces which are of free stone, but nothing so stately built as might be expected from the pride and riches of the great Turkes chiefe servants. And these houses (as those of the adjacent territories of Europe) are built only 2 stories high, with a low roofe without any windowes, after the manner of Italy, whereas the houses of Asia have a plaine and plaistered roofe to walke upon, especially in Asia the greater. The streetes of this Citie are narrow, and shadowed with pentises of wood, and upon both sides the way is raised some foot high, but of little breadth, and paved for men and women to passe, the middest of the street being left low and unpaved, and no broader, then for the passage of Asses or beasts loaded. In many places of the streetes lye carcases, yea sometimes the bodies of dead men, even till they be putrified, and I thinke this uncleanlinesse of the Turks (who otherwise place Religion in washing their bodies, and keeping their apparrell, especially their Tulbent pure and cleane) is the chiefe cause that this Citie, though most pleasantly seated, yet above all the Cities of the world

[I. iii. 265.]

The buildings of the City.

The streetes.

is continually more or lesse infected with the plague. They say, that Job, famous for his pietie and patience, is buried in this Citie: but I did not see his monument, and thinke it probable, that the same and all like Christian monuments, were defaced by the Turkes when they tooke the Citie.

Master Edward Barton.

The worthie English Ambassadour, Master Edward Barton most curteously entertained me with lodging and dyet so long as I staied in this Citie, so as for them I spent not one Asper: but I passe over the due praises which I owe to the memory of this worthy Gentleman, being hereafter to speake more of him, I will onely adde, that I attended him once to the great Turkes Court, and when I had nothing satisfied my curiositie in viewing the Citie by occasions casually happening, that hee commaunded a Janizare to guide mee round about the same, till I had taken full view thereof. And with this guide the first day I viewed the foresaid monuments within the walles, and the second day compassed the Citie without the walles, beginning at the passage over the water called Tapano, and noted with the letter (K), and so passing by water (in a boat, vulgarly called Pyrame, and hired for fortie aspers) to the Castle of the seven Towers, noted with the letter (T), then passing by land to the Pallace of Constantine, noted with the letter (V.)

An old woman's mirth.

And by the way as we passed by land, an old woman meeting us, and taking me for a Captive to be sold, demaunded my price of the Janizare; who for mirth entertained her offer to buy me and another Gentleman, servant to the Ambassadour, whom hee had sent to beare me company: but because I was very slender and leane after my long sicknes, he could not induce her to give more then one hundred aspers for me, though she offered foure hundred aspers for the other Gentleman in my company, as the Janizare told me in the Italian tongue, when he had intertained this discourse with her to passe away the time in our long walke. From the foresaid Pallace of Constantine we hired a boat for eight aspers, and so by water returned to the passage Tapano, from whence we set forth, having gone by land and water the full circuit of the Citie, being nine miles by water, and five by land. Thence wee returned to the Ambassadours house, where I gave the Janizare my guide fifty aspers for his paines.

The ship called the great Lion. A Venetian ship called the great Lion was now ready to set sayle from Constantinople to Venice, which commoditie of my speedy returne I thought good to take, and having agreed with the Patron or Master of the ship, and being promised by the chiefe of the Marriners (whom I had bound unto me with some curtisies) that they would without faile call me before they were to set sayle, I passed the time in the sweete conversation of this worthy Ambassadour, more securely then I should have done, til one evening I heard a great piece of Ordinance discharged, and thereupon suspected (as indeede it fell out) that this ship ready to set sayle, gave this warning piece to call aboard the Marriners and passengers. And so I made all the haste I could to the water side; but when I came thither, saw that my labour was in vaine, the ship being under sayle, and gone out of the Haven. My selfe, my servant, and a Gentleman, the Ambassadours
[I. iii. 266.] servant, and sent by him into England with letters to the Queene from the great Turke, being thus left behind, presently tooke one of the Ambassadours Janizares for our Guide, and upon the last day of Februarie (in the end of the yeere 1596 according to the English computation,
Ann. 1597. or in the beginning of the yeere 1597, according to the computation of most Kingdomes, beginning the yeere the first of January) hired a boat (called Pyrame) for one thousand Aspers to Gallipoli, in hope to overtake the great ship sayling slowly, before it could passe the straight of Hellespont. And the same evening in which the great ship set sayle, wee in our little boat sayled by the shoare
Selebris. of Thrace fortie miles to Selebris, a towne of Thraice, not without great feare and farre greater danger of being cast away. For when we found the little boate unfit to

passe the great waves of the Sea (though much calmer then other Seas), and therefore willed our Marriner to sayle close by the shoare, he told us, that there was greater danger from theeves upon the shoare, then from the waves of the sea, and so easily persuaded us to imitate the Prophet David, committing our selves rather to the hands of God by sayling in the deepe, then into the hands of men by coasting the shoare. When we had passed the darke night without sleepe in this obscure harbor, the next morning early being Tuesday, and the first of March, we sayled twenty miles to Erylis, seated upon the same *Erylis.* shore of Thracia, not without extreme danger of being cast away, which we often and justly feared, and our Janizare no lesse, who either for feare, or repentance of his sins, shed abundance of teares. Erylis was of old called Heraclea, famously knowne by having been the seat of the Greeke Patriark and many Christian Emperours. Here we left the boat which we had hired at Constantinople, having found it unfit for this passage: but howsoever wee had hired it to Gallipoli, yet the Marriner would remit nothing of the covenanted price. From hence to Gallipoli we hired for eight hundred aspers a greater Barke called Cayke. The second of March, notwithstanding the rage of the windes and the waves, we set saile, and landed at the Iland Marmora after fiftie *Marmora.* miles sayle, in which Iland I had formerly been, and to the mention thereof formerly made, let me now adde, that it is inhabited only with Greeks, and these Greeks fearing lest our Janizare (after their maner) would pay them nothing for our necessaries, and he being a yong unexperienced man, and so not carrying himself with such authoritie as other Janizares doe, we could not get lodging nor diet in any house, til at last our selves promising to pay honestly for al we took, we were received into a house (where as we were wont) we slept upon our owne bedding, they having no convenient beds, and we paied for two Egges one asper; for a Caponet five and twentie aspers; for our fier five and twentie aspers; and for the use of the house five and twentie aspers; as likewise in other places where we landed, wee paied commonly sixteene aspers or there-abouts, each night for our lodging, and the use of the house. The third of March wee set sayle after midnight, and having sayled sixtie miles, came before breake of day to Gallipolis, and the same day hiring a boat with two Oares for two hundred aspers, we passed eight and twentie miles, and found the great ship of Venice at anchor, but not daring to goe aboard in the night, wee slept in our little boat fastened to the shoare, with no little inconvenience, because it rained all night. The fourth of March we gave the Janizare our guide three hundred twentie eight aspers for his paines, and to beare his charges back, which was a small sum for so great a journey. Yet after some repining he was satisfied therewith, because he served the English Ambassadour. Then we went aboard the Venetian ship, called the great Lion, and when I remembred that the ship wherein I sailed from Venice to Jerusalem was called the little Lion, I was stirred up to give praise and humble thankes to the great Lion of the Tribe of Juda, who through so many dangers preserved mee in this voyage. This Venetian ship was forced heere to expect the pleasure of the Turkish Searchers and Customers, namely, at the two Castles upon the entrie of the Straight of Hellespont, wherof I made mention in my sayling from Candia to Constantinople, and in the description of that Citie have noted them with the letters (W) and (X). For the ships that come from Constantinople, use to bee detained here some three daies, to the end that in case they carry away private men's slaves, the Masters may have time to follow after them; and in like case if they carrie away any prisoners or offenders, the publike Magistrates may have meanes to bring them backe. Besides,these searchers and Customers looke, that they carry no prohibited wares, neither can the ship, nor any passenger be suffered to passe these Castles, except they bring the Pasport of the great Turke, which the

Gallipolis.

Two Castles.

[I. iii. 267.]

chiefe Visere or Basha useth to grant unto them. Thus when no ship without the knowledge of the chiefe Visere can either passe these Castles leading to the Mediteranean Sea, or the two Castles above leading into the Euxine Sea, noted with (D E), surely these foure Castles are the greatest strength of Constantinople by Sea.

I said, that these Castles, where we found the Venetian ship, are in the description of Constantinople noted with the letters (W) and (X), and they are now commonly called the Castles of Gallipolis: but of old that noted with the letter (W) was called Sestos, being a Citie in Thrace, in which the most faire Hero was borne and dwelt; and the other noted with the letter (X) was called Abydos, being a Citie of Asia the lesse, in which Leander dwelt, famous for his love to Hero, and these Castles are divided by the Hellespont some two miles broad, at least so narrow, as Leander is said often to have swomme over it to his beloved Hero. The Castle of Sestos more specially is seated in a most fertile soyle; for Nairo, the next adjoyning towne, yeeldes excellent Wines, and all necessaries to sustaine life plentifully. Howsoever the ships ought, and use to bee staied here for three daies, yet a very faire winde blowing, and all duties being performed, the Patrons of the ships by a large gift to the Officers, sometimes obtaine leave to depart sooner. They say, that each passenger by Pole payeth here one zechine for tribute: but perhaps this belongs onely to Merchants, for my selfe, my servant, and the English Gentleman in my company, having given betweene us one zechine to the substitutes of the Venetian Bailiffe (so their Ambassador is called), we were dismissed upon their motion, yet we moreover gave fortie aspers to a Janizare, and fiftie aspers to a Chiauslar for the fees of their offices.

Sestos.

Abydos.

It being unwholsome to sleep above the hatches of the ship at this time of the yeere (though in summer time I made choice to sleepe so, when I sailed from Venice to Jerusalem), we three, namely, my selfe, the English Gentleman and my servant, gave for each of us three

Unwholsome aire.

zechines to the Pilot to be partners with him in his cabin, which by his Office hee had proper to himselfe in the Castle of the ship; and to the Patron or Master of the ship for our diet, we paid each of us after the rate of five zechines and a halfe by the moneth, as well at Sea, as in Harbors; and for our passage we joyntly paid ten ducats of Venice, (so as I still paid two parts of three in all expences); besides that, wee brought with us some hundreds of Egges, and a vessell of excellent Wine of Palormo, which our Ambassadour at Constantinople gave us.

Upon Monday the seventh of March (after the old stile used in Turky by all Christians and others) in the afternoone we set sayle, and passed the straight of Hellespont, and the same night sayled by the foresaid Iland of *Tenedos.* Tenedos. This Sea is called Pontus of the adjacent Province of Asia the lesse, named Pontus, which Province containes Colchis (famous by the old Argonauticall expedition), Capidocia, and Armenia. The eight of *Lemnos.* March, early in the morning, we did see the Iland Lemnos (famous for a kind of earth there digged, and in Latin called Terra Sigillata) upon our right hand, and the Ilands *Metelene.* Metelene, and Chios (now called Zio), and the Citie *Zio.* Smyrna (upon the continent of Asia the lesse) upon our *Smirna.* left hand, (to omit Ephesus, not farre distant upon the same continent.) And being now entred into the Ægean Sea (now called Archipelagus of fiftie Ilands standing like Arches, and not farre distant one from the other, which are called Cyclades, or Sporades), the ninth of March, having now sailed eightie miles, and being to sayle by the Iland Saint George of Skyra, the windes were so contrary, as wee were forced to strike sayles, and lie at hull (that is, tossed to and fro by the waves.) The same *Andros.* day we set sayle, and left the Iland Andros (one of the Cyclades) and the Iland Tyno (subject to the Venetians) on our left hand, or towards the East, and the Iland Negropont (lying close to the continent of Attica, and *Athens.* right over against the ruines of famous Athens) on our right hand, or towards the West. The tenth and eleventh of March, wee sayled 100 miles in the same Sea full of Ilands, and sailed by the Ilands Gia and Makarone. But [I. iii. 268.] towards night contrary windes rising high, and we fearing to bee cast upon some shoare of many adjacent Ilands, againe we struck sayle and lay at hull, tossing to and fro, but making small or no progresse. The twelfth of March, early in the morning, we set sayle, and sayled by the Iland Milo (of old called Miletum), where Saint Paul landed, Acts 20, 15), and a neere Iland Sdiles (of old called Delos, and most famous for the Oracle of Apollo), *Delos.* and the Promontory of Morea (of old called Peloponesus, containing many Provinces of Greece), which promontory is called Capo Malleo. The thirteenth of March, having sayled one hundred and ninety miles, we passed by the Iland Cerigo, not subject to the Turkes (as most of the Ilands are), but to the Venetians, who in a Castle on the South side keepe a Garrison of souldiers. It is one of the Cyclades, seated at the entrance of the Archipelagus towards the South, scarce five miles distant from Morea (the foresaid continent of Greece) and some one hundred and fiftie miles from Candia, the chiefe Citie of the Iland Candia, and was of old called Scotera, also Porphoris, of that precious kind of Marble there digged, and also Citherea, of which as her *Citherea.* chiefe seate Venus is often so called. And to this day there are seene the ruines of a Temple dedicated to Venus, and of a Pallace belonging to Menelaus the husband of Helena. From the thirteenth to the seventeenth of March, the windes were so contrary or scant, as wee onely sayled one hundred and twenty miles, and tooke harbour in the Iland Zante, subject to the Venetians *Zante.* (whereof I made mention in my voyage from Venice to Jerusalem.) Here some English Merchants continually reside, and the Haven being commodious, and most ships that trade in these Seas using to put into this Harbor, the goods that are diversly transported thence, are vulgarly, but falsely, esteemed the native commodities of the Iland. It hath scarce sixtie miles in circuit, and the Mountaines round about upon the Sea-side, inclose a pleasant and fruitfull Plaine. The Haven is like an halfe Moone increasing, and the chiefe Towne called Zante, lies in a little Plaine upon the innermost part thereof in length. The buildings of the houses are two stories high, with a tyled, but low roofe without any windowes (according to the building of Italy) but are poore and base for the matter, so as the onely beautie of the Towne lies in the Castle built at the East end upon a high Hill, being of a large circuit, and containing many houses and Churches within the walles thereof. In which Castle the Governour (called il Podestà) and the other Venetian inferiour Magistrates dwell, and give Law to the people of that Iland.

Turkish Pirats.

The Turkish Pirats of Saint Mauro in Morea, having lately set upon and taken a huge Venetian ship, did lade seventeene of their little barques with the most pretious goods thereof, namely, clothes of Gold, Damasks and Grogerans, to the value of a thousand thousand zechines (as the report went), and setting the ship on fire, tooke away the marriners for slaves. And the very time of my being in this Iland, seven Turkish Gallies lay upon this coast, and robbed all the Venetian ships falling into their hands, so as howsoever they had peace then with the Turkish Ottoman, yet their ships durst not stirre out of this haven. Whereupon they having now occasion to send out ships for Corne, the Magistrate forced the Master of an English ship then harbouring there, to waft these ships, though much against his will, when there were some 20 Venetian ships in the same Haven, whereof divers were of 400 or 500 tuns. Also at this time it hapned, that a Spanish ship of Catolonia was driven into this Harbor, and the Magistrate calling our Merchants before him, would have forced them to give caution, that the English ships then lying there, should not assaile the same, though betweene England & Spaine war had now long time bin proclaimed: but they contesting against this course

A Spanish ship.

as injurious to them, yet could not be dismissed, till they gave their words, that our ships should not assayle the same by day or night, so long as it lay in this Haven. And this Spanish ship for long time not daring to goe forth, at last upon occasion of Venetian Gallies landing there, was wafted by them, and so escaped. Upon the robbing and burning of the foresaid Venetian ship by Turkish Pyrates, the Venetian Baliffe, (so they call their Ambassadour) lying then at Constantinople, had obtained the Great Turkes Mandate, that these Pyrates gallies being burnt, they should presently be sent in bonds to [I. iii. 269.] his Court, and this Mandate was brought by a Chiauss, (or Pencioner) who came in the same ship with us, whereupon the Pyrates being more inraged against the Venetians, did at this time take and spoyle another Venetian ship of some foure hundred and fifty Tunnes, called the Sylvester, and not content with the most rich booty, did cast into the Sea many Marriners yeelding to mercy, and could hardly be perswaded by the intercession of Turkes passengers in the same ship, to spare the lives of some twenty chiefe Marriners yet alive, and to forbeare the burning of the ship. The Italians of best judgement, did not expect that the great Turke would duly punish these outrages, but rather were of opinion that himselfe and his chiefe Visere would draw the greatest part of the prey to their own hands, and that the Turkish Governours inticed by like participation, would endevour to free these Pyrates, and doe their best to nourish them, yea, that this very Chiauss now sent with a Mandate to suppresse them, would be induced by bribes, to returne to Constantinople, with relation that the Pyrates could not be found, so they did (as no doubt they would) for a time hide themselves, and in conclusion, that the Venetians after having spent much money in obtaining new Mandates for their apprehension, should find no other remedy, but to repell force by force.

Another Venetian ship taken by the Pyrates.

Upon Wednesday the thirtieth of March, (after the old stile) in the beginning of the yeere 1597, we set sayle,

March 30. Ann. 1597.

but by contrarietie of winds, were againe driven backe into the Haven of Zante. Upon Friday the first of Aprill after dinner, againe we set saile, and the second of Aprill sayling by the Iland of Cefalonia, (whereof I spake in our voyage from Venice to Jerusalem), we cast anchor in the outward Haven of the Iland Corfu, because the Master of our ship was sicke, and this his sickenesse increasing, we set saile to returne backe to the chiefe City of that Iland, the Haven whereof we entered the sixth of Aprill. From Zante to Cefalonia are seventy miles, and from thence to Corfu are 120 miles.

Cefalonia.

Corfu.

This Iland Corfu inhabited by Greekes is very fertile, yeelding plenty of fruites, corne, wines, and Currands, and this Haven is fortified with two Forts cut out off a Rocke, namely, the old and the new Fort, (which is more then a mile in circuit), both being very strong and held unexpugnable, so as this Iland is worthily reputed one of the chiefe Keyes of Christendome. The Master of our ship having recovered his health, wee set saile upon Tuesday the twelfth of Aprill, and returned againe to the foresaid outward Haven of Corfu Iland, where an old woman a passenger died, and her kinsemen carried her body to be buried on Land. Here againe we were forced to stay, the winds being contrary.

Corfu a Keye of Christendome.

At last upon the nineteenth of Aprill towards evening, with a faire wind we joyfully set saile, and the twentieth day we sailed over the streight Sea, betweene Greece and the Province of Apulia in Italy. Upon Friday the two and twentieth of Aprill towards the evening, having sayled some two hundred miles from the said streight, we were carried by the shoare of the City Raguza, with a faire gale of wind, and had the wind beene never so contrary, yet our Master knowing some late difference risen betweene the Raguzeans and Venetians, would not willingly have landed in that Haven. The blame of which difference some imputed to the Raguzeans, in that they favoured the Scocchi, a Neighbour people upon the shoare of Sclavonia, who being subject to the Emperour

Raguza.

and Christians, yet robbed all kinds of ships passing these Seas, and had lately spoiled and burnt a Venetian Gally in the Port of Rovingo. But other alleaged a more probable cause thereof, namely, that some Venetian Gentlemen for some venerious insolencies there committed, had lately beene slaine in a tumult. Raguza of old called Epidaurus, and the chiefe City of Sclavonia, is foure hundred miles distant from Venice, built at the foot of an high mountaine, upon the Sea shoare, and hath great trafficke by those Seas, and huge ships, which the Kings of Spaine have often hired and joined to their Navy. The governement is popular, and this City to the wonder of many, doth to this day maintaine the liberty, though it be seated betweene the very jawes of the two powerfull States of the great Turke and Venetians, to one of which all other neere Townes Ilands and Countries are subject. For the Venetians are loath to drive them being Christians to such despaire, as they might be forced to yeeld themselves to the great Turke, and the City is very strongly fortified towards the sea, whence the Venetians can onely assaile them: besides, that they pay great customes of their trafficke to the State of Venice, for which reason that State attempts nothing against the freedome of the City. Againe, the Turkes knowing that if they should besiege the City by Land, the Citizens would with all their best moveables flie into Italy by Sea, and receiving also a great yeerely tribute from the trafficke of this City, (where the great Turke hath his owne Officer called Chiaussagha to gather the same,) are also content not to molest them by warre, especially since they know that the Pope, the King of Spaine, and the State of Venice, would assist the Raguzeans against them, and no way indure that the Turkish Ottoman should make himselfe Lord of that Haven.

The governe-ment of Raguza.

[I iii. 270.]

Upon the three and twenty of Aprill towards evening, we sayled by the little Iland Augusta, (being yet of a good large circuit, and populous, and subject to the Raguzeans, but the Coast is dangerous for ships arrivall, by reason

The Iland Augusta.

of the Rockes called the Augustines,) and by the little Iland Corsolari. Some Ilands in this Sea are subject to the Raguzeans, and some neere to the Northerne continent, have the Great Turke for their Lord, but the rest are subject to the Venetians, and are very many in number, but little, and good part of them little or not at all inhabited. The Italians our consorts, told us of

Pelaguza. an Iland not farre distant, called Pelaguza, and lying neere the continent of Italy, upon the Coast whereof the famous Turkish Pyrate of Algier, (a Haven in Africa) was lately wont to hover and lie hidden, and made rich booties of the Venetian and Italian Merchants. Upon Sunday the foure and twenty of Aprill, we had in sight, and little distant, the little Ilands, Catza and Lissa, and in the afternoone on our left hand towards Italy the Iland Pomo, and in the evening towards Dalmatia, two Ilands, and upon the continent the City Zaga, being some two hundred miles distant from Venice. And the night following we sailed over an arme of the Sea some thirty miles broade, lying betweene Dalmatia and Istria, called

Il Cornaro. Il Cornaro, which we passed without any appearance of danger, though otherwise it be generally reputed so dangerous, as the Venetians offended with any Marriner, use this imprecation; Maledetto sia il Cornaro che t' ha lasciato passare; that is: Cursed be the Cornaro for letting thee passe. Upon Monday the five and twenty of Aprill, as we sailed by the Coast of Istria, one of the Marriners aged, and (as we thought) honest, and of some authority among the rest, privately admonished me, that I should safely locke up our goods in our chests, lest the inferior Marriners should steale our shirts, or any other thing they found negligently left, which they used to doe, especially at the end of any voyage. Upon Tuesday the sixe and twenty of April, we cast anchor beyond Pola, in the continent of Istria, a City now ruined, and upon the

Rovingo. seven and twenty day we entred the Haven of Rovingo in Istria, subject to the Venetians, where the ships use to take a Pilot for their owne safety, or els are tied so to doe by some old priviledge of that City. Here the Provisors for health gave us liberty of free conversation, (as they had formerly done at Zante), seeing no man in our ship to be sicke or sickely. And I did not a little wonder, when I observed each second or third person of this City to halt and be lame of one foot, which made me remember the Citizens of Islebe in Germany, and in the Province of Saxony, where almost all the men have wry neckes; whereof I knew the cause, namely because they used daily to dig in mines, with their neckes leaning on one side: but of this common lamenes of the Inhabitants in Rovingo, I could not learne any probable cause, except it were the foule disease of lust, raigning in those parts, which I rather thought likely, because the lamenesse was common to weomen as men.

Lame Rovingians.

Now the sayling in our great ship was like to be more troublesome, dangerous, and slow, whereupon five of us joyning together, did upon the thirtieth of Aprill (after the old stile) hier a boate of sixe Oares, for seven Venetian Duckets to Venice, where we arrived the next day towards evening, and staied in our boat upon the wharfe of the Market place of Saint Marke, till the Provisors of health sitting in their Office neere that place, came unto us, and after some conference, understanding that we and our ship were free of all infection or sicknesse, gave us free liberty of conversation. Wee staied three dayes at Venice to refresh our selves, and paied each man three lyres for each meale in a Dutch Inne.

Venice.

[I. iii. 271.]

Then having received money of a Merchant, I went to the Village Mestre, and there bought of Dutchmen newly arrived in Italy, two horses for my selfe and my man, the one for thirtie, the other for twentie ducates. These horses I sold at Stode in Germany after my journey ended, at, or about the same rate. He that hath the Dutch tongue, and either knowes the waies of Germany himselfe, or hath consorts skilfull therein, being to travell from Stode, or those parts into Italy, shall finde more profit in buying a horse in those parts of Germany, for

Profit in the Dutch Tongue.

so hee shall save great summes usually paid for coches, and at the journies end, or rather by the way towards the ende of his journey, may in Italy sell his horses with good profit. In the Village Mestre, each of us paid each meale fiftie soldi, that is, two lires and a halfe.

From hence we took the right way to Augsburg in Germany, to Nurnberg, Brunswick, and to Stode, an old Citie lying on the Northern Sea of Germany. The particulars of which journey I here omit, having in my journey to Jerusalem passed the very same way from Stode to Venice.

Charges in Italy.

So as it shall suffice to adde some few things in generall. Within the confines of Italy, each man of us paid for each meale fortie, and sometimes fiftie Venetian soldi, and for hay and stable for his horse commonly at noone foure soldi, at night twelve soldi, and for ten measures of oates given each day to each horse fiftie soldi.

After we entred Germany, each man paid each meale commonly twenty creitzers, at Inspruch twentie foure, and somtimes twentie six creitzers, for hay six creitzers a day, or there-abouts, and for ten measures of oates, serving one horse for a day wee paid fiftie creitzers. In the middle Provinces of Germany, each of us paid for each meale commonly sixteene creitzers, that is, foure batzen, and in the parts upon the Northerne sea some foure Lubeck shillings. And from the Citie Armstat (seated betweene Augsburg and Nurnberg) to the said Northern sea side, we had a new measure of oates called Hembd, one of which measures was sold for some tenne Lubeck shillings, and served three horses for our baite at noone, and another was almost sufficient for them at night.

Charges in Germany.

From Stode seated upon the German Sea, we passed in a boat to the outmost Haven, where wee went abroad an English ship upon the fourth of July (after the old stile) being Tuesday. The sixt of July early in the morning we set sayle, and the eight of July we came upon the most wished land of England, and cast anchor neere Orford, a Castle in Suffolke. Upon Saturday the ninth of July (after the old stile) we landed at Gravesend, and without delay with the night-tide passed in a boat to London, where we arived on Sunday at foure of the clock in the morning, the tenth of July, in the yeere 1597, our hearts being full of joy, that our mercifull God had safely brought us thither. This early hower of the morning being unfit to trouble my friends, I went to the Cocke (an Inne of Aldersgate streete) and there apparrelled as I was, laid me downe upon a bed, where it happened, that the Constable and watchmen (either being more busie in their office then need was, or having extraordinary charge to search upon some foraine intelligence, and seeing me apparrelled like an Italian) tooke me for a Jesuit or Priest (according to their ignorance; for the crafty Priests would never have worne such clothes as I then did.) But after some few bowers when I awaked, and while I washed my hands, did inquire after my friends health, dwelling in the same streete, the Host of the house knowing me, dismissed the watchmen that lay to apprehend me, and told me how I had been thus mistaken.

July 10, an. 1597.

The Constable's errour.

Chap. V.

[I. iii. 272.]

Of the journey through England, Scotland, and Ireland.

HE that desires to see the Cities and Antiquities of England, Scotland and Ireland, let him reade the Chapter of the usuall manner of all kingdomes to journey, and to hire Coches and horses, and also the Chapter, wherein these Kingdomes are Geographically described out of Camden, or if he list, rather let him reade Camden himselfe of this point: and lastly let him in the same last named Chapter peruse the diet of these Kingdomes, and the entertainement in Innes. Touching the distances of places by miles: first, for England he shall easily find

Camden.

a little printed booke particularly setting downe the same. For Scotland I will briefley set downe my journey therein. And for Ireland, the Cities being rare and farre distant, hee must have a guide, who may without great trouble inquire them out. Onely give me leave for the helpe of strangers to adde this one thing, namely, how they being curious to search antiquities, and loth to omit the sight of things worthy of observation, may to this purpose best dispose of their journies, which all other men may fit to their endes and purposes. First, let them passe out of Normandy to Rhye, an English Haven in Sussex, then let them visit such of the five Kentish Ports as they please, let them see Canterbury, famous for the Seate of the Metropolitan Archbishop; then the Castle of Quinborrough, in the Iland of Sheppey, and the Regall Navy; then let them passe by Rochester (a Bishops Seate), the Regall Pallace at Greenewich, and Depford the Navall storehouse, and not farre thence see the broken ribbes of the ship, wherein famous Sir Francis Drake compassed the World, and so let them come to London. When they have viewed the Monuments of London and Westminster, and seene the Kings Court, they may take a cursory journey to view such antiquities in Middlesex, Surry, and Barkshire, as upon the reading of Camden they shall most desire to see, and especially all, or the chiefe Pallaces of the King. Againe, from London they may take a cursory journey to see the University of Oxford, and so by Worcester returne to London. In their journey to the confines of England and Scotland, they may see the Universitie of Cambridge, and view the most choise antiquities mentioned by Master Camden in Harfordshire, Northamptonshire, Lincolnsheire, Yorkeshire, Durham and Northumberland.

Places worthy of observation.

Sir Francis Drake's Ship.

My selfe upon occasion of businesse in the month of Aprill, and the yeere 1598, tooke a journey to these said confines, namely, to Barwick, a Towne then very strongly fortified by the English, to restraine the sudden incursions of the Scots, and abounding with all things necessary for

Aprill, Anno. 1598.

food, yea with many dainties, as Salmons and all kindes of shell-fish, so plentifully, as they were sold for very small prices. And here I found that for the lending of sixtie pound, there wanted not good Citizens, who would give the lender a fàire chamber and good dyet, as long as he would lend them the mony. Being to returne from Barwicke, I had an earnest desire, first, to see the King of Scots Court. So from hence I rode in one day fortie miles to Edenborrow the chiefe Citie of that Kingdome. And in this said daies journey after foure miles riding I came to Aton, a Village where the Lord of Humes *Aton.* dwelles, whose Family was powerfull in those parts. After sixteene miles more I came to Dunbar, which they said to have been of old a Towne of some importance, but then it lay ruined, and seemed of little moment, as well for the povertie, as the small number of inhabitants. After the riding of eight miles more, on the left hand towards the West, and something out of the high way, the pleasant Village of Hadrington lay, which the English, *Hadrington.* in the raigne of Queene Elizabeth, tooke, and kept against the French, who drawne over in the time of faction, kept [I. iii. 273.] the Towne of Dunbar, and fortified the same. When I had ridden five miles further, I came to the ancient and (according to the building of that Kingdome) stately Pallace of the L. Seton, beautified with faire Orchards and Gardens, and for that clime pleasant. Not farre thence lyes the Village Preston-graung, belonging to the Family of the Cars, powerfull from these parts to the very borders of England within land. After I had ridden three miles more, I came to the Village Fisherawe, neere *Fisherawe.* which beyond a Brooke lyes the Village Musselborrow in a stony soyle, famous for a great Victorie of the English against the Scots. On the left hand towards the West, and something out of the high way, the Queene of Scots then kept her Court (in the absence of the King) at the Village Dawkeith, in a Pallace belonging to the Earle of Murray.

From the said Village Fishrawe, I rode the rest of the

way, being foure miles, and so in one dayes journey (as I said) came to Edenborow, seated in Lodovey, (of old called Pictland) the most civill Region of Scotland, being hilly and fruitfull of corne, but having little or no wood. This City is the seat of the King of Scotland, and the Courts of Justice are held in the same. Of old according to the changeable fortune of warre, it was sometimes in the possession of the Scots, sometimes of the English inhabiting this Easterne part of Scotland, till the English Kingdome being shaken with the invasions of the Danes, at last about the yeere 960. it became wholly in the power of the Scots. This City is high seated, in a fruitfull soyle and wholsome aire, and is adorned with many Noblemens Towers lying about it, and aboundeth with many springs of sweet waters. At the end towards the East, is the Kings Pallace joyning to the Monastery of the Holy Crosse, which King David the first built, over which, in a Parke of Hares, Conies, and Deare, an high mountaine hangs, called the chaire of Arthur, (of Arthur the Prince of the Britanes, whose monuments famous among all Ballad-makers, are for the most part to be found on these borders of England and Scotland.) From the Kings Pallace at the East, the City still riseth higher and higher towards the West, and consists especially of one broad and very faire street, (which is the greatest part and sole ornament thereof), the rest of the side streetes and allies being of poore building and inhabited with very poore people, and this length from the East to the West is about a mile, whereas the bredth of the City from the North to the South is narrow, and cannot be halfe a mile. At the furthest end towards the West, is a very strong Castle, which the Scots hold unexpugnable. Camden saith this Castle was of old called by the Britaines, Castle meyned agned; by the Scots, The Castle of the Maids or Virgines, (of certaine Virgines kept there for the Kings of the Picts), and by Ptolomy the winged Castle. And from this Castle towards the West, is a most steepe Rocke pointed on the highest top, out of which this

Edenborow.

The mountaine called the chaire of Arthur.

The Castle.

Castle is cut: But on the North & South sides without the wals, lie plaine and fruitfull fields of Corne. In the midst of the foresaid faire streete, the Cathedrall Church *The Cathedrall Church.* is built, which is large and lightsome, but little stately for the building, and nothing at all for the beauty and ornament. In this Church the Kings seate is built some few staires high of wood, and leaning upon the pillar next to the Pulpit: And opposite to the same is another seat very like it, in which the incontinent use to stand and doe pennance; and some few weekes past, a Gentleman, being a stranger, and taking it for a place wherein Men of better quality used to sit, boldly entred the same in Sermon time, till he was driven away with the profuse laughter of the common sort, to the disturbance of the whole Congregation. The houses are built of unpolished stone, *The houses.* and in the faire streete good part of them is of free stone, which in that broade streete would make a faire shew, but that the outsides of them are faced with wooden galleries, built upon the second story of the houses; yet these galleries give the owners a faire and pleasant prospect, into the said faire and broad street, when they sit or stand in the same. The wals of the City are built of little and unpolished stones, and seeme ancient, but are very narrow, and in some places exceeding low, in other, ruined.

From Edenborow there is a ditch of water, (yet not running from the Inland, but rising of springs) which is carried to Lethe, and so to the Sea. Lethe is seated *Lethe.* upon a creek of the Sea, called the Frith, some mile from [I. iii. 274.] Edenborow, and hath a most commodious and large Haven. When Monsieur Dessy a Frenchman, did fortifie Lethe, for the strength of Edenborow, it began of a base Village to grow to a Towne. And when the French King Francis the second had married Mary Queene of the Scots: againe the French, (who now had in hope devoured the possession of that Kingdome, and in the yeere 1560. began to aime at the conquest of England) more strongly fortified this Towne of Lethe:

but Elizabeth Queene of England, called to the succour of the Lords of Scotland against these Frenchmen, called in by the Queene, soone effected that the French returned into their Countrey, and these fortifications were demolished.

King-Korn in Fife.

From Leth I crossed over the Frith, (which ebs and flowes as high as Strivelin) to the Village King-korn, being eight miles distant, and seated in the Region or Country called Fife, which is a peninsule, that is, almost an Iland, lying betweene two creekes of the Sea, called Frith and Taye, and the Land yeelds corne and pasture and sea-coales, as the Seas no lesse plentifully yeeld (among other fish,) store of oysters & shel fishes, and this Countrey is populous, and full of Noblemens and Gentlemens dwellings commonly compassed with little groves, though trees are so rare in those parts, as I remember not to have seene one wood.

Falkeland.

From the said Village King-korn, I rode ten very long miles to Falkeland, then the Kings House for hunting, but of old belonging to the Earles of Fife, where I did gladly see James the sixth King of the Scots, at that time lying there to follow the pastimes of hunting and hawking, for which this ground is much commended; but the Pallace was of old building and almost ready to fall, having nothing in it remarkeable. I thought to have ridden from hence to Saint Andrewes a City, seated in Fife, and well known as an University, and the seate of the Archbishop: But this journey being hindred, I wil onely say, that the Bishop of Saint Andrewes, at the intercession of the King of Scotland James the third, was by the Pope first made Primate of all Scotland, the same Bishop and all other Bishops of that Kingdome having formerly to that day beene consecrated and confirmed by the Archbishop of Yorke in England. Likewise I purposed to take my journey as farre as Strivelin, where the King of the Scots hath a strong Castle, built upon the front of a steepe Rocke, which King James the sixth since adorned with many buildings, and the same

Saint Andrewes.

hath for long time beene committed to the keeping of the Lords of Eriskin, who likewise use to have the keeping of the Prince of Scotland, being under yeeres. And from thence I purposed to returne to Edenborow, but some occasions of unexpected businesse recalled me speedily into England, so as I returned presently to Edenborow, and thence to Barwicke, the same way I came. *Striveling.*

I adde for passengers instruction, that they who desire to visit the other Counties of England and Ireland, may passe from Edenborow to Carlile, chiefe City of Cumberland in England, and so betweene the East parts of Lancashire and the West parts of Yorke, and then through Darbyshire, Nottinghamshire, Warwickeshire, Staffordshire, and Chesshire, may take their journey to the City Westchester, whence they shall have commodity to passe the Sea to Dublin in Ireland, and while they expect this passage, they may make a cursory journey into Flintshire, and Caernarvenshire in Northwales, to see the antiquities thereof, or otherwise may goe directly to Holy Head, and thence make a shorter cut to Dublyn in Ireland. From Dublyn they may passe to see the Cities of the Province Mounster, whence they may commodiously passe to the South parts of Wales, and there especially see the antiquities of Merlyn, and so taking their journey to the West parts of England, may search the antiquities of these severall Counties, and easily find commoditie to passe into the West parts of France: And all this circuit beginning at London, may (with ordinary favourable winds according to the season of the yeere) be easily made, from the beginning of March, to the end of September. Alwaies I professe onely to prescribe this course, to such as are curious to search all the famous monuments and antiquities of England, mentioned in Camdens compleat description thereof. *Journeys through England.* *Ireland.* *Wales.*

[Chap. VI.

[I. iii. 275.]

Chap. VI.

Of the manner to exchange Moneys into forraine parts, and the divers moneys of divers parts, together with the divers measures of miles in sundry Nations, most necessary for the understanding of the former journall.

The Travellers most commodious course.

He Travellers most commodious course, is to deliver into the hands of some Merchant those kinds of gold or silver coynes, which are of greatest value in those parts to which he takes his journey, with covenant to deliver him by his Factor the same, both in the Species or kind, and in the number, or to send them in that sort to him by a trusty messenger. But the first course is not in use, besides that, it is a difficult taske, to find such divers kinds in any particular place, except it be from the Exchangers and Usurers, who use not to serve another mans turne for profit or otherwise, without their owne gaine; and being most expert in such affaires, are like to draw all the hoped profit to themselves. And the second course threatens many dangers, by robberies, by confiscations of the transmitted Coynes, and by the doubtfull credit of the messengers. Particularly in England and France, he that is knowne to carry great summes of money about him, shall runne great danger to be robbed, and in England the Law forbids any Traveller upon paine of confiscation, to carry more money about him out of the Kingdome, then will serve for the expences of his journey, (namely, above twenty pounds sterling). As likewise in France, the like Law restraines the exporting of money, allowing an Horseman from Lyons to Rome, eighty crownes, from Turine to Rome fifty, and no more, for his expences; all greater summes found about him, being subject to confiscation: yet I confesse that many wary Travellers

The exporting of money restrained.

have exported greater summes out of England into France, and out of France into England; and thereby with these hazards, have made great gaine: But upon the confines of Italy, and the severall principalities thereof, yea, at the gates of each City in Italy, most crafty Officers so curiously search into the breach of these Pænall Statutes, and so narrowly prie into all mens carriage, never wincking at any delinquent, as there is no hope upon breach of the Law to escape the penalty: for these searchers are tied to more strict attention in this businesse, that (according to their Office) they may beware least their Princes be defrauded of their Tributes. And since very Jewels, and the least toyes carried about passengers, are subject to frequent Tributes (according to the frequent Principalities) these good fellowes leave nothing unassaied, in the wished discovery of these fraudes, yea, where they have no just suspition of fraud; yet cease they not to trouble passengers in this kind, till they have extorted some bribe or gift from them. Behold here a two horned danger, (as I may tearme it of the captious argument, called Dilemma) which travellers cannot possibly escape in Italy, who carry about them Jewels or great summes of money, where they are in danger of confiscation, if they hide them warily, and of theeves, if they shew them, and pay due tributes for them. For theeves (namely, men banished for notorious crimes) lie continually upon the confines of Princes (very frequent in Italy), and more specially of the Kingdome of Naples and of the Popes territory. In Germany, Bomerland, Sweitzerland, the Low-Countreys, Denmarke, Poland, and Turkey, passengers may carry summes of money about them with more security, neither have I there observed any great danger therein, so that the passenger affect not solitarinesse, and be so wary as not to boast of his plenty.

Jewels subject to Tributes.

Dangers of Confiscation and theeves.

Touching the divers kinds of Coynes to be transported, I forewarne the Reader, that the gold Coynes of England and of France, and aswell the silver as gold Coynes of Spaine, are in generall spent abroad with greatest gaine:

but even the gold and silver Coynes of other Princes, are rarely currant out of their owne Dominions, and can
[I. iii. 276.] hardly be exchanged among Merchants without some losse. Againe, that hee who exports any gold coynes, must take care to have them of just weight, for such hee may disburse with gaine, but shall beare losse in others that are lighter, because they want the helpe of their Princes Prerogative, where no man can be forced to receive them. Now I wil briefly shew, which kinds of foraine coines are most valued in divers states. In England the gold and silver coynes of Spaine and French Crownes are highly valued. In Scotland the same coynes, and as well in Scotland as Ireland; moreover, the gold and silver coynes of England are valued. For Germany: at Stode the English angels, and all the gold coynes of England, France and Spaine are most esteemed: but if you passe into the upper parts of Germany, you must for your expences there change these coynes at Stode into the Rhenish gold guldens, and silver dollers of Germany. But at Vienna and the confines of Hungary, the Hungarian ducats are most currant. In Bohmerland the Rheinish gold guldens, the silver dollers of Germany, and the Hungarian ducats. In Sweitzerland, first, the French Crownes of gold, then the gold guldens and silver dollers of Germany. In Denmarke the silver and gold coynes of England. At Dantzk in Prussen, and throughout all Poland, the gold coynes of England, and the gold guldens and silver dollers of Germany, and especially Hungarian ducats. In France upon the Sea coasts, the Angels and gold coynes of England are currant: but for your journey further into the land, you must change them into French Crownes, and the silver coynes of that Kingdome, and the gold coynes of Spaine are very currant in all the Cities even within the land. In the Low Countries, all coynes are currant, they being most cunning exchangers, and wanting many things, yet drawing to them abundance of all forraine commodities, so as they have skill to draw gold out of the dung (as he said of Ennius.) Yet they

Value of foraine coines.

most esteeme the coynes of England, Spaine, and France. In Turkey the gold zechines of Venice are most currant, and preferred even before their owne Sultanones of gold. The coynes after them most esteemed and to be spent with most gaine, are the silver ryals of Spaine (which the Italians call Pezzi d' otto, and Pezzi di quattro, pieces of eight, and pieces of foure, and the Turks call piastri, and halfe piastri.) In Italy generally the gold coynes of Spaine are spent with most advantage. In the next place, and more particularly at Venice and Naples the French Crownes are esteemed, but in Italy more then any other place; you must have care they be of just weight. In generall, all gold coynes may be put away with gayne at Venice, but they being in other parts of Italy lesse valued, or not currant, hee that travels higher, must change them there into silver Crownes of Italy, and least the weight of them should be burthensome, and he should chance to fall into the hands of theeves (called Banditi, banished men), he shall do well to carry no more about him then will suffice for the expences of his journey, and to deliver the rest to some Venetian Merchant of credit, taking his bils of exchange, or letters, by which he may receive them in any other Citie or Cities, as his occasions require.

Value of foraine coines.

But in respect of the foresaid difficulties to export coynes in specie, that is, in the kinde, the Traveller shall doe better who takes the second and most usuall course, taking care to have his moneys delivered to the exchangers (or Merchants) by the hands of some trustie friend, to be exchanged over (according to the exchange variable in respect of the time, and the place to which it is to bee made) and sent to him in forraine parts for his expence (by severall sums, and at set times of the yeere.) This exchange is so variable upon many usuall accidents, as a constant manner of so unconstant a thing cannot be prescribed. But the rate & course therof may be inquired in the Burse (or publike meeting place for the Merchants.) For the alteration thereof is weekely made knowne particularly to the Merchants, that by letters they presently

Exchange of moneys.

may certifie the same to their severall Facters beyond the Seas. Now this daily alteration of the exchange commeth, partly of the quantitie of moneys for the present to be exchanged to the Princes or Merchants uses, and of the greater or lesser number of those that desire moneys in exchange. For when small summes are to be exchanged, either by the Prince for payment of his Army, or by the Merchants for their traffick, and when many desire moneys upon exchange, then the rate thereof is raised, and the Traveller loseth more thereby, as on the contrary, the rates are abased, and so the traveller gaines by his exchange. But a farre greater cause of this alteration, is the change of the moneys value by the Princes Edicts. Thus at Antwerp (in our memory) when an English Angell of gold was worth twelve Belgick shillings and eight pence, then hee that in London paid twentie English shillings, received at Antwerp five and twentie Belgick shillings and foure pence. But at this time when the said Angel was at Antwerp worth five Belgick or Flemish guldens and two blancks (that is, seventeene Belgick shillings, wanting a stiver), he that at London paid twentie English shillings, received at Antwerp foure and thirtie Belgick shillings wanting two stivers. And this divers valuation of the Angel (as of other coynes) seemes to proceede of this Flemish custome, that when the united Provinces have great store of any coyne in their coffers, then they raise the value thereof, that they may issue it with advantage in the payment of their Army; and when the same coynes are to be brought into their coffers by tributes and taxes, then they in like sort use to decry them, that the State may also receive them with advantage. For howsoever this raising and decrying of moneys by publike Edict, savoureth of tyranny, yet the necessitie of the united Provinces affaires in their long and dangerous civill warres, or the hidden skill they have to make gaine of all things with an unseene, and so lesse felt oppression of the common people, hath made this course ordinary among the Flemings, which to al other

Alteration of the Exchange.

[I. iii. 277.]

Flemish Exchanges.

subjects is offensive in high degree. Yet howsoever a certaine value of moneys cannot be set downe, notwithstanding the value of English Angels, and gold coynes of Spaine, France, and Germany is more constant then of others, and subject to little increase or decrease. And (to say truth) howsoever this alteration may oppresse the subject, yet it imports little to travellers, whether forraine coynes be raised or decryed, since the prices of al things necessary to life, answere in due proportion to the present valuation of moneys, and use to be changed as the value of money is altered. But to make the manner of exchanges more manifest, by one example conjecture of the rest. English Merchants taking money to be exchanged, doe give the traveller, or his friend for him, three severall billes of exchange for the same money, for his better securitie to receive it, yet in each of them inserting a caution, that onely one be paid. Of these three bills the traveller useth to retaine one with himselfe, and to take order that the other two be sent before him by severall messengers to the Merchants Factor, who received his money and gave him these billes for it. Or in the Travellers absence, his friend receiving these billes, sends them all by severall messengers to him living beyond the Seas. And to avoide all fraudes, I advise the traveller to have his billes so made, as the Species, or kinde of money be therein named, in which the Factor is to pay him in forraine parts, and the number of the pieces in that kind, and the just waight of the coyne (as the Italians for French Crownes write, Scudi d' oro in oro del Sole.) And because the Factors use to delay and put off the paiment of these billes; first, lest they should object, that they know you not to be the man, except you prove it by the testimony of countrimen, who in all places are not to bee found, or may perhaps be unknowne to you, and you to them as to the Merchant, you shall doe well besides these billes of exchange, to send the Merchants letters to his Factor, expressing the most rare markes of your body, by which

Billes of Exchange.

you may be made knowne to him, together with caution, that your money bee paid to no other then your selfe, lest any deceive you, and receive it in your name, having by fraude or violence gotten one of your three billes, and arriving at the place before you. Moreover, since travellers use to remove twice in the yeere from one Citie or Countrey to another, namely, at the Spring and at the Fall of the leafe, lest your billes of exchange should negligently bee sent, or slowly come to your hands, and so you be forced to leese the season of the yeere most fit for taking of journeys, take order that the money you are to use at the fall of the leafe in Italy, bee sent by billes from England at the Spring, or if you be in nearer places, that it bee sent three, or at least two moneths before the time you are to use it. And lest the Factor should protract paiment, let it be expressed in your bill that the money be paid upon sight. Our Merchants write their bils of exchange for neere places in 4 kinds, namely, to bee paid, at sight, at usance, at halfe usance, and at double usance; which word usance being not English, I take to be borrowed of the Italian word usanza, signifying a manner or custome. The word (at sight) imports present payment; at halfe usance a fortnight after the date; at usance, a moneth; at double usance, two moneths. And thus to him that goes from London to Hamburg in Germany, it is all one, whether his bill of exchange be paid at sight, or at halfe usance, since hee can hardly arrive there in lesse space then a fortnight. But touching the exchange from London to Venice farther distant, by the word usance three moneths are signified, and by double usance six moneths. The Turks Empier is so farre distant, and the journeys are so uncertaine, as our Merchants use no certaine rate of exchange thither, neither indeed use they to give any billes of exchange, but onely letters of credit, to receive set summes of money, or at large, as much as the traveller shall want, (of which third kinde of receiving money in forraine parts, I shall hereafter speake.) By the foresaid billes of exchange, accord-

Advice to travellers.

[I. iii. 278.]

Usance.

ing to the foresaid opportunities, the traveller commonly loseth, and sometimes gaineth. For my selfe am familiarly acquainted with a Merchant, who tooke up one hundred pounds at London, to be paid by his Factor at Stode in Germany, which Factor againe tooke up the same hundred pounds at Stode, to be paid by his Master at London, and at foure moneths end, he paied the same, having by these bils of exchange made use there of all this time, without one penny losse. But in generall, when great quantitie of money is to bee made over to any place from London, the traveller shall lose after five in the hundred by the yeere; and when small quantitie is to bee made over, he shall lose after the rate of fifteene in the hundred by the yeere, and ordinarily he shall lose about the rate of ten in the hundred by the yeere.

Loss in Exchange.

By reason of the aforesaid uncertaintie in receiving money by billes of exchange, as well by the slow sending of them, as by the delay which Factors use to make in paying them, as also by the usuall negligence of the travellers friend, who is to make over his mony, or by his want of ready mony at the time, I say for this uncertaintie, lest the traveller should lose the season of the yeere fit to take journeys, by the expecting of his mony, a third course of receiving mony in forraine parts hath growne in use, namely, that the traveller should take with him letters of credit, from some Merchant of great trade to his Factor, to furnish him from place to place of money, either according to his want, or for a certaine yeerely summe. I confesse it is a more frugall course, that he should first pay his money at home, and after receive it beyond the Seas, then that he should first receive it there, and after repay it at home: but I would advise him to make over his money after the foresaid manner by billes of Exchange, and withall to carry these letters of credit for abundant caution of all events, so as upon any crosse accident, he may rather incurre a small losse of money, then the unrecoverable losse of time. Yet even in money taken by letters of credit, reckoning the time of the repai-

Uncertaintie in receiving money by billes of Exchange.

ment, Merchants use not to exact greater gaine, then ten in the hundreth by the yeere, especially if they be honest men, or have any bond of friendship with the traveller, or his friends at home, and be confident of repaiment, without any doubt, arising either by the travellers sicknesse or by his friends ill keeping of their credit.

My experience of the rate of Exchanges.

It remaines that I adde somewhat in generall out of my experience, of the rate at which my selfe received money by the foresaid bils of exchange, or letters of credit. And first I will confesse my negligent omission, in noting the rates of my exchanges, whereof (as a matter of moment) I much repent me; but for this reason the Reader must beare with me, if I set the same downe more briefly then were fit for his instruction. Out of England into Scotland, and Ireland, a Traveller shall have many opportunities to carry monies in specie, (that is, in kind), or to exchange them without any losse. The exchange out of England, to Stoade or Hamburge in Germany, useth to beare this rate, for a pound, (or twenty shillings sterling) to receive there five and twenty Hamburge shillings and sixe pence. My selfe delivered forty pounds in England, and after the rate of twenty foure Hamburg shillings and eight pence, for each English pound, or at the rate of an imperiall doller, vallued at foure shillings six pence English I received at Stoade forty nine Hamburg pounds six shillings and eight pence. Hereof I kept in my purse ten dollers, (that is, two Hamburg pounds and fifteene shillings), the rest I left in a Merchants hands, who sent me at divers times to Leipzig, first nine and thirty dollers, (that is, ten Hamburg pounds foureteene shillings and six pence), & at another time threescore dollers, (that is, sixteene Hamburg pounds ten shillings) and the third time seventy dollers, (that is, nineteene Hamburg pounds five shillings). These joined together with two shillings, paied to the Carrier for my letters, make the foresaid summe of forty nine Hamburg pounds sixe shillings eight pence, received upon bill of exchange for my forty pound first paid in

Hamburg.

[I. iii. 279.]

London. Againe, I tooke up at Stode from an English Merchant, seventy dollers upon my letters of credit, and rating each doller at foure shillings eight pence English, I gave him a bill of sixteene pound sterling, to be paid him by my friend in London. From these parts in Germany, a Traveller must carry with him the foresaid kinds of moneyes most currant in Germany, when he takes his journey to the upper parts of Germany, to Bohemia, and to Sweitzerland, or the confines of Hungary. The exchange out of England into the Low-Countries, usually rateth an English pound sterling, first paid in England, at foure and thirty Flemmish shillings, wanting two stivers, to be paid after in the Low-Countries. In Denmarke Travellers seldome make any long aboad, and the trade of our Merchants is more rare in that Kingdome, wanting native commodities; so as there is no usuall exchange from London thither. From London to Dantzk in Prussen, the exchange of an English pound sterling, first paid in London, useth to be rated at foure and twenty Hamburg shillings and six pence, to be paid there. My selfe by letters of credit received fifty dollers at Dantzk, and after the rate of foure shillings six pence English for each doller, I gave my bill for the payment of eleven pound five shillings English, to be repaied by my friend at London. And at Dantzk the same Merchant for the same fifty dollers gave me one and thirty Hungarian duckets of gold, and foureteen grosh in silver, being the fittest money for my journey to Crakaw in Poland, and to Vienna in Oestreich (or Austria). Out of England to Venice in Italy, the exchange of foure shillings and sixe or eight pence English, useth to bee rated at a Venetian Ducket. My selfe tooke no bils of exchange from England to Venice, but had letters of credit, to receive money of a Venetian Merchant, to be repaid in London upon my bill, after the rate of foure shillings three pence for each Venetian ducket. And at first being to take my journey for Rome and Naples, I tooke up two hundred silver

The Low-Countries.

Dantzk.

Venice.

crownes, most fit for that journey, which at Venice were rated at two hundred five & twenty duckets, and nineteene grosh, and I gave my bill for three and fifty pound sterling, twelve shillings and sixe pence English, to be repaied by my friend in London. Then I retained with my selfe as many of those crownes, as were necessary for my journey, leaving the rest in the hands of a Venetian Merchant, who gave me a bill to receive so many crownes in specie, (that is, in kind) at Florence, where I purposed to make my aboad for some few moneths. Out of England into Turkey, I formerly said that for the uncertainty of the journey, upon the great distances of places, there is no certaine value of exchange, neither use our Merchants to send bils of exchange thither, but to give letters of credit, first to receive money there, either at large according to the passengers wants, or for a certaine yeerely summe, to be after repaied in England, upon the passengers bill. And the Merchants there, for each zechine of gold of Venice, delivered at Heleppo, use to exact nine or ten shillings English, to be repaied in London, to the passengers great losse, which he that will avoid, may exchange his money to Venice, and there receive zechines of gold, or silver moneys of Spaine, to carry with him in specie, (that is, in kind). From London into France, the exchange of sixe shillings English, useth to be rated at threescore French soulz, or three French pounds, which make a common French crowne, but a French crowne in specie, and of just waight, is valued there at threescore and foure soulz, (as in England an Angell of gold is worth more then ten shillings silver among the Exchangers, though in expences it is given out for no more then ten shillings) and not onely bils of exchange into France are given at the foresaid rate for moneys first received in England: but he that hath a merchant to his friend or acquaintance, may easily compound to receive money, first, in France upon his letters of credit, and to repay it in London after the rate of sixe shillings English, for sixtie French soulz.

Turkey. *Haleppo.* *France.* [I. iii. 280.]

A.D. 1617.

To this I will adde two generall cautions, most necessarie for travellers; first, whereas in Germany and Italy, the Territories of absolute Princes are frequent, and of small extent, and each of these Princes doth coyne small pieces of brasse money, it behooveth the passenger to take heede, that he spend each Princes brasse moneys within his Territory, or else that upon the confines hee change them into brasse moneys currant in the next Territory; which if hee neglect, the subjects of the new Prince, howsoever they bee neighbours to the former Prince, and may daily change these coynes for their owne, yet they will not receive them without great gaine, they being of themselves little worth, and onely by the prerogative of each Prince, currant among their owne subjects. Secondly, the passenger must take speciall care, to leave a faithfull friend at home, to pay the bils readily, which he sends over to his Merchant, for so doing, hee shall never want in forraine parts (at least among Christians, and knowne places of trafficke), yea, out of his good report hee shall bee furnished with more money, then is warranted by his letters of credit: but on the contrary, if his friend deny or delay paiments, hee shall not have credit to borrow a penny upon his occasions, more then that for which the Factors shall have warrant by billes of exchange, or letters of credit; and if he fall into any misfortune, he shall not find a friend to deliver him from penurie and shame.

Caution as to brasse moneys.

Caution to pay bills readily.

These things being sayed in generall, nothing remaines now, but to set downe the particular moneys of severall Kingdomes, and the value of them, at the time when I lived beyond Seas, which value is subject to change, at the pleasure of each absolute Prince. And in this discourse I thinke most fit to begin with the moneys of England, being more familiarly knowne unto me.

Being to write of the Standard, weight, and value of English moneys, I thinke fit first to give some few admonitions to the Reader.

Of the divers Monies of England.

First, that the purest gold containes foure and twentie

caracts in the ounce, and foure graines make a caract.

The purest silver.

Secondly, that the purest silver containes twelve ounces in each pound Troy weight: And that Edward the first, King of England, keeping the Feast of Christs Nativitie at Barwick, in the yeere 1300, did upon Saint Stevens day decrie the value of base silver moneys, and after did altogether forbid the use of them, and shortly after commanded sterling money to be coyned, so called of the Easterlings, who first coyned silver money of that Standard, which is of eleven ounces two penny weight.

The English pound.

Thirdly, that the English pound, as well of gold as silver (meaning the pound of the Ballence, not the pound of twentie shillings commonly spent) containes twelve ounces Troy weight. And that each ounce of silver is worth five shillings of the currant money, and each ounce of Angel gold is worth three pound five shillings (or sixtie five shillings) of Queene Elizabeths silver money, and each ounce of Crowne gold is worth three pound (or sixtie shillings) of the same coyne.

Fourthly, that the Mint-Master gave account before the Queenes Examiners for the money they coyned, as well by the tale (or number of the pieces) as by the sheere: for it being not possible to coyne moneys of the just prescribed weight, yet the Mint-master was held to have performed his contract with the Queen for the standard prescribed by her, so the silver were not more then 2 penny weight in the ounce heavier or lighter, then her standard prescribed: and in like sort for the coyning of gold, a certaine proportion of some eight graines in the ounce, was allowed to the Mint-Master in this account by the sheere.

Fiftly, that 20 penny weight makes an ounce, and 24 graines make a penny weight.

Queene Elizabeth and the Mint-Master.

Now I returne to the discourse in hand. Queene Elizabeth in the yeere 1600, contracted with the Mint-Master, that of gold of the standard of twenty three caracts three graines and a halfe, he should coyne pieces of Angels, halfe Angels, fourth parts of Angels, pieces of an Angel and a half, & of 3 Angels. Now this Angel was of three penny weight and 8 graines, and this gold was commonly called Angel gold. Also she contracted [I. iii. 281.] with him, that of gold of the Standard of twentie two caracts, he should coyne pieces of twentie shillings, and pieces of tenne shillings, and pieces of five shillings; and the piece of tenne shillings was three penny weight fifteene graines. And this gold called Crowne gold, was almost *Crowne gold.* two caracts baser then the former, and two caracts after the rate of this standard, are worth five shillings of Queene Elizabeths silver. Lastly, she contracted with him, that of silver of the standard of eleven ounces two penny *Silver pieces.* weight, he should coyne shillings, halfe shillings, fourth parts of shillings, and pieces of two pence, and of one penny, and of halfe pence. And the shilling was foure penny (or ninety sixe graines) waight. The same Queene not long before her death, reduced her silver to the Standerd of eleven ounces, which was two-penny weight baser then the former in each ounce, and the Mint Office was said to have gained thereby one halfepenny in each ounce, or about five in the hundreth.

King James in the yeere 1604 published a Proclamation, *King James* whereby new pieces of gold were to be coyned, of a *Proclamation.* standard uniforme to the standards of other Nations: for it appeares by the Proclamation, that the gold coynes of England, were not of a just proportion betweene gold and silver, according to the proportion used by all Nations, so as the English coynes of gold, being given in England for lesse, then indeed they were worth, it came to passe, that they were transported into forraine parts, where they were esteemed at higher rate; which mischiefe his Majestie desired to take away by this uniforme standard, published in the same Proclamation; for the better understanding whereof, this following Table was joyned to the same.

King James in the yeere 1609, contracted with the [I. iii. 283.] Mint-Master, that of gold of the Standard of three and

B. C. It is to be remembred, that the pound weight English, being twelve ounces Troy, doth over-poix the pound weight of Scotland foure-penny weight, and nine graines English : Whereupon this Table is made to distinguish every severall piece of Gold and Silver Coyne, according to the true weight of both Nations.

B. English Weight.

		Pennyweight 20.	Graines 24.	Mites 20.	Droits 24.	Periots 20.	Blancks 24.	
Pieces of Gold of	xx.s.	06	10	16	18	10		Of these 37.li.4.s. make a pound weight Troy.
	x.s.	03	05	08	09	05		
	v.s.	01	14	14	04	12	12	
	iiij.s.	01	06	09	08	10		
	ij.s.vj.d.	00	19	07	02	06	06	
Pieces of Silver of	v.s.	19	08	10	08			Of these 3.li.2.s. make a pound weight Troy.
	ij.s.vj.d.	09	16	05	04			
	xij.d.	03	20	18	01	10		
	vj.d.	01	22	09	00	15		
	ij.d.	00	15	09	16	05		
	j.d.	00	07	14	20	02	12	
	ob.	00	03	17	10	01	06	

C. Scottish Weights.

		Deniers 24.	Graines 24.	Primes 24.	Seconds 24.	Thirds 24.	Fourths 24.		
Pieces of Gold of	xx.s.	07	21	07	01	09	19		A Of these 36.li.10.s.3.d. q.make 12 oz. Scottish. Or 48.li.3.s.8.d.
	x.s.	03	22	15	12	16	21	$\frac{1}{2}$	
	v.s.	01	23	07	18	08	10	$\frac{3}{4}$	
	iiij.s.	01	13	20	14	16	08	$\frac{3}{4}$	
	ij.s.vj.d.	00	23	15	21	04	05		
Pieces of Silver of	v.s.	23	15	21	05	00	13		B Of these 3.li.10.d.q.or 4.li. 1.s. 1.d.ob.di.q. di.di.q.
	ij.s.vj.d.	11	19	22	14	12	06	$\frac{1}{2}$	
	xii.d.	04	17	13	20	01			
	vi.d.	02	08	18	22	00	12		
	ii.d.	00	18	22	07	08	04		
	i.d.	00	09	11	03	16	02		
	ob.	00	04	17	13	20	01		

twentie caracts, three graines and a halfe, he should coyne pieces of thirty shillings, called Rose Ryals; pieces of fifteene shillings, called Spur Ryals. And the foresaid Rose Ryall was nine penny weight and five graines. Also he contracted with him, that of gold of the Standard of two and twentie caracts, hee should coyne pieces of twentie shillings called Unites; pieces of ten shillings, called double Crownes, pieces of five shillings, called Brittan Crownes, pieces of 4 shillings, called Thistle crownes, and pieces of 2 shillings 6 pence, called halfe Brittan crownes; and lastly, that all these pieces should bee proportioned to the foresaid Table. But the first Standard of this yeere 1609 was lighter then the Standard of the yeere 1600 by ten pence in each Angell, and the second standard of the yeere 1609, was lighter in like proportion, then the second standard of the yeere 1600. Moreover, the Goldsmiths of this time said, that of old a wedge of gold (or any gold uncoined) being brought into the Mint, was coyned there for six silver shillings in each pound of gold, whereas at this time the Mint exacted thirtie silver shillings for the same, whereupon the Merchants carried their wedges for the most part into Flaunders to be coyned, and few of them being brought into England, the Goldsmiths could not procure any of them for the exercise of their trade, but were forced to melt coyned gold and silver for that purpose. In the same yeere 1609, the King contracted with the Mint-master, that of silver of the standard of 11 ounces, he should coyne divers pieces above mentioned in the former Table, according to the rule therein prescribed. To conclude, Cæsar in his Commentaries, mentions brasse coynes of the Brittans, but the Kings of England have now for many ages, cast out of England all use of brasse or copper moneys, using none but coynes of gold and silver, and that of a pure allay.

King James' pieces coyned in 1609.

King James in like sort as he did for the English coyne, did also joyne to his foresaid Proclamation the foresaid Table of the Scottish weights, whereby the correspon-

Of the divers moneys of Scotland.

dencie of the Scottish money to the English, and the just value, weight and purenesse thereof may be distinguished; to which end I have also formerly joyned those tables.

The Scots also coyne a silver money of 13 pence halfe penny, and another piece of halfe the same value, and both these pieces of money are of the same purenes & value with the English silver. And the Scots of old called 20 English pence, a pound, as wee in England call 20 silver shillings a pound. And in like sort thirteene pence halfepenny English, was by the Scots called a Marke, as in England thirteene shillings foure pence is so called. Also the Scots have of long time had small brasse coynes, which they say of late are taken away, namely, Babees, esteemed by them of old for 6 pence, wherof 2 make an English peny; also Placks, which they esteemed for 4 pence, but 3 of them make an English penny; also Hard-heads, esteemed by them at one penny halfe-penny, whereof eight make an English penny.

Of the divers moneys of Ireland.

The Irish Histories report, that a Bishop, Justice of Ireland under John King of England, did coyne moneys in Ireland, of the same purenes and weight with the English. And the Irish had a Mint-house at the beginning of Queene Elizabeths raigne. But in our memory the Irish have not enjoyed any priviledge of coyning moneys, but have continually received them from the Mint of England. And for the most part of Queene Elizabeths Raigne, they had the same coyne with the English, save that the Irish shillings were stamped with a Harpe, the Armes of the Kingdome, and being called Harpers, were only worth 9 pence English. But civill warre having set all Ireland in a combustion, the same Queene more easily to subdue the rebels, did take silver coyne from the Irish, some few yeers before her death, & paid her Army with a mixed base coyne, which by Proclamation was commanded to bee spent and received for sterling silver mony, for no pieces of gold were at any time expressely coyned for the Irish. And this base mixed money had 3 parts of copper, and the fourth part of silver, which proportion of silver was in some part consumed by the mixture, so as the English Goldsmiths valued a shilling thereof at no more then 2 silver pence, though they acknowledged the same to be worth 2 pence halfe penny. At last the civill warre being appeased immediately before the Queenes death, King James her successor in the yeere 1605 took away this mixed coine, & restored their old silver harpers to the Irish. Moreover in the happy [I. iii. 284.] beginning of King James his Raigne, the Irish had the under written old coynes, which Sir George Carey Knight, at that time Lord Deputie, and yet continuing Treasurer at wars for that Kingdome, did so gather up, as at this day none of them are to be found. These coynes were thus called; First, they had silver groats, called broad faced groates, which of old were coyned for foure pence, though some of them were now worth eight pence. Also they had silver groats, called crosse-keele groats, stamped with the Popes tripple Crowne, likewise coined for foure pence, but being of more value. And these groats were either sent hither of old by the Popes, or for the honour of them had this stampe set upon them. Lastly, they had silver groats of like value, called Dominus groats, of the Kings of England, then called Domini (that is, Lords) of Ireland. Also they had Rex groats, so called of the Kings of England, after they had the stile of Kings of Ireland, which were coyned for foure pence, but by the mixture of copper were onely worth two pence. Also they had white groats, which were coyned for foure pence, but of such base allay, as nine of them were given for an English shilling. They had little brasse pence, and pence of a second kinde, called Harpers, being as big as an English shilling. They had also brasse farthings, called smulkins, whereof foure made a penny. Lastly, there were lately found brasse coynes by plowing up the earth, whose stampe shewed, that the Bishops of Ireland had of old the priviledge of coyning. And of all these moneys aforesaid, some were coyned at London, some at the

Old coynes used in Ireland.

The Bishops of Ireland coyned money.

Mint, at Yorke, and some at the Mint at Bristow in England.

Of the divers moneys of Germany.

Being to write of the divers moneys of Germany, I thinke fit first to set downe some Lawes of the Empire about coyning of moneys. In the Diet (or Parliament) at Augsburg in the yeere 1551. it was decreed by the Emperour, together with the Electors, Princes, States, the Counsellors of those that were absent, the Ambassadours, and Substitutes; that in the greater pieces of coynes to that piece included, which is worth six creitzers, the Mint-masters, of a marke of Colen pure silver, should make eight gold guldens and a halfe, with halfe a creitzer (the gold gulden being esteemed at seventie creitzers) making in silver ten guldens, twelve creitzers and a halfe, (the silver gulden being esteemed at sixtie creitzers.) And that hereafter in the sacred Empire, the under written pieces of moneys should be coyned; namely, the great silver piece, and two balfes of the same, answering in value to a gold gulden. Also pieces of twenty creitzers, twelve, ten, sixe, three, and one. Also that the States, according to the conditions of their Countreys, should coyne for common use certaine pieces of small moneys, with pence and halfe pence. That the Rhenish guldens of the Electors, and the guldens answerable to them, should be worth seventie two creitzers. And that all dollers being worth sixty six creitzers (and so half dollers) should be admitted by the Counsellers, but for the rest, that they should certifie the Emperor the true value of each, to the end he might prescribe how each coyne, according to the value made by them, should be received and spent or prohibited. And lest the Empire should by fraudes suffer losse, in the carrying out of uncoyned silver, and bringing in of forraine moneys, it was in the meane time decreed, that no man should carry out of the Empire any uncoyned silver, and that those who had the Regall priviledge of coyning, should not sell the same to any other, but use it themselves, with this condition, that hereafter, of a silver marke of Colen weight, they should

Pieces of money in the sacred Empire.

make ten silver guldens, with twelve creitzers and a halfe (the gulden being esteemed at sixtie creitzers), so as in that summe there should be found a silver Marke of the said weight, excepting alwaies the charges of coyning for the smaller pieces of moneys. And this to bee done upon penaltie of losing that priviledge. Moreover, it was decreed, that upon paine of burning, all men should abstaine from clipping, and washing of coynes, or any abasing of them with like fraudes. Lastly, it was decreed, that the States having the priviledge of coyning, should not hereafter, upon penaltie, bring any dollers, guldens, groshes, or halfe, or fourth parts of groshes to the mint, excepting those who had mines of their owne, who were not forbidden to coyne as much gold and silver as they had in their owne mines, so they coyned according to the foresaid decree; and that no other should coine any other gold, then according to the value and weight used by the Emperor, and the Princes of the Empire upon the Rheine. In the Dieta at Spyre, in the yeere 1557, it was decreed, that hereafter the stipends should be increased to the Assessors of the Imperiall Chamber, so as a Gulden having beene given hitherto for 16. Batzen, or sixty foure Creitzers, should hereafter be paied from the Callends of Aprill, in the yeere 1558, for seventy seven Creitzers.

Abasing coynes.

[I. iii. 285.]

Likewise in the Dieta at Augsburg, in the yeer 1558, it was decreed, that the following stipends should be paid to the Judge and Assessors of that chamber. Namely, that the Judge, being an Earle, or Baron, should have 2000. guldens, and if he were a Prince, his stipend should be increased. That an Assessor being an Earle or Lord, should have seven hundred guldens, a Doctor licentiate, or a gentleman, should have five hundred Guldens, an Advocate in Exchequer causes, should have three hundred guldens, each Gulden being esteemed at sixteene batzen, till agreement were made for equall mony in the Empire. The Princes and divers States, and free Cities, have from old times by the gifts of Emperours, the priviledges of coyning. The Electors and Princes of Austria, doe

Stipends decreed by the Diet at Augsburg, A.D. 1558.

stampe their Coynes upon one side with their owne Image, having the imperiall apple over their heads, and upon the other side with their owne armes: but the Coynes of other Princes and free Cities, are stamped with the Imperiall Eagle. The Coynes that are not of just value, are prohibited by Imperiall Edicts, but the greatest gaine which the Princes and Cities make by their Priviledge, is by the coyning of smal brasse peeces, which peeces are not of any value out of the Territory where they are coyned, and cannot be spent upon the confines without losse. As these priviledges of Coyning are derived from the Emperours, so were they subject to the Emperours censure, while their power was yet unbroken. For I find these words, under the Emperours name, in the abstract of the Imperiall lawes, (vulgarly called Reichs Abscheydt.) Let every one which hath the priviledge of coyning, send their Counsellers to me at Nurnberg, &c. In the meane time let coyning cease in all places, upon penalty of losing that priviledge. In the same Booke by an imperiall Edict, with the consent of the Princes and States, in the yeere 1559, the weights and stampes of all Coynes are prescribed, and it is decreed, that none should coyne more small moneys then for the necessity of their Subjects, and that these moneys increasing, they should presently be forbidden to coyne any more. By like Edicts divers Coynes are either decried for the value, or altogether taken away, and the bringing in of forraine moneys, and transporting the Coynes of Germany, are for the time forbidden. Otherwise each Prince may convert forraine moneys into the Coynes of Germany for the use of his subjects. The transporting of uncoyned Gold or Silver into the Low-Countreys is there forbidden for the time. Great punishments are decreed therein, to be inflicted on those, that use frauds to abase the Coynes. Likewise it is decreed, that Gold-smiths should not use any coyned moneys in the exercise of their Art, except uncoyned wedges were not to be had, in which case they are restrained to melt no more coyne then necessity

Priviledges of coyning.

Imperiall Edicts.

requires. Lastly, therein decrees are made, that for the time none should sell or lay to gage their priviledge of coyning, and that hereafter like priviledge should not be granted to any, without being subject to the prescribed lawes, and that a silver marke should be worth foureteene halfe ounces, (which weight the Germans call Loth, being halfe an ounce); and that Gold-smyths offending herein, should be punished, according to the quality of the fraud. *Loth.*

Now I will set downe the divers moneys of Germany, with the severall values of them. And first I will forewarne the Reader, that most reckonings of Germany are made by common silver guldens, yet is there no such coyne in the Empire; and these Guldens are esteemed at fifteene batzen in Germany, neere the value of three shillings foure pence English. Also that in reckoning of payments, the Germans use to make them by markes of Colen and Lubecke, yet is there no such money at all coyned. Now I returne to the purpose. The Gold Rhenish Guldens of Germany, are almost of the same standard with the Crowne Gold of England: but the difference of the value shall hereafter appeare. The Gold Ducket of Hungary, is of the purest gold of twenty foure Caracts, and it is two penny weight and sixe graines, (for I will apply all values to the English Coynes); and in England they are worth seven shillings and two pence. The silver Doller of the Empire (called Reichs Doller) is of the standard of ten ounces or thereabouts, and is eighteene penny weight sixteene graines. And at this time in England a Doller is worth foure shillings and five pence, which of late, before the reducing of our money, was given for foure shillings foure pence. The Phillips Doller, is of the standard of nine ounces ten penny weight, and it is an ounce halfe quarter weight, & at this time in England it was worth foure shillings ten pence. *Generally.* [I. iii. 286.]

At Stoade, Hamburg, and Lubecke, the Gold Rhenish Gulden was worth eight and twenty silver Misen Grosh, and a halfe, and a fourth part of a Grosh. And the Imperiall Doller was worth foure and twenty Grosh. *At Stoade and those parts.*

The same Rhenish gold Gulden, was worth sixe and thirty Lubecke shillings and a halfe, and the Imperiall Doller was worth three and thirty Lubecke shillings, though in all reckonings it were accounted but two and thirty shillings. A common silver Gulden was worth eight and twenty Lubecke shillings. A French Crowne of Gold was worth foure and forty. An English Angell of Gold was worth two Dollers, with the fourth part of a Doller and two Lubecke shillings, (or otherwise it was worth twelve Flemmish Shillings, and foure Lubecke shillings.) Seven Lubecke shillings and a halfe, made an English Shilling sterling, and sixe Lubecke shillings made a Flemmish Shilling, and likewise a shilling of Hamburg.

At Hamburg. The Hamburgers coyned a peece of Gold called a Portegue, which was worth foure pounds and eight shillings of Hamburg, or three and thirty Markes of Lubecke, (a Marke being esteemed for two shillings eight pence of Hamburg). At Stoade the silver shilling of England was worth seven stivers, and the Groates of England, being of the same standard, yet were currant for two stivers and a halfe, because seven stivers in that money could not be divided into three equal parts. Whereupon it fell out, that he who bought any thing for an Hamburg penny, if he paied three English groats, had an English shilling given him backe, and so had the thing bought for nothing.

At Emden. At Emden upon the confines of the Empire and the Low-Countreys, a silver Gulden of Emden was worth twenty stivers, an Imperiall Doller five and forty (which since that time is worth seven and forty) a Doller of Emden was worth thirty stivers, (for Princes and Cities coyne gold and silver Guldens, which often in their value differ from the Imperiall, as likewise Dollers in specie, (that is, kind) differ in value from Dollers, as they are esteemed in contracts), a French crowne was worth three Flemmish Guldens and sixe stivers. Now sixe stivers (as also sixe Lubecke shillings) make one Flemmish shilling.

At Breme, Oldenburg, and those parts. At Breme and Oldenburg, they have these small moneys currant, namely, Groates, and peeces (of the stampe) called Copstucks, and a Doller was there worth foure copstucks and a halfe, or five and fifty Groats. A French crown was worth six Copstucks, and one Copstucke was worth ten stivers, or twelve groats or there abouts. A Groat was worth little more then an English penny. A Sesling was worth halfe a Lubecke shilling, and they have also halfe Seslings in these parts. At Brunswicke a Doller was worth six and thirty Maria Grosh, which are of equall value with foure and twenty silver Misen Grosh, and also nine Maria Grosh, make eight Lubecke shillings. The same Doller was worth eighteene spitz-groshen, whereof each was worth two Maria Groshen. Here also I changed sixe Dollers into five Rhenish Gold Guldens and nine Grosh. At Magdeburg, Leipzig, Misen, and in all the Electorate of Saxony, and in the Neighbour Territories, to the confines of Bohemia, a Doller was worth foure and twenty silver Groshen, which are as much worth as eighteene spitz-groshen, or as sixe and thirty Maria Groshen. A Rhenish Gold Gulden was worth seven and twenty silver Groshen, and the silver Phillips Doller, was of the same value. A common silver Gulden was esteemed at one and twenty silver Groshen, a French Crowne at three and thirty, a Spanish pistolet at two and thirty, an halfe Milreise at sixe and thirty, the short and long Crusado, at five and thirty, the Hungarian Ducket at thirty silver Groshen. The Rose Noble was esteemed at three Dollers and a halfe, the English Angell at two Dollers, and little more then an Ort, or fourth part of a Doller. And the silver Grosh is worth more then two pence, lesse then 2. pence halfepenny English. And for the small Coynes, a Grosh was worth foure drier, & one drier was worth two Dreyhellers, and one Dreyheller was worth a pfenning and a halfe, and twelve pfenning made a Grosh, and two schwerdgroshen made one schneberger. In generall, through all the upper parts of Germany, a doller was esteemed at eighteene batzen, a silver Gulden at fifteene, a Phillips doller at twenty, a Rhenish Gold

At Brunswicke.

At Misen and those parts.

[I. iii. 287.]

In upper Germany.

Gulden at twenty, a French Crowne at foure and twenty and a halfe, a Gold Crowne of Italy was esteemed at Heidelberg and at Strassburg at foure and twenty batzen, at Augsburg a silver Italian Crowne at two and twenty batzen and a halfe. And the silver Grosh of Misen being carried out, & currant in all Germany, a Rhenish gold Gulden through higher Germany was worth seven and twenty silver Misen Grosh, a silver Gulden there (as in Saxony) was esteemed at one and twenty Grosh. The Batz is worth three English pence, and foure Creitzers make a Batz, foure pfenning make a Creitzer, and three Creitzers make a Zwelver, and twenty zwelvers make fifteen batzen, which is a common silver Gulden.

In all Princes Territories.

More particularly know, that in all Princes Territories, new and divers small moneys are found. At Nurnberg eight pfund (that is, Pounds) with twelve pfenning, make a silver Gulden, thirty pfenning make one pfund, two haller make one pfenning, five pfening make one finfer, seven pfening make a Maria Grosh, thirty six Maria Grosh make a silver gulden. In Austria two haller make one pfening, foure pfening one creitzer, seven Creitzers and a halfe make a shilling, eight shillings make a silver Gulden. At Augsburg seven haller make one creitzer, eight pfening make one Bemish, three creitzers make one plappart, twenty plappart (as also sixe and twenty Bemish with 2 pfening) make a silver Gulden. In Franconia, six pfening (whereof twelve make nine pfening of Misen) make one gnack. In Suevia and Bavaria towards the Rheine, three Creitzers make one shilling, or one plappart, and twenty plappart make a silver gulden. At Lindaw, and from thence to Costnetz, three pfening of Costnetz make one creitzer, twelve pfening make a batzen, and there be also halfe batzen. From thence to Basil, these moneys are spent before named. At Strasburg and Spira, foure pfening of the Phaltz, (that is, Palatinate) make one Creitzer, and at Heydelberg, and so to Francfort, two Strasburg pfening, make one Creitzer. At Francfort seven and twenty weispfening make a silver Gulden, and eight haller make a weispfening. At Wien (that is, Vienna) and upon the confines of Hungary, foure pfening make a creitzer, thirty pfening (or seven creitzers and a halfe,) make a shilling, and one shilling makes a pfund (or pound).

In generall. Alwaies let the Reader understand, that the value of these moneyes is subject to change, in divers Provinces, and more at divers times. And let him know, that an Imperiall Doller is now in Germany worth nineteene batzen, which at my being there was given for eighteene batzen; and that a Phillips doller is now worth twenty two batzen, which then was given for twenty, and that a Rhenish Gold Gulden is now worth three and twenty batzen, which then was given for twenty. Likewise that in the Territory of the Elector of Saxony, a doller is now worth sixe and twenty Misen Grosh and a halfe, which then was given for foure and twenty. Also that the great Coynes of Germany, are now worth more in England, then they were at that time, in respect of our silver somewhat debased. And if any object, that our English coynes of silver are now worth more in the Low-Countreys, then they were at that time when they were more pure, let him know, that all great Coynes, as well of silver as Gold, as well forraine as domesticall, have since that time beene increased in value in the Low Countreys; yet he that will change an English Angell into dollers, or great silver Coynes in the Low-Countreys, shall gaine no more at this time then formerly, since now they esteeme a doller at seven shillings sixe pence, which formerly was given for five shillings foure pence, and all the gayne which this raising of the Coynes seemes to promise a passenger, is by changing his great Coynes into stivers and small brasse moneys, which being of none or small value in themselves, are despised by Merchants, who are to receive great summes. But I will referre the change of the value of Coynes in the Low-Countries, to the proper place, and returne to the value of Coynes, increased in Germany: Wherein no man is to wonder, that the great Coynes still remaining of the old standard, yet are [I. iii. 288.]

given for more of their owne small moneys, then formerly they were, since divers reasons therof may be readily brought. Either for that the Merchants, being to receive great summes, desire rather with losse to receive great Coynes, then with gaine to receive the base, and brasse Coynes. Or perhaps for that the small Coynes are now either more abased, or altogether made of brasse: And most of all, for that forraine Merchants doe more carry out the moneys of Germany for their wares, then any native commodities thereof, so as the increased value of Coynes in Germany, turnes onely to the losse of strangers, and to the gaine of the Empire.

Divers moneys of Bohemia.

Bohemia now long subject to the Family of Austria, having long held the dignity of Emperours, doth admit all the great Coynes of Germany, in the same value as the Germans held them. And as well the Bohemians, as the Hungarians, in the yeere 1551 gave consent, that thenceforward their moneys should be made agreeable to those of the Empire, in weight, matter, and value. Touching the small moneys in Bohemia, and upon the confines of Hungary and Poland, I remember that three potschandels or pochanels made one creitzer, and nine creitzers with a pochanell made foure weissgrosh, and that thirty Grosh of Moravia (or weissgrosh) made a doller. And that in Bohemia they had a kind of Grosh, which answered in value to the Grosh of Polonia. Lastly, that Merchants reckoned two hallers for a pfenning, and six pfenning for a grosh, and sixty grosh for a shocke, and forty grosh for a marke.

Divers moneyes of Sweitzerland.

The Common-wealth of the Sweitzers consisting of divers Cities and Villages, and Territories, doth also admit divers moneys. The priviledge of Coyning is granted in common to Zurech, Basil, and Schaphusen, and each of these Cities hath his peculiar mynt, with Officers to oversee that the moneys stamped with the markes of the Cities, be of just weight, and due mixture: but each of these Cities hath their peculiar moneys. They of

Basil.

Basil, with the Neighbour townes of Alsetz, doe coyne

a peece of money, which of a Crow stamped upon it, is called Rappen Múntz, whereof five and twenty pound Troy weight, (called in Latin, Assis) make a common gold gulden, esteemed at sixty creitzers. They of Schaphusen, doe coyne money of the same mixture and value, together with the usuall money of the Empire. They of Zurech coyne dollers and halfe dollers, after the value of those in the Empire; but they have a lesse money of their owne, whereof forty pounds Troy weight, (called in Latin Assis) make a common gold Gulden. They also coyne Batzen, whereof sixteene make a gold Gulden. More particularly to explane the value of these moneys: Six Rappen of Basil, make a plappart or three creitzers, and twenty plappart or sixty creitzers, make a common Gulden. And as I formerly said in the discourse of German moneys, from Lindaw to Costnetz, three pfenning of Costnez make a Creitzer. Now I adde that the money of Schaphusen and Costnetz is spent to the confines of Schaphusen, and the money of Basil is spent from thence to Basil. At Zurech sixe pfenning make a shilling, (worth a penny English), and three pfenning make a Sicherling. Two great finfers of Basil, and one little finferlin, make a batz of Basil, and in like sort five finferlin make a batz, and five finfers make two batzen, and these moneys are spent to Strassburg, and so to Spire in Germany. Bern, Friburg, and Solothurn, have a peculiar money, whereof two and forty pounds Troy weight (in Latin Assis) and twice foure ounces (in Latin Trientes) make a gold Gulden. Besides they (and especially those of Solothurn, in great quantity) coyne a peece of mony, which the Sweitzers call Dickenpfenning, & the French call Testoone, but it is lesse worth by the tenth part then the Testoone of France. Those of Bern did first coyne Batzen, so called of a Beare, the Armes of the City, (for the words Baren, and also batzen, signifie Beares in the Sweitzers tongue), and the Cities of Suevia, imitating them, drew the same money and word into Germany. At Bern sixteene batzen are esteemed for a rhenish gold

Schaphusen.

Zurech.

Peculiar money of Bern.

Gulden. The money of Lucerna, is like to that of Basil, but onely sixe ounces Troy weight more base, and fifty of these moneys make a Rhenish gold Gulden. As the French gold is spent with gaine in Sweitzerland, so in all places upon these confines of France the French silver Coynes called Francks, are commonly spent. In the Cantons dwelling scattered in Villages, (namely, the [I. iii. 289.] Sweitz, those of Undervald, the Tugians, those of Glarona, and Abbatiscella), a pound is a doller. In Rhætia (or the Grisons) the Bishop and the Citizens of *Chur.* Chur coyne money, and the Abbot of Disent hath an old priviledge of coyning. And here sixty creitzers make a common gulden, foure Angster make a Creitzer, and twelve Angster make a Behmisch. But in this Province confining upon the State of Venice, the Lires or Berlingots, and the gagets of Venice, are vulgarly spent, and I remember that when I came out of the state of Venice into this Province, I spent Crownes of Italy; and I find in my notes, that at Lasagna I changed a silver crowne for eight and twenty batzen: but since seven batzen of Germany make two lires of Venice, and a gold crowne of Italy, is there given for eight lires; I thinke that either it was a gold crowne that I changed, or that the batzen of this Province are of lesse value then those of Germany. For a gold crowne of Italy, and the French crowne are both of a value, and I said before, that at Strassburg I changed each of these Crownes for foure and twenty batzen: yet to the contrary I find, that passing forward in this Territory of the Grisons, I exchanged at Lanzi a silver crowne of Italy for seven and twenty batzen, and that three batzen were there esteemed at foureteene creitzers, which in Germany are onely worth twelve creitzers. So as I am doubtfull, and cannot determine the value of the Italian coynes, in the small moneys of the Grisons.

Of the divers Coynes of the Low-Countreys. In the foresaid Imperiall Dieta (or Parliament) held at Augsburg, in the yeere 1551. these words are added to the Imperiall Edict. We wil that this our Edict shall be propounded to our Hereditary States of the Low-Countreys, and we will take care that they apply themselves thereunto, as much as they possibly can. The States of the Low-Countreys, coyne divers peeces of gold, as Archiducall Angels and Crownes. And the Angell is of the standard of twenty two Caracts, and of three penny weight seven graines. Also they coyne gold Lyons, called Riders, whereof each is worth foure Flemmish Guldens and a halfe. The Noble of Gant, is of the same standard with the French Crowne, and in England it is worth thirteene shillings foure pence. They spend commonly Phillips dollers, the value whereof I have set downe with the moneys of Germany. To conclude, they coyne any peece, of which they can make gayne, yea, the Merchants report, that they coyne the great moneys of Spaine, England, and all Dominions, stamped with the same Image and Armes, and for such utter the same in their trafficke with the Indians. But they coyne little gold or silver of their owne, having a singular Art to draw all forraine coynes when they want them, by raising the value, and in like sort to put them away, when they have got abundance therof, by decrying the value. And when their Exchequer aboundeth with any money, & they are to pay their Army, then they increase the value thereof; but having aboundance of the same coyne, and being to receive their revenues, then they decry the value thereof. And while they thus raise the value of forraine great coynes, in their small moneys, it fals out, that they have plenty of gold and silver, with the onely losse of base stivers and brasse moneys. And indeed, as well the art, as industry of this Nation, hath in our age become wonderfull to all other Nations. For they have no woods, yet by the commodity of their rivers and ditches, they are become terrible to their enemies in the strength of their Navy. They have not corne to suffice their owne wants, yet by fetching it from other parts, they relieve therewith all Nations that want corne. Of late, when they had no skill in trafficke, the Italians trading at Antwerp, did

Gant.

Hollanders skill in coyning.

rashly take their children to write their letters, and be their cashiers, and they too late complaine, that when these children grew to age, they did not onely take all forraine trafficke from them, and send them backe into Italy, but also followed them thither, and living dispersed through all the Cities of Italy, and spending at a low rate, did also draw all that trafficke to themselves. In like sort they have no mines of gold and silver, yet by their singular wit, and rare industry, doe abound both with gold and silver. To conclude, as they are most practicall in all kinds of businesse, so are they most subtile in the art of the mynt, and money matters. But I will returne to the moneys of the Low-Countreys. At this day the English Angell being esteemed at five Flemmish guldens and two blancks, two English Angels (or twenty shillings) [I. iii. 290.] are there worth foure and thirtie Flemish shillings, wanting 2 stivers, and a hundreth pounds Flemish make sixty English pounds sterling. Two English shillings are three shillings foure pence Flemish, and make a Flemish silver gulden, twentie Flemish shillings make a Flemish pound, twentie stivers make a Flemish gulden, sixe stivers make a Flemish shilling, two blancks make one Flemish stiver and a halfe, foure orkees (or doights) of brasse make a Flemish stiver. A French crowne was given for three Flemish guldens, and foure stivers: (but in Holland onely three stivers, and in some places but two stivers more then three guldens.) An Imperiall doller was given for fortie five stivers, a Spanish pistolet for three flemish guldens, and two or three stivers, a gold Rhenish gulden for two Flemish guldens and nine stivers, and a Phillips doller of silver for two Flemish guldens and eight stivers, or very little more.

Of the divers moneys of Denmark.

The marke of Denmarke was esteemed at 16 Lubeck shillings, and two shillings of Denmark made one Lubeck shilling, and thirtie three Lubeck shillings were given for an Imperiall Doller, yet two and thirtie of Lubeck, or sixtie foure shillings of Denmark made a common Doller in contracts. The gold of England was commonly spent in Denmark, and they esteemed an English Angell at two Dollers, and little more then the fourth part of a Doller; and they esteemed the English Rose Noble of that time at three Dollers and a halfe, which coyne they had almost drawne altogether into Denmark, by the exacting the same for the tributes of ship-masts, and other Merchandizes, passing the narrow straight of their Sea.

Of the divers moneys of Poland.

The Polonians coyne gold Duckets of the same value with the Hungarian Duckets (whereof I have spoken among the moneys of Germany), and these Duckets at this day are given for seventy Polish grosh, which of late were worth no more then sixtie five. Venceslaus King of Bohemia was crowned King of Poland about the yeere 1300, who first brought silver money into Poland, namely, Bohemian groshen (I meane those of silver, not the white grosh), which to this day are currant in Crakaw, and those parts. For before that time the Polonians did traffick with little pieces of uncoined silver, and with exchange of skins and other commodities. At this day the Polonians, aswell as the Germans, make all contracts by silver guldens, but have no such coyne stamped. Thirty Polish grosh make a silver gulden, and a doller at this day is worth fortie Polish grosh, at the least, which not long since was worth no more then thirtie five grosh, but to this day in contracts thirtie sixe Polish grosh make a doller, howsoever a doller in specie (that is, in kinde) be worth fortie grosh at the least. Three Pochanels make a Creitzer, and seven pochanels make a Polish and Bohemian groshen of silver. At Danske in Prussia (of old a Province of Germany, but lately annexed to the Crowne of Poland) they coyne Hungarian dukets of gold (as they doe in Poland), and they have two coynes of gold, called Milreis, and halfe Milreis. And I received of a Merchant there, each Hungarian ducket, and each halfe milreis, for a doller and a halfe with one sesling, and each milreis for three dollers and two seslings. And thirtie sixe Polish grosh did there make a doller. But I remember, that I did there change an Hungarian ducket for fiftie sixe Polonian grosh, which value passeth the former about a grosh and a halfe. For a sesling of Hamburg makes a Danish shilling, and that is little more worth then a halfe Polish grosh. The Muscovites Empire lyes upon this Province, and therefore I will adde a word of their coynes. They make all contracts by a money called Rubble, which is altogether imaginarie, for they have no such coyne, and it is esteemed in England at thirteene shillings foure pence sterling, and in the Muscovites money, it is rated at thirtie three altines and two Diagoes. And sixe single or three double diagoes make one altine.

Of the divers moneys of Italy. In generall.

The Italian Crowne of gold, and the Spanish pistolet, and double pistolet (being there current), are of the same standard, allay, and value, with the after mentioned French Crowne, save that the double pistolet containes two French Crownes. The Venetian zecchine is of the same standard, finenesse, and value as the Hungarian ducket, above mentioned in the moneys of Germany. The Popes giulii of silver, and so likewise the poali, are of the same standard finenesse and value with the English sixe pence, but the lire of Venice being worth about nine pence [I. iii. 291]. English, is of a little baser standard. The Spanish coynes of silver are currant in Italy, and they are called Pezzi d' otto, pieces or rials of eight, and they be of the standard of 11 ounces and two penny weight, and are three quarters of an ounce and a halfe weight, and in England each of them is worth foure shillings foure pence half peny, this Spanish mony being two and twentie pence in each twentie shillings English, more worth then the English silver. All Crownes of gold are currant in Italy, and all at one rate, excepting the French Crownes, which at Venice and Naples are esteemed somewhat higher then other, though in all the other Cities of Italy, it is more commodious to spend Spanish pistolets or crownes, then French crownes. In generall, the Italian silver crowne, given for seven lires of Venice, is worth almost five shillings English, and the Italian gold crowne vulgarly called d' oro, given for seven lires, and about fifteene sols of Venice, is worth almost five shillings sixe pence English, and the gold crowne, vulgarly called d' oro in oro del sole, given for eight lires, and some odde sols of Venice, is currant in England for sixe shillings. To conclude, greater summes paid in little brasse moneys, are in Italy delivered by weight, not by tale or number. And more particularly to explaine the values of moneys. At Venice *At Venice.* a zechine of Venice is given for ten lires, and ten or twelve sometimes more sols. A double pistolet of Spaine, called Dublon', is there given for seventeene lires. A French crowne is given for eight lires, and eight, or sometimes ten sols. An Italian crowne of gold is there given for eight lires, and some for seven lires sixteene sols (for the weight of Venice being heavier then in other parts of Italy, the light crownes are lesse esteemed.) The Spanish piastro of silver is given for sixe lires, the silver ducket for sixe lires and foure sols, the silver crowne for seven lires, the justino for two lires, the mutsenigo for a lire, and foure sols. Besides, the Venetians have silver pieces of 4 lires, of eight soldi (or sols), and of sixe soldi, and a piece of two soldi called Gagetta, which are of a baser standard. Touching the brasse moneys, twentie soldi make a lire, two soldi or three susines make a gagetta, two betsi or three quatrines, make a soldo or marketta, and foure bagatines make a quatrine. In the Dukedome of Ferrara, the silver crowne is spent for seven *At Ferrara.* lires of Venice, and in the money of the Dukedome twelve bolignei make a Venetian lire, three susines make a boligneo, and two bolignei make one amoray, seven make one Saint Georgio, foure make one cavalot, foure and a halfe make one berlingasso, nineteene make one carli, and ten bolignei make one bianco, and two brasse quatrines make a susine, sixe make a boligneo, seven make a gagetta of Venice. At Bologna, a silver crowne is given for ten *At Bologna.* poali, and a French crowne of just weight for thirteene poali. The poalo, and the giulio in other parts of Italy are both of one value, but here the giulio is given for sixe bolignei, and foure brasse quatrines, or for fortie brass quatrines, and the poalo is given for eight bolignei, or for fortie eight brasse quatrines. Also hee that changeth any crowne, shal have more gaine, if he change it into bolignei (which are good for expences there), then if he change it into poali (because the poali are currant in other parts, but the bolignei onely in the territory of Bologna.) At

At Pesara. Pesaro, and in the Dukedome of Urbino, a gold crowne is spent for twelve poali, and fifty two brasse quatrines make a poalo: but if you will change your gold crowne into brasse quatrines, which are not current out of the Territory, you may have 182 quatrines for the crowne, which make fifteene poali, which is a fifth part more then it is worth in silver. At Ancona, and in the Marca of

At Ancona. Ancona, a gold crowne is given for eleven poali and a half, or to the value of twelve poali, if you receive it in brasse quatrines, and there fortie quatrines of brasse make a giulio, fortie three make a poalo. A silver crowne is given for ten poali, and if you receive brasse quatrines for poali, they will give seven baocci more, and ten baocci

At Rome. make a poalo. At Rome a gold crowne is sometimes given for eleven poali and a halfe, somtimes for twelve, sometimes for twelve and a halfe, according to the abundance and want of gold, and all gold crownes are of one value. And a silver crowne is given for ten poali or giulii, and ten baocci make one giulio or poalo, and foure brasse quatrines make a baocco. Lastly, at Rome more then any other where, he that changeth crownes into quatrines, which cannot be spent out of that State, shal in appearance make great gaine: but in the Market those

[I. iii. 292.] which sell, use to looke into the buyers hands, and if he have quatrines therein, they hold the thing to be sold at a higher rate, if he bring silver, they sell cheaper. And I remember, that the Gentlemen of Rome refusing to take quatrines for their rents, the people, when the Pope came abroad, falling on their knees before him, in stead of asking his blessing, did with humble cries crave a remedie for that oppression. At Naples a gold Spanish crowne, or a French crowne of just weight, was given for thirteene carlini, an Italian gold crowne for twelve carlini and a halfe, a silver crowne for tenne carlini, and nine carlini make eight reali, or giuli, or poali, and five carlini make one paraque, and fortie brasse quatrines make one carlino, ten quatrines make one sequin, three quatrines one turnas, & two cavali make one quatrine. In the Dukedome of Florence, a gold crowne is given for twelve giulii (or reali, or poali, for they bee all of one value) and for halfe a giulio more. And a silver crowne called Piastro (which is most commodious to bee carried for expences in all Italy, and especially here) was given for ten giulii and a halfe. Touching smaller monys, ten brasse deners make a quatrine, three brasse quatrines make a soldo, five quatrines make a baello (or creitzer, which is a little coyne of silver), and eight baelli make a giulio or carlino, and fortie giulii make twentie shillings sterling English. At Genua and in Liguria, gold crowne of just weight (aswell Spanish, as French, Venetian, Florentine, Neapolitan, and that of Genoa) is given for foure lires and a halfe of Genoa. A silver crowne there called ducaton, is given for three lires of Genoa, fifteene soldi or bolinei, and somewhat more. And a chanfron of Naples for one and thirtie soldi. Fifteene lires of Genoa make twenty shillings sterling English, twentie soldi or bolinei of Genoa make a lire of Genoa, and twelve soldi of Genoa make a lire of Venice, seven soldi and a halfe of Genoa make a reale, foure soldi make a cavalotto, sixe quatrines make a soldo, or bolineo, and two deners make a quatrine. Also at Genoa they coyne a silver piece of eight reali, which is given for three lires and one or two soldi. Likewise they coyne a piece of foure reali, and another of two reali. Also they coyne silver pieces, of one, two, and foure lires, and a silver piece of ten soldi or bolinei. Lastly, they coyne brasse pieces of foure soldi, called cavalotto, of one soldo or bolineo, of eight deners, of foure deners, and of one denere. In the Dukedome of

At Naples.

At Fiorenza.

In Liguria.

At Milano. Milan, a gold crowne of Italy being of just weight, is given for one hundred twentie one soldi. A Spanish dublon of just weight, is given for two hundred and sixty soldi, and more sometimes. A dublon of Milan for two hundred and fiftie soldi, a light gold crowne for one hundred and seventeene soldi, a silver crowne called ducaton for one hundred and foureteene soldi. And twentie soldi make a lire, two lires of Genoa make about three lires of Milan, foure brasse quatrines make a soldo, nine soldi make a bianco, ten quatrines make one parpoyolle, forty quatrines make a terso. My selfe at Milan changed a gold crowne for sixe lires and sixe soldi, and at Marignano, hiring a horse for sixe lires, and giving a *In Piemont.* gold crowne, I received backe eight soldi. In Piemont, a French crowne is given for ten florines somewhat more, a silver crowne for eight florines. And twelve grossi make a florine, foure quatrini make a grosso, foure soldi make a bianco, seven quatrines make a soldo, sixe soldi and sixe quatrines make a florino, twelve quatrini make a cavalotto, and foure cavalotti make a florino. Lastly, in *At Mantua.* the Dukedome of Mantua, a zecchine of Venice is given for eight lires and twelve soldi, a gold crowne of Mantua for seven lires, a silver crowne for sixe lires and foure soldi. Foure trantis make a soldo, two soldi make a parpayollo, sixe soldi make a Barbarino, ten soldi and a halfe make a giulio, twelve soldi and a halfe make a Spanish riall, 20 soldi make a lire, 2 trantis make a susine, and 3 deners of Mantua make a trantis.

The divers moneys of Turkey. The great Turke coynes a piece of gold called Sultanon', and it is of the same standard, finenesse, and value with the Hungarian ducket, above mentioned among the moneys of Germany. In Affrick, those of Barbary have a gold Ducat, commonly current among Christians, which is so rare in Turkey, as I do not remember to have seene any piece thereof spent there. Neither have the Affricans any mines of gold, but they carry salt to Ganger, and thence bring this gold. And this Barbary duckat of gold is of the standard of three and twentie caracts, and the fourth part of a graine, and three penny weight wanting two graines, and at this day in England it is given for nine shillings two pence sterling, which of late was worth [I. iii. 293.] no more then eight shillings foure pence sterling. To conclude, the gold zechine of Venice, and the Spanish peeces of silver, of foure and eight Reali, and the very silver of Venice, are so commonly spent in Turkey, as the gold and silver of Turkey seemes dispised, or at least is seldome spent. But because this vast Dominion hath large circuit, it will not be amisse to name the moneys currant in divers places. And first I forewarne the passenger, that in all places, he is in danger, who shewes his money, but most of all among the Turkes, where to be rich, is more dangerous then the greatest crime can be objected, either in respect of the covetous Judge in publike, or the ravinous nature of each man in private, neither doth any thing more provoke the Turkes to lay snares for the unwary passenger. So as howsoever it be not improvidently done, to carry summes of gold or silver by sea, & in Barks of Christians; yet I would advise a passenger to be wary how he shew them among Christians, and much more among Turkes, and advise him rather to make shew, to draw his money from a little purse, hiding his greater store, then in payments to pull it out by heapes. The Greeke Iland Zante, subject to the Venetians, hath Venice money, and a gold zechine was given there for eleven Lires, and two gagets.

At Zante.

Likewise the Greeke Iland Candia, subject to the Venetians, hath the moneys of Venice, where a gold zechine was given for eleven lires, and to the Turkes (landing there) at a higher rate. The silver crowne called piastro, was there given for six lires, and about foure soldi. And here I found a silver peece, which I never found to be spent in the State of Venice, namely, a perper, worth eight soldi, and eight baggatini of Venice.

At Candia.

The Greeke Iland Cyprus, subject to the Turkes, spends the Venetian gold and silver lires, but receives not the peeces of eight soldi, nor the lesser moneys of

At Cyprus.

Venice, neither are the Venetian lires currant any further then this Iland, though perhaps they may be spent with some losse upon the Coast adjoyning. At Cyprus the gold zechine was given for eleven lires of Venice, and for 120 aspers of Turkey; and the silver crown called piastro, or a piece of eight Reali Spanish, was given for seventy Aspers, and the gold Sultanon of Turkey, was of the same value with the zechine of Venice: yet the very Subjects more willingly received the zechines. The Turkish Asper is a little peece of silver, which at Haleppo in Syria was worth some three farthings English: and eight aspers at Cyprus made one scahy (a Turkish money which the Italians call Seya) being esteemed at little more then sixe pence English, and fifteene scahy made a zechine, twelve scahy made a French or Spanish Crowne, ten scahy made a piastro or Spanish peece of eight Reali. And sixteene brasse Mangouri made one silver Asper, neither can any money of Cyprus be spent in Palestine without losse.

At Jerusalem. At Jerusalem and through all Palestine, and those parts, the gold zechines of Venice are more esteemed (as in all Turkey,) then any other peeces of gold, and the very Turkes more willingly receive them then the Turkish Sultanons. At Jerusalem a zechine was given for five and forty meidines of Cairo in Ægypt, the Spanish peece of eight Reali called piastro, was given for eight and twenty meidines; and halfe a piastro at the same rate, neither have they any Aspers there, but these meidines onely, where of each is worth three Aspers, so as the five and forty meidines given for the zechine, are worth 135 Aspers, and the eight and twenty meidines given for the piastro, are worth eighty foure aspers. The gold crownes of France and Spaine, are not spent here without losse, but the silver duckets of Italy are commodious to be spent here. *At Tripoli.* At Tripoli in Syria, and at Haleppo, and in the territories adjoyning, the foresaid silver aspers are commonly spent. The gold zechine of Venice is there worth ninety meidines, and the Spanish piastro worth sixty; but these meidines of Tripoli, differ from the other of Cayro in Ægypt, for those of Tripoli are each worth one asper and a halfe, but those of Cayro are each worth three Aspers. At Constantinople all contracts are made by aspers, howsoever the foresaid peeces of gold and silver be there also currant. And in small contracts they pay aspers by the weight, because they cannot easily number them, but in great contracts they reckon by Asses loades of aspers, as the English doe by hundred and thousand pounds. Lastly, at Constantinople, I exchanged gold zechines each at 125 aspers, a French Crowne at one hundred aspers, and a doller of Germany at 75 aspers.

At Constantinople.

[I. iii. 294.]

Of the divers moneys of France.

The gold French Crowne is of the standard of two and twenty caracts, and is two penny weight, foure graines and a quarter. The silver peece called Quart d' escu, that is, the fourth part of a crowne, is of the standard of eleven ounces, and is six penny weight foure graines, and is worth two Venice Lires, or eighteene pence sterling English. The peece of Silver called Francke, is of the standard of nine ounces ten penny weight, and eighteene penny weight sixeteene graines, and is worth two shillings English. The French Crowne is exchanged for three Franckes, or for foure Quarts d' escu, or for little more then foure testoones. For foureteen soulz and a halfe make a testoon, fifteene soulz make a Quart d' escu, and twenty soulz make a francke, and sixty soulz make a French crowne, and twelve deniers make a soulz. Yet a gold French crowne in specie, (that is, in kind) is changed for sixty five soulz. As in like sort in England, a French crowne is worth no more then six shillings, and the English Angell is worth no more then 11 shillings in common estemation, yet he that brings a weighty a French crowne in specie to the Gold-smyths, they will give him sixe shilling six pence for it, and he that brings to them an old Angell of gold, they will give him 11. shillings and six pence, or more for it. And in the last civill warre, the value of the French crowne was raised to 120, soulz, till the King reduced the same to the old value after the warre composed. The same King Henry the fourth since that time raised the value of gold crownes, to the end he might draw backe his gold which was carried into forraine parts. My selfe passing through Lorayne, before the French civil warre was fully appeased, did at Monwicke, upon the confines of Lorayne and Germany, exchange a French crowne for foure franckes and nine grosh, and shortly after comming to Shallons, exchanged a French crowne for no more then sixty soulz, so as I guesse that either the Franckes of Loraine differ from the Franckes of France, or that the tumult of the warre, and the making of peace shortly after, made this difference.

Of the divers measures of miles, through divers parts of the world.

The difference of miles. FUrther being to write of the divers measures of miles, through the divers parts of the World, it seemed good to me to adde the measure of miles, vulgarly received, namely that five Italian miles, or three French, or two and a halfe English, make one Dutch mile, and that one Dutch mile and a halfe makes a mile of Sweitzerland.

It remaines now that according to my owne experience, I should speake something of the divers kindes of miles. And in generall, this my opinion hath respect to the difficult or easie passages of the way, since even in England, the miles seeme, and indeed are more short, neere London, where the waies are faire and plaine, and frequently inhabited, as they seeme, and indeed are more long and tedious, through the desart places of the North, over mountaines, and through uninhabited and difficult passages.

Italian. The Romans of old held a thousand paces for a mile, and such are the miles of Italie.

English. A common English mile makes one & a halfe Italian, but towards the North, & in some particular places of

England, the miles are longer, among which the Kentish mile (being a Southerne County) is proverbially held to be extraordinarily long.

The Irish miles among the English, and the Irish-English are answerable to the English; howsoever for the solitary and disinhabited wayes, and many foards often overflowed, they are more troublesome to passe. *Irish.*

In like sort the miles of Scotland, answere to the Northerne miles of England, save that the frequent climing of mountaines, and the unbeaten waies, make them seeme longer, and indeed require more time for the passage. *Scottish.*

Villamont a French gentleman in the book of his travels witnesseth, that one French mile containes two Italian miles. *French.*

The common Germain mile, being for the most part in plaines, makes more then three English, or five Italian miles; but in some places the solitude of Woods, and the ascent of Mountaines, make the miles of Germany seeme much longer, and Suevia extraordinarily hath long miles, though it be a plaine Countrey. The miles of Sweitzerland, being over continuall Mountaines, are so long, as passengers distinguish their journey more by the spaces of howers, then by the distances or numbers of miles. And I remember, that finding no horse to be hired, I went on foote from Scaphusen to Zurech, which journey I was going ten howers, being accounted but foure miles. And in Rhætia among the Grisons, upon the confines of Italy, one mile is held for sixe Italian miles. And upon the foote of the Alpes towards the North, one mile is accounted for seven miles and a halfe of Italy, where having a good horse, I could ride with an ordinarie pace no more then one Dutch mile in foure howers space. By which appeares, that the measure of miles is very uncertaine among the Sweitzers, who for the most part reckon their journeys by howers riding, or going with an ordinary pace, and not by miles. *German.* [I. iii. 295.]

The miles of Bohemia and Moravia are no lesse tedious, *Bohemia.*

and I remember, that my selfe passing there on horseback, did commonly ride no more then foure miles in a dayes journey. And howsoever the length of the Sweitzers and Bohemian miles may in part be attributed to the climbing of Mountaines, and bad waies, yet no such reason can be given for the miles of Moravia, which Country is either a plaine, or little pleasant Hilles, and the waies faire, and the Countrey well inhabited.

Flemish. The Low-Countrey miles are of a middle length betweene the German and French miles. But in the very County of Holland they differ much one from another, since foure miles of great Holland make sixe miles of little Holland. And I remember, that about the Citie Horne, I esteemed each mile longer then three English. Also next to the Holland miles, those of Freesland are longer then the rest.

Danish. A mile of Denmark is somewhat longer then three English miles, and answereth to the common mile of Germany.

Polonian. The miles of Poland generally are like the miles of Denmarke, but they differ in length one from the other. For I remember, that in Prussia each dayes journy I passed by coach some seven miles, and in middle Poland nine or ten miles, but in upper Poland towards Germany I commonly rode on horse-back no more then five miles or there-abouts each day, in my passage from Crakaw to Moravia. In Russia among the Moscovites confining upon Poland, a mile is called a ferse, and answeres to five Italian miles, or one common mile of Germany.

Turkish. In Turkey those that guide Christians, having the Italian tongue, doe in my opinion number the miles to them, much after the Italian manner.

The Rebellion

[II. i. 1.]

of Hugh Earle of Tyrone, and the appeasing thereof; writen in forme of a Journall.

PART II. BOOKE I.

Chap. I.

Of the Induction or Preface to my Irish Journall, and a compendious narration, how Charles Blount, Lord Mountjoy (my Lord and Master of happy memorie) was chosen Lord Deputy of Ireland; and of this worthy Lords qualitie, as also of the Councels in generall, by which he broke the Rebels hearts, and gave peace to that troubled State. Together with his particular actions in the end of the yeere 1599.

AT my returne from Scotland about the month of September in the yeere 1598, I retyred my selfe to Healing (my deare Sister Faith Mussendines house, being situate neere the South banke of Humber, in the Countie of Lincolne.) In which place (and my deare sister Jane Alingtons house neere adjoyning) whilest I passed an idle yeere, I had a pleasing opportunitie to gather into some order out

Faith Mussendine.

Jane Alington.

of confused and torne writings, the particular observations of my former Travels, to bee after more delibrately digested at leasure. After this yeere spent in Countrey solace, the hopes of preferment drew me into Ireland. Of which journey being to write in another manner, then I have formerly done of other Countries, namely, rather as a Souldier, then as a Traveler, as one abiding in Campes, more then in Cities, as one lodging in Tents, more then in Innes; to my former briefe discourse of the journeys through England and Scotland, I have of purpose added there, out of my ordinary course, the like of Ireland, onely for travellers instruction.

Hugh Earle of Tyrone. I am now to treate of the famous and most dangerous Rebellion of Hugh, Earle of Tyrone, calling himselfe, The Oneale, (a fatall name to the chiefe of the sept or Family of the Oneales), and this I will doe, according to the course of the former Part namely, in this place not writing Historically, but making only a Journall, or bare narration of daily accidents, and for the rest referring the discourse of Ireland for all particulars to the severall heads, wherein each point is joyntly handled, through all the Dominions of which I have written. Onely in this
[II i. 2.] place for the better understanding of that which I principally purpose to write, I must crave leave to fetch some short remembrances (by the way of preface) higher then the time of my owne being in Ireland, in the Lord Mountjoy his Governement.

Ann. 1169. About the yeere 1169 (not to speake of the kind of subjection which the Irish are written to have acknowledged, to Gurguntius, and some Brittan Kings), Henry the 2 being himself distracted with French affaires, gave the Earle of Strangbow leave by letters Patents, to aide Dermot Morrogh King of Lemster, against the King of Meath. And this Earle marrying Eva, the daughter of Dermot, was at his death made by him heire of his Kingdome. Shortly after King Henrie himselfe landed at Waterford, and whilst he abode in Ireland, first Dermott MacCarthy, King of Corcke, and the South part of

Mounster, and Dunewald Obrian King of Limrick, and the North part of Mounster, then Orwark King of Meath, and Roderick King of Connaght, (by singular priviledge over the rest, called the King of Ireland), and the above named King of Lemster yet living, did yeeld themselves vassals unto King Henrie, who for the time was saluted Lord of Ireland (the title of King being first assumed by acte of Parliament to King Henrie the eight many yeeres after.) In the said Henrie the seconds raigne, Sir John de Courcy with foure hundred voluntary English souldiers sent over, did in five battailes subdue Ulster, and stretcht the bounds of the English pale as farre as Dunluce in the most Northerne parts of Ulster.

Ulster subdued.

About 1204, John Courcy of English bloud, Earle of Ulster and Connaght, did rebel, and was subdued by Hugh Lacy. About 1210 the Lacies of English bloud rebelling, were subdued by King John, who after some three moneths stay returned backe into England, where the Lacies found friends to be restored to their Earledome of Ulster. About 1291 O-Hanlon & some Ulster Lords troubling the peace, were suppressed by the English Colonies. From 1315 to 1318 the Scots made great combustions in Ireland to whom many Irish families joyned themselves, and both were subdued by the English Colonies. In the yeere 1339 generall warre was betweene the English Colonies and the Irish, in which infinite number of the Irish perished. Hitherto Ireland was governed by a Lord Justice, who held the place sometimes for few yeeres, sometimes for many. In the yeere 1340, John Darcy, an Englishman, was made Justice for life, and the next yeere did exercise the place by his owne Deputy (which neither before nor after I find to have been granted to any, but some few of the Royall bloud.)

Anno 1339.

About the yeere 1341, the English-Irish (or English Colonies), being degenerated, first began to be enemies to the English, and themselves calling a Parliament, wrote to the King, that they would not indure the insolencies

The English-Irish enemies to the English.

of his Ministers, yet most of the Justices hitherto were of the English-Irish (or English, borne in Ireland.)

The Duke of Clarence made Lord Lieutenant. About the yeere 1361, Leonel, Duke of Clarence, was made Lord Lieutenant of Ireland, and sometimes left his Deputy to governe it. This Duke being Earle of Ulster and Lord of Connaght by the right of his wife, came over with an Army of some 1500 by pole, and quieted the borders of the English Pale in low Lemster. He reformed the English-Irish, growne barberous (by imbracing the tyrannicall Lawes of the Irish, most profitable to them, which caused them likewise to take Irish names, and to use their language and apparrell.) To which purpose good Lawes were made in Parliament, and great reformation followed, aswell therein, as in the power of the English, for the seven yeeres of his Lieutenancy, and after, till the fatall warres of Yorke and Lancaster Houses. And hitherto most of the Justices were English-Irish.

Ann. 1400. *Richard II.* About the yeere 1400, Richard the second, in the eighteenth yeere of his Raigne, came with an Army of foure thousand men at Armes, and thirtie thousand Archers, fully to subdue the Irish: but pacified by their submissions, and no act of moment otherwise done, he returned with his Army into England. After, to revenge the death of the Earle of March his Lieutenant, he came againe with a like Army: but was suddenly recalled by the arrivall of Henry the 4 in England. During the said Kings Raigne, Ireland was governed by his Lord Lieutenants, sent from England, and in the Raignes of Hen. the 4, and Hen. the 5, by Justices for the most part chosen of the English-Irish, only the Lord Scroope for 8 yeres was Deputy to Thomas the second son to Hen. the 4, who was L. Lieutenant of Ireland.

[II. i. 3.] This I write out of the Annals of Ireland printed by Camden. In which, from the first Conquest of Ireland, to the following warres betweene the Houses of Yorke and Lancaster in England, I find small or no mention of the Oneals greatnesse among the Irish Lords. And I find very rare mention of any seditions in Ulster, especially among the Northerne Irish, so as that Province, from the first Conquest to these civill English warres, doth thereby seeme to have beene one of the most peaceable and most subject to the English. Neither reade I therein, of great forces or summes of mony sent out of England into Ireland, (except voluntaries, and the cursary journeys of King John and King Richard the second); but rather that for the most part all seditions as well betweene the English-Irish, and the meere Irish, as between the English-Irish themselves, were pacified by the forces and expences of the same Kingdome.

The civill warre betweene Yorke and Lancaster.

During the said civill warre betweene Yorke and Lancaster, for England, most of the Noble Families were wasted, and some destroied; whereupon the English Irish, which hitherto had valiantly maintained their Conquest, now began to repaire into England, partly to beare out the factions, partly to inherit the Lands of their Kinsmen, of whom they were discended: And the meere Irish boldly rushed into the possessions, which the other had left void in Ireland. And from that time, under the governement of English Liefetenants and Deputies, seditions and murthers grew more frequent, the authority of the English Kings became lesse esteemed of the Irish, then in former times, and the English Pale had sometimes larger, sometimes straighter limits, according to the divers successes of the Irish affaires at divers times.

Perkin Warbeck.

After the appeasing of the said bloody warre, I finde some 1000 men sent over by Henry the seventh to suppresse Perkin Warbeck, an English Rebell, and 500 men sent by Henry the eight to suppresse the Geraldines of English race, rebelling against him. Otherwise the said Annals mention no great or generall rebellion in Ireland, especially such, by which either much blood of the English was spilt, or much of our treasure exhausted, till the happy raigne of Queene Elizabeth. For in this onely age, Religion rather then Liberty first began to be made the cloake of ambition, and the Roman Locusts, to maintaine the Popes usurped power, breathed every where *Papists combinations.* fier and sword, and not onely made strong combinations against those of the reformed religion in all Kingdomes, but were not ashamed to proclaime and promise Heaven for a reward, to such cut-throates as should lay violent hands on the sacred persons of such Princes, as opposed their tyranny. Amongst which, this famous Queene being of greatest power, and most happy in successe against them; they not only left nothing unattempted against her sacred person, and her Crowne of England, but whither incouraged by the blind zeale of the ignorant Irish to Popery, or animated by an old Prophesie

He that will England winne,
Must with Ireland first beginne,

did also raise two strong and dangerous rebellions in Ireland, the one of the Earle of Desmond, & the other of the Earle of Tyrone, (not to speake of the troubles made by Shane Oneale, the easie setling whereof shall be onely mentioned in the treating of Tyrones Ancestors.) Howbeit the wonted generall peace seemes to have continued till after the 19. yeere of the Queenes raigne, being *Anno* 1577. 1577: at which time the Lords of Connaght, and Ororke, for their particular, made a composition for their lands with Sir Nicholas Malby, Governour of that Province, wherein they were content to yeeld unto the Queen so large a rent, and such services, (both of labourers to worke upon occasion of fortifying, and of horse and foote to serve upon occasion of war), as it seems the Popish combinations had not yet wrought in them any alienation of mind from their wonted awe and reverence of the Crowne of England.

The rebellion of the Earle of Desmond. Touching the rebellion of Gerald Earle of Desmond: John Gerald the sonne of Thomas (whose Progenitors of English race, had long behaved themselves valiantly in subduing the Irish) had Kildare given him by King

Edward the second, with title of an Earle. And this Family of the Fitz Geralds, or Geraldens, (as they are now called) long flourished, (not onely keeping Ireland in obedience to the King; but infesting the sea coasts of the Welsh, not yet united to the Crowne of England,) and never raised armes against England, till Thomas Fitz Gerald, the sonne of Gerald Fitz Gerald, Earle of Kildare, and Lord Deputy of Ireland, under King Henry the eight, [II. i. 4.] (whom the King had called into England, and there brought in question for his ill Governement), hearing by light and false rumour that his father was executed, rashly tooke Armes against the King, inviting the Emperor Charles the fifth to invade Ireland, which he in the meane time wasted with fire and sword. This Thomas and five of his Uncles were shortly after hanged, the father being before dead of griefe. But Queene Marie restored this Family to honour and lands, though they never after recovered their former dignity. Of these Geralds most of the greatest Lords in Mounster are descended, (though for divers causes, many of them have taken other Sirnames) and particularly the Earles of Desmond.

Maurice Fitz-thomas first Earle of Desmond.

Maurice Fitz-thomas a Geraldine was first created Earle of Desmond by Edward the third. Of whose posteritie many excelled in wealth, vertue, and honourable reputation, farre extending their power. But James invaded his Nephewes inheritance by force, and imposed heavy exactions on all depending upon him, whose sonne Thomas following his fathers steps, was by the Lord Deputie beheaded in the yeere 1467: his sonnes were restored, and the Earledome remained in his posterity, till Gerald Earle of Desmond in the yeere 1578 rebelled *Ann.* 1578. against Queene Elizabeth. To whose aide certaine bands of Italians and Spaniards, sent by Pope Gregory the twelfth, and Philip King of Spaine, landed at Smerwic, who besieged by the Lord Arthur Grey, then Lord Deputy, in a Fort they had built, and called the Fort del ore, shortly after yeelded themselves, in the yeere 1583, and were put to the sword, as the necessitie of that State, and their manner of invading the land, was then said to require. And the Earle of Desmond flying into the Woods, was there in a cottage killed, and his head cut off, (being, as they say, betrayed by his owne followers, wherein the Ulster men challenge an honour of faithfulnesse to their Lords, above those of Mounster; for in the following warres none of them could be induced by feare or reward, to lay hands on their reverenced Oneale.) Thus with an Army of sixe thousand men, whereof some foure-thousand were newly sent over at divers times, this Rebellion of Desmond in Mounster was soone appeased. The Earledome of Desmond was by authoritie of Parliament adjudged to the Crowne, and made a County, with Sheriffes appointed yeerely to be chosen by the Lord Deputie.

The Earledome of Desmond adjudged to the Crowne.

Upon the attainter of the said Earle of Desmond and his confederats, all the lands falling to the Crowne, were in Acres of English measure about - - - - - - - -	574628 Acres.

Hereof great part was restored to the offenders, as to Patrick Condon his Countrey, to the White Knight his Countrey, to some of the Geraldines, and to other their confederats no small portions. The rest was divided into Seigniories, granted by letters patents to certaine English Knights and Esquires, which upon this gift, and the conditions whereunto they were tied, had the common name of Undertakers.

Land grants in Kerry and Desmond.

In Kerry and Desmond, by patent, to Sir William Harbert, to Charol Harbert, to Sir Valentine Browne, to Sir Edward Denny, besides an uncertaine portion to George Stone and John Chapman and their beires, were granted - - - -	30560 Acres with yeerely rents five hundred foure and twentie pound sixe shillings eight pence sterling.

A.D. 1583.

Land grants in Limerick.

In Limerick by Patent to Sir Henrie Billinsley, to William Carter, to Edmund Mannering, to William Trenchard, to Sr. George Bourcher, to Sr. George Thornton, to Richard Fitton, to Robert Annesley, to Edward Barkley, to Sir Henry Uthered, to Sir William Courtney, to Robert Strowde, and to their heires, were granted - - -	96165 Acres, with rents nine hundred three & thirty pound foure shillings halfe penny, sterling.
In Corke, by patent to Vane Beacher, to Henrie North, to Arthur Rawlins, to Arthur Hide, to Hugh Cuffe, to Sir Thomas Noris, to Warham Sent-leger, to S Thomas Stoyes, to Master Spencer, to Thomas Fleetwood, and Marmaduke Edmunds, and to their heires were granted - - - - -	88037 Acres, with rents five hundred twelve pound seven shillings sixe pence halfe penny sterling.
In Waterford and Tipperary by Patent to the Earle of Ormond, to Sir Christopher Hatton, to Sir Edward Fitton, to Sir Walter Rawleigh, and to their heires were granted - - - - -	22910 Acres with rent three hundred and three pound, three pence sterling.

Land grants in Corke.

[II. i. 5.]

Land grants in Waterford and Tipperary.

These Undertakers did not people these Seigniories granted them and their heires by Patent, (as they were bound) with well affected English, but either sold them to English Papists, (such as were most turbulent, and so being daily troubled and questioned by the English Magistrate, were like to give the most money for the Irish land) or otherwise disposed them to their best profit, without respect of the publike good: neither did they build Castles, and doe other things (according to their covenants) for the publike good, but onely sought their private ends, and so this her Majesties bounty to them, turned not to the strengthning, but rather to the weakening of the English Governement in that Province of Mounster.

Tyrones Rebellion.

Touching the Rebellion of the Earle of Tyrone, the worthy Antiquary Camden mentioneth Neale the Great, tyrannising in Ulster, and great part of Ireland, before the comming of Saint Patrick into that Kingdome, about the yeere of our Lord 431, adding that this Family notwithstanding lived after more obscurely, not onely till the English entered to conquer Ireland, about the yeere 1169: but after that, to the time that the Scots under Edward Bruce, attempted to conquer that Kingdome, about the yeere 1318. In which turbulent time, Donevaldus O Neale started up, and in his letters to the Pope stiled himselfe King of Ulster, and true Heire of all Ireland. Further, Camden addeth, that after the appeasing of these troubles, this new King vanished, and his posteritie lurked in obscuritie, till the Civill warres of England, betweene the Houses of Yorke and Lancaster. The seede whereof was sowne by Henry the fourth of Lancaster Family, deposing Richard the second of Yorke Family, and usurping the Crowne, though Henrie the fourth and his sonne Henrie the fifth by their valour so maintained this usurpation, as no Civill warre brake forth in their time, nor so long as the noble Brothers of Henrie the fifth, and Uncles to Henrie the sixth lived. After, betweene Henrie the sixth of Lancaster Family, and Edward the fourth of Yorke Family, this bloudy war was long continued, but ended in the death of the next successor Richard the third, a double Usurper, both of the House of Lancaster, and the Heires of his Brother Edward the fourth of the House of Yorke. After, in the marriage of Henrie the seventh with the Daughter and Heire of Edward the fourth, both these Houses were united; and so this bloudie warre well ended. From this time, behold the Pedigree of the Oneales.

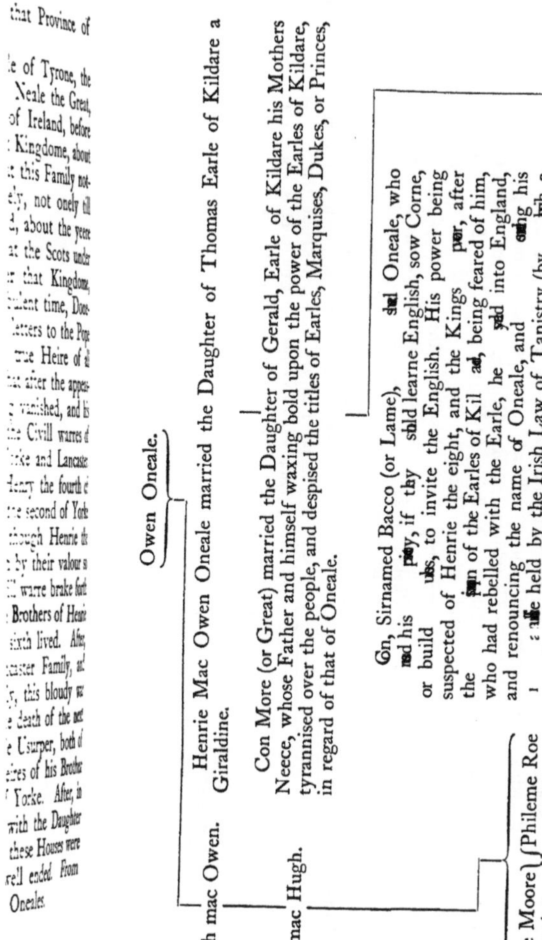

Owen Oneale.

Hugh mac Owen.

Henrie Mac Owen Oneale married the Daughter of Thomas Earle of Kildare a Giraldine.

Art mac Hugh.

Con More (or Great) married the Daughter of Gerald, Earle of Kildare his Mothers Neece, whose Father and himself waxing bold upon the power of the Earles of Kildare, tyrannised over the people, and despised the titles of Earles, Marquises, Dukes, or Princes, in regard of that of Oneale.

Con, Sirnamed Bacco (or Lame), [illegible] Oneale, who [illegible] his [illegible], if they [illegible] learne English, sow Corne, or build [illegible], to invite the English. His power being suspected of Henrie the eight, and the Kings [illegible], after the [illegible] of the Earles of Kil[illegible], being feared of him, who had rebelled with the Earle, he [illegible] into England, and renouncing the name of Oneale, and [illegible] his [illegible] held by the Irish Law of Tanistry (by [illegible] a man is [illegible] to a boy, and the Uncle to that Nephew, whose Grandfather [illegible] the Father, and commonly the most active Knave, not the next Heire, is chosen), had his land regraunted to him from the King, under the great Seale of England, as to his Vassall, with title of Earle of

D

Neale Moore mac Art.

A

Phileme Roe mac Art.

B

Neale Connelagh.

F

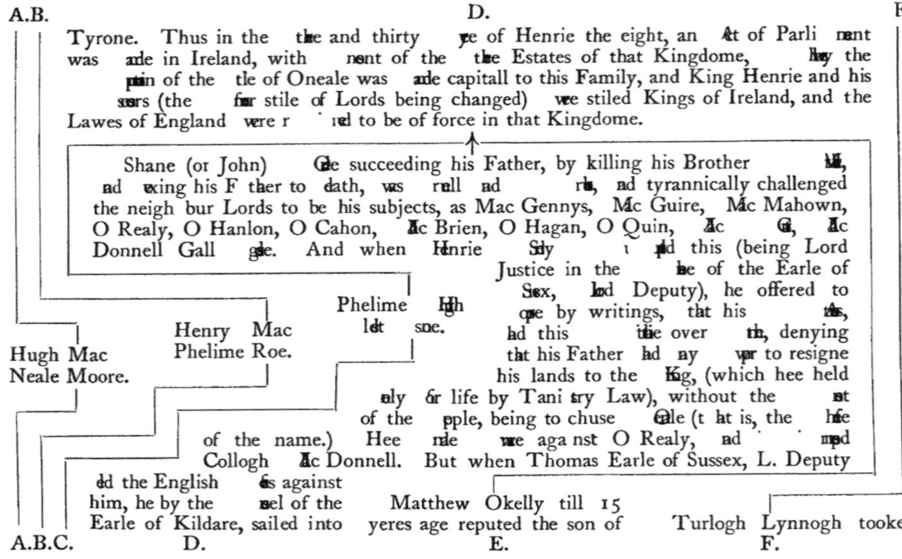
A.B.
D.
F.
Tyrone. Thus in the three and thirty yere of Henrie the eight, an Act of Parliament was made in Ireland, with consent of the three Estates of that Kingdome, whereby the ... of the title of Oneale was made capitall to this Family, and King Henrie and his successors (the former stile of Lords being changed) were stiled Kings of Ireland, and the Lawes of England were ... to be of force in that Kingdome.
Shane (or John) Oneale succeeding his Father, by killing his Brother Mathew, and vexing his Father to death, was rebell and ..., and tyrannically challenged the neighbour Lords to be his subjects, as Mac Gennys, Mac Guire, Mac Mahown, O Realy, O Hanlon, O Cahon, Mac Brien, O Hagan, O Quin, Mac ..., Mac Donnell Gall ... And when Henrie Sidney ... this (being Lord Justice in the absence of the Earle of Sussex, Lord Deputy), he offered to ... by writings, that his ... had this ... over them, denying that his Father had any power to resigne his lands to the King, (which hee held only for life by Tanistry Law), without the consent of the people, being to chuse Oneale (that is, the chiefe of the name.) Hee made warre against O Realy, and ... Collogh Mac Donnell. But when Thomas Earle of Sussex, L. Deputy led the English forces against him, he by the counsel of the Earle of Kildare, sailed into
Phelime Hugh lost sone.
Henry Mac Phelime Roe.
Hugh Mac Neale Moore.
Matthew Okelly till 15 yeres age reputed the son of
Turlogh Lynnogh tooke
A.B.C.
D.
E.
F.

PEDIGREE OF THE O'NEILLS

A.B.C. | D. | E. | F.

England, and submi ted him-selfe to Q. Elizabeth, and after for a while reduced the rest to obedience and civil life. But when he tir-ani ed over the Irish Lords, and they craved of Henrie Sidney Lord Deputy in the yeare 1565, he leading an Army against him, sent Edward Randolph with seven of Foote, and a Troope of Horse by Sea to Derry and Loughfoyle, to assault the Rebell on the back. Against whom the Rebell turning all his fo es was so defeated, as he fled for to the Scots, whose he had killed, and they at first taining him well, after fell to words, & killed him in the yeare 67. After in a Parliament at Dublin, he was of treason, and his lands confiscated, and a Law that no man should for that to take the name and title of Oneale.

a Black Smith at Dudalke, gi en Con O Neale by a Smiths wife at This Bastard he to him by the Kings Pattents, at which he was Baron of Dungannon: but he was killed in his Fathers life by Shane, the of whose Bastard this that thw

the title of Oneale Shane: he was aged, and so loved qui the for feare of the chil of Shane and of the He was obedient to the Queene, but Odonnel, & the Scots, of whom he killed in the field Al ex- Oge, who Shane

Sir Arthur O Neale Knight, living in this Rebellion. This Sir Arthur served the Queene against Hugh the Arch-Rebell, who had two of his sons in prison, but two or htee sonnes were with their father at Loughfoyle among the English.

Owen Mac Hugh Neale Moore, offered to serve against trai-tor Hugh.

A.

Turlogh Mac Henry of the Fuse, Rebell with Hugh.

B.

Turlogh Brasilogh.

C.

He had three sonnes, Henry, Con, and Tirlogh, cast in prison by Hugh the Rebell.

D.

E.

A.

Four sonnes, Tirlogh, Hugh, Bryan, and Henry, living when Hugh Oneale rebelled.

B.

Five sonnes then living.

C.

Six sonnes at least then living, and able to serve the Queene.

E.

Brian killed by O donnel, at the instance of Shane O Neale.

Hugh preserved by the English from Shane, married the Daughter of Tirlogh Linnogh Oneale, whom he put away by divorce, and after prooved an Arch Rebell.

Cormoc preserved from Shane by the English, now rebelling with Hugh.

This Hugh, sonne to the base Baron Matthew, (borne of a Smiths wife, and reputed the Smiths sonne till he was fifteene yeeres of age) lived sometimes in Ireland, and much in the Court of England, and was supported against Turlogh Lynnogh Oneale, with the title of Barron of Dungannon, by his fathers right. He had a troope of horse in Queene Elizabeths pay, in the late warres of the Earle of Desmond, in which and all occasions of service he behaved himselfe so valiantly, as the Queene gave him a yeerely pension of one thousand Markes. He was of a meane stature, but a strong body, able to indure labours, watching, and hard fare, being withall industrious and active, valiant, affable, and apt to mannage great affaires, and of a high dissembling subtile and profound wit. So as many deemed him borne, either for the great good or ill of his Countrey. In an Irish Parliament he put up his petition, that by vertue of the letters Patents granted to his Grand-father, to his Father & his heires, he might there have the place and title of the Earle of Tyrone, and be admitted to this his inheritance. The title and place were there granted to him, but the inheritance (in regard the Kings of England by the attainder of Shane, were thereof invested) was referred to the Queenes pleasure. For the obtaining whereof, Sir John Perrot then Lord Deputie, upon his promise of a great rent to be reserved to the Crowne, gave him his letters of recommendation into England, where he so well knew to humour the Court, as in the yeere 1587 he got the Queenes Letters Pattents under the great Seale of England, for the Earledome of Tyre-Oen, without any reservation of the rent he had promised to the L. Deputy, wherwith, though his Lordship were offended, in that the Pattent was not passed in Ireland, and so the said rent omitted, yet in reverence to the great Lords, who had procured this grant in England, he did forbeare to oppose the same. The conditions of this grant were, that the bounds of Tyrone should be limited; That one or two places (namely, that of Blackwater) should be reserved for the building of Forts, and keeping of Garrisons therein; That the sonnes of Shane and Tirlogh should be provided for; and that he should challenge no authoritie over the neighbour Lords bordering upon Tyrone, or any where out of that County. And such were his indeavours in the Queenes service, such his protestations of faith and thankfulnesse, as Tirlogh Linnogh, by the Queenes intercession, was induced (upon certain conditions for his maintenance) to surrender the County, and all command in those parts unto him.

Sir John Perrot, Lord Deputie.

The Spanish (forsooth) invincible Navy, sent to invade England, in the yeere 1588, being dispersed, and proving nothing lesse then invincible, many of them were wrecked

[II. i. 8.] *Ann.* 1588.

on the Coasts of Ireland, whereof some were harboured by the Earle of Tyrone, with whom since he was thought to have plotted the following mischiefes.

Anno 1589. *Sir William Fitz-williams Lord Deputie.* And shortly after (in the end of this yeere, or beginning of the next) Sir John Perrot being revoked, Sir William Fitz-williams, was sent Lord Deputy into Ireland. I have heard that he having been formerly Lord Deputy, when he returned and sued for recompence of his service, a great Lord should answer him, that such imployments were preferments, and not services to challenge reward: And therefore, if in this new imployment any shall thinke that he followed this counsell, seeking to make it a preferment to him and his family, I doe not much marvell thereat. This I write of hearesay, but as in the generall relation following, I purpose to write nothing which is not warranted either by relations presented to the Queene, by the principall Councellers of Ireland, or by Letters interchanged betweene the States of England and Ireland, or like authenticall writings; so for the particular of the above named Lord Deputy, if perhaps some may thinke any thing observed by me to derogate from him, I protest, that whatsoever I write is in like sort warranted, and may not be omitted without the scandall of Historicall integrity, being objections frequently made by the Rebels, for excuse of their disloyalty, aswell in all their petitions, as treaties of peace: But howsoever I cannot but mention these imputations, yet I advise the Reader to judge of them, as objections of the Rebels, who in their nature are clamorous, and could no way make their excuse so plausible, as by scandalizing the chiefe Governor. And I further protest, that as I shall in the due place once mention an honorable answer of this L. Deputy, to part of the chief complaints made by the Irish against him, so I would most willingly have inserted his full justification, if any such memoriall had come to my hands.

Sir William Fitz-williams, being Lord Deputy of Ireland, Sir John Norreys was Lord President of

Mounster, (who made his brother Sir Thomas his Vice-president), and Sir Richard Bingham was Governor of Connaght. This Lord Deputy now againe entering the governement of Ireland, that Kingdome was in the best estate that it had beene in of long time, not only peaceable and quiet, (so as any the greatest Lord called by letter or messenger, readily came to the State there, and none of them were known to be any way discontented), but also most plentifull in corne, cattel, and all manner of victuals. But within three moneths after his taking of the sword, some Irish informed him, that the above named Spaniards, last yeere wrecked on the Coasts of Connaght and Ulster, had left with the Inhabitants (in whose hands they fell) great store of treasure and other riches. This the Lord Deputy (as the Irish say) did greedily seeke to get into his hands, but surely he pretended the Queenes service, as may appeare by a commission, by which he first assaied to sease the same. This not taking any effect, he tooke a journey himselfe into those parts, with charge to the Queene and Countrey (as they said) and that in an unseasonable time of the yeere, after Allhallontide. Where altogether failing of his purpose, he brought thence with him as prisoners, two of the best affected Gentlemen to the State in those parts, whom he deemed to possesse the greatest part of those riches, namely, Sir Owen mac Tooly (father in law to the Earle of Tyrone, who had long enjoied a yeerely pension of one hundred pound from the Queene, and had kept Odonnel in a good course of opposition against Tyrlogh Lynnogh Oneale) and Sir John Odoghorty, (of Ulster Lords best affected to the English.) Wherof the first refusing (as they object) to pay for his inlargement, continued prisoner til the beginning of Sir William Russels governement, who in pitty discharged him, but the old gentlemans heart was first broken, so as shortly after he died. The second was released after two yeeres restraint, not without paying for his liberty, (as the Irish say). At this hard usage of those two Ulster gentlemen, all the

Ireland peaceable and quiet.

Sir Owen Mac Tooly and Sir John Odoghorty taken prisoners by the Lord Deputy.

great men of the Irish, (especially in those Northerne parts) did much repine.

Ann. 1590. In the moneth of May 1590, the Earle of Tyrone came into England, where he was after an easie manner restrained of his liberty, because he came without the [II. i. 9.] Lord Deputies Licence, which fault repaired by his submission, he was freed of his restraint. In the moneth

The Earle of Tyrone agrees to keepe peace. of June, the Earle agreed before the Lords, to enter bonds with good sureties of the Pale, to keepe peace with all his Neighbours, namely Sir Tirlogh Lynnogh (who since the renouncing the title of Oneale, and yeelding at the Queenes intercession, the governement of those parts to the Earle, was Knighted); and at his returne to put in pledges, to be chosen by the Lord Deputy and Counsell, for more assurance hereof, and of his loyalty, as also the performance of certaine Articles signed by him: Provided that the pledges should not lie in the Castle, but with some gentlemen in the Pale, or Merchants in Dublyn, and might be changed every three moneths, during her Majesties pleasure.

The Articles. The Articles were to this effect: To continue loyall and keepe the peace: To renounce the title of Oneale, and all intermedling with the Neighbour Lords: That Tyrone should be limited, and made a shire or two, with Gaoles to be built for holding of Sessions: Not to foster with any neighbour Lord, or any gentleman out of his Countrey, not to give aid to the Iland and Irish-Scots, nor take any of them: That if for his defence he needed forces, he shall levy none out of his Countrey without speciall licence of the State, in which case he might have English bands. To conclude, with the Lord Deputy within ten moneths, about a composition of rents and services to her Majesty for all his Countrey, according to the above mentioned composition of Connaght, made in the yeere 1577. Not to impose any exactions without licence of the State on his Country above ordinary, except it be for necessary forces for his defence, and that also with licence: Not to make any roades into Neighbour

The Articles.

Countreys, except they be within five dayes after a prey taken: That none of his Countrey receive any stelths from Neighbour-Countreys, nor steale from them, but he to bring forth the theeves, or drive them out of Tyrone: That he execute no man, except it be by Commission from the Lord Deputy, under the broad seale for martial law, and that to be limitted. That his Troope of 50 horse in her Majesties pay, be kept compleat for her service; and that besides he answer a rising out at every generall hosting. That he meddle not with spirituall livings, nor lay any charge on them. Not to maintaine any Monkes or Friers in his Countrey: Not to have intelligence with forraine traytors. That he take no blacke rent of any Neighbours. To cause the wearing of English apparell, and that none of his men weare glibbes (or long haire): That he answere for his brother Tyrlogh Mac Henry, Captaine of the Fewes: That in time of necessity he sell victuall to the Fort of Blackewater. These he promised to performe upon his honour before the Lords in England, and that his pledges to be put in, should lie for performance of them, to his power. And order was given, that all the Neighbour Lords should be drawne to like conditions, that so they might not spoile Tyrone.

Ann. 1590. Con mac Shane's accusation.

In the moneth of July 1590, Con mac Shane, (that is, the son of Shane Oneale,) accused Hugh Earle of Tyrone, of many practices, to make himselfe great in the North, and that after the wrecke of the above named Spaniards, he conspired with those which fell into his hands, about a league with the King of Spaine, to aid him against the Queene. These Articles the Earle answered before the Lords in England, denying them, and avowing the malice of Con to proceed of her Majesties raising him to be Earle of Tyrone, and Cons desire to usurpe the name of Oneale, as his father had done, which name he laboured to extinguish. He could have spoken nothing more pleasing to this State (as he well knew), and therefore his answere was approved: But the event

shewed his dissembling; for within two or three yeeres, Sir Tyrlogh Lynnogh died, and then the Earle tooke this title of Oneale to himselfe, (which was treason by act of Parliament in Ireland,) still excusing himselfe subtilly that he tooke it upon him, lest some other should usurpe it, promising to renounce it, yet beseeching that he might not be urged to promise it upon oath. Camden affirmes that Hugh ne-Gavelocke, bastard to Shane Oneale, exhibited these Articles against the Earle, who after got him into his hands, and caused him to be hanged, (hardly finding any, in regard of the generall reverence borne to the blood of the Oneals, who would doe the office of hangman,) and that the Queene pardoned the Earle for
[II. i. 10.] this fact. I doubt not but he writes upon good ground, and I find good warrant for that I write the same to be exhibited by Con mac Shane, and both may be reconciled by the exhibiting of the petition by Hugh, in the name of Con.

Death of Sir Tyrlogh Lynnogh.

Sure I am that the Earle durst never enter into rebellion, till he had gotten the sons of Shane Oneale to be his prisoners. Two of them, in this time of Sir William Fitz-williams his governement, were now in the Castle of Dublyn, and if they had beene safely kept, they being true heires of Tyrone before their fathers rebellion, would have beene a strong bridle to keepe the Earle in obedience: But they together with Phillip Oreighly, (a dangerous practiser), and with the eldest sonne and heire of old Odonnel, (both imprisoned by Sir John Perrot, in his governement), shortly after escaped out of prison, being all prisoners of great moment, whose inlargement gave apparant overture to ensuing rebellion. Neither did the Irish spare to affirme, that their escape was wrought by corruption, because one Segar, Constable of the Castle of Dublin by Patent, having large offers made him to permit the escape of Oreighly, and acquainting the Lord Deputy therewith, was shortly after displaced, and one Maplesdon, servant to the Lord Deputy, was put in his place, in whose time those prisoners

Shane Oneale's sons.

escaped. To returne to the orderly course of my relation.

The Earle on the last of August, and the same yeere 1590, did before the Lord Deputy and Counsell of Ireland, confirme the above mentioned Articles, sent thither out of England, faithfully promising by word and under his hand, to performe them. But still he delaied and put off the performance, by letters unto both States, intreating that equall security might be taken of Sir Tyrlogh Lynnogh, and in generall of all the bordering Lords, (which he knew at that time most difficult to effect), and by many subtile shifts, whereof he had plenty.

The Articles confirmed.

About this time Mac Mahown, Chiefetaine of Monaghan died, who in his life time had surrendered this his Countrey, held by Tanistry the Irish law, into her Majesties hands, and received a regrant thereof, under the broad seale of England, to him and his beires males, and for default of such, to his brother Hugh Roe mac Mahowne, with other remainders. And this man dying without beires males, his said brother came up to the State, that he might be setled in his inheritance, hoping to be countenanced and cherished as her Majesties Patentee, but he found (as the Irish say) that he could not be admitted, till he had promised to give about sixe hundred Cowes (for such and no other are the Irish bribes). After he was imprisoned (the Irish say for failing in part of this payment), and within few daies, againe inlarged; with promise that the Lord Deputy himselfe would go to settle him in his Countrey of Monaghan, whither his Lordship tooke his journey shortly after, with him in his company. At their first arrivall, the gentleman was clapt in bolts, and within two dayes after, indited, arraigned, and executed, at his owne house all done (as the Irish said) by such Officers, as the Lord Deputy carried with him to that purpose. The Irish said, he was found guilty by a Jury of Souldiers, but no gentlemen or freeholders, and that of them foure English souldiers were suffered to goe and come at pleasure, but the other being

Ann. 1590. Death of Mac Mahown Chieftaine of Monaghan.

Irish kerne, were kept straight, and starved, till they found him guilty. The treason for which he was condemned, was because some two yeeres before, he pretending a rent due unto him out of the Ferney, upon that pretence, levied forces, and so marching into the Ferney in warlike manner, made a distresse for the same, (which by the English law may perhaps be treason, but in that Countrey never before subject to law, it was thought no rare thing, nor great offence). The greatest part of the Countrey was divided, betweene foure gentlemen of that name, under a yeerely rent to the Queene, and (as they said) not without payment of a good fine under hand. The Marshall Sir Henry Bagnoll had part of the Countrey, Captaine Henslowe was made Seneshall of the Countrey, and had the gentlemans chiefe house, with a portion of land, and to divers others smaller portions of land were assigned, and the Irish spared not to say, that these men were all the contrivers of his death, and that every one paid something for his share. Hereupon the Irish of that name, besides the former allegations, exclaimed that their kinsman was trecherously executed, to intitle the Queene to his land, and to extinguish the name of Mac Mahowne, and that his substance was divided betweene the Lord Deputy and the Marshall, yea, that a pardon was offered to one of the Jury for his son, being in danger of the Law, upon condition hee would consent to find this his kinsman guilty.

The Ferney divided.

[II. i. 11.]

Complaint against the Lord Deputy.

Great part of these exclamations was contained in a complaint exhibited, against the Lord Deputy after his returne into England, to the Lords of her Majesties Councell, about the end of the yeere 1595, in the name of Mac Guire, and Ever Mac Cooly (one of the Mac Mahownes, & chiefe over the Irish in the Ferny.) To which Sir William Fitz Williams, then sicke at his house, sent his answere in writing. There first he avowes to the Lords, that the fact of Mac Mahowne, was first adjudged treason in England, and that his calling in question for it was directed from thence, and for the manner of proceeding herein, not prescribed, that it was just, and contrary to their calumnious allegations, who complained against him. He further answered, that the most part of the Countrey was not bestowed on the Marshall Sir Henrie Bagnall, but that seven of the chiefe in that Countrey had the greatest part of it, that three hundred Freeholders were raised to her Majestie, with eight hundred pound yeerely rent, and that all the Country seemed then glad of his execution, and joyfully received the English Lawes. The rest of the complaint he denied, and for the bribe of Cowes in particular, did avow, that Ever Mac Cooly, one of the plaintiffes, offered him seven thousand Cowes to make him chiefe of the name, when he might have learned, that his mind was not so poore, to preferre Cowes or any bribes before the Queenes service.

The Lord Deputie's Answers.

To returne to our purpose, certaine it is, that upon Mac Mahownes execution, heart-burnings and lothings of the English governement, began to grow in the Northerne Lords against the State, and they shunned as much as they could, to admit any Shiriffes, or any English to live among them, pretending to feare like practises to overthrow them.

Ann. 1591.

The sixteenth of July 1591, the Earle of Tirone wrote unto the Lords of England, excusing himselfe, that Sir Tirlogh Lynnogh was wounded by his men, while he sought to prey his Countrey. In the same moneth he suffered his Countrey of Tyrone to be made Shire ground, being by certaine Commissioners bounded on every side, and divided into 8 Baronies, and the Towne of Dungannon made the Shier Towne, where the Gaole should be. In the moneth of October he wrote againe to the Lords, justifying himselfe against the complaint of the Marshall Sir Henry Bagnoll, avowing that he had not stolne his sister, or taken her away by force, but that after her brothers many delayes, she willingly going away with him, hee married her. And that he had no other wife, being lawfully divorced from her, whom the Marshall

The Countrey of Tyrone made shire ground.

termed his wife. He complained against the Marshall, that he reaped the benefit of all that in Ulster, which by his endeavours had been brought to her Majesties obedience. That he had obtained under the great Seale a superioritie over Ulster, which he exercised over him. About this time the Northerne Lords are thought to have conspired, to defend the Romish Religion (for now first among them Religion was made the cloake of Treason), to admit no English Shiriffes in their Countries, and to defend their libertie and rights against the English.

Ann. 1592. In the Moneth of August 1592, the Earle of Tyrone by his letters to the Lords in England, justified himselfe against the complaint of Sir Tyrlogh Lynnogh, apparantly shewing that his sonne Con Oneale did not disturbe the Commissioners sitting in Monaghan, but that they, having one hundred Foote for their guard, were afraid of two Horsemen; which they discovered. He wrote further, that he had brought Odonnel into the State, (who since his above-mentioned escape out of prison, had stood upon his defence), and that he would perswade him to loyalty, and in case hee were obstinate, would serve against him as an enemy. And further craftily intreated the Lords, that he might have the Marshalls love, that they being neighbours, might concurre the better for her Majesties service, and that their Lordships would approve of his match with the Marshals sister, for whose content he did the rather desire his love.

Ann. 1593. In the beginning of the yeere 1593, or about this time,
[II. i. 12.] a Northerne Lord Mac Guire, began to declare himselfe discontent, and to stand upon his defence upon the execution of Mac Mahowne, and the jelousies then conceived by the Northerne Lords against the English. This Mac Guire, Chieftaine of Fermannagh avowed, that he had given three hundred Cowes to free his Countrey from a Shiriffe, during the Lord Deputies Government, and that notwithstanding one Captaine Willis was made Shiriffe of Fermannagh, having for his guard one hundred men, and leading about some one hundred women and

boyes, all which lived on the spoile of the Countrey. Hence this barberous Lord taking his advantage, set upon them, and drove them into a Church, where he would have put them all to the sword, if the Earle of Tyrone had not interposed his authoritie, and made composition for their lives, with condition that they should depart the Countrey. Whereupon the Lord Deputy Sir William Fitz Williams sent the Queenes forces into Fermannagh, wonne Mac Guires Castle of Eniskillen, and proclaimed him Traytor. And the Irish avow, that the Lord Deputy there let fall threatning speeches in publike against the Earle of Tyrone, calling him Traytor.

These speeches comming to the Earles hearing, he ever after pretended, that they were the first cause that moved him to misdoubt his safetie, and to stand upon his defence, now first combining himselfe with Odonnell, and the other Lords of the North, to defend their Honours Estates, and Liberties. When Tyrone first began to plot his rebellion, he is said to have used two notable practises. First, his men being altogether rude in the use of Armes, he offered the State to serve the Queene against Tyrlogh Lynogh with sixe hundred men of his owne, and so obtained sixe Captaines to traine them (called by our men Butter Captaines, as living upon Cesse) and by this meanes (and his owne men in pay, which he daily changed, putting new untrained men in the roome of others) he trained all his men to perfect use of their Armes. Secondly, pretending to build a faire house (which our State thinkes a tye of civilitie) he got license to transport to Dungannon a great quantitie of Lead to cover the Battlements of his house: but ere long imployed the same only to make bullets for the warre. But I returne to my purpose.

Tyrone plots his rebellion.

Sir Henrie Bagnoll Marshall of Ireland, had formerly exhibited to the State divers articles of treason practised by the Earle of Tyrone, who now would not come to the State without a protection. To these articles the Earle answered by letters, saying, that the Marshall accused him upon envy, and by suborned witnesses, and that he

Treason practised by Tyrone.

together with the Lord Deputy, apparantly sought his overthrow. Further complaining, that the Marshall detained from him his sisters portion, whom hee had married, and that (according to his former complaint) he usurped jurisdiction over all Ulster, and in particular exercised it over him. Yet these articles of treason against the Earle were beleeved in England, till he offered by his letters to stand to his triall either in England or Ireland. And accordingly he answered to the said Articles before the Lord Deputy and Councell at Dundalke, in such sort as they who had written into England against him, now to the contrary wrote, that hee had sufficiently

Ann. 1594. *The Lords of England's Letters.*

answered them. Whereupon the Lords of England wrote to the Earle of Tyrone, in the moneth of August of the following yeere, that they approved his answeres, and that in their opinion he had wrong, to be so charged, and that publikely before Judges, and especially, that his answeres were for a time concealed. Further, they commended him for the token of loyalty he had given, in dealing with Mac Guire to submit himselfe, exhorting him to persist in his good course, and charging him (the rather for avoiding his enemies slaunder) not to medle with compounding of Controversies in Ulster out of Tirone, without the Lord Deputies speciall warrant. At the same time their Lordships wrote to the Lord Deputy, taxing him and the Marshall, that they had used the Earle against Law and equitie, and that hee the Lord Deputy was not indifferent to the Earle, who offered to come over into England to justifie himselfe. Thus was the Earle cleared in shew, but whether through feare of his enemies, or the guiltines of his conscience, he shewed himselfe ever after to be diffident of his owne safety.

[II. i. 13.] *MacGuire's Rebellions.*

In the beginning of the yeere 1594 Mac Guire brake into open Rebellion, he entered with forces into Connaght (where the Burkes and Orwarke in Letrim, commonly called Orwarkes Countrey, for disobediences to the State, had been prosecuted by Sir Richard Bingham, Governour of that Province.) This forerunner of the greater conspirators (shortly after seconded by Mac Mahowne) was perswaded to enter Connaught by Gauranus a Priest, whom the Pope (forsooth) had made Primate of all Ireland, and was incouraged thereunto, by his ominating of good successe. But by the valour of Sir Richard Bingham the Governour, Mac Guire was repelled, with slaughter of many of his men, among whom this pretended Primate was killed.

The Earle of Tyrone serves against Mac Guire.

Against this Mac Guire, the Earle of Tyrone served with the Queenes forces, and valiantly fighting, was wounded in the thigh, yet this Earle providing for his securitie, about this time imprisoned the above mentioned sonnes of Shane Oneale, who had escaped out of Dublin Castle, and if they had been there kept, would have been a sure pledge of his obedience, neither would he restore them to libertie, though he were required so to doe, but still covering his treacherous heart with ostentation of a feare conceived of his enemies, he ceased not daily to complaine of the Lord Deputies and Marshals envy against him, and of wrongs done him by the Garrison souldiers. Thus the fier of this dangerous Rebellion is now kindled, by the above named causes, to which may be added, the hatred of the conquered against the Conquerors, the difference of Religion, the love of the Irish to Spaine (whence some of them are descended), the extortions of Sheriffes and sub-Sheriffes buying these places, the ill governement of the Church among our selves, and the admitting Popish Priests among the Irish, and many such like. And this fier of rebellion now kindled, shall be found hereafter to be increased to a devouring flame, by slow & slender oppositions to the first erruptions, before they had libertie to combine and know their owne strength; by not laying hands timely on suspected persons of quality, to prevent their combining with the rest (especially in Mounster, being as yet quiet): by intertaining and arming of Irish men (a point of high oversight begun by Sr Joh. Perrot, & increased by Sr Will. Fitz Williams, the present

The love o the Irish to Spaine.

Causes of the Rebellion.

L. Deputy, who at the first sending of forces into Formannagh, gave power to certaine Irish men to raise companies, which they did of their own Country men, so as this ill custome being after continued, it both furnished the enemy with trained men, and filled our Bands with such false hearted souldiers, as some doubted, whether we had not better have them enemies then friends): By a Treatie entertained at the very entrance of the Rebellion, before any blow was strucken, which made the Traytors proud, and daunted the hearts of good subjects; By ensuing cessations, long continuing and giving liberty to the Traytors to strengthen their combination, and to arme themselves in forraine parts and at home, whereupon all idle and discontented people had opportunitie to draw into Tyrone, and the Traytor Earle of Tyrone had meanes to oppresse the bordering Lords of Countries adjoyning, whereof many feeling once his power, some for feare, some for love, joyned with him. Besides that, the Army in the meane time was not onely an excessive charge to the Queene, but lay idle, and in stead of hurting the enemy, oppressed the subject, thereby daily driving many into Rebellion. Lastly (for I will not more curiously search the causes, being not suteable to so briefe a narration as I intend), the Rebellion was nourished and increased by nothing more, then frequent Protections and Pardons, granted even to those, who had formerly abused this mercy, so as all entred and continued to bee Rebels, with assurance to be received to mercy at their pleasure, whereof they spared not to brag, and this heartened the Rebell no lesse, then it discouraged the subject.

Anno 1594. Sir William Russel Lord Deputie.

This present yeere 1594, about the month of August, Sir William Fitz-williams, the Lord Deputy being recalled into England, Sir William Russell tooke the sword. About this time Ulster men in open hostility distressed her Majesties forces, and Tyrone (so I will hereafter call him, deserving no addition of title), having long absented himselfe from the State, was undoubtedly reputed a party in their rebellion, when his sudden & voluntary appearance before this new Lord Deputy at Dublin, in the very first moneth of his governement, made many hope better of him. He most assuredly promised al humble obedience to the Queene, as well before the State at Dublin, in his own person, as to the Lords in England by his letters, [II i. 14.] and making his most humble submission to her Majesty, besought to be restored to her former Grace, from which he had fallen by the lying slanders of his enemies, not by any his just desert. The Marshall Sir Henry Bagnoll was then ready to prove before the Lord Deputy Articles of high treason against Tyrone, and to avow that he sent mac Guire with his Primate into Connaght. That hee had secret intelligence with the Traytors mac Guire and Odonnell, and had communicated counsels with them, and gave them aide in the wasting of Monnaghan, and the besieging of Eniskellin, by his brother Cormac mac Baron, and by Con his owne base son; and that he by threats had drawne the Captaines of Kilulto and Kilwarny from their faith and alleageance to the Queene. It was in Councell debated, whether Tyrone should be staied to answere hereunto; and the Lord Deputy was of opinion he should be staied: but most of the Counsellers, either for idle feare, or inclination of love to Tyrone, thought best to dismisse him for that time, and the counsell of these, as more in number, and best experienced in Irish affaires, the Lord Deputy followed. This much displeased the Queene, since this Foxes treasonable practises were now so apparant, and her selfe had forewarned, that in case he came to the State, he should be staied, till he had cleered himselfe of all imputed crimes. And the Lords in England by their letters thence, sharpely reproved the Lord Deputy, for so dismissing him, which might give the Rebels just cause to thinke that they durst not charge him with treason, for feare of his forces, and their Lordships professed to doubt, that Tyrones performance would not be such, as might warrant this act.

Sir Henry Bagnoll proves Articles of high Treason against Tyrone.

Tyrone dismissed.

The Lord Deputy reproved.

The Lord Deputy shortly after tooke the field, and

The Lord Deputy takes the field.

leaving for martiall causes the Earle of Ormond, for civell causes the Lord Chanceller, to governe Lemster and those parts in his absence, drew the forces into Fermannagh, that he might releeve Enis-Kellin, and expell mac Guire out of his Countrey. This winter following, it seemes there was some negotiation on both sides about peace. For in the moneth of February, the Lords of England wrote to the Lord Deputy, of her Majesties dislike of certaine writings sent over from Odonnel and Sir Arthur Oneale, namely that in their petitions, they included the pardon of mac Guire, and Orwarke (commonly called Orurke). That they indented with the Lord Deputy, that he should come to Dundalke within a moneth, and especially that the Lord Deputy by Sir Edward More should desire a fortnight more for his comming thither. Their Lordships also signified, that the Queene sent over 2000. old souldiers, which had served under General Norreys in Britanny; (giving order that they should be divided into hundreds, and so many Captaines) besides that 1000. souldiers were levied in England, to be sent thither. And because their Lordships judged, that all the practises of the Northern Lords, came out of Tyrones schoole, (howsoever he grossely dissembled the contrary), their Lordships advised the Lord Deputy to offer Odonnel pardon, so as he would sever himselfe from Tyrone: And that the rather, because he was put into rebellion by Sir John Perrots imprisoning him without any cause.

3000. souldiers sent over.

Tyrone hearing that supplies of souldiers, & namely the old souldiers of Britany, were comming for Ireland, and that Garrisons of English were to be planted at the Castles of Ballishanon; and Relike, lying upon the Lake Earn, thought it no longer time to temporise. Wherefore about this time of this yeere ending, or the first entrance of the yeere 1595, he drew his forces together, and in open hostilitie, suddenly assaulted the Fort of Black-water, built upon the passage into Tyrone on the South side, and taking the same, raced it, and broke

Ann. 1595
Tyrone takes the Fort of Black-water.

downe the Bridge. And now the Northerne Rebels with Banners displaied, entred the Brennye. Yet at this time Tyrone subtilly made suite for pardon, and promised the Treasurer at warres, Sir Henrie Wallop, that he would continue his Alleageance to the Queene. At this time likewise Feagh Mac Hugh, Walter Reagh, and many Lemster men, began to enter into actions of hostility against the English.

Tyrone's subtilty.

The Lord Deputy, who saw this storme of Rebellion would lye heavy on his shoulders, in his letters to the Lords in England had let fall a request, that some old experienced Commander might be sent over to him, for his better assistance, meaning (no doubt) such a Captaine as should be commanded by the supreame authority of the Lord Deputie. But the Lords either mistaking his intent, or because they so judged it best for her Majesties service, sent over Sir John Norreys, a great Leader, and famous in the warres of the Low Countries and France, giving him the title of Lord General, with absolute command over military affaires, in the absence of the L. Deputie. This great Commander was not like to be willingly commanded by any, who had not borne as great or greater place in the warres then himselfe. So as whether through emulation, growing betweene him and the Lord Deputy, or a declining of his Fortune, incident to the greatest Leaders, howsoever he behaved himselfe most valiantly and wisely in some encounters against Tyrone, and the chiefe rebels, yet he did nothing against them of moment. About the beginning of June, the L. Deputie and the Lord Generall drew their Forces towards Armagh, and now Tyrone had sent letters of submission to them both (intreating the Lord Generall more specially for a milder proceeding against him, so as he might not be forced to a headlong breach of his loyaltie.) These letters should have been delivered at Dundalke, but the Marshall Bagnoll intercepting them, stayed the messenger at the Newrye, till the Lord Deputies returne, at which time because in this journey

L. Deputy, L. Generall together.

[II. i. 15.]

Sir John Norreys Lord General.

Tyrone had been proclaimed Traytor, he refused to receive them, in respect of her Majesties Honour.

Sir Henrie Wallop and Sir Robert Gardner to conferre with Tyrone.

Yet shortly after at Tyrones instance, Sir Henrie Wallop, Treasurer at Warres, and Sir Robert Gardner chiefe Justice of Ireland, were by Commission appointed to conferre with him and his confederate Rebels. Tyrone in this conference complained of the Marshall for his usurped jurisdiction in Ulster, for depriving him of the Queenes favour by slaunders; for intercepting his late letters to the Lord Deputie, and Lord Generall, protesting that he never negotiated with forraine Prince, till he was proclaimed Traytor. His humble petitions were, that hee and his might be pardoned, and have free exercise of Religion granted (which notwithstanding had never before either been punished or inquired after.) That the Marshall should pay him one thousand pound for his dead Sisters, his wives portion. That no Garrisons nor Sheriffes should be in his Country. That his troope of fiftie horse in the Queenes pay might be restored to him. And that such as had preyed his Country, might make restitution.

Odonnell's complaint.

Odonnell magnifying his Fathers and Progenitors services to the Crowne, complained that Captaine Boyne, sent by Sir John Perrot with his Company into his Countrey, under pretence to reduce the people to civilitie, and being well entertained of his Father, had besides many other injuries, raised a Bastard to be Odonnel, and that Sir John Perrot, by a ship sent thither, had taken himselfe by force, and long imprisoned him at Dublin. And that Sir William Fitz Williams had wrongfully kept Owen O Toole above mentioned seven yeeres in prison. His petitions were for pardon to him and his, and for freedome of Religion. That no Garrisons or Sheriffes might bee placed in his Countrey. And that certaine Castles and lands in the County of Sligo might bee restored to him.

Shane Oneale's complaint.

Shane Mac Brian Mac Phelime Oneale, complained of an Iland taken from him by the Earle of Essex, and that he had been imprisoned till he surrendered to the Marshall a Barrony, his ancient Inheritance. Hugh Mac Guire complained of insolencies done by Garrison souldiers, and by a Sheriffe, who besides killed one of his nearest Kinsmen. Brian Mac Hugh Oge, and Mac Mahowne (so the Irish called the chiefe of that name surviving), and Ever Mac Cooly of the same Family of Mac Mahownes, complained of the above-mentioned unjust execution of Hugh Roe Mac Mahowne, in the Governement of Sir William Fitz Williams.

The Commissioners judged some of their petitions equall, others they referred to the Queenes pleasure. But when on the Queenes part, they propounded to the Rebels some Articles to bee performed by them, they were growne so insolent, as judging them unequall, the conference was broken off, with a few dayes Truce granted on both sides, when the Queene, for sparing of bloud, had resolved to give them any reasonable conditions.

The conference broken off.

This Truce ended, the Lord Deputy and the Lord Generall, about the eighteenth of July, drew the Forces to Armagh, with such terror to the Rebels, as Tyrone left the Fort of Blackwater, burnt the Towne of Dungannon, and pulled downe his House there, burnt all Villages, and betooke himselfe to the Woods. They proclaimed Tyrone Traytor in his owne Countrey, and leaving a Guard in the Church of Armagh, they for want of victuals, returned to Dublin, and by the way placed a Garrison in Monaghan. And when the Army came neere to Dundalke, the Lord Deputie according to his instructions from England, yeelded the command of the Army to the Lord Generall, and leaving him with the Forces in the Northerne Borders, returned to Dublin. The third of September Hugh Earle of Tyrone, Hugh O Donnel, Bryan O Rourke, Hugh Mac Guire, Bryan Mac Mahowne, Sir Arthur Oneale, Art Mac Baron, Henry Oge Oneale, Turlogh Mac Henry Oneale, Cormac Mac Baron (Tyrones Brother), Con Oneale, Tyrones base Sonne, Bryan Art Mac Brian, and one Francis Mounfoord,

[II. i. 16.]

Tyrone betakes himself to the woods.

Tyrone proclaimed Traytor.

were for forme of Law indited, though absent, and condemned judicially of Treason in the Countie of Lowthe, neere the Borders of the North.

The Lemster Rebels. From this time the Lemster Rebels began to grow very strong: for Feogh Mac Hugh of the Obirns, & Donnel Spanniah of the Cavanaghs, when they were declining, & in want of munition, were not prosecuted, but upon fained submission were received into protection, and so had meanes to renew their Forces, and supply their wants, so as this yeere, about this moneth of September, they began to oppresse al the subjects, from the Gates almost of Dublin, to the County of Wexford (the most ancient English County, and ever much cared for by the Queene), which they spoiled, wanting forces to defend it, and so deprived the English souldier of great reliefe he might have found therein. The like may be said of the Oconnors in Ophalia.

Generall Norris being left by the Lord Deputie on the Northerne Borders, with full command of the Army, the Winter passed without any great exploit. There was in *Emulation betweene the Lord Deputie and the Lord Generall.* many things no small emulation betweene the Lord Deputie and him, and no lesse in Tyrones particular. The Lord Deputie seemed to the Lord Generall, to be unequall and too sharpe against Tyrone, with whom he wished no treaty of Peace to bee held, (which he wisely did, having experienced his false subtiltie, and knowing that he sought delaies, onely till hee could have aide from Spaine.) But the Lord Generall (whether it were in emulation of the Lord Deputy, or in his favour and love to Tyrone) was willing to reclaime him by a Gentle course (which that crafty Fox could well nourish in him.) And it seemes some part of the Winter passed, while this project was negotiated betweene them.

Ann. 1596. For in the beginning of the yeere 1596, a Comission was procured out of England, whereby her Majestie, though justly offended with Tyrone and his associates, about their demaunds, in the former conference with Sir Henry Wallop, and Sir Robert Gardner, yet in regard

A Commission procured out of England.

of their letters of humble submission, since that time presented to her, doth signifie her gratious pleasure to Sir John Noreis Lord Generall, and Sir Geffry Fenton, her Majesties Secretary for Ireland, giving them authoritie to promise pardon of life, and restoring of lands and goods to the said Lords, seeking with due humilitie her Royall mercy, and to heare them, with promise of favourable consideration in all their complaints. And thus much the Commissioners signified to Tyrone and Odonnell, by Captaine Sant Leger, and Captaine Warren, sent of purpose unto them, with instructions dated the eleventh of Aprill, this present yeere 1596, and with reference of other particulars, to a meeting appointed to be at Dundalke. The twentie of the same month Tyrone at Dundalke before these Commissioners craved the Queenes mercy on his knees, signing with his hand a most humble submission in writing, vowing faith in the presence of Almightie God, who seeth into the secrets of all mens hearts, and (to use still his owne words) most humbly craving her Majesties mercy and pardon on the knees of his heart. His first petition for liberty of Religion, was utterly rejected. For the second, touching freedome from Garrisons and Sheriffes, he was answered, that her Majestie would not be prescribed how to governe. In the third, interceding for Orelyes pardon, it was disliked that he should capitulate for others, yet giving hope of his pardon upon his owne submission. For the fourth, concerning the Jurisdiction of Armagh, the answer was, that her Majesty would reserve all the Bishops right. For the fifth, concerning the freeing of Shane Oneales sons, it was referred to her Majesties further pleasure. Finally, he promised to desist from aiding the Rebels, and from intermedling with the neighbor Lords. To make his Country a Shiere: to admit a Shiriffe. To renounce the title of Oneale. To confesse (upon his pardon) all his intelligences with forraine Princes, and all his past actions, which may concerne the good of the State. To rebuild the Fort and Bridge of Blackwater, and to relieve the

Tyrone craves the Queenes mercy.

[II. i. 17.]

Tyrone's promises.

Garrison for ready money at all times. To deliver in sufficient Pledges. To dismisse all his Forces, & to pay such reasonable fine to her Majesties use, as should be thought meete by her Majestie. Hugh Odonnel at the same time did agree to divers articles, for the good of his Countrey, and made his like humble submission. The like did Hugh mac Guire, Bryan mac Hugh, Ever Oge Roe mac Cooly, Bryan Orewark (called Ororke), Shane Mac Bryan, Phillip O Reyly, and others. To each one was given (under the Commissioners hands) a promise of her Majesties pardon, upon putting in of Pledges. And Proclamation was made, to give notice hereof to all the Queenes subjects, that in the meane time no acts of hostilitie might be done against any of those, who had thus submitted themselves.

Tyrone solicites aide from Spaine.

Thus the Ulster Rebels, by a submission too honest to be truly intended by them, whilest Pledges were expected, and Pardons drawne, were freed from the prosecution of the Queenes Forces this Summer. And even at this time did Tyrone solicite aide in Spaine, and two or three messengers came secretly to the rebels from thence, by whom many of them (as Ororke, Mac William, &c) sent a writing signed, to the King of Spaine, covenanting, that if hee would send sufficient Forces, they would joyne theirs to his, and if he would at all relieve them, in the meane time they would refuse all conditions of Peace. But Tyrone, though consenting, yet was too craftie to signe this Covenant, yea, craftily he sent the King of Spaines answere to the Lord Deputie, whilest hee notwithstanding relied on the promised succours. I finde nothing of moment done this Summer by the Forces with the Generall, being restrained by the last agreement at Dundalke; onely about the end of August, hee wrote out of Connaght unto the Lord Deputie, complaining of divers wants, and desiring more Forces to be sent him. To whom the Lord Deputie answered, that his Lordship had warrant to supply some of his wants in the Countrie, and denied the sending of any

Forces to him, because himselfe was to goe into the Field.

The rebels of Lemster growne strong.

By this time the rebels of Lemster were (as I formerly mentioned) growne strong, Feogh Mac Hugh breaking his protection entred into acts of hostilitie, and he together with the O Mores, O Connors, O Birnes, O Tooles, the Cavenaghs, Butlers, and the chiefe names of Connaght, animated by the successe of Ulster men, combined together, and demaunded to have the barbarous titles of O and Mac together with lands they claimed, to be restored to them, in the meane time spoiling all the Country on all sides.

Sir Richard Bingham.

About the moneth of January, Sir Richard Bingham, Governour of Connaght, who had valiantly beaten Ororke out of his Countrie, and prosecuted the Bourks, and other Rebels, was called into England, upon complaints of the Irish, and Sir Conyers Clifford was sent to governe Connaght. This Gentleman complained off by the Irish, was valiant and wise; but some of our English Statesmen thought him too severe, and that he had thereby driven many into rebellion, howsoever himselfe very well experienced in the Country, and those who best understood the Irish nature, found nothing so necessarie for keeping them in obedience, as severitie, nor so dangerous for the increase of murthers and outrages, as indulgence towards them. His answers to their complaints could not be so admitted as for the time some discountenance fell not on him, which reward of services he constantly bore, till in short time after, to his great grace, the State thought fit againe to use his service, in a place of great commaund in the Armie.

Sir Conyers Clifford.

Another Commission appointed.

[II. i. 18.]

Sir John Norreys Lord Generall, Sir George Bourcher, Master of her Majesties Ordinance, and Sir Geffery Fenton her Majesties Secretary for Ireland, being by Commission directed to treat againe with Tyrone, did by their letters dated the twenty of Januarie remember him of the favour he had received at the last treatie at Dundalke, and charged him (as formerly he had been charged) with high crimes since that committed by him, to the violation of the Articles then agreed on, therefore advising him, that since they were for her Majesties service to draw to the Borders, he would there testifie to them his penitencie for offences done since his pardon, by such an humble and heartie submission, as they might recommend into England from him. Tyrone by his answere of the two and twentie of Januarie, acknowledged under his hand her Majesties mercy therein extended to him, and confessed offences and breaches of the Articles there signed, withall desiring them, to examine the wrongs and provocations, by which he had beene driven thereunto, and protesting his sorrow for these offences. The same day he met the Commissioners neere Dundalke, where he being on the one side of the Brooke, they on the other, hee put of his hat, and holding it with great reverence in his hand, said to them. That hee was come thither, not onely to shew his duty to them, as her Majesties Commissioners, but his inward desire to bee made & continued a subject. When he would have remembred the wrongs since his late Pardon provoking him to disloialtie, they cut him off by remembring him of all the benefits, and that of his last pardon, received from the Queene, which should have counterpoised his wrongs, and have kept him in duty. He confessed this, with shew of great remorse, and protested before God and heaven, that there was no Prince nor creature, whom he honoured as he did her Majestie; nor any Nation of people that he loved or trusted more, then the English. Protesting further, that if her Majestie would please to accept of him againe as a subject, and to take such course as hee might bee so continued, (thus still he reserved pretence of wrongs to shaddow his future disloialties), then he doubted not but to redeeme all his faults past with some notable services. Besides, hee gave answers to divers questions, and signed them after with his hand. First, asked what messages and letters had passed betweene Spaine and him; he answered, never to have received any,

Meeting with Tyrone neere Dundalke.

Tyrone's Answers.

but incouragements from Spaine, and assurances of an Army to aide him: that he never had further contract with the Spaniards, and that he had sent the King of Spaines letter above mentioned to the Lord Deputie and Counsell: that he never received thence any money or ought of value, nor any of his confederates to his knowledge. Only Odonnel had some fifteene barrels of powder, whereof he should have had a portion, but never had it. Secondly, for the late Submitties, Pardons, and Pledges, hee undertooke that with all speede the Pledges should be sent to Dublin, with Agents to sue out the Pardons granted in the last Treatie at Dundalke. Thirdly, for his making O Realy, he vowed that the Gentlemen of the Countrie made him, and that he would hereafter never meddle in the causes of the Brenny. Fourthly, for the Rebels of Lemster and the Butlers, he answered, that he never had confederacy with any but Feogh Mac Hugh, and for the Butlers, hee never had any thing to doe with them. Fiftly, for Agents in Spaine, he denied to have any, or to know any his confederates had. Sixthly, for his jealousie of the State, hee avowed it to be upon just causes, which hee would after make knowne. This done, hee desired Captaine Warren might come over the Brooke to him, and then by him he requested that himselfe might come over to the Commissioners, in token of his faithfull heart to her Majestie, which granted, he with great reverence saluted them, and with hat in hand, lifting up his eyes to Heaven, desired *His oathe.* God to take vengeance on him, if (her Majestie vouchsafing to make him a subject, and to cause the Articles of Dundalke to be kept to him) he would not continue faithfull, and desired never to see Christ in the face, if he meant not as he spake. He confessed, that the Spanish ships lately arrived in the North, had brought Odonnel the Kings letter, signifying that he heard the Earle of Tirone to be dead, and the Irish to have received a great overthrow, desiring to be advertised of their State. And that Odonnel before his comming had given answere, that if the King sent an Army, he would take his part, and hoped the like of the other Irish. But at his comming, that the Spanish Captaine excusing that the King had not written to him, he only told him, that promise had not been kept with him by the English, and therefore he would not refuse the Kings promised aide. And with many execrations swore, that the Captaine left neither Munition nor Treasure with him, and that he never received any thing from the King of Spaine, but that letter above mentioned, which he sent to the Lord Deputy. And that he never wrote but three letters into Spaine, all about one time, and (as he thought) all intercepted. Lastly, he vehemently denied to have incited any Mounster men to rebellion, since his last pardon. So with like reverence as formerly, he tooke his leave.

[II. i. 19.]

The King of Spaine's help.

Commissions power to meet with Tyrone.

Upon advertisement hereof into England, the Commissioners received ample power to conclude all things with Tyrone. Thus much they made knowne to him by letters, sent to him by his old friend Captaine Warren, the ninth of March, with instructions to appoint the second of Aprill the day of meeting at Dundalke, which Tyrone accepted, with shew of joy to be received to her Majesties mercy, the sweetnes whereof he had often experienced, and of feare to be pursued by her forces, which he professed himselfe not able to resist. But by his letters the fifteene of March, he made doubt of meeting, pretending that his pledges were not changed according to covenant, nor restitution made him by those that had preyed his Country, and that his confederates could not come so soone. The Commissioners replyed by letters the two and twenty of March, that these were but delayes, since the pledges at the meeting (upon his putting in his eldest sonne for pledge) should be restored, and he in all things reasonably satisfied, protesting that if he refused this occasion, they could doe no more for him, since her Majesty would be no longer abused by his faire promises and delayes: Adding, that he must conforme himselfe to the directions they had, and could not alter. Master

Tyrone delays.

Secretary wrote out of England unto the Commissioners the two and twenty of March; That her Majesty was displeased to have the treaty thus delayed, and charged to have the meeting in a Towne, as a submission of the Rebels, not in the field as a parley. That her Majesty prepared for the warre, resolving not to have any more treaties, if this tooke not effect. Lastly, desiring them to acquaint the Lord Deputy with all their directions, and the issues, and to excuse his not writing to his Lordship, thinking that the Commissioners were not at Dublyn with him.

The Queene prepared for warre.

Upon the tenth of Aprill, in the yeere 1597, the Commissioners againe pressed Tyrone by letters, not to slacke his owne greatest good by delayes, and appointed for the last day of meeting, the sixteenth of that present moneth, and that his confederats not able then to come, should draw after as soone as they could, protesting that this was the last time that they would write unto him. Tyrone on the seventeenth of April, sent his reasons of not comming: First justifying his relaps into disloialty by the truce not observed to him, and because restitution was not made him of preyes taken from him, which was promised. Then excusing his not meeting, because his pledges, by the truce being from three moneths to three moneths to be changed, were still detained, yea, his pledges the second time put in, were kept together with the first; And saying, that he durst not come to the Lord Generall, because many promises by him made, being not kept, he knew it was much against his honourable mind, and so could not be perswaded, but that the Lord Generall was overruled by the Lord Deputy, so as he could not make good his promises without the Lord Deputies consent, who shewed malice to him, and was no doubt the cause of all the breaches of such promises, as had beene made unto him. Againe, in regard he heard that the Lord Bourgh was to come over Lord Deputy, who was altogether unknowne to him, he protested to feare that the acts of the Lord Generall with him, would not be made

Ann. 1597.

Tyrones excuses.

good, wishing that rather the Lord Generall might be continued in his command, for then he would be confident of a good conclusion. Finally, he desired a meeting neere Dundalke the sixe and twenty of Aprill, but this appointment for the day being against the last finall resolution, and for the place against her Majesties directions, there was no more speech of this treaty.

Sir William Russell called home.

In the meane time Sir William Russell Lord Deputy, by the managing of those and like affaires, finding himselfe not duly countenanced out of England, in the place he sustained, had made earnest suit to be called home,
[II. i. 20.] and accordingly about the end of May he was revoked, and the Lord Bourgh, (so he himselfe writes, others write Burke, and Camden writes Borough) came over Lord Deputy. The ill successe of the treaties and small progresse of the warres, together with this unexpected change of the Lord Deputy, comming with supreme authority, as well in martiall as civill causes, brake the heart of Sir John Norryes Lord Generall, a leader as worthy and famous as England bred in our age. Of late (according to vulgar speech) he had displeased the Earle of Essex, then a great favourite in Court, and by his merites possessed of the superintendency in all martiall affaires: For Sir John Norryes had imbraced the action of Brest Fort in Britany, and the warres in those parts, when the Earle himself had purpose to entertaine them, and prevailed against the Earle, by undertaking them with lesse forces, then the Earle desired for the same. And it was thought that the Earle had preferred the Lord Bourgh, of purpose to discontent him, in regard the said Lord Bourgh had had a private quarrell with the said Generall in England, and that besides the superiour command of this Lord, (though otherwise most worthy, yet of lesse experience in the warres then the Generall had), could not but be unsupportable to him, esteemed one of the greatest Captaines of his time, and yet having inferiour command of the Presidentship of Mounster in the same Kingdome. Certainely upon the arrivall of this new

L. Bourgh. L. Deputy.

The Earle of Essex and Sir John Norryes.

Lord Deputy, presently Generall Norryes was commanded to his governement of Mounster, and not to stirre thence without leave. When he came thither, this griefe so wrought upon his high spirit, as it apparantly brake his brave and formerly undaunted heart, for without sickenes or any publike signe of griefe, he suddenly died, in the imbrace of his deere brother Sir Thomas Norreys, his vicepresident, within some two moneths of his comming into Mounster.

Death of Generall Norryes.

The Lord Bourgh at his entry into the place of Lord Deputy, found all the North in Rebellion, except seven Castles, with their Townes or Villages, all but one lying towards the sea, namely Newry, Knockfergus, Carlingford, Greene-Castle, Armagh, Dondrom, and Olderfleet. And all Connaght was likewise in Rebellion, together with the Earle of Ormonds nephewes the Butlers, in Mounster.

All the North in Rebellion.

In this moneth of May, Ororke was sent into England, by the King of Scots, and there executed. This Ororke seemes to have beene expelled his Countrey, when Sir Richard Bingham was Governour of Connaght, but those of his name, and the chiefe of them, usurping the Countrey of Letrym, still continued Rebels.

Ororke executed.

Tyrone hitherto with all subtilty and a thousand sleights abusing the State, when he saw any danger hanging over him, by fained countenance and false words pretended humblest submission, and hearty sorrow for his villanies; but as soone as opportunity of pursuing him was omitted, or the forces were of necessity to be drawne from his Countrey, with the terror of them all his loyalty vanished, yea, he failed not to mingle secretly the greatest Counsels of mischiefe with his humblest submissions. And these courses had beene nourished by the sloth of our Leaders, the frugality of some of our counsellers, and the Queenes inbred lenity: yet of all other, he had most abused the late Lord Generals love to him, and his credulity, which specially grew out of his love. Now of this new Lord Deputy, by letters hee requested a truce or cessation, which it seemed good to the Lord Deputy to grant for

Tyrone's craftinesse.

a moneth, in regard of the conveniency of her Majesties present affaires, not any way to gratifie the Rebell, for he had no purpose to entertaine more speech of his submission, or to slacke the pursuit of him and his confederates, to which he was wholly bent. He saw the lamentable effects, which these cessations, together with protections, had hitherto produced, and among other evils, did specially resolve to avoid them.

The Lord Deputy takes the field.

Therefore assoone as the moneth of truce was expired, the Lord Deputy aswell by his first actions, to give luster and ominous presage to his governement, as because he judged it best for the service to strike at the head, presently drew the Forces towards Tyrone. The Irish, in a fastnes neere Armagh, (so they call straight passages in woods, where to the natural strength of the place is added the art of interlacing the low bowes, and casting the bodies of trees acrosse the way) opposed the passage of the English, who made their way with their swords, and found that
[II. i. 21.] the Irish resolutely assaulted, would easily give ground.

The Fort of Blackwater retaken.

Then the Lord Deputy assaulted the Fort of Blackewater, formerly built by the English upon the passage to Dungannon, whence the Earle at his first entering into rebellion, had by force expelled the English, as carefully as he would have driven poyson from his heart. This Fort he soon wonne, and repayring the same, put a company of English souldiers into it, to guard it. But whilst the Lord Deputy with the whole army were rendering thanks to God for this good successe, the Rebels shewed themselves out of the thicke woods neere adjoyning on the North-side of the Fort, so as the prayers were interrupted by calling to armes. The English entered

Conflict in the woods.

skirmish, and prevayled against them, driving them to flye into the thickest of their dens. In this conflict were killed Francis Vaughan, brother to the Lord Deputies wife; and Robert Turnour Serjant Major of the Army, and two foster brethren to Henry Earle of Kildare, who with his troope of Horse valiantly served upon the Rebell, and tooke the death of his foster brethren so to heart, (after the education of the Irish) as he shortly after died. Many also were wounded, among whom Thomas Walker was of chiefe name.

When the Lord Deputy first resolved to draw up to Blackewater, he sent directions to Sir Conyers Clifford to come up with the Connaght forces by the way of Ballyshannon, and to meete him there, which he in like sort attempted, but being overmatched by the Rebels lying in his way, could not peirce so farre, but was forced to retire, and by that retreat wonne great reputation to himselfe and the men under him: for having with him some sixe or seven hundred foote onely; of which part was of the old Britan Souldiers, and being assayled by more then 2000. Rebels, during thirty miles march he valiantly repelled them, and safely retired to the garrison.

Sir Conyers Clifford's skillful retreat.

The Lord Deputy leaving the Fort at the Blackewater well guarded to the charge of Captaine Thomas Williams, withdrew the Forces towards the Pale. Now the Rebels tossed betweene hope, feare, and shame, resolved to besiege the Fort, and Tyrone thought his reputation lost, if he recovered it not, and so with joynt force they compassed and assayled the same. Whereof the Lord Deputy being advertised, with all possible expedition gathered the forces, to leade them to the reliefe of that fort, and the Rebels hearing of his Lordships approach, quitted the siege of the Fort, and retired into their strengths. Whereupon the Lord Deputy marched forward, and having passed the Blackwater Fort, and purposing to enter and passe the place leading to Dungannon Tyrones chiefe House, he fel suddenly sicke, and being carried backe in his horse litter to Armagh, and thence to the Newry, died in the way, to the great joy of the Rebels, dejected with his sharpe prosecution and bold adventures, and to the no lesse griefe of the English, erected with hope of good successe. Howsoever many of good judgement held his purpose of passing to Dungannon very dangerous, and altogether fruitlesse, since no garrisons being planted to gaine ground, no other

The Rebels beseige the Blackewater Fort.

Death of the Lord Deputy.

issue could be hoped in the best event, then a bragge of courage in passing to Tyrones cheefe seate, which no other Deputy had yet attempted. And as they greatly commended the Lord Deputies valour in these actions, so they feared the ingaging and losse of the Queenes Army, by this or some like bold attempt.

Lord Justice. After his death, Sir Thomas Norreys, Lord President of Mounster, was under the great seale of Ireland provisionally made Lord Justice of the Kingdome, (as the custome is in such sudden changes) who repaired to Dublin, and there executed his place for one month (as I thinke of September) and no longer, for he being sick & cast down in minde by the great sorrow he had conceived for the late death of his worthy brother, made great suite to the Queene and the Lords in England, to be eased of this burthen of being Lord Justice, and to have leave to retire himselfe to his governement of the Province of Mounster.

Lord Liefetenant, and Lords Justices. And so Adam Loftus Lord Chauncellor of Ireland, and Lord Archbishop of Dublin, and Robert Gardner chiefe Justice of Ireland, by letters out of England, the thirteene of October were made Lords Justices for the civell governement, and the Earle of Ormond with title of Lord Liefetenant of the Army, was authorized to command in cheefe for all martiall affayres. Tyrone after [II. i. 22.] his old custome, flies unto the Lord Lieftenant, with protestations of loyalty, and complaines of wrongs, inforcing his disloiall courses, which his Lordship advertising into England, received authority from thence, to treat with Tyrone about his submission, having Sir Geffery Fenton Secretary of Ireland joyned with him *Meeting with Tyrone.* for an assistant. Hereupon ensued a meeting at Dundalke on the 22 of December, where Tyrone made his most humble submission in writing, acknowledging her Majesties great mercie in giving him and his Associates their pardons upon former submissions, and upon the knees of his heart (as he writes) professed most heartie penitencie for his disloialtie, and especially his foule

A.D. 1597.

relapses thereinto, humbly beseeching the Lord Lieutenant to be a meanes to her sacred Majestie for his pardon, withall making knowne his grievances, which howsoever they could not justifie his offence, yet might in some measure qualifie the heinousnesse thereof. And till these might be booked, to be sent over with his Submission, most humbly craving of his Lordship to grant a truce or cessation of Armes for eight weeks following. And further, to the end it might appeare that his submission proceeded from his heart, promising that for the time of this cessation, there should be no impediment given to her Majesties Ministers bringing victuals to Blackwater Fort, yea, that for a poore token of his humblest duty, hee would voluntarily give to the hands of the Captaine fortie Beeves, and suffer the souldiers to cut and fetch in wood, or any other provisions. For his performance whereof hee offered presently to give Pledges to his Lordship.

Tyrone craves a truce.

The same day hee subscribed the following articles, propounded to him by the Lord Lieutenant. First, he promiseth for him and his associates, faithfully to keepe her Majesties Peace during the cessation. Secondly, that hee will presently recall all Ulster men sent by him into Lemster, leaving those who should not obay his directions to the Lord Lieutenants discretion. Thirdly, if any during the Truce shall breake into Rebellion, he promiseth not to aide them, so as none depending on his Truce, be in the meane time taken in by the State without his consent. Fourthly, he agreeth to a generall Liberty, of buying necessaries for his men in the Pale, and for the Queenes subjects in Ulster, and nothing to be forceably taken on either side. Fiftly, that upon pretended wrongs no revenge be taken, but restitution be made within ten dayes after complaint. Sixthly, that during the Truce hee shall have no intelligence with the King of Spaine, or other forraine Prince, but acquaint the State with any message hee shall receive, or project he shall heare. Seventhly, that he shall presently

He subscribes these Articles.

draw a booke of his grievances, such as he can prove, without mention of frivolous matters unworthie her sacred Majesties view. Eightly, that he will deliver into the Fort forty Beeves, and give safe conduct to her Majesties Ministers to vittaile the said Fort of Blackwater, and suffer the souldiers to cut and fetch wood on the South-side of Armagh, and for all other necessaries permit them to agree with the owners, so as they come not of themselves into his Countrie, but have his men with them in company. Ninthly, that any prey being tracked into his Countrie, he shall make restitution, and deliver the theeves to be executed, and if any be stopped from following of his track the stopper shall answere the goods so tracked; which course the Lord Lieutenant promised likewise to hold towards him and his associates.

Beeves sent by Tyrone.

The foure and twentie of December, Tyrone advertised the Lord Lieutenant, that he served the Fort with fortie Beeves, but the Captaine had refused ten of them, wherein his discretion was taxed by the Lord Lieutenant, since they were of voluntarie gift. Yet Tyrone promised to send ten other of the best he had in lieu of them.

Submission of Brian Ororke.

The eighteenth of Februarie Brian Oge Orwarke (commonly called Ororke) Lord of Letrym (commonly called Ororkes Country) submitted himself in a great assembly on his knees to her Majestie, before Sir Conyers Clifford Governour of Connaght, subscribing further to these Articles. First, that he and his followers promised in all humblenesse to performe all duties to her Majestie, as becommeth good subjects. Secondly, that he will receive her Majesties Sheriffes, and yeeld them all due obedience. Thirdly, that he will pay to her Majestie her composition or rent, and yeeld to her Highnes all services, according to his new Patent to be granted. Fourthly,
[II. i. 23.] that hee shall send out of his Countrie all strangers to their owne dwelling places. Fifthly, that hee will apprehend all Rebels, Theeves or Malefactors comming into his Countrie, sending them and their goods to the Governour. Sixthly, that hee will deliver Pledges for

Sir Conyers Clifford's advice.

his Sept (or Family) and the chiefe Septs with him, within twentie dayes. Hereof Sir Conyers Clifford advertised the Lords Justices, praying that in regard of the strength and fastnesse of Ororkes Country, he might not bee discontented, with having Beeves taken from him for reliefe of the Army, without payment of ready money for them, since that course had already grieved all the Submitties. Further, he shewed that the Countrie of Ororke was most necessary to be defended. For howsoever it was held by Sir Richard Bingham the last Governour as by Conquest (upon expelling of the above mentioned Ororke), yet then it was all waste, so as the Rebell could make little use of it, whereas now it was most replenished with cattle, and therefore like to be assaulted by Tyrone and Odonnel, incensed against Ororke by reason of this his submission. Besides that, the Queenes forces could lie no where so fitly for service, as upon the Earne, nor there bee relieved but by Ororke, nor receive reliefe with his contentment but by paying ready money. Lastly, hee shewed that all the people upon the Earne, and in those parts, excepting Mac William, had submitted themselves to her Majestie, and delivered Pledges for their Loyalty, being glad to live under her Majesties Lawes, and onely terrified with the burden of relieving the souldiers, without paiment for their cattle. Therefore he desired that two of the privy Counsell might bee sent over, to take knowledge of such grievances, as the Submitties should present unto them, and to take order for their satisfaction. This goodly submission had all the same issue, as followeth in that of the famous Faith-breaker Tyrone.

Since the last meeting of the Lord Lieftenant with Tyrone at Dundalke, his Lordship had sent over into England Tyrones humble submission, and the Booke of his grievances, and had received authority from her Majesty, to make a finall conclusion with the Rebels, and now at another meeting in Dundalke, on the fifteene of March, the Lord Lieftenant signified to Tyrone, that her

Conditions of pardon for Tyrone.

Majesty by his humble submission had beene induced
againe to receive him to mercy, and to give him and all
the Inhabitants of Tyrone her gracious pardon, upon
1. conditions following. First, that he renew his humble
submission to the Lord Liefetenant on her Majesties
2. behalfe in some publike place. 2. That he promise due
obedience of a Subject, and not to intermeddle with the
Irish, nor his adherents, not onely hereafter, but now,
leaving them to themselves, that they may become humble
suitors for their owne pardons, in which case it is promised
3. them also. 3. That he dispierce his forces, upon receit of
his pardon, and dismisse all strangers, Irish, Scots, or
4. others. 4. That he renounce the name and title of
5. Oneale. 5. Not to intermeddle with her Majesties
Vriaghtes, (so the Irish call the bordering Lords, whom
the Ulster Tyrants have long claimed to be their vassals).
6. 6. That he build up againe, at his owne charges, the Fort
and Bridge of Blackewater, and furnish the souldiers with
7. victuals, as formerly he did. 7. That he deliver to the
Lord Lieftenant the sonnes of Shane Oneale, who were
her Majesties Prisoners; till breaking out they fell into
8. his hands, and were imprisoned by him. 8. To declare
faithfully all intelligence with Spaine, and to leave it.
9. 9. That he receive a Sheriffe for Tyrone, as all other
10. Countries doe. 10. That he put in his eldest sonne for
pledge, and at all times come to the state being called.
11. 11. That he pay a fine in part of satisfaction for his
12. offence, according to her Majesties pleasure. 12. That
he aid no Rebell, nor meddle with the Inhabitants on the
East side of the Ban, yet so as he may enjoy any lands
13. or leases he hath there. 13. That he receive not any
disloyall person, but send such to the chiefe Governour.

Tyrone agreeth to all the Articles save two.

To the first and second Articles Tyrone agreeth, so as time might be given for the other Lords his associates to assemble, that they might herein lay no imputation on him. To the third he agreeth, craving a generall pasport for all such strangers. To the fourth he agreeth. For the fifth, he saith that he desireth nothing of the Vriaghts,

but such duties as they yeelded, since his Grandfathers time. To the sixth he agreeth. The seventh he refuseth, because he had not those prisoners from the State. To the eight he agreeth. To the ninth he agreeth, according [II. i. 24.]
to the statute appointing a gentleman of the Countrey to be chosen, yet craving forbearance for a small time. The tenth he refuseth, for the pledges (in particular). For the eleventh he agreeth to a fine of five hundred Cowes, yet praying the Lord Lieftenant to be a meanes to her Majesty for the remittall thereof. To the twelfth he agreeth. To the last he agreeth, provided that he would deliver no man to the State, who came to him for cause of conscience. Finally, in regard Odonnell and other of Tyrones associates, did not then appeare, and in that respect the Lord Liefetenant had beene pleased to grant him further day till the tenth of Aprill following, he 10. *April.*
promised upon his credit and honour, and by his hand writing, that in case they or any of them should not then appeare, and submit themselves; yet he at that time would make his submission, and humbly crave and receive her Majesties gracious pardon, and goe thorow with all things requisite for a perfect conclusion, and to deliver in two pledges of his faith, to be chosen out of a schedule presented to the Lord Lieftenant, the same to be changed according to the agreement, and if the Mores and Conners, for whom he had obtained protection, should violate this peace, that he would no way give aide or assistance to them. Hereupon at the instance of the Lord Liefetenant, the Lords Justices caused Tyrones pardon to be drawne, and sealed with the great seale of Ireland, bearing Date the eleventh of Aprill, in the fortith yeere of her Majesties Raigne, and of our Lord the yeere 1598.

The pardon sealed.

An. 1598.

Tyrone received his generall pardon, but continuing still his disloyall courses, never pleaded the same, so as upon his above mentioned indictment, in September 1595. you shall find him after outlawed, in the yeere 1600.

The Irish kerne were at the first rude souldiers, so as two or three of them were imployed to discharge one

Peece, and hitherto they have subsisted especially by trecherous tenders of submission, but now they were growne ready in managing their Peeces, and bold to skirmish in bogges and wooddy passages, yea, this yeere and the next following, became so disasterous to the English, and successefull in action to the Irish, as they shaked the English governement in this kingdome, till it tottered, and wanted little of fatall ruine. Tyrone wanted not pretences to frustrate this late treaty, and to returne to his former disloyalty, and the defection of all other submitties depending on him, followed his revolt.

The Irish Kerne growne skillful.

Tyrone's trecherie.

First he sent aid to Phelim mac Feogh, chiefe of the Obirnes, the sonne of Feogh mac Hugh, (killed in Sir William Russels time), to the end he might make the warre in Lemster against the English: And because the English Fort of Blackewater was a great eye sore to him, lying on the cheefe passage into his Countrey, he assembled all his forces, and assaulted the same. But Captaine Thomas Williams, with his company under him, so valiantly repelled the great multitudes of the assaylants, with slaughter of many and the most hardy, attempting to scale the fort, (which was onely a deepe trench or wall of earth, to lodge some one hundred Souldiers), as they utterly discouraged from assayling it, resolved to besiege it a farre off, and knowing they wanted victuals, presumed to get it by famine.

Siege of Blackewater Fort.

This Captaine and his few warders, did with no lesse courage suffer hunger, and having eaten the few horses they had, lived upon hearbes growing in the ditches and wals, suffering all extremities, till the Lord Lieftenant in the moneth of August sent Sir Henry Bagnoll Marshall of Ireland, with the most choice Companies of foote and horse troopes of the English Army, to victuall this Fort, and to raise the Rebels siege. When the English entered the Pace, and thicke woods beyond Armagh, on the East side, Tyrone (with all the Rebels forces assembled to him) pricked forward with rage of envy and setled rancour against the Marshal, assayled the English, and turning his full force against the Marshals person, had the successe to kill him, valiantly fighting among the thickest of the Rebels. Whereupon the English being dismaied with his death, the Rebels obtained a great victory against them: I terme it great, since the English from their first arrivall in that Kingdome, never had received so great an overthrow, as this commonly called, The defeat of Blackewater; Thirteene valiant Captaines, and 1500. common Souldiers, (whereof many were of the old companies which had served in Brittany under Generall Norreys) were slaine in the field. The yeelding of the Fort of Blackwater followed this disaster, when the assaulted guard saw no hope of reliefe: but especially upon messages sent to Captaine Williams, from our broken forces retired to Armagh, professing that all their safetie depended upon his yeelding the Fort into the hands of Tyrone, without which danger Captaine Williams professed, that no want or miserie should have induced him thereunto.

The Marshal killed.

The defeat of Blackewater.

[II. i. 25.]

Shortly after Sir Richard Bingham (above mentioned) late Governour of Connaght, and unworthily disgraced, was sent over to succeede Sir Henrie Bagnoll in the Marshalship of that Kingdome.

Sir Richard Bingham marshal.

By this Victory, the rebels got plenty of Armes and victuals, Tyrone was among the Irish celebrated as the Deliverer of his Country from thraldome, and the combined Traytors on all sides were puffed up with intolerable pride. All Ulster was in Armes, all Connaght revolted, and the Rebels of Lemster swarmed in the English Pale, while the English lay in their Garrisons, so farre from assailing the Rebels, as they rather lived in continuall feare to be surprised by them.

After the last yeeres navall expedition out of England into the Ilands, certaine old Companies of one thousand and fiftie foote, drawne out of the Low Countries, were appointed to Winter in the West parts of England, To these, nine hundred and fiftie new men were added this Summer, and the command of these two thousand Foote, and of one hundred Horse, was given to Sir Samuel

New forces for Ireland.

Bagnol, who was appointed to goe with them to Loughfoyle, in the North of Ireland: but after the defeate of Blackwater, they were countermaunded to goe into Lemster, to strengthen the Queenes Forces in the heart of the Kingdome.

The Captaines.

The old Companies.

Sir Samuel Bagnol, Colonell -	150	1050 Foot.
Captaine John Jephson - -	100	
Captaine Josias Bodley - -	100	
Captaine John Sidney - -	100	
Captaine Foulke Conway - -	100	
Captaine Nicholas Pynner - -	100	
Captaine Edward Blaney - -	100	
Captaine Tobey Calfeild - -	100	
Captaine Austin Heath - -	100	
Captaine Owen Tewder - -	100	

To these were added new men, partly under old Captains, as Captaine Francis Roe, Captaine Charles Egerton, Captaine Ralph Bingley, and partly under new Captaines - } 950 Foot.

Besides, Sir Samuel Bagnol the Colonell had the command of a Troope of Horse new raised } 100 Horse.

Rebellion in Mounster.

After the defeate of Blackwater, Tyrone sent Ony Mac Rory O More, and one Captaine Tyrel (of English race, but a bold and unnaturall enemy to his Countrie, and the English), to trouble the Province of Mounster. Against whom Sir Thomas Norreys Lord President opposed himselfe: but assoone as he upon necessarie occasions had with-drawne his forces to Corke, many of the Mounster men now first about October 1598, brake into rebellion, and joyned themselves with Tyrones said forces, spoyled the Country, burnt the Villages, and puld downe the houses and Castles of the English, against whom (especially the femall sex) they committed all abominable outrages. And now they raised James Fitzthomas as a Geraldine to be Earle of Desmond, (which title had since the warres of Desmond bin suppressed), with condition,

Anno 1598.

that (forsooth) he should be vassall to Oneale. The Mounster Rebellion brake out like a lightning, for in one moneths space, almost all the Irish were in rebellious Armes, and the English were murthered, or stripped and banished. Thus having inflamed Mounster with the fire [II. i. 26.] of Rebellion, and leaving this sedition to be cherished and increased by this new Earle of Desmond, and other Rebels of that Province, the Ulster forces returned backe to Tyrone: The infection which Mounster men had drawne from the corrupted parts in Rebellion, did more and more spread it selfe, so as the old practises long held by the Arch-Traytor Tyrone to induce them to a revolt, now fully attained their wished effect. To the working whereof in the hearts of the seditious, there wanted not many strong motives, as the hatred which the Geraldines bare to those English Undertakers (of whom I formerly spake, in Desmonds warre), which possessed their Ancestors lands; also the incouragement they received by the good successe of the Rebels, and no lesse the hope of pardon upon the worst event. And to speake truth, Munster undertakers above mentioned, were in great part cause of this defection, and of their owne fatall miseries. For whereas they should have built Castles, and brought over Colonies of English, and have admitted no Irish Tenant, but onely English, these and like covenants were in no part performed by them. Of whom the men of best qualitie never came over, but made profit of the land; others brought no more English then their owne Families, and all entertained Irish servants and tenants, which were now the first to betray them. If the covenants had been kept by them, they of themselves might have made two thousand able men, whereas the Lord President could not find above two hundred of English birth among them, when the Rebels first entred the Province. Neither did these gentle Undertakers make any resistance to the Rebels, but left their dwellings, and fled to walled Townes; yea, when there was such danger in flight, as greater could not have been in defending their owne, whereof

Spread of the Rebellion.

The Munster Undertakers.

many of them had wofull experience, being surprised with their wives and children in flight. Among the Mounster Rebels were the Vicount Mountgarret, the Earle of Ormonds neere Kinsman, and the Baron of Cahir, a Butler, and of the Earles Kindred. Both these pretended their discontent and malice against the said Earle, for cause of their revolt. But more dangerous causes were suspected, and except a Royall Force were quickly opposed to the Rebels bold attempts, a generall revolt was feared.

The chiefe Rebels.

Tyrone's double dealings.

May you hold laughter, or will you thinke that Carthage ever bred such a dissembling fædifragous wretch as Tyrone, when you shall reade, that even in the middest of all these garboyles, and whilest in his letters to the King of Spaine he magnified his victories, beseeching him not to beleeve that he would seeke or take any conditions of Peace, and vowing constantly to keepe his faith plighted to that King, yet most impudently he ceased not to entertaine the Lord Lieutenant by letters and messages, with offers of submission. This hee did, but not so submissively as before, for now the Gentleman was growne higher in the instep, as appeared by the insolent conditions he required.

Earle of Essex Lord Lieutenant.

Ireland being in this turbulent State, many thought it could not bee restored but by the powerfull hand of Robert Earle of Essex. This noble Lord had from his youth put himselfe into military actions of greatest moment, so farre as the place he held in Court would permit, and had of late yeeres wonne much honour in some services by Sea and Land, so as he had full possession of a superintendencie over all martiall affaires, and for his noble worth was generally loved, and followed by the Nobilitie and Gentrie. In which respects the Queene knew him fit for this service. He had long been a deare favourite to the Queene, but had of late lien so open to his enemies, as he had given them power to make his imbracing of military courses, and his popular estimation so much suspected of his Soveraigne, as his greatnesse was now judged to depend as much on her Majesties feare of him, as her love to him. And in this respect he might seeme to the Queene most unfit for this service. But surely the Earle was perswaded, that his Honour could not stand without imbracing this Action; and since he affected it, no man durst be his rivall. Besides that, his enemies gladly put forward this his designe, that they might have him at more advantage by his absence from Court. Finally, the vulgar gave ominous acclamations to his enterprise, but the wiser sort, rather wished then hoped happy effects, either to his private or the publike good, in regard of the powerfull enemies hee left in Court, (whence all seconds were to come to him), and of his owne [II. i. 27.] distracted ends (though enclined to the publike good, yet perhaps, in aiming at the speedy end of this warre, and some other particulars, not fully concurring with the same.)

The Earle of Essex's Forces.

The Earle of Essex, when he first purposed to intertaine the managing of the Irish warres, advised and obtained, that two Regiments of old souldiers should be transported out of the Low-Countries into that Kingdome: namely,

The first Regiment.

Sir Charles Pearcy Colonell -	200	1050 Foote.
Captaine Richard Moryson Lieutenant Colonell - - -	150	
Sir Oliver Lambart - - -	150	
Captaine Henrie Masterson -	150	
Captaine Randal Bret - -	150	
Captaine William Turret - -	150	
Captaine Turner - - -	100	

The second Regiment.

Sir Henry Dockwra, Colonel (and Conductor of all) - -	200	950 Foote.
Captaine John Chamberlin Lieutenant Colonel - - -	150	
Captaine Edmond Morgan - -	150	
Captaine Edward Michelburne -	150	
Captaine Walter Floyd - -	150	
Captaine Garret Harvy - -	150	

A.D. 1598.

These Regiments landed in Ireland before the Earles comming over, and were then dispersed by the Earle into divers Regiments of new men, to season them, and to replenish them with sufficient Officers.

The Earles Patent.

The Earles Patent was granted with title of Lord Lieutenant, and with more ample authoritie, then many other Lord Deputies had formerly granted them: for whereas others had power to pardon all Treasons, Felonies, and all offences, except such treasons as touched her Majesties person, her heires, &c, and the counterfeiting of money. This exception was by the Earles importunitie left out, which hee extorted with wise providence, since the Lawyers held all Treasons to touch the Princes person. And whereas other Lord Deputies had power to bestow all Offices excepting the chiefe reserved to the Queenes gift, his Lordship had power to bestow some of the chiefest, and to remove all Officers not holding by Patent, and to suspend such as held by Patent. Besides his Lordship had power in many things, which never had been formerly given to any: as to make Martiall Lawes (he being Lord Martiall of England), and to punish the transgressors. And to let the lands of Tyrone and other Rebels named, to any persons whatsoever, and to their heires Males, reserving due rents to her Majestie. To command the Ships already sent, and to be sent into Ireland, except the Lord Admirall were sent forth to Sea, and commandement were given of joyning the said ships to his Fleete. And lastly to issue the Treasure according to the two establishments, with liberty to alter that which was signed by the Lords in England, with the advise and consent of the Counsell of Ireland, so as he exceeded not the summe of the Establishments. He had an Army assigned him, as great as himselfe required, and such for number and strength, as Ireland had never yet seene.

The Establishment.

The establishment was signed by the Queene the foure and twenty of March, being the last day (after the English account) of the yeere 1598. It contained: first, the pay of the chiefe Officers in the Army: the Lord Lieutenant

Generall ten pound a day. The Lieutenant of the Army three pound a day. The Generall of the Horse fortie shillings a day: the Marshall of the Campe thirtie shillings a day: the Sergeant Major twentie shillings a day: the Lieutenant of the Horse twentie shillings a day: The Quartermaster twentie shillings a day: the Judge Marshall twentie shillings a day: the Auditor Generall thirteene shillings foure pence a day: the Comptroler generall of the victuals ten shillings a day: the Lieutenant of the Ordinance ten shillings a day: the Surveyer sixe shillings eight pence: two Clerkes of Munitions each five shillings a day: foure Corporals of the field sixe shillings eight pence a day a peece: one Commissarie of victuals eight shillings, and three other, each sixe shillings a day: The Carriage Master sixe shilling eight pence a day: and twentie Colonels, each ten shillings a day; whereof the totall in the yeere amounts to thirteene thousand one hundred twentie seven pound sixteene shillings eight pence. [II. i. 28.] *The yeerely totall* 13,127 *li.* 16*s.* 8*d.*

It contained further the pay of thirteene hundred Horse, divided into sixe and twentie Bands, each Band having a Captaine at foure shillings a day, a Lieutenant at two shillings sixe pence a day, a Cornet at two shillings a day, and fiftie horsemen each at fifteene pence a day, whereof the totall in the yeere amounts to one and thirtie thousand foure hundred eight pound five shillings. *The Horse.* 31,408 *li.* 5*s.*

It contained further the pay of sixteene thousand footemen, distributed into one hundred and sixty Bands, each Band having a Captaine at foure shillings a day, a Lieutenant at two shillings a day, an Ensigne eighteene pence a day, two Sergeants, a Drum, and a Surgeon, each at twelve pence a day, and ninetie foure souldiers, and sixe dead paies (allowed to the Captaine) at eight pence each by the day; whereof the totall in the yeere amounts to two hundred twenty eight thousand two hundred fortie sixe pound thirteene shillings foure pence. *The footemen.* 228,246 *li.* 13*s.* 4*d.*

Lastly, it contained an extraordinarie supply of six thousand pound to be allowed by concordatum, for Spies,

Guides, Messengers, Barkes hiring, keeping of Prisoners, buildings, reparations, rewardes, and like charges; the totall of the Establishment by the yeere amounts to two hundred seventy seven thousand seven hundred eighty two pound fifteene shillings.

Charges not contained in the Establishment.

Besides her Majesty was at great charge for many things not contained in the establishment as followeth. First for Officers generall. The Lord Lieftenant for his ordinary entertainement by the yeere, one thousand three hundreth pound. His Lordships Band of Horse by the yeere, one thousand five hundred thirteene pound two shillings six pence. His Lordships fifty footmen by the yeere, six hundred eight pound sixe shillings eight pence. Both these bands of horse and foot being not of the Army, I take to be allowed him for his followers, and the servants in his family, besides his company of horse and foot in the Army; the Treasurer at warres by the yeere sixe hundred eight and thirty pound fifteene shillings. The Marshall of the Army by the yeere one hundred foure pound eighteene shillings and nine pence. The Master of the Ordinance for himselfe by the yeere foure hundred fifty pound three shillings foure pence, and for Clerkes, Gunners, and Ministers of the Ordinance by the yeere, foure hundred fifty nine pound five shillings ten pence. The Muster-Master generall by the yeere two hundred nine pound seventeene shillings six pence.

Newly erected officers.

Secondly for chiefe Officers newly erected. The Governour of Loghfoyle, by the yeere three hundred sixty five pound. The Governour of Caricfergus by the yeere one hundred eighty two pound ten shillings. The Governour of Dundalke as much. The Commander of the Forces at Rathdrum and Wickelow as much. The Commander of the Forces in Ophaly as much. The Commander of the Forces at Cavan as much.

These payments being made in sterling money, doe amount to sixe thousand five hundred fourescore ten pound nineteene shillings seven pence.

Observe that all these above named Officers (excepting

the Muster-Master) as also the Lieftenant of the Army, The Generall of the Horse, The Serjant Major, And likewise the Governours of Provinces and Garrisons, have all beside their fees, the command of a band of Horse, or of Foot, or of both. Thirdly for Officers in the foure Courts and certaine Pattentees: In the Exchequer the Earle of Ormond Lord Treasurer of Ireland hath for his fee, forty pound. The Treasurer at warres, threescore sixe pounds thirteene shillings and foure pence. The chiefe Baron threescore and eleven pound ten shillings, and in augmentation fourescore eight pound seventeene shillings and nine pence. The Chancellor foureteene pound. The second Baron foure and thirty pound. The Auditor Generall two hundred pound. The Surveyor Generall fourescore pound. The Remembrancer forty pound. The Serjant at Law seventeene pound sixe shillings and eight pence. The Attourney Generall one hundred forty nine pound sixe shillings eight pence. The Solicitor one hundred forty nine pound sixe shillings eight pence. The Escheator six pound thirteene shillings and foure pence. The second Remembrancer ten pound ten shillings. The chiefe Ingrosser fourteene pound. The second Ingrosser nine pound sixe shillings and eight pence. The chiefe Chamberlaine thirteene pound six shillings and eight pence. The second Chamberlaine sixe pound thirteene shillings and foure pence. The Clerke of the first fruits ten pound. The keeper of the Records thirteene pound sixe shillings and eight pence. The Usher of the Court three pound sixe shillings and eight pence. The Clerke of the Common Pleas three pound sixe shillings eight pence. The Transcriptor fifty three shillings foure pence. The Deputy Auditor eleven pound. The Vicetreasurers Deputy eleven pound. The Somoniter one hundred sixe shillings eight pence. The Marshall of the Court one hundred sixe shillings eight pence. A Messenger foure and forty shillings five pence farthing. Two Pursivants each eighteene pound five shillings fee; In the Kings Bench the chiefe Justice foure hundred

Officers in the foure Courts and Pattentees.

The Exchequer.

[II. i. 29.]

The King's Bench.

pound. The second Justice one hundred three and thirty pound sixe shillings eight pence. The Clerke of the Crowne ten pound.

The Common Pleas.

In the Common Pleas the chiefe Justice threescore seven pound ten shillings, and in augmentation fourescore eight pound seventeene shillings nine pence farthing. The second Justice forty pound, and in augmentation twenty pound. The Protonotor ten pound. In the Chauncery.

The Chauncery.

The Lord Chauncellor foure hundred and fifteene pound sixe shillings eight pence. The Master of the Roles fifty pound, and in augmentation fourescore eight pound seventeene shillings nine pence. Two Ministers each seven & twenty pound thirteen shillings foure pence. The Clerke of the Crowne sixe pound thirteene shillings foure pence, and in augmentation six & twenty pound thirteene shillings foure pence. The Clerke of the Hamper foureteene pound. Divers Officers in the Starre-chamber sixe and fifty pound thirteene shillings foure pence. Divers Ministers of the Ordinance holding by Patent one hundred thirty five pound thirteene shillings five pence farthing. The Constable of the Castle of Dublyn and his warders with divers other Constables and Porters three hundred thirty five pound thirteene shillings two pence farthing.

Officers of the State.

For Officers of the State. The Secretary one hundred sixe pound thirteene shillings foure pence. The Clerke of the Counsell threescore and two pound thirteene shillings foure pence. The Surveyer of the victuals one hundred forty three pound sixe shillings eight pence. The King at Armes thirty five pound sixe shillings eight pence. The Serjant at Armes eighteene pound two shillings two pence halfe penny farthing. The Pursivant at Armes thirteene pound sixe shillings eight pence. The Irish Interpreter seven and twenty pound seven shillings sixe pence. Officers about the Custome forty pound. For Creation money to Noble men; the Earle of Ormond thirty pound. The Earle of Kildare twenty pound. The Earle of Clanrickard forty pound. The Earle of

Thomond twenty pound. The Baron of Kaber fifteene pound. Divers annates & procurations two hundred fourescore & nineteene pound nineteene shillings three pence halfe penny. For Parchment, Paper, Inke, Bagges, &c. in the Exchequer, Kings Bench, and Common Pleas, two hundred fourescore two pound, ten shillings eight pence: For other payments by warrant two hundred sixe and twenty pound two shillings foure pence. In the County of Wexford, the Justice of the liberties twenty pound. The Senescall five & twenty pound. The Receiver twenty pound. The Marshall forty shillings.

The totall of these being paid in Irish mony, is foure thousand six hundred fifteene pound thirteene shillings halfe penny; which reduced to sterling money, makes three thousand foure hundred threescore one pound thirteen shillings 9 pence.

Officers in Lemster.

Fourthly for Officers in Lemster. The Lieftenant of the Queens County one hundred twenty one pound thirteene shillings foure pence. The Provost Marshall of the Army threescore and seventeene pound eleven shillings three pence. The Provost Marshall of Lemster one [II. i. 30.] hundred and two pound thirteene shillings one penny halfe penny. These paid in sterling money, amount to three hundred one pound sixteene shillings eight pence halfe penny.

Officers in Mounster.

Fifthly, for Officers in Mounster, the Lord President one hundred three and thirty pound sixe shillings eight pence. His diet with the Counsell allowed at his table, five hundred twenty pound. His Retinue of twenty foot with the Officers, and of thirty Horse, eight hundred and three pound. The chiefe Justice one hundred pound. The second Justice threescore sixe pound thirteene shillings foure pence. The Queenes Attourney thirteene pound sixe shillings eight pence. The Clerke of the Councell twenty pound. The Clerke of the Crowne twenty pound. The Serjant at Armes twenty pound. The Provost Marshall two hundred five and fifty pound ten shillings. The totall being paid in sterling mony, is one thousand nine hundred fifty one pound sixteene shillings eight pence.

Officers in Connaght.

Sixtly, for Officers in Connaght, the chiefe Commissioner (or Governour) one hundred pound: his diet with the Counsel at his table, one hundred fourescore two pound ten shillings. An allowance to himselfe forty pound. The Justice one hundred pound. The Queenes Attourney twenty pound. The Clarke of the Crowne twenty pound. The Clarke of the Counsell twenty pound. The Serjant at Armes twenty pound, the Provost Marshall two hundred threescore and foure pound, twelve shillings sixe pence. An increase of pay to the present chiefe Commissioner, two hundred fourescore two pound ten shillings.

The totall being paid in sterling money, is nine hundred forty nine li. twelve s. sixe d.

Irish Kerne.

Seventhly, certaine bands of Irish kerne, five hundred threescore nineteene pound eight shillings nine pence.

Warders.

Eightly, for warders in severall Provinces, three thousand five hundred threescore and seventeene pound two pence halfe penny.

Commissaries of Musters.

Ninthly, for Commissaries of Musters, five hundred threescore seventeene pound eighteene shillings foure pence.

Pensioners.

Tenthly, Pensioners of all sorts, as well recorded in the Office of Musters, as those holding by Patent, and recorded with the Auditor, some holding for tearme of yeers, some during life, some during good behaviour, some during pleasure, three thousand two hundred forty nine l. nine d.

Almes-men.

Lastly, Almes-men, fourescore eight l. nineteene s. foure d. ob.

The totall of the above named charge not contained in the establishment, is twenty one thousand three hundred twenty eight l. eight s. seven d. ob.

Adde to this the establishment, two hundred threescore seventeene thousand seven hundred fourescore two pound, fifteene shillings.

The totall of the yeerely charge, is two hundred fourescore and nineteene thousand, one hundred eleven pound three s. seven d. ob. *The totall of the yeerely charge.*

To which if you adde the great charge of all sorts of Munitions, with the like extraordinary expences, and doe also consider that the thirteene hundred Horse, and sixeteene thousand Foot, by new supplies were made fully twenty thousand: the heavy burthen of this yeeres warre in Ireland will appeare.

The Earle of Essex had in speciall charge from the Queene, to bend all his forces against the chiefe Traitor Tyrone, (and the Ulster Rebels his confederates), and withall to plant Garrisons at Loughfoyle and Balishannon, to the end they might at the same time assayle him (and them) at the backe (both which courses his Lordship had in all counsels perswaded, and often taxed the omissions of them). Thus with happy acclamations of the people (who to so worthy a Generall in the head of so strong an Army, did ominate nothing but victory and triumphes), yet with a Sunne-shine thunder happening (as Master Camden notes for an ominous ill token): This noble Lord (accompanied with the flower of the English Gentry, and conducted on his way with many of the Nobility), tooke his journy from London towards Ireland, in the end of the Moneth of March, and the beginning of the yeere 1599, and though crossed with tempestuous weather, (wherein the Earle of Kildare, and some gallant gentlemen accompanying him in a little barke, chosen of purpose for speed, were unfortunately cast away), landed within few dayes at Dublin, where according to the manner of other Governours, he received the Sword. *Special charge to the Earle of Essex.* *An. 1599.* [II. i. 31.]

Upon his Lordships demaund to bee advertised from the Counsell of the present state of that Kingdome, a Collection thereof, debated and agreed upon in Counsell, and signed by the Counsellers, was presented to his Lordship the seventeenth of Aprill, being to this effect. First, for the Province of Lemster, in the Countie of Dublin, all the Mountainers were in actuall rebellion, *The present state of Ireland.* *Dublin.*

The present State of Ireland. as Phelim Mac Feagh, and his brother Redmond, with their Sept (or name) of the Obyrns, and Phelim Mac Feagh with his Sept of the Otooles, and Walter Mac Edmond chiefe of the Galloglasses, with his Sept of Mac Donnels; onely two Castles, Newcastle and Wickloe, Sir Henrie Harrington held for the Queene, and all the rest of the Countrie continued loyall. The Rebels thereof were in number foure hundred eightie Foot, and twentie Horse. *Kildare.* In the County of Kildare James Fitz-pierce a Geraldine, two Geraldines, base brothers to the late Earle of Kildare, some of the Delahides, some of the Odempsies, and some of the Eustaces (of which Sept was the late Vicount Baltinglasse attainted), all in action of Rebellion, were in number two hundred and twentie Foote, and thirtie Horse. All the rest of the Countrie being wasted by the Rebels, yet held for the Queene. *Carlogh.* In the County of Carlogh, being little and all wasted, the Castles of Carlogh and Laughline, and her Majesties house of Fernes, held by the Queenes Wardes, and sixe Castles belonging to the Earle of Ormond, held for the Queene; but the Cavanaghs, and Keytons, were in Rebellion. *Wexford.* In the County of Wexford being wasted, all the Castles held for the Queene, and Sir Thomas Calclough, Sir Richard Masterson, and Sir Dudly Loftus, the onely English there inhabiting, held for the Queene. But Donnel Spaniagh (alias Cavanagh) with all that Sept, the Omorroghs, Mac ony More, all the Kinsellaghes, Dermot Mac Morice, and divers others with their followers, were all in rebellion, and in those two Counties the Rebels were in number seven hundred and fiftie Foote, and fiftie Horse. In the County of Leax, called the *Queenes Countie.* Queenes Countie, lately all English, now usurped by the Rebels Owny Mac Rowry Omore, and all the Sept of O Mores, and the chiefe of the Galloglasses in that County, of the Sept of Mac Donnel, the Sept of O Dempsies (except Sir Terence O Dempsey) the Sept of O doynes (except Teig Oge O Doyne), were al in rebellion, and the base son of the Earle of Kildare, a

Geraldine, lately came in upon protection. The Rebels were in number five hundred seventie Foote, and thirty Horse. Master Hartpol, Master Bowen, and Master Pygot, were the onely English Inhabitants, by whom and some others, certaine Castles were kept for the Queene, besides the Fort of Mariaborough kept by the Queenes Garrison. In the Countie of Ophalye, called (of Phillip King of England) the Kings County, lately English, the Fort of Phillipstowne was kept by an English Garrison, Sir George Colley, Sir Henrie Warren, Mast. John Moore, and Mast. Phillips, held their Castles for the Queene, the rest of the Castles were kept by the sept of the Oconners then rebels, and al the land was wasted, the Sept of the Omollyes and Odonners were likewise in rebellion, and they were all in number foure hundred sixtie and eight Foot, and twelve Horse. In the County of Kilkenny, the Vicount of Mountgaret, a Butler, of the Earle of Ormonds Family, and sonne in Law to Tyrone, was in rebellion, with his brethren, and with some of his sonnes, and with his followers, being in number one hundred and thirty Foote, and twentie Horse, and held the Castles of Balliragge and Colekil; the rest of the Castles, and the whole County were held by the Earle of Ormond for the Queene. In the County of Meath, the sonne and heire of Sir William Nugent was in rebellion, and the Countie lying in the heart of the Pale, was greatly wasted by the Ulster Rebels, and many Castles lay waste without inhabitants, but no Rebels possed either Towne or Castle therein. In the County of Westmeath, lying for the most part waste; the Omollaughlines, and the Magoghegines, many of the Nugents, and the Geraldines were in rebellion, being in number 140 Foot, and twentie Horse, besides Captaine Tyrel (a Rebel of English race), who had of Ulster men and other strangers two hundred Foote. In the County of Lowthe, Sir Edward Moore and Sir Francis Stafford were the only English house-keepers, al the lands were wasted by the Ulster rebels; but the Lord of Lowthe, [II i. 32.]

The present state of Ireland.

Kings County.

Kilkenny.

Meath.

Westmeath.

Lowthe.

The present state of Ireland.

an English-Irish Barron, and all the Townes and Castles stood firme for the Queene. In the County of Lonford, all the Ofarrols were in rebellion, except two chiefe men of that Family, and the Castle of Longford was held by an English Warde, and the Rebels were in number one hundred and twenty Foot. The whole number of the Rebels in this Province of Lemster was three thousand fortie and eight Foote, and one hundred eighty two Horse.

Lonford.

The Province of Ulster.

Secondly, for the Province of Ulster (consisting all of Irish Septs, except the Scots possessing the Rowt and Clinnes), those of Lecale, and the little Ardes held for the Queene, but overawed by Tyrone, were forced to give way to him to tirannize in their Countries. Dundalke the frontier Towne betweene the Pale and Ulster, and Knockfergus (or Carickfergus) a frontier Towne towards Scotland, were kept by English Garrisons, as likewise the Newry, Carlingford, Greene Castle, and Narrow water (all neare Dundalke), and the Castle of Ballinecargie in the Brenny, the rest were all in Rebellion. Neale Brian Fertough in the upper Clandeboyes, had in number eighty Foote and thirtie Horse. Shane Mac Brian in the lower Clandeboyes had eighty foote and fiftie Horse. The Whites Countrie (or the Duffery) had twentie Foote. Mac Arten and Sleaght Mac Oneale had one hundred foote, and twentie horse. Mac Rorye Captaine of Kilwarlin had sixtie foote, and ten horse. Cormack Mac Oneale, Captaine of Kilultogh had sixtie foote and ten horse. Hugh Mac Murtagh beyond the Min water had fortie foote. Shane Mac Brian Carogh upon the Ban side, had fiftie foote, ten horse. Sir James Mac Surleyboy, and his Scots, possessing the Rowt and the seven Glynnes, had foure hundred foote, and one hundred horse. The Iland of Magee, belonging to the Earle of Essex, was altogether waste. Mac Guire in Fermannagh had sixe hundred foot, one hundred horse. Mac Mahowne in Monaghan, and Ever Mac Coolye in the Ferney, and others of that name in Clankarvil, had five hundred foote, one hundred and sixtie horse. The Oreylyes in the Brenny (or the County of Cavan) had eight hundred foot, two hundred horse. Ocane in his Countrie had five hundred foote, two hundred horse. Sir Art Oneale in Sleught Art had three hundred foot, sixtie horse. Henry Oge in his Countrie had two hundred foot, and fortie horse. Turlough Mac Henrie Oneale in the Fues, had three hundred foote, sixty horse. Ohagan in his Countrie had one hundred foote, thirtie horse. Oquin in his Countrie eightie foote, twentie horse. The Donolaghes in their Countrie one hundred foote, sixtie horse. Mac Can in Clancan one hundred foote, twelve horse. Tyrone the Arch-traytor in Tyrone seven hundred foot 200 horse. Carmack Mac Baron his brother, in his Countrie had three hundred foot and sixtie horse. Mac Gennis in Yuogh (or Mac Gennis Countrie) had two hundred foot, fortie horse. In Tyrconnel Odonnels Country, Sir John Odogherty for his Countrie had three hundred foot, and fortie horse. Odonnels sonne in the Conologhs Countrie one hundred and fiftie foote, and fiftie horse. Mac Swine for his Countrie five hundred foote, and thirtie horse. Oboyle for his Countrie one hundred foot and twenty horse. O Donnel himselfe in the County of Donnegal two hundred foote, sixtie horse. O Gallohore for his Countrie (in which his chiefe house is Ballashannon) had two hundred foote, sixtie horse. Sleught Rorie for his Countrie one hundred foote, and fiftie horse. The forces of the Rebels in Ulster are in all one thousand seven hundred and two horse, and seven thousand two hundred and twentie foote.

The present state of Ireland.

The Province of Ulster.

Thirdly, for the Province of Mounster, In the County of Tipperary. The Lord Baron of Cahir a Butler, with his brother and followers, had three hundred foote twelve horse. Edmond Fitzgibbon called the White Knight (this nickname given to one for his grey heares, comming as hereditarie to his posteritie), in his Country foure hundred foote, thirtie horse. Richard Pursell Baron of

The Province of Mounster.

Tipperary.

The present state of Ireland. Loughwey 200 foot, 6 horse. The Omulrians three hundred foote, sixe horse. The Omaighirs sixtie foote, three horse. The Okennydayes five hundred foot, thirty horse. The Burkes in the Lord Burkes Countrie, two hundred foote, foure horse. *Corke.* In the County of Corke, James Fitz thomas, the supposed Earle of Desmond, two hundred and fifty foote, thirtie horse. The Lord of Dowallough two hundred foote, eight horse. Barry Oge, and the Lord Barryes brother in the Muskerye, one hundred and twentie foote, three horse. Davy Burke in [II. i. 33.] the Carbrye five hundred foote. *Limrick.* In the County of Limrick, Pierce Lacy, with divers septs, had three hundred foote, and fifteene horse. *Kerrie.* In the County of Kerrie, the Lord Fitz Morrice, Thomas Oge, John Delahyde, with others, five hundred foote, thirtie horse. *County of Desmond.* In the County of Desmond, called Oswyllivan Beare, and Oswillivan Mores Countrie, Dermod Mac Owen (usurping the name of Mac Arty Moore) had five hundred foote, six horse. *Waterford.* In the County of Waterford, the Rebels had two hundred foote, and ten horse. In all the Rebels of this Province of Mounster were strong five thousand thirtie foote, and two hundred fortie two horse. This number the Earle of Ormond judged to bee the least, and thought the horse one hundred more in number. Observe, that all the Cities and Port-townes, and almost all the Castles in this Province of Mounster, and many great Lords and Gentlemen, held for the Queene.

Connaught. Fourthly and lastly, for the Province of Connaught; *Roscommen.* In the County of Roscommen, the Castles of Roscommen, Athlone, Tulske, Boyle, and Ballineslawe, were kept at her Majesties charge, and the Rebels of divers septs had five hundred foote, sixtie horse. *Sligo.* In the County of Sligo, O Conner Sligo, and divers septs of rebels, had three hundred foot, and thirtie horse, and onely the Castle of Calony held for the Queene. *Leytrim.* Orworke in Leytrim (called Ororkes Countrie) had sixe hundred foote, sixtie horse, and not any Castle was kept for the Queene. *Maio.* In the County of Maio, some three Castles lately held for the Queene, but were thought to be rendred up to Mac William, who with his followers had sixe hundred foot, sixtie horse. In the County of Galloway, the towne of Galloway, of Athenrie, and the Castle of Milech, held for the Queene, but many septs of the Country were in rebellion, who had some foure hundred ninetie foote. In the County of Clare, the Earle of Thomonds brother (who first was upon suspition committed to prison by the said Earle, and after released), with the Obryans, and Mac Marres, and other septs, had sixe hundred foote, fiftie horse, and not one Castle was there kept for the Queene. In all, the rebels of this Province of Connaught were strong three thousand and seventie foote, two hundred and twentie horse. And the Rebels in all the foure Provinces were strong eighteene thousand two hundred fortie sixe foote, and two thousand three hundred forty sixe horse.

The present state of Ireland.

Galloway.

Clare.

The Earle of Essex in the moneth of Aprill dispatched two letters to the Lords in England; by the first whereof he advertised them of this strength of the rebels; and by the second, that Tyrone had in counsell resolved, first, to hearten his confederates, and strengthen them in their dependency on his protection; then to make two heads against the Queenes forces, the one in Ulster, of some sixe thousand horse and foote, under his owne commaund, and the other in Connaght of some foure thousand horse and foote under O donnells commaund: and further advertised their Lordships, that many in Mounster had taken a solemne oath at a publike Crosse in that Province, to be stedfast in their rebellion. And that no traytor sought pardon, but used such insolent behaviour, as might well shew they had no such thought. That the mindes of the very subjects were so alienated from the English, as well for Religion as Governement, as some who could bring one hundred horse, and three hundred foote into the field upon private revenge, would protest not to be able to serve the State with sixe horse or foote. That every active borderer had a solliciter with the Rebels,

Letters from the Earle of Essex.

and almost every one of the greatest in the State had some Rebell or other to his Client. Concluding, that small or no assistance could be promised from the Irish, so as howsoever the Queenes Army was great, yet he durst boldly say, that the playster would doe no more then cover the wound.

After few dayes of rest, good part of the English forces being drawne together, this noble Lord Lieutenant gave entrance to his first actions, from which the progresse commonly receiveth a kind of ominous luster or staine. And therein hee attempted not the head of the Rebellion, according to his own advise in England, and the Queens expresse commaund, but was induced by some of the Counsell in that State, aiming at their owne private interest, more then the publike good, to leade his forces against some few Rebels in Mounster, where he tooke the Castle of Cahir, belonging to Edward Butler, Baron of Cahir, and making a great prey of the rebels cattle
[II. i. 34.] in those parts, he cast the terror of his forces on the weakest enemies, whom he scattered and constrained to flie into Woods and Mountaines, to hide themselves.

Two ships from Spaine.

The fifteenth of June, while the Lord Lieutenant was yet in this Mounster journey, he received advertisement from a Captaine, whom he had imployed by sea into the North, to spie out Tyrones actions, that two ships lately come from Spaine, had put confidence in Tyrone, who went from Dungannon to Loughfoyle about that businesse, but they brought onely munition, not any treasure. That Tyrone had given forces to Brian Mac Art, sonne to Art Mac Baron, that hee might take pledges, and watch over Neale Mac Brian, whom he suspected, and had charged Mac Genis to doe the like over Mac Cartan, also suspected by him, so as there was no possibilitie to parley with them, according to the instructions given by his Lordship. That Tyrone kept his great pledges, Shane Oneales sonnes, in an Iland, within a strong fastnesse, but as yet had neither gathered at home, nor received from forraine parts any treasure. That both Tyrone and

O donnel had their Agents in the out Iles of Scotland, to sollicite the Redshankes to assist them for pay. That the King of Spaine had promised them aide of men, which they would not have landed in Ulster, but in some Port of Mounster, or at Galloway in Connaght. That Scots daily carried Munition to them, which trafficke might be hindred by two Gallies with Oares, but no ship using sayles could stop their passage. That the grosse of the Northerne Rebels in Ulster, and part of Connaght drawne together, would be nine thousand foote, and one thousand foure hundred horse. That they were confident to draw the warre into such a length, as should be unsupportable to the State of England. To which end Odonnel had hired a Masse of Redshankes, who were to be cessed in Connaght and Mounster, because Tyrone, having deadly fewde with some of the chiefe Leaders, durst not trust them in Ulster. Besides that upon arrivall of forraine treasure, great multitudes of those Scots were like to flocke unto them. And to the same end Tyrone had made strong fastnesses or intrenchments, aswell upon the passages of Loughfoyle and Ballishanon, (where he left forces to resist the English Garrisons to be sent thither), as at the Blackewater, and Ballinemoyree, himselfe purposing to meet the English Army in the woods of Ballinemoyree, betweene Dundalke and the Newry, where he hoped to make some of the best to drop, and after to fall backe at his pleasure to like fights of advantage, which he had prepared at the Blackewater. So as the onely meanes suddenly to breake those rebels, was to hier 4000. Redshankes, to breake in upon them, (by advantage of their rowing boates) into the heart of Tyrone, betweene these intrenchments, where they might easily take from him all his wealth, consisting in cattell, and there intrench themselves, and in despite of all Tyrones forces, be supplied with all necessaries from the Scottish Ilands. And indeed to this purpose, the Lord Bourgh, if he had not beene prevented by sudden death, had contracted with those Scots, promising

Aide promised by the King of Spaine.

Tyrone's fastnesses.

Meanes to breake the rebels.

Pay to the Scots. 4000. men for the first moneths pay, 1200. pound, the chiefe Leader a Colonels pay, and certaine Captaines the pay of a Captaine of 100, men. After which moneth, their Septs were to be cessed for their victuals, upon such countreys, as they must have fought with the Rebels for every morsell: Namely, the sons of Agnus mac Connell with their Sept, upon the Route, the Glinnes, and North Clandeboy, who for the pretence they had to inherite that Countrey, would prosecute James mac Surley, the possesser thereof to the uttermost. Donnel Grome and his Sept, uppon Yuogh, being Mac Genis his Countrey. The Mac Lanes and their Sept, upon the South Clandeboy, and the Duffren. All which Septs were to put in pledges to the Lord Bourgh, not to prey any under the Queenes protection, and to depart the Kingdome, when his Lordship should please no longer to make use of their service.

The five and twenty of June, during the said Mounster journey, the Lord Liefetenant wrote unto the Queene this Letter following.

Letter from the Lord Liefetenant to the Queene. WHen this shall come to your Majesties hands, I know not; but whensoever it hath that Honour, give it leave (I humbly beseech your Majesty) to tell you, that having now passed through the Provinces of Lemster and Mounster, and been uppon the Frontire of Connaght, (where the Governour and the chiefe of the
[II i. 35.] Province were with me); I dare begin to give your Majesty some advertisement of the state of this Kingdome, not as before by heare-say, but as I beheld it with mine owne eyes. The people in generall have able bodies by nature, and have gotten by custome ready use of armes, and by their late successes boldnes to fight with your Majesties troopes. In their pride they value no man but themselves, in their affections they love nothing but idlenesse and licentiousnesse, in their rebellion they have no other end, but to shake off the yoake of obedience to your Majesty, and to root out all remembrance of the

English Nation in this Kingdome. I say this of the people in generall, for I find not onely the greater part thus affected, but that it is a generall quarrell of the Irish, and they who doe not professe it, are either so few, or so false, that there is no accompt to be made of them. The Irish Nobility and Lords of Countreys, doe not onely in their hearts affect this plausible quarrell, and are divided from us in religion, but have an especiall quarrell to the English governement, because it limitteth and tieth them, who ever have beene, and ever would be as absolute Tyrants, as any are under the Sunne. The Townes, being inhabited by men of the same religion and birth as the rest, are so carried away with the love of gaine, that for it, they will furnish the rebels with all things that may arme them, or inable them against the State, or against themselves. The wealth of the Kingdome, which consisteth in cattle, oate-meale, and other victuals, is almost all in the Rebels hands, who in every Province, till my comming, have beene Masters of the field. The expectation of all these Rebels is very present, and very confident, that Spaine will either so invade your Majesty, that you shall have no leisure to prosecute them here, or so succour them, that they will get most of the Townes into their hands, ere your Majesty shall relieve and reinforce your Army. So that now if your Majesty resolve to subdue these Rebels by force, they are so many, and so framed to be Souldiers, that the warre of force will be great, costly, and long. If your Majesty will seeke to breake them by factions amongst themselves, they are covetous and mercinary, and must be purchased, and their Jesuites and practising Priests, must be hunted out and taken from them, which now doe sodder them so fast, and so close together. If your Majesty will have a strong party in the Irish Nobility, and make use of them, you must hide from them all purpose of establishing English governement, till the strength of the Irish be so broken, that they shall see no safety but in your Majesties protection. If your Majesty will be assured

The state of the Kingdome.

Spaine.

Rebels covetous and mercinary.

Worth of the Townes. of the possession of your Townes, and keepe them from supplying the wants of the Rebels, you must have garrisons brought into them, able to command them, and make it a capital offence for any Merchant in Ireland, to trade with the Rebels, or buy or sell any armes or munition whatsoever. For your good subjects may have for their mony out of your Majesties store, that which shall be appointed by order, and may serve for their necessary defence, whereas if once they be tradable, the Rebels will give such extreme and excessive prices, that they will never bee kept from them. If your Majesty will secure this your Realme from the danger of invasion, *Defence of the Country.* assoone as those which direct & mannage your Majesties intelligences, give notice of the preparations and readinesse of the enemy, you must be aswell armed, and provided for your defence: which provision, consists in having forces upon the Coast, inroled and trained, in having Magazines of victuall in your Majesties West and North-west parts, ready to be transported; and in having ships both of warre and transportation, which may carry and waft them both, upon the first allarum of a discent. The enroling and training of your subjects, is no charge to your Majesties owne cofers: The pro- *Magazines.* viding of Magazines, will never be any losse, for in using them, you may save a Kingdome, and if you use them not, you may have your old store sold, and (if it be well handled) to your Majesties profit. The arming of your Majesties ships, when you heare your enemy armes to the Sea, is agreeable to your owne provident and Princely courses, and to the pollicy of all Princes and states of the World. But to returne to Ireland againe, as I have shewed your Majesty the dangers and disadvantages, which your servants and Ministers here shall and doe meete withall, in this great worke of reducing this Kingdome. So I will now (as well as I can) represent to your Majestie your strengths and advantages. First, [II i. 36.] these Rebels are neither able to force any walled Towne, Castle, or House of strength, nor to keepe any that they get, so that while your Majesty keeps your Army in strength and vigor, you are undoubtedly Mistresse of all townes and holds whatsoever. By which meanes (if your Majesty have good Ministers) all the wealth of the Land shall be drawne into the hands of your subjects; your soldiers in the winter shall be easefully lodged, & readily supplied of any wants, and we that command your Majesties forces, may make the warre offensive and defensive, may fight and be in safety, as occasion is offered. Secondly, your Majesties Horsemen, are so incomparably better then the rebels, and their foot are so unwilling to fight in battell or grosse, (howsoever they be desirous to skirmish and fight loose); that your Majesty may be alwaies Mistress of the champion Countries, which are the best parts of this Kingdome. Thirdly, your Majesty victualling your Army out of England, and with your Garrisons burning and spoyling the Countrey in all places, shall starve the Rebell in one yeere, because no place els can supply them. Fourthly, since no warre can be made without Munition, and munition this Rebell cannot have, but from Spayne, Scotland, or your owne Townes here, if your Majesty will still continue your Ships and Pinaces upon the Coast, and be pleased to send a Printed Proclamation, that upon paine of death no Merchant, Townes-man, or other Subject, doe trafficke with the Rebell, or buy or sell in any sort any kinde of Munition or Armes, I doubt not, but in short time I shall make them bankerout of their old store, and I hope our Seamen will keepe them from receiving any new. Fifthly, your Majesty hath a rich store of gallant Colonels, Captaines, and Gentlemen of quality, whose example and execution is of more use, then all the rest of your troopes; whereas the men of best qualitie among the rebels, which are their Leaders, and their horsemen, dare never put themselves to any hazard, but send their Kerne, and their hirelings to fight with your Majesties Troopes; so that although their common souldiers are too hard for our new men, yet are they not able to stand before such

1. The Rebels cannot take the Townes.

2. Rebels poore horsemen.

3. Victualling.

4. Munition.

5. Gallant Leaders.

gallant men as will charge them. Sixthly, your Majesties Commanders being advised and exercised, know al advantages, and by the strength of their order, will in all great fights beate the rebels. For they neither march, nor lodge, nor fight in order, but only by the benefit of their footmanship, can come on, and goe off at their pleasure, which makes them attend a whole day, still skirmishing, and never ingaging themselves. So that it hath been ever the fault and weakenesse of your Majestis Leaders, whensoever you have received any blow. For the rebels doe but watch and attend upon all grosse oversights. Now if it please your Majestie to compare your advantages and disadvantages together, you shall finde that though these Rebels are more in number then your Majesties Army, and have (though I doe unwillingly confesse it) better bodies, and perfecter use of their Armes, then those men which your Majestie sends over; yet your Majestie, commanding the walled Townes, Holdes, and Champion Countries, and having a brave Nobilitie and Gentry, a better Discipline, and stronger order then they, and such means to keep from them the maintenance of their life, and to waste the Countrie, which should nourish them, your Majestie may promise your selfe, that this action will (in the end) be successefull, though costly, and that your Victorie will be certaine, though many of us your honest servants must sacrifice our selves in the quarrell, and that this Kingdome will be reduced, though it will aske (besides cost) a great deale of care, industry, and time. But why doe I talke of victorie, or of successe? is it not knowne, that from England I receive nothing but discomforts and soules wounds? Is it not spoken in the Army, that your Majesties favor is diverted from me, and that alreadie you do boad il both to me and it? Is it not beleeved by the Rebels, that those whom you favour most, doe more hate me out of faction, then them out of dutie or conscience? Is it not lamented of your Majesties faithfullest subjects both there and here, that a Cobham, or a Raleigh (I will forbeare others for

6. Orderly Commanders.

The Lord Liefetenant's complaint.

their places sake) should have such credit and favour with your Majestie, when they wish the ill successe of your Majesties most important action, the decay of your greatest strength, and the destruction of your faithfullest servants? Yes, yes, I see both my owne destiny, and your Majesties decree, and doe willingly imbrace the one, and obey the other. Let me honestly and zealously end [II. i. 37.] a wearisome life, let others live in deceitfull and unconstant pleasure; let me beare the brunt, and die meritoriously; let others achive and finish the worke, and live to erect Trophies. But my prayer shall be, that when my Soveraigne looseth mee, her Army may not loose courage, or this Kingdome want phisicke, or her dearest Selfe misse Essex, and then I can never goe in a better time, nor in a fairer way. Till then, I protest before God and his Angels, that I am a true Votarie, that is sequestred from all things but my duty and my charge; I performe the uttermost of my bodies, mindes and fortunes abilitie, and more should, but that a constant care and labor agrees not with an inconstant health, in an unwholsome and uncertaine clymate. This is the hand of him, that did live your dearest, and will die,

Your Majesties faithfullest servant
Essex.

Towards the end of July his Lord^P. brought back his forces into Lemster, the souldiers being wearie, sicke, and uncredibly diminished in number, and himselfe returned to Dublin. All that his Lordp. had done in this journey, besides the scattering of the Rebels weake troopes, was the taking of Cahir Castle, and receiving the L. of Cahir, the L. Roche and some others into her Majesties Protection, who after his departure did either openly fall againe to the rebels party, or secretly combine with them. While his Lordp. was in this journy, some 600 men left in the Glinnes, by the unskilfulnesse of some young Captaines and souldiers, and the ill affection of some Irish Officers, received a disgracefull blow from the

Cahir Castle taken.

A disgracefull blow. Obirns, whereupon his Lordp. now severely punished their fault, disarming the souldiers, and executing the tenth man, calling the Captaines to a Martiall Court, and discharging them, and condemning to bee shot to death an Irish Lieutenant, who had parlied with the Rebels, and was thought to have animated them. Then his Lordp. understanding that the Queene was much offended with this Mounster journy, he cast in his letters the fault on the Counsell of Ireland, whose advise, by reason of their long experience in those warres, he thought fittest to follow, at his first entry, but withal gave her Majesty ful assurance that he would presently leade the Army into Ulster against Tyrone himselfe. Yet these letters were scarce delivered, when by others he signified a *Journey into Ophalia and Leax.* necessity of a journey into Ophalia and Leax neere Dublin, against the Oconnors and Omores, whom he brake with ease, himself leading some 1500 into Ophalia, & sending Sir Christopher Blunt the Marshal into Leax with 1000 men, under the command of Sir Charles Pearcy and Sir Richard Moryson. Then at his returne, taking a view of the Army, he found it so weakened, as by letters signed by himselfe and the Counsell there, hee desired a supplie of 1000 foot out of England, to inable him presently to undertake the Ulster journey.

Thus resolved to march Northward, he commaunded *Sir Conyers Clifford* Sir Conyers Clifford, Governour of Connaght to draw his forces up to Belike, that hee might force Tyrone to send some of his forces that way, while he assailed him on the other side. Sir Conyers Clifford accordingly marched this way with one thousand foure hundred foote by Pole, and the Earle of Southamptons Troop of one hundred horse, under the leading of Captaine John Jephson, with some other Irish horse: & comming to the Curlew mountaines he left the munition and carriages under the guard of the horse, til he passing forward with the Foote had tried the passage. He had not gone farre, before Ororke and other rebels with him, upon the advantage of Woods, Bogges, and, a stony causey, assailed our men, who at the first valiantly repelled them, till the rebels finding the munition our men had about them beginning to faile, renewed the charge with greater fury then before; at which time our men, discouraged with the want of powder, (almost all they had about them being spent, and their store being behind with the carriage), as also wearied with a long march they had made before the skirmish, began to faint, and take themselves to flight, whom the rebels pursued, & killed some one hundred and twenty in the place, among which the Governour Sir Conyers Clifford, and a worthy Captaine Sir Alexander Ratcliffe, were lost, besides as many more hurt, whereof the greatest part recovered. And no doubt the rest had all perished, if the Horse had not valiantly succored them. For the Lord of Dunkellyn (who that day had most valiantly behaved himselfe) sent word to Captaine John Jephson of their distresse, who presently charged upon the causey, and to the very skirts of the Wood, with such resolution, as the rebels either thinking Horse could not have served there, or expecting advantages upon them in that boggy place, stood gaping on them, and gave way, without any resistance for a good space, in which our men had leasure to retire over a Ford, into the Plaine, where the carriages were, and thence to the Abby of the Boyle, being very neere the place. Afterwards the rebels began to charge our Horse, but their powder being almost spent, Captaine Jephson safely retyred, with the losse of some few horses. In a Consultation, some were earnest to have marched forward the next day: but the Lord of Dunkellin, Sir Arthur Savage, Captain John Jephson, and many of the best judgement, considering the Governor was lost, our troopes utterly dismaied, and Odonnel come downe with all his forces into those parts, thought fit our men should retire to their Garrisons. So Captaine Jephson all that night kept the Ford, while our Foote in the silent night retired, and in the morning when they were in safetie, hee with the Horse under his command went softly after

A rebel victorie.

[II. i. 38.]

Valiant horse.

Captaine Jephson.

them to the Castle of Athlone. It is strange, the rebels then present being but some two hundred, and most of our men being old soldiers, how this defeate could be given, but small accidents in militarie affaires, are often causes of strange and great events: for I have heard this mischance fully attributed to an unorderly turning of the whole body of the Van; which though it were toward the enemy, yet being mistaken by some common souldiers for a flight, it caused a generall rowte.

Supplies from England.

In the meane time the foresaid supply of one thousand foote was sent out of England to the Lord Lieutenant, according to his and the Counsels request. But few daies after, his Lordship signified by his letters into England, that he could doe no more this season of the yeere, then to draw thirteene hundred Foote, and three hundred horse to the borders of Ulster. Whether he came about the Ides of September, and Tyrone two dayes together shewed himselfe and his troopes upon distant hilles, to the English. Then Tyrone sent Hagan to the Lord Lieutenant, to intreat a Parly betweene his Lordship and him; which his Lordship refused, answering, that if Tyrone would speak with him, he should find him next day in Armes, in the head of the Army. The next day, after a light skirmish, one of Tyrones horsemen cried with a loud voice, that Tyrone would not fight, but would speake with the Lord Lieutenant, and that unarmed, and both withdrawne aside from the forces. The next day, when his Lordship marched forwards, Hagan met him againe, and declared to him, that Tyrone besought the Queenes mercy, and that he would vouchsafe to speake one word with him, which granted, he would in all humblenesse attend his Lordship at the Foard Balla-clinch, neere the chiefe Towne of the County of Louth. His Lordship sent some before, to view the Foard, who found Tyrone there, and hee assured them, that howsoever the waters were something risen, yet they might easily heare one another from each side. His Lordship being come thither, Tyrone leaving a troope of horse upon a hill

Tyrone intreats a Parly.

Conference with Tyrone.

A mutuall truce.

not far off, came downe alone, and putting his horse up to the belly in the water, with al humblenesse saluted his Lordship standing on the other banke, and there they passed many speeches. Then Tyrone called his brother Cormack, Mac Gennys, Mac Guire, Ever Mac Couley, Henrie Ovington, and O Quin, to the Foard, the Lord Lieutenant having first called the Earle of South-hampton, Sir George Bourcher, Sir Warham Sant Leger, Sir Henrie Davers, Sir Edward Wingfeld, and Sir William Constable, to come downe. Tyrone very Courtly saluted each one, and after short conference, it was concluded, that the next day Commissioners, should meete to treate of Peace, and they made a mutuall Truce from that day for sixe weekes, and so from sixe weekes to sixe weekes, till the Callends of May, with caution, that it should bee free to either side, upon foureteene dayes warning first given, to renew the warre. And if any of the Earle of Tyrones confederates should not assent hereunto, hee left them to bee prosecuted, by the Lord Lieutenant.

[II. i. 39.]

Judgement of the chiefe Commanders.

By this time the Queene had received his Lordships last letters above mentioned, signifying that he could onely for this winter, draw to the confines of Ulster, with one thousand three hundred foot and three hundred horse; At which time, to justifie his resolution, he sent the judgement of the chiefe Commanders of the Army, subscribed with their hands, dated the one twentie of August, that for that time more could not be enterprised for these reasons; that the Army was unwilling to bee drawne towards Ulster, so as many ran away from their Colours; that many were sicke; that no Plantation could be made this yeere at Loughfoyle, nor any course taken to divert Tyrones forces; that the Connaght Army was defeated; that his Lordships Army had not above foure thousand able men at the most; that these were unable to stand against the rebels, being six thousand shot, and lying within strong intrenchments; that much lesse any strong Garrisons could bee left in the North, and a safe retreit made; And lastly, that those Garrisons, if they could bee left there, would more endanger the English (being continually to supply them with vittles in winter time) then annoy the rebels. Her Majestie being highly offended, that so royall an Army, maintained with her excessive charge, had in sixe moneths effected nothing, and now gave no hope of any important service to be done against the rebels, wrote a sharpe letter to the Lord Lieutenant, and the Counsell of Ireland, as followeth.

The Queene offended.

Elizabeth Regina. By the Queene.

The Queene's sharpe Letter to the Lord Lieutenant and the Counsell of Ireland.

Right trusty and right well beloved Cosen and Councellor, and trusty and welbeloved, We greet you well. Having sufficiently declared unto you before this time, how little the manner of your proceedings hath answered, either our direction, or the worlds expectation. And finding now by your letters by Cuffe, a course more strange, if stranger may be, we are doubtful what to prescribe you at any time, or what to build upon by your owne writings to us in any thing. For we have clearely discerned of late, that you have ever to this hower possessed us with expectations, that you would proceede as we directed you. But your actions shew alwaies the contrary, though carried in such sort, as you were sure we had no time to countermaund them.

Before your departure, no mans counsell was held sound, which perswaded not presently the maine prosecution in Ulster, all was nothing without that, and nothing was too much for that. This drew on the sudden transportation, of so many thousands to be carried over with you, as when you arrived we were charged with more then the liste, or which wee resolved, to the number of three hundred horse; Also the thousand which were onely to be in pay during the service in Ulster, have been put in charge ever since the first journey. The pretence of which voyage, as appeareth by your letters was to doe some present service, in the Interim, whilest the season grew more commodious for the maine prosecution; for the which purpose, you did importune with great earnestnesse, that all manner of provisions might be hastned to Dublin against your returne. *The Queene's letter.*

Of this resolution to deferre your going into Ulster, you may well thinke that wee would have made stay, if you had given us more time, or if we could have imagined by the contents of your owne writings, that you would have spent nine weekes abroad. At your returne, when a third part of July was past, and that you had understood our mislike of your former course, and making your excuse of undertaking it onely in respect of your conformitie to the Councels opinions, with great protestations of haste into the North, we received another letter, of new reasons to suspend that journey yet a while, and to draw the Army into Ophalia. The fruit whereof was no other at your comming home, but more relations of further miseries of your Army, and greater difficulties to performe the Ulster warre. Then followed from you and the Councell a new demaund of two thousand men to which if we would assent, you would speedily undertake what wee had so often commanded. When that was granted, and your going onward promised by divers letters, wee received by this bearer now fresh advertisement, that all you can doe, is to goe to the frontier, and that you have provided only for twentie daies victuals. In which kinde of proceeding, wee must deale plainely with you & that Councell, that it were more proper for them, to leave troubling themselves with instructing us, by what rules our power & their obedience are limitted, & to bethink them, if the courses have bin only derived from their Counsels, how to answere this part of theirs, to traine us into a new expence for one end, and imploy it upon another; to which we could never have assented, if we could have suspected it should have beene undertaken, before we heard it was in action. And therefore we doe wonder how it can be answered, seeing your attempt is not in the capitall Traytors Countrey, that you have increased our list: but it is true as we have often saied, that we are drawne on to expence, by little and

Camden saith onely one thousand.

[II. i. 40.]

The Queene's letter.

little, and by protestations of great resolutions in generalities, till they come to particular execution. Of all which courses, whosoever shall examine any of the arguments used for excuse, shall find, that your owne proceedings beget the difficulties, and that no just causes doe breed the alteration. If lacke of numbers, if sickenesse of the army be the causes, why was not the action undertaken, when the Army was in better state, if winters approch: why were the summer moneths of July and August lost? if the spring was too soone, and the summer that followed otherwise spent, if the harvest that succeeded was so neglected, as nothing hath beene done, then surely must we conclude, that none of the foure quarters of the yeere will be in season for you and that Counsell, to agree of Tyrones prosecution, for which all our charge was intended. Further we require you to consider, whether we have not great cause to thinke, that the purpose is not to end the warre, when your selfe have so often told us, that all the petty undertakings in Lemster, Mounster, and Connaght, are but losse of time, consumption of treasure, and waste of our people, untill Tyrone himselfe be first beaten, on whom the rest depend. Doe you not see, that he maketh the warre with us in all parts by his Ministers, seconding all places where any attempts be offered: who doth not see, that if this course be continued, the warres are like to spend us and our Kingdome beyond all moderation, as well as the report of the successe in all parts hath blemished our Honour, and incouraged others to no smal proportion. We know you cannot so much fayle in judgement, as not to understand, that all the World seeth, how time is dallied, though you thinke the allowance of that Counsell, whose subscriptions are your Ecchoes, should serve and satisfie us. How would you have derided any man else, that should have followed your steps? How often have you told us, that others which preceded you, had no intent to end the warre? How often have you resolved us, that untill Loughfoyle and Ballishannon were planted,

All the World seeth.

The Queene's letter.

there could be no hope of doing service upon the capitall Rebels? We must therefore let you know, that as it cannot be ignorance, so it cannot be want of meanes, for you had your asking, you had choice of times, you had power and authority more ample then ever any had, or ever shall have. It may well be judged, with how little contentment, wee search out this and other errours: for who doth willingly seeke for that, which they are so loth to find, but how should that be hidden which is so palpable? And therefore to leave that which is past, and that you may prepare to remedy matters of weight hereafter, rather then to fill your papers with many impertinent arguments, being in your generall Letters, savouring still in many points of humours, that concerne the private of you our Lord Liefetenant; we doe tell you plainely, that are of that Councell, that we wonder at your indiscretion, to subscribe to Letters which concerne our publike service, when they are mixed with any mans private, and directed to our Counsell Table, which is not to handle things of small importance.

To conclude, if you will say, though the Army be in list twenty thousand, that you have them not, we answere then to our Treasurer, that we are ill served; and that there need not so frequent demands of full pay: If you will say the Muster-master is to blame, we much muse then why he is not punished, though say we might to you our Generall, if we would Ex Jure proprio judicare, that all defects by Ministers, yea though in never so remote Garrisons, have beene affirmed to us, to deserve to be imputed to the want of care of the Generall. For the small proportion you say you carry with you of three thousand five hundred foot, when lately we augmented you two thousand more. It is to Us past comprehension, [II. i. 41.]
except it be that you have left still too great numbers in unnecessarie Garrisons, which doe increase our charge, and diminish your Army, which We command you to reforme, especially since you, by your continuall reports of the state of every Province, describe them all to be

The Queene's letter.

in worse condition, then ever they were before you set foote in that Kingdome. So that whosoever shal write the story of this yeeres action, must say, that We were at great charges to hazard Our Kingdome, and you have taken great paines to prepare for many purposes, which perish without understanding. And therefore because We see now by your own words, that the hope is spent of this yeeres service upon Tyrone and O Donnel, We doe command you and our Councell, to fall into present deliberation, and thereupon to send Us over in writing, a true declaration of the State to which you have brought our Kingdome, and what be the effects which this journy hath produced, and why these Garrisons which you will plant farre within the land in Brenny and Monaghan, as others whereof We have written, shall have the same difficulties.

Secondly, We looke to heare from you and them joyntly, how you thinke the remainder of this yeere shal be imployed, in what kind of warre, and where, and in what numbers, which being done and sent Us hither in writing with al expedition, you shal then understand Our pleasure in all things fit for our service, untill which time, We command you to be very carefull to meete with all inconveniences, that may arise in that Kingdome, where the ill affected will grow insolent upon Our ill successe, and the good subjects grow desperate, when they see the best of Our preserving them.

The cartell.

We have seene a writing in forme of a cartell, full of challenges that are impertinent, and of comparisons that are needelesse, such as hath not been before this time presented to a State, except it be done now with a hope to terrifie all men, from censuring your proceedings. Had it not bin enough to have sent Us the testimony of the Counsell, but that you must call so many of those, that are of slender experience, and none of Our Counsell, to such a forme of subscription. Surely howsoever you may have warranted them, Wee doubt not but to let them know, what belongs to Us, to you, and to themselves. And thus expecting your answere, We ende, at Our Mannor of Nonsuch the fourtenth of September, in the one and fortieth yeere of Our Raigne, 1599.

Lords Justices.

The Lord Lieutenant being nettled, or rather galled with this letter, resolved to leave Adam Loftus the Lord Archbishop of Dublin, and Sir George Cary Treasurer at Warres, to governe the Kingdome in his absence, and presently sayling into England, posted to the Court, where altogether unlooked for, he arrived the eight and twentie of September, and presented himselfe on his knees to the Queene, early in the morning, being in her private chamber, who received him not with that chearefull countenance, which she was wont to shew him, but after a briefe conference, commanded him to retire to his chamber, and there to stay, untill hee knew her further pleasure; from whence his Lordships next remove, was to the Lord Keepers house, in state of a prisoner.

The chiefe Officers of the Kingdom.

The list of the chiefe Officers of the Kingdome, and the Army, and the disposall of the forces made in September, 1599, when the Lord Lieutenant left the Kingdome.

Officers and Governours.

Lord Lieutenant the Earle of Essex. Lord President of Mounster void by the death of Sir Thomas Norreys. Place of chiefe Commissioner of Connaght void or provisional. Lieutenant of the Army Earle of Ormond. Treasurer at Warres Sir George Carey, The Marshals place of Ireland void. Master of the Ordinance Sir George Bourcher. Marshall of the Campe provisionally Sir Oliver Lambert. Lieutenant of the Horse Sir Henrie Davers. Serjeant Major Sir Arthur Chichester.

Colonels of Horse.

[II i. 42.]

Sir William Evers. Sir Griffin Markham.

Colonels of Foote.

Earle of Kildare. Earle of Thomond. Lord of Dunkellin. Lord Audley. Lord Dunsany. Sir Edward Denny. Sir Matthew Morgan. Sir Charles Piercy. Sir Henry Dockwra. Sir Christopher Saint Laurence. Sir John Bolles. Sir Edward Harbert. Sir Charles Wilmott. Sir Henrie Power. Sir Arthur Savage.

Foure Corporals and a Provost-Marshall of the Army.

The disposall of the forces.

The disposall of the forces.

Horse in Mounster.

The Earle of Thomond, 25. Sir Anthony Cooke, 50. Sir Warham Saint Leger, 25. Captaine Thomas White, 50.

Mounster.

Foote in Mounster.

Earle of Thomond, 200. Master Treasurer, 100. Sir Henrie Harington, 100. Sir Henry Power, 200. Sir Edward Denny, 150. Sir Anthony Cooke, 100. Sir Charles Wilmott, 150. Sir Francis Barkley, 100. Sir John Dowdal, 100. Captaine William Power, 150. Captaine Clare, 150. Captaine Browne, 100. Captaine Keamys, 100. Captaine Bostock, 100. Captaine Brooke, 100. Captaine Rande, 100. Captaine Flower, 100. Captaine Diggs, 100. Captaine William Tirwhit, 150. Captaine Parker, 100. Captaine William Hartpoole, 100. Captaine Francis Kingesmil, 100.

Horse in Connaght.

Earle of Clanrickard, 50. Provost Marshall, 10. Sir Theobald Dillon, 15. Captaine George Blunt, 12.

Connaght.

Foote in Connaght.

Earle of Clanrickard, 100. Lord of Dunkellyn, 150. Sir Arthur Savage, 200. Sir Thomas Bourke, 100. Sir Gerrald Harvy, 150. Sir Hugh O Connor, 100. Sir Theobald Dillon, 100. Captaine Badbye, 150. Captaine Richard Pluncket, 100. Captaine Mostion, 100. Captaine

A.D. 1599.

Tibot ne long, 100. Captaine Walter Floyd, 150. Captaine Thomas Roper, 150. Captaine Oliver Burke, 100. Captaine Thomas Burke, 100. Captaine David Bourke, 100. *The disposall of the forces.*

Horse at Carrickfergus.

Neale Mac Hugh, 30.

Foote at Carrickfergus.

Sir Arthur Chichester, 200. Sir Richard Percy, 150. Captaine Eington, 100. Captaine Norton, 100.

Horse at the Newry.

Sir Samuel Bagnol, 50.

Foote at the Newrie.

Sir Samuel Bagnoll, 200. Captaine Edward Blaney, 150. Captaine Freckleton, 100. Captaine Josias Bodley, 150. Captaine Francis Stafford, 100. Captaine Toby Cawfeild, 150. Captaine Leigh, 100.

Foote at Dundalke.

Captaine Egerton, 100. Captaine Bingley, 150. Captaine Basset, 100.

Foote at Atherde. [II i. 43.]

Sir Garret Moore, 100. Captaine Roe, 100.

Horse at Kells and Navan.

Lord of Dunsany, 50. Sir Garret Moore, 25.

Foote at Kells and Navan.

Lord Audley, 200. Lord Dunsany, 150. Sir Fulk Conway, 150. Sir Christopher Saint Laurence, 200. Sir Henry Dockwra, 200. Sir John Chamberlaine, 150. Captaine John Sidney, 100. Captaine Ralph Sydley, 100. Captaine Roger Atkinson, 100. Captaine Heath, 150. Captaine Nelson, 100. Captaine Hugh Rely, 100.

Horse at Trym.

Sir Griffin Markham, 50.

The disposall of the forces.

Foote at Trym.

Sir Charles Piercy, 200. Captaine Roger Orme, 100. Captaine Alford, 100.

Foote at Leax and the Barow side.

Sir Warham Saint Leger, 150. Sir Francis Rush, 150. Captaine John Fitz-Piers, 150. Master Hartpoole, 10.

Foote at Eniscorthy.

Sir Oliver Lambert, 200. Sir Richard Masterson, 150.

Horse in and about the Nasse.

The Earle of Kildare, 50. Captaine Richard Greame, 50. Captaine Thomas Gifford, 25. Captaine George Greame, 12. Captaine Thomas Lee, 12.

Foote in and about the Nasse.

Earle of Kildare, 150. The Earle of Southampton, 200. Sir Matthew Morgan, 150. Sir Thomas Loftus, 100. Captaine Walter Mac Edmond, 100. Captaine Edward Loftus, 100. Captaine Thomas Williams, 150. Captaine Thomas Lee, 100. Captaine William Eustace, 100. Captaine Esmond, 150. Captaine John Masterson, 100. Captaine Ellys Flood, 100. Captaine R. Trevor, 100.

Foote at Mullingar.

The Lord of Delvin, 150. Captaine Thomas Mynne, 100. Captaine William Stafford, 100. Captaine Lionel Ghest, 100. Captaine William Winsor, 100. Captaine Thomas Cooche, 100. Captaine Garret Dillon, 100.

Foote in Ophaly.

Sir Henrie Cooly, 20. Sir Henry Warren, 100. Sir Edward Fitz-gerald, 100. Sir George Cooly, 20.

Horse at Kilkenny.

The Earle of Ormond, 50. Sir Oliver Lambert, 25. Sir Walter Butler, 50. Sir Cristopher Saint Laurence, 30. Captaine Garret Fleming, 25. Captaine William Taffe, 50.

The disposall of the Forces.

Foote at Kilkenny.

The Earle of Ormond, 200. Sir Carew Reynel, 150. Sir Henrie Follyot, 150. Captaine Richard Croft, 100. Captaine Henry Sheffeild, 100. Captaine Nicholas Pinner, 100.

Foote at Ballymore, and O Carrols Countrie.

Captaine Francis Shane, 100. Captaine Edward Lister, 100. Sir Charles O Carrol, 100.

Horse and Foote at Newcastle.

Sir William Warren, 50 horse. Sir William Warren, 100 foote.

Foote at Athboy and Phillipstown. [II. i. 44.]

Sir Richard Moryson, 200. Sir George Bourcher, 100.

Foote at Dublin.

Sir Henrie Foulkes, commanding the Lord Lieutenants Guard, 200.

Horse at Fingall, and at Navan.

Sir William Evers, 100. The Earle of Southamptons troope, commanded by Captaine John Jephson, 100. Sir Henry Davers, 100.

Horse in the Countie of Dublin.

Sir Henrie Harrington, 25. Sir Edward Herbert, 12. Sir Gerald Aylemer, 13. Murrogh Mac Teig, Oge, 10.

Foote undisposed.

Sir John Talbot, 22.

The Totall of the Horse and Foote.

Totall of Horse, one thousand two hundred thirtie one.

Totall of Foote, fourteene thousand foure hundred twenty two.

The foresaid Lords Justices being left to governe Ireland, upon the Lord Lieutenants sudden departure, did easily rule the unweldy Helme of this Kingdome so long, as the Sea was calme, by the continuance of that truce formerly mentioned to bee made, betweene the Lord Lieutenant and Tyrone, which was then concluded for sixe weekes, and so from sixe to sixe weekes, till the Calends of May, except either of them should give fourteene daies warning of their purpose to breake the same. But about the beginning of December, Tyrones party entring into acts of hostility, the Lords Justices sent Sir William Warren, to expostulate with him the cause of this breach. He answered, that he had not broken the Truce, having (according to the condition thereof) given them fourteene dayes warning. And that he had so done, because the Earle of Essex being imprisoned in England, in whom he had placed all the confidence of his life and estate, he was resolved not to relye on the Councell of that Kingdome, who had formerly delt deceitfully with him therein. Finally, that he could not now renew the truce, though hee never so much desired it, since hee had already sent Odonnel into Connaght, and divers of his confederates into other parts to renew the warre.

Tyrone's hostile acts.

Thus much their Lordships advertised into England, by letters full of diffidence, professing that they feared the rebels would presently assault the English Pale. Likewise some ill affected to the Earle of Essex, advertised, that among the Rebels a common rumor was spread, and that no doubt from Tyrone, that England would shortly be in combustion within it selfe, which increased the suspitions already conceived of the foresaid conference had betweene the Earle and Tyrone, to the great prejudice of the Earle being in durance.

England to be in combustion.

Now her Majestie receiving these advertisements, and further understanding, that the rebels daily increased in number and courage, that the meere Irish aspired to liberty, and that the English Irish, if perhaps well affected, yet were daunted by the ill successe of the Queenes affaires, (whose great expences, and Royall Army they had seene vanish into smoke), and were besides exasper-

A.D. 1599.

ated with an old griefe, to be excluded themselves from the Governement, while English Deputies were daily sent to command them. And having intelligence, that Tyrone full of pride, did every where bost himselfe as Champion of the Irish Liberty and Romish Religion (every where receiving to his protection, and cherishing all seditious persons, helping the weake with succours, confirming the diffident with strong hopes), and that he was growne confident to roote out the English Governement, aswell by former successes, as by the succour of the King of Spaine, (who already had sent him some munition and a little mony, with bragging promises of greater supplies), and by the faire promises and large indulgences sent from the Pope, with a Crowne of Phœnix fethers (perhaps in imitation of Pope Urban the third, who sent John, the sonne to King Henry the second, then made Lord of Ireland, a little Crowne woven of Peacocks feathers.)

Tyrone Champion the Romish Religion.

Her Majestie (I say) having these advertisements, & finding thereby, that it was high time, to make strong opposition to this rebellious monster, made choice of Charles Blount, Lord Mountjoy to be Deputy of Ireland, whom her Highnesse had the last yeere purposed to imploy in that place: At which time, the Earle of Essex, though linked in neere friendship with him, yet secretly opposed this her Majesties determination, alleaging that the Lord Mountjoy had small experience in martiall affaires, save that he had gained in the small time he served in the Low-Countries, adding that he was too bookish, and had too few followers, and too small an estate, to imbrace so great a businesse. So as the Earle not obscurely affecting this imployment himselfe, (to the end he might more strongly confirme that dependancy which all military men already had on him) and his enemies willingly giving second to this his ambition, (that by his absence they might have better advantages to hurt him, and to benefit themselves), at that time the said Earle easily drew this fatall governement on his owne

[II. i. 45.] *Charles Blount, L. Mountjoy, L. Deputy.*

shoulders, which was one of the first steps, and not the least cause of his ruine.

Being now to write of this Honourable Lord Mountjoy, my deceased Lord and Master, I doe faithfully professe, and pray the Reader confidently to beleeve, (which I hope most easily to obtaine of those, who best know me), that as in the duty of a servant I will not omit any thing I remember, which may turne to his Lordships Honor, so in my love to truth, I will be so farre from lying and flattering, as I will rather be bold modestly to mention some of his defects, whereof the greatest Worthies of the World cannot be altogether free. To which I will onely adde, that as I esteeme lying and flattery by word of mouth, among the living, to be unfallible notes of basenesse and ignorance, so I judge these vices infamous and sinfull, when they are left in print to deceive posterity. Since the first may detect falshood by inquiring the truth, but the latter have no meanes to rectifie their misinformed judgements.

The Lord Deputy's person.

Thus I returne to proceed in my former narration; and first I will delineate (after my best skill) the true portraiture of this worthy Lords body and mind, then I will collect the Councels, by which he tamed this Monster of Rebellion; and lastly, I will discend by order of time to his Lordships particular actions. But ere I take my pensill in hand to figure this Noble Lords person, I must acknowledge my weakenesse such, as I cannot fully apprehend his compleat worthinesse, and therefore desire, that those of greater judgement to discerne the same, will impute all defects to the unskilfulnes of the workeman, and that with others, to whom his Lordship was lesse knowne, my rude Pen may not derogate any thing from his due praise. Againe, give me leave to remember, that which I received from his mouth, that in his childhood when his Parents would have his picture, he chose to be drawne with a Trowell in his hand, and this Mot; Ad reædificandam antiquam Domum, To rebuild the ancient House: For this noble and ancient Barrony was decaied, not so much by his Progenitors prodigality, as his Fathers obstinate addiction to the study and practise of Alchumy, by which he so long laboured to increase his revenues, til he had almost fully consumed them. Now to the purpose, let us observe how he fulfilled this ominous presage, in rebuilding that Noble House, till by his untimely death, the same was fatally eclipsed againe.

His bodily presence.

He was of stature tall, and of very comely proportion, his skin faire, with little haire on his body, which haire was of colour blackish (or inclining to blacke), and thinne on his head, where he wore it short, except a locke under his left eare, which he nourished the time of this warre, and being woven up, hid it in his necke under his ruffe. The crown of his head was in his latter dayes somthing bald, as the forepart naturally curled; he onely used the Barber for his head, for the haire on his chin (growing slowly) and that on his cheekes and throat, he used almost daily to cut it with his sizers, keeping it so low with his owne hand, that it could scarce bee discerned, as likewise himselfe kept the haire of his upper lippe something short, onely suffering that under his nether lip to grow at length and full; yet some two or three yeeres before his death, he nourished a sharpe and short pikedevant on his chin. His forehead was broad and high; his eyes great, blacke, and lovely; his nose something low and short, and a little blunt in the end; his chin round; his cheekes full, round, and ruddy; his countenance cheerefull, and [II. i. 46.] as amiable as ever I beheld of any man, onely some two yeeres before his death, upon discontentment, his face grew thinne, his ruddy colour failed, growing somewhat swarthy, and his countenance was sad and dejected. His armes were long, and of proportionable bignes, his hands long and white, his fingers great in the ende, and his leggs somewhat little, which hee gartered ever above the knee, wearing the Garter of Saint Georges order under the left knee, except when he was booted, and so wore not that Garter, but a blew ribben in stead thereof above his knee, and hanging over his boote.

The description of his apparrell.

The description of his apparrell may be thought a needelesse curiositie, yet must I adde some few words thereof, be cause having promised the lively portraiture of his body, aswell as his minde, the same cannot otherwise bee so lively represented to the imagination, besides that by his clothes, some disabilities of his body to undertake this hard war may be conjectured, and especially the temper of his mind may be lively shadowed, since the Wise man hath taught us, that the apparrell in some sort shewes the man. His apparrell in Court and Cities was commonly of white or black Tafetaes or Sattens, and he wore two (yea sometimes three) paires of silke stockins, with blacke silke Grogran cloakes guarded, and ruffes of comely depth and thicknesse (never wearing any falling band) blacke beaver hats, with plaine blacke bands, a taffaty quilted wastcoate in summer, a scarlet wastcoate, and sometimes both in winter. But in the Country, and specially keeping the Field in Ireland (yea, sometimes in the Cities), he ware Jerkins and round hose (for hee never ware other fashion then round) with laced panes of russet Cloath, and clokes of the same cloth lined with Velvet, and white Bever hats with plaine bands, and besides his ordinarie stockings of silke, he wore under bootes another paire of Wollen or Wosted, with a paire of high linnen bootehose, yea three wastcotes in cold wether, and a thick ruffe, besides a russet scarfe about his necke thrice folded under it. So as I never observed any of his age and strength to keepe his body so warme. He was very comely in all his apparrell, but the Robes of Saint Georges order, became him extraordinarilie well.

His diet.

For his diet, he used to fare plentifully, and of the best, and as his meanes increased, so his Table was better served, so that in his latter time, no Lord in England might compare with him in that kinde of bountie. Before these warres, he used to have nourishing brackefasts, as panadoes, and broths; but in the time of the warre, he used commonly to breake his fast with a drie crust of bread, and in the Spring time with butter and sage, with a cup of stale beere, wherewith sometimes in Winter he would have suger and Nutmeg mixed. He fed plentifully both at dinner, and supper, having the choisest and most nourishing meates, with the best wines, which he drunk plentifully, but never in great excesse; and in his latter yeeres (especially in the time of the warre, aswell when his night sleepes were broken, as at other times upon full diet) he used to sleepe in the afternoones, and that long, and upon his bed. He tooke Tobacco abundantly, and of the best, which I thinke preserved him from sicknes, (especially in Ireland, where the Foggy aire of the bogs, and waterish foule, plentie of fish, and generally all meates with the common sort alwaies unsalted and greene rosted, doe most prejudice the health), for hee was very seldome sicke, onely he was troubled with the head-ach, which duly and constantly like an ague, for many yeeres, till his death tooke him once every three moneths, and vehemently held him some three daies, and himselfe in good part attributed, aswell the reducing of this paine to these certaine and distant times, as the ease he therein found, to the vertue of this hearbe. He was very neat, loving clenlinesse both in apparrell and diet, and was so modest in the necessities of nature, as my selfe being at all howers (but time of sleepe) admitted into his chamber, and (I thinke) his most familiar friends, never heard or saw him use any liberty therein, out of the priveledge of his private chamber, except perhaps in Irish journeys, where he had no with-drawing roome.

The tender using of his body, and his daintie faire before the warres, gave Tyrone occasion, upon hearing of his comming over, to jeast at him, as if all occasions of doing service would be past, ere he could be made ready [II. i. 47.] and have his breakfast, but by wofull experience he found this jeasting to bee the laughter of Salomons Foole. His behaviour was courtly, grave, and exceeding comely, especially in actions of solemne pompes. In his nature he loved private retirednesse, with good fare, and some few choice friends. He delighted in study, in gardens,

His behaviour.

an house richly furnished, and delectable for roomes of retrait, in riding on a pad to take the aire, in playing at shovelboard, or at cardes, in reading play-bookes for recreation, and especially in fishing and fishponds, seldome using any other exercises, and using these rightly as pastimes, only for a short and convenient time, and with great varietie of change from one to the other. He was undoubtedly valiant and wise. Hee much affected glory and honour, and had a great desire to raise his house, being also frugall in gathering and saving, which in his latter daies declined to vice, rather in greedy gathering, then in restraining his former bounties of expence. So that howsoever his retirednes did alienate his minde from all action, yet his desire of Honour and hope of reward and advancement by the warres, yea of returning to this retirednesse after the warres ended, made him hotly imbrace the forced course of the warre; to which hee was so fitted by his wisedome, valour, and frugalitie, that in short time hee became a Captaine no lesse wise, wary, and deliberate in counsell, then chearefull and bold in execution, and more covetous in issuing the publick treasure, then frugall in spending his owne revenewes. And his care to preserve his Honour, and maintaine this estate, made him (though coldly) intertaine the like forced course of a State Counseller at home after the warres. To the mannaging of which affaires, he was no lesse inabled by the same valour, wisedome, and many other vertues, had not the streame of his nature, prevailed to withdraw him from attending them, further then to the onely obtaining of these his owne private endes. But surely these dispositions of nature (besides others hereafter to be mentioned), and these his private endes, made him of all men most fit for this Irish imployment, wherein the Queene and State longed for an ende of the warre, and groned under the burthen of an unsupportable expence.

His affecting honour and glorie.

Touching his affecting honour and glorie, I may not omit, that his most familiar friends must needes observe,

ERARY

le for roomes of
aire,
; play
shponds, seldome
these rightly as
at time, and with
e other. He was
uch affected glory
o raise his house,
ving, which in his
greedy gathering,
s of expence. So
ate his minde from
ad hope of reward
f returning to this
made him body
rre; to which hee
and frugalitie, that
o lesse wise, wary,
refull and bold in
suing the publick
owne revenews.
and maintaine this
ine the like forced
after the warres.
he was no lesse
, and many other
ture, prevailed to
rther then to the
vate endes. But
ides others bare-
vate endes, made
loyment, wherein
de of the warre,
n unsupportable

lorie, I may not
needes observe,

the discourses
ordinarily *pleas*
not *prone to*
observed *him*
nature, which
into any other.
yea necessary
fight & mannage
set forth his
observed any
hee used to
mention the

Touching
imputed to *him*
an active
grounded from
London, he so
able to direct
skill in tongues.
the Italian and
to speak *them*,
Cosmography and
owne ends; he
naturall Phylos
held by him with
without marve
remember of
subtilest objectio
chiefe delight
especially in
for I have
his youth
prejudicate
have convers
e Fathers
bsurd distinc
heir opinions,
confirmed in the

the discourses of his Irish actions to have been extraordinarily pleasing to him: so that, howsoever hee was not prone to hold discourses with Ladies, yet I have observed him more willingly drawne to those of this nature, which the Irish Ladies entertaining him, then into any other. And as hee had it that commendable, yea necessary ability of a good Captaine, not only to fight & mannage the war well abroad, but to write and set forth his actions to the full at home, so I have seldome observed any omission of like narrations in him, whereof hee used to delate the more weightie seriously, and to mention the smallest, at least by way of a jeast.

His studies.

Touching his studies or Bookishnesse, (by some imputed to him in detraction of his fitnes to imbrace an active imployment), he came young and not well grounded from Oxford University; but in his youth at London, he so spent his vacant houres with schollers best able to direct him, as besides his reading in Histories, skill in tongues, (so farre as he could read and understand the Italian and French, though he durst not adventure to speak them), and so much knowledge (at least in Cosmography and the Mathematikes) as might serve his owne ends; he had taken such paines in the search of naturall Phylosophy, as in divers arguments of that nature held by him with schollers, I have often heard him, (not without marvelling at his memory and judgement) to remember of himselfe the most materiall points, the subtilest objections, and the soundest answers. But his chiefe delight was in the study of Divinity, and more especially in reading of the Fathers and Schoolemen: for I have heard himselfe professe, that being in his youth addicted to Popery, so much as through prejudicate opinion no Writer of our time could have converted him from it, yet by observing the Fathers consent, and the Schoolemens idle and absurd distinctions, he began first to distaste many of their opinions, and then by reading our Authours, to be confirmed in the reformed doctrine, which I am confident

His chiefe delight in the study of Divinity.

[II. i. 48.] he professed and beleeved from the heart, though in his innated temper he was not factious against the Papists, but was gentle towards them, both in conversation and in all occasions of disputation. And I will be bold to say, that of a Lay-man, he was (in my judgement) the best Divine I ever heard argue, especially for disputing against the Papists, out of the Fathers, Schoolemen, and above all, out of the written Word, (whereof some Chapters were each night read to him, besides his never intermitted prayers at morning and night). Insomuch as I have often heard him, with strange felicity of memory and judgement, discover the Papists false alleagings of the Fathers, and Texts, or additions, & omissions in them, and to urge arguments strongly, and (as much as beseemed him) schollerlike, as well in discourses with Jesuites and Priests in Ireland, (more specially at Waterford, where he made the very seduced Irish ashamed of them), as upon divers occasions with other Papists his friends.

His nature. Further, in his nature he was a close concealer of his secrets, for which cause, least they should be revealed, and because he loved not to be importuned with suites, a free speaker, or a popular man, could not long continue his favorite: He was sparing in speech; but when he was drawne to it, most judicious therein, if not eloquent. He never used swearing, but rather hated it, which I have seene him often controle at his Table with a frowning brow, and an angry cast of his blacke eye: He was slow to anger, but once provoked, spake home. His great temper was most seene in his wise carriage betweene the Court factions of his time: He was a gentle enemy, easily pardoning, and calmely pursuing revenge; and a friend, if not cold, yet not to be used much out of the high way, and something too much reserved towards his dearest Minions; besides that, the strength of his judgement made him so confident, as they had more power in seconding his Counsels, then in diverting or altering them. To his servants he was milde, seldome reproving them, and never with ill words: for his looke of displeasure was sufficient to checke them, and the best sort nearest him, did so well know him, as they served and observed him, as much almost by his lookes as his words. He made no servant partner of his secrets, further then his place necessarily gave him knowledge thereof, neither could any of them leade him, or if any did, it was more by art to know his humours, then power to sway them. I cannot say that he was bountifull to them, some of their places drew profit, which could no more be stopped, then the Miller can stay the draining of his water through his damme gates; otherwise his gifts to them were rare and sparing, so as if it were above an hundred pound, it was no morsell for a servant, yet still he kept their hopes so greene, as might continue their diligence, and at his death he gave a thousand pound by will, to be divided by his executors discretion among them. They who had his eare, might easily season him with good or ill opinion of his servants and strangers, by reason he dranke in their speeches, without uttering them, onely his judgement was excellent, to discerne the truth of the relation, aswell out of the informers passions, as observing the others actions. He kept his word in publike affaires inviolably, without which he could never have beene trusted of the Irish: but otherwise in his promises, he was delatory and doubtfull, so as in all events, he was not without an evasion. Lastly, in his love to Weomen, (for as wanton peace succeeds bloody warre, so in the last period of his life, after the Irish warres, griefe of unsuccessefull love brought him to his last end): He was faithfull and constant, if not transported with selfe-love more then the object, and therein obstinate.

His love to Weomen.

This worthy Lord Mountjoy was he, whose knowne valour, sound wisdome, grave constancy, and singular temper, two old Counsellers of Ireland well observing, did on their death bed, (as it were by divining faculty) pronounce to be the man, by whom Tyrones fatall rebellion (in which their thoughts and endevours had long beene wearied) was to be suppressed, if ever the English were to recover the helme of that governement. Neither did their presage deceive us herein: for like another Fabius, he did by the ensuing deliberate and slow counsels, restore his Countries declining power.

[II. i. 49.]

He cherished active spirits.

1. He entertained & cherished (especially at his first entering the government, when he was yet unskilfull in the affaires of that State and warre) all active spirits, whose endevours he saw like to be of good use in that great action; and this he did, rather with a pleasing familiarity, then with any large bounty.

His care for his souldiers.

2. The hearts of the English common souldiers broken with a currant of disasterous successes, he heartned and incouraged, by leading them warily, especially in his first actions, being more carefull, that our men should not bee foiled, then that the rebels should be attempted with boldnesse. To this end also, and that he might bee ever at hand, as well to incourage and direct them fighting, as to second them by any accident dismaied, he bravely adventured his person, more then in the opinion of Militarie wise men, a Generall should ordinarily hazard himself (howsoever I must confesse, the nature of the Irish fights, maintained upon passages, by sudden eruptions of hidden rogues, doth more expose the Generall to these dangers, then any other warre.) And such was his forwardnesse, as his Lordships servants may without offence boldly say, they were a small part of this great action. For howsoever we had neither stipend in the warres with the souldier, nor pensions with them after the warre ended, yet by reason of this our Lords extraordinarie forwardnesse to put himselfe into danger, and for that the Rebels use most commonly to assault upon Woody paces, and difficult passages, where every man must needes be in danger, and they most who ride in the best troope, it could not be but that we should have our share in the adventure of our persons. And lest I should seeme to arrogate that to my selfe and my fellowes, which is not due to us, the event may cleare this point. Since in this short warre (not to speake of many lesse

dangers), my Lord himselfe had his horse shot under him, his Galloglasse carrying his helmet, had the same brused with the grasing of a bullet upon it, yea, his Lordships very Grayhound, likewise using to waite at his stirrop, was shot through the body. Among his Lordships Chaplaines, Doctor Lattware was killed, and Mast. Ram had his horse shot under him. Among his Lordships Secretaries, Master Cranmer was killed, and my selfe had my thigh brused with a shot I received in my saddle. Among the Gentlemen of his Lordships Chamber, Master Chidley had his horse killed under him, Master Done was shot in the legge, and Master Saint John, a Gentleman attending neere his Lordship, was killed. I have heard a pleasant report of a Generall in our age, who on the contrary was so sparing to hazard himself: as a Gentleman his follower, hearing some marvel at a cold peece of service performed by his Mast merily replied for his own excuse, that he went to follow his General, and not to go before him. But I wil boldly say, that if our noble Lords followers did well attend his person, they found danger enough without seeking it. But enough (and I feare too much) of this point, I will now returne to this worthy Lords Counsels, by which he effected this great worke. *His dangers.*

3. The Rebels being swolne to the height of pride by their full numbers, and much more by continuall successe in their actions, hee proceeded in like sort with them, as formerly with his owne men, at the first warily tasting them with light skirmishes, yet he so prudently and bravely pursued his attempts, as he stil caried what he atempted. *His warinesse.*

4. The wise distribution of the forces availed him much: for first he planted Garrisons upon the chiefe rebels Countries, as likewise he compassed Tyrone on every side with them, which kept the rebels at home, so as they could not second one another, for feare of loosing their owne goods. *Wise distribution of his forces.*

5. And whereas other Deputies used to make some two

or three journies in a Summer against the rebels, and then did leade a great Army with them. And whereas this kind of service never tooke any good effect, as well because the bruit thereof came long before to the rebels, as because these great forces could not long be kept together. So as the rebels hearing the bruit of any such journy, took victuals with them for certaine daies, and assembling themselves together, did lie upon the bogs and hard passages, where without danger to themselves, they were able to annoy the greatest Army could be led against them. This noble Lord Mount-joy on the contrary (as I said) by Garrisons keeping them at home, *His keeping the field.* himselfe kept the field with some thousand foot and two hundred horse (whereof my selfe have many times [II. i. 50.] observed the greater part to be English Irish), and not onely was able to affront Tyrone himselfe (specially since the Garrisons lying upon his Country drew towards him at the same time, on all sides together), but also (by reason of his singular secrecy, in keeping his purposes unknowne, and casting out false reports of them to deceive the rebels) had the opportunitie to assaile and spoyle any one of the rebels on the sudden, while he kept all the rest like dared larkes in continuall feare, aswell of himselfe, as of the Garrisons adjoyning.

6 Againe, where other Deputies used to assaile the rebels onely in Summer time, this Lord prosecuted them *The Lord Deputy fought in winter.* most in the Winter, being commonly five daies at least in the weeke on horsebacke, all the Winter long. This brake their hearts; for the aire being sharpe, and they naked, and they being driven from their lodgings, into the Woods bare of leaves, they had no shelter for themselves. Besides that, their cattle (giving them no milke in the Winter) were also wasted by driving to and fro. Ad that they being thus troubled in the Seede time, could not sowe their ground. And as in Harvest time, both the Deputies forces, and the Garrisons, cut downe their Corne, before it was ripe, so now in Winter time they carried away, or burnt, all the stores of victuals

in secret places, whether the Rebels had conveied them.

His speciall care to cut downe the difficult passages.

7 Againe, he had a speciall care to cut downe and cleare the difficult passages, that so our forces might with more safetie meete together, and upon all occasions second one another.

His protections and pardons.

8 For protections and pardons (the easie obtaining whereof had formerly incouraged the rebels, aswell to enter into rebellion, as to breake their faith after submissions, in hope to be againe received to mercy), although it was necessary for the State in this generall rebellion, like a mother, to open her bosome to her children, lest being driven to dispaire, they should plunge themselves into all mischiefes, yet he never received any to mercy, but such as had so drawne bloud on their fellow rebels, and were themselves made so poore, as there was small danger of their relaps. To which ende he forbad al conferences and parleys with the rebels, by pretence whereof many treacherous plots had formerly beene drawne, by the false-hearted subjects, and many corruptions had been practised by some covetous commanders. But to such as were received to mercy, (that he might take away the diffidence they had long conceived of the State), he kept his word inviolable.

His patience with the Irish Lords.

9 And whereas these rebellious people, are by nature clamorous (which made them tedious in complaints), and also use great oppression under the shadow of Justice, (which made them continually importune the Governors with petitions, which being signed by them, gave those Irish Lords a shadow of authoritie to oppresse the people, by shewing the Governours hand, and concealing the matter to which he subscribed. This worthy Lord Deputie, for their incouragement in the first, used singular patience in hearing their tedious complaints, and for the second, gave them such delatory answers, as might well hearten them in obedience, but could no way strengthen their tyranny over the poore people.

10 To conclude, nothing furthered this noble Lord

His singular temper.

more in his designes, then his singular temper, not so much in secrecy, and in sparingnesse of speech (though many great Captaines have hindered their proceedings by letting fall rash speeches), as more specially in Court factions: for he used in such sort the familiar love of the Earle of Essex, in his doubtfull courses, as he not onely kept him from intertaining dangerous counsels, so long as hee lived with him in England, but demeaned himselfe towards his enemies with such moderation, as he little provoked their envy, yea, rather gained an inclination of their good affection towards him. So as they at this time governing all the affaires in England, were readie to give all possible seconds to his ends, which (as I formerly shewed) did aime at nothing but the speedy ende of this warre. By these counsels this worthy Lord restored the declining State of Ireland, from the desperate termes wherein he now found it.

I have before set downe, in the Earle of Essex his Governement, the power of the rebels, through al the Provinces of Ireland, and have shewed, that at his Lordships leaving that Kingdom, the same was nothing abated, and from that time, the rebels were in all parts increased. [II. i. 51.]

The Rebels strength.

The Mountaine rebels in the County of Dublin, then 480 foote 20 horse, now by the going out of the Walshes and Harrols were increased 100. In the County of Kildare, the rebels then in number 220 foot, and 30 horse, were now more then doubled, by the going out of the Briminghams, all the Leynaghs, & many of other Septs. In the two Counties of Catherlough and Wexford, the rebels then 750 foote and 50 horse, were now increased an hundred. In the County of Ophaly, five strong Castles then held by the English, were now betraied, & above 468 foot, & 12 horse then were in rebellion, but now Mac Coughlan was gone out with 200 more, and the Odoines with 100 more, were now in rebellion. In the County of Meath the rebels were increased in number 150; by the Delahides, the Rochfords, Hussies, and Darcies. And beyond the River, Capt. John O Rely, having then 100 foote in her Majesties pay, well armed, was now revolted. In the County of West-Meath, the rebels then 140 foote and 20 horse, were now increased 100 at least, by the revolt of the eldest sonne of William Nugent, second brother to the Lord of Delvin, with divers of the Pettyes and Daltons. In the County of Longford, the rebels then 120 foote, were now increased 180: so the rebels in Lemster being then in the whole number 3048 foote, and 182 horse, were now increased 1280, and made in all 4510.

The Province of Mounster.

For the Province of Mounster, Tyrone in his present journy thither, taking pledges of almost all the Irish Lords and Gentlemen, the number of the rebels were now there increased beyond estimation.

The Province of Connaght.

For the Province of Connaght, the rebels were increased three hundred, by the revolt of O Connor Sligo, besides the uncertainty of Tybot ne Long, who had one hundred Irish men in her Majesties pay.

The rebellion at the greatest strength.

So as at this time, I may boldly say, the rebellion was at the greatest strength. The meere Irish puffed up with good successe, and blouded with happy incounters, did boldly keepe the field, and proudly disdaine the English forces. Great part of the English-Irish were in open action of rebellion, and most part of the rest temporised with the State, openly professing obedience, that they might live under the protection thereof, but secretly relieving the rebels, and practising with them for their present and future safeties. Among the English, the worthy Generals of this age, partly by this fatall warre, partly by the factions at home, were so wasted, as the best judgements could hardly finde out any man fit to command this Army in chiefe. The English common souldiers, by loosenesse of body, the natural sicknesse of the Country, by the poverty of the warre, in which nothing was to bee gained but blowes, and by the late defeates, wherein great numbers of them had perished, were altogether out of heart. The Colonels and Commanders, though many in number, and great in courage and experience, yet by these considerations of the Armies weakenesse, were somewhat dejected in mind. Yea, the very Counsellors of State were so diffident, as some of them in late conferences with Tyrone, had descended (I know not upon what warrant) to an abject Intreaty for a short cessation. Not to speake of the Generall distraction of the hearts of all men in England, and much more of the souldiers, by the factions of this age, between the worthy Earle of Essex now imprisoned and his enemies, able to ruine a great Kingdome, much more to divert the successe of any great action. And the generall voyce was of Tyrone among the English, after the defeat of Blackwater, as of Hanibal among the Romans, after the defeat of Cannas; Thou knowest how to overcome: but thou knowest not how to use victorie. To conclude, not onely the remote parts, but the very heart of the Kingdom now languished under the contagion of this rebellion. Leax and Ophalia being possessed by the O Mores, and the O Conners; and the Glynnes or Mountainous, Country on the South-West side of Dublin, being in the hands of the Obyrnes and O Tooles (and more remotely of the Cavanaghs), who nightly made excursions to the very Gates of the City, giving alarum of warre to the long gound Senate, and (as it were) to the chaire of Estate. In this miserable estate was Ireland, when the Lord Mountjoy, like a good Planet, with a fortunate aspect began to shine thereon, whose happy actions I will now set down particularly, yet as briefly as I can.

The contagion of the rebellion.

[II. i. 52.] *An.* 1599.

The tenth of January, towards the end of the yeere 1599, the Lords of England signified by their letters, to the Lord Archbishop of Dublin, and Sir George Carey Treasurer at warres, which were then Lords Justices of that Kingdome, that from that day forward, the entertainement due to them as Lords Justices, should cease, and bee conferred on Charles Blount Lord Mountjoy, whom her Majestie had made Lord Deputie.

And now Tyrone (who hitherto had contained himselfe in the North, onely making short excursions from thence into the Pale), being proud of victories, and desirous to shew his greatnesse abroad, resolved with his forces to measure the length of Ireland, and to the end hee might, by his presence strengthen, and increase the rebellion in Mounster (which in absence by practises he had raised), under the religious pretence of visiting a piece of Christs Crosse, kept for a holy relike in the Monastery of the holy Crosse in the County of Tipperary, he entred this journy about the twentieth of Januarie. On the three and twenty the rebels of the Brenny met him in the Cavan, from whence he marched forward, taking the rebels of Lemster in his company, and leading with him some two thousand five hundred foot, and two hundred horse, leaving the rest of his forces, & the Gentlemen of the North to guard those parts. The intent of his journey, was to set as great combustion as he could in Mounster, and so taking pledges of the rebels, to leave them under the command of one chiefe head.

Tyrone's journy to Mounster.

This Moneth of January, her Majestie signed that warrant, which is vulgarly called the great Warrant for Ireland, whereby authority is given to the Lord Treasurer and Chamberlaine of the Exchequer in England, that according to an Establishment, after signed by her Majesty the first of February, and to begin that day, (wherein the Army is reduced to twelve thousand foote, and one thousand two hundred horse), they should pay to the Treasurer at warres for Ireland such summes, as should bee signed by sixe of the privy Counsell of England, the Lord Treasurer, the Principall Secretary, and the under-Treasurer alwaies being three of them. Secondly, above the foure thousand pound for extraordinaries therein mentioned, to pay him such sums as should by the same be signed. Thirdly, to pay in like sort according to an Establishment or list of Officers and others not contained in the former Establishment, it not exceeding yeerely fifteene thousand pound, which List was then to bee signed by the Lords of her Majesties Counsell. Fourthly, to pay in like sort divers Officers payable out of the

The great Warrant for Ireland signed.

revenues, in case the revenues extended not to pay them. Fifthly, to pay in like sort all summes for reinforcing the Army, for leavyes of men, for conducting, transporting, and victualling them at Sea, according to the rates of the first Establishment.

The Establishment signed by her Majestie, the first of February, 1599.

The Establishment signed by her Majestie.

The Lord Deputies entertainement to be paid according to the List after following, which List was to be signed by the Lords. Officers of the Army: Lieutenant of the Army per diem three li. Serjeant Major per diem twenty s. Comptroler Generall of the victuals per diem ten s. Foure Commissaries of victuals, whereof three at sixe s. per diem, and the fourth at eight s. per diem. Twelve Colonels, each at ten s. per diem. A Provost Marshall for Loughfoyle, another for Ballishannon, each at foure shillings per diem.

Summa per annum, foure thousand foure hundred fiftie three pound.

The pay of three hundred horse, divided into sixe Bands, each Band consisting of fiftie, viz, the Captaine foure shillings per diem; Lieutenant two shillings sixe pence per diem; Cornet two shillings per diem; and fiftie Horsemen at eighteene pence per diem a piece. The pay of two hundred Horse, divided into foure Bands, each Band consisting of fiftie, viz. Captaine foure s. per diem; Lieutenant two s six d. per diem. Cornet two s. per diem, and fiftie Horsemen at fifteene d. a piece per diem. The pay of seven hundred Horse, divided into fourteene Bands, each Band consisting of fiftie viz.
[II. i. 53.] Captaine, foure shillings per diem. Lieutenant, two shillings sixe pence per diem, Cornet two shillings per diem. Fiftie horsemen at twelve pence a peece per diem.

Summa per annum twenty nine thousand two hundred threescore thirteene pound.

The pay of twelve thousand footmen, divided into 120

Bands, each Band consisting of a hundred heads, viz. Captaine foure s. per diem. Lieutenant two shillings per diem, Ensigne eighteene d. per diem, two Serjeants, a Drum, and a Surgion, at twelve d. a peece per diem, and fourescore fourteene Souldiers, and sixe dead payes, at eight d. a peece per diem.

Summa per annum one hundred threescore eleven thousand one hundred fourescore and five pound.

Extraordinaries, viz. for sending of letters, hyring of Barkes, for passage of packquets, for gifts and rewards, for espyes from abroad or at home, carriage of treasure, victuall, or munition, and the like, &c. for a whole yeere, foure thousand pound.

Summa totale per annum, two hundred eight thousand nine hundred and eleven pound.

The Lord Mountjoy's petition.

The Lord Mountjoy hastened away from Court, did not stay for the Lords signing of the above mentioned second establishment, as a thing of ordinary course continued for many yeeres, with little or no alteration. And being now in this journey towards Ireland, the tenth of Februarie he wrote to Master Secretarie from Daintrie, intreating him, that whereas her Majestie, notwithstanding the contrary opinion of all admitted to that consultation, had reduced the Army to twelve thousand foote, and that hee found by letters from the Counsell and other Commanders in Ireland, a general concurring in opinion, that these forces were not sufficient (especially since the Plantation of Loughfoyle and Ballyshanon Garisons were presently to be made, and that Tyrone was now Master of the field, having led his forces in person as farre as Mounster), he would move her Majestie to give him power, to retaine one or two thousand in Lyst, of those English, which otherwise he was to cast.

[The above

The above mentioned second Establishment, or Lyst of divers Officers and Servitors, not contained in the former Establishment, which list was signed by the Lords the eleventh of Februarie, the end of the yeere 1599.

Officers Generall. THe Lord Deputies ordinarie entertainement per mensem one hundred pound, per annum thirteene hundred pound. To him for a Band of horsemen in his family foure pound foure shillings per diem. To him for fiftie footemen in his family, eight pence a man per diem. The Treasurer at Warres per diem thirtie five shillings. The Marshall at five shillings nine pence per diem. The Master of the Ordinance per diem three and twentie shillings eight pence. Note that the above named, as also the chiefe Governours of Provinces undernamed, had besides in the Army the command of a Band of foote, or horse, or both. Divers Ministers of the Ordinance per diem twentie five shillings two pence. Mustermaster two shillings eight pence per diem.

Summa per annum five thousand three hundred seven d. seven shillings eleven d.

Mounster. The Lord President per annum one hundred thirtie three d.; his diet at ten pound a weeke, and so per annum five hundred twenty pound. His guard of horse and foote at thirtie shillings seven pence halfe-penny per diem. Chiefe Justice per annum one hundred pound. Second Justice sixty sixe pound, thirteene shillings foure pence. Queenes Atturney thirteene pound sixe shillings eight pence. Clerke of the Counsell twentie pound. Provost Marshall two hundred fiftie five pound ten shillings.

Summa per annum one thousand sixe hundred threescore seven pound eight shillings two pence halfe penny.

Connaght. Governour of Connaght per diem ten s., for increase per annum one hundred d. Chiefe Justice per annum one hundred pound: for his diet fortie pound. Clerke of the Counsell twenty pound, for his diet twenty pound.

Provost Marshall one hundred two pound thirteene shillings one peny half-peny, besides twelve Horse out of the Armie.

Summa per annum five hundred sixtie five pound three s. two pence halfe-penny.

Governor at Loughfoyle per diem foure shillings foure pence, besides his entertainement as a Colonel. Governour of Carickfergus and Dundalke no entertainement, but as Colonels of the Army. [II. i. 54.] *Ulster.*

Summa per annum threescore pound sixteene shillings eight pence. *Lemstor.*

Governour of the Queenes Countie at sixe shillings eight pence per diem. Provost Marshall of the Army per diem foure shillings three pence. Provost Marshall of Lemster five shillings seven pence per diem. And to both Provosts, Horses to bee assigned out of the Army, at the Lord Deputies discretion.

Summa per annum three hundred one pound two shillings seven pence.

Warders and Pensioners.

Warders in divers Provinces three thousand thirtie one pound seven pence halfe-penny. Pensioners, fortie foure, at foure pound nineteene shillings two pence per diem. Almesmen foureteene, at sixe pence Irish a peece per diem. Commissaries of Musters, twenty, at sixe shillings eight pence a peece per diem.

Summa per annum three thousand one hundred twenty two pound five s. sixe d.

Summa totalis per annum fourteene thousand fiftie five pound foure shillings eight pence halfe-penny.

The same day this List was signed, being the eleventh of Februarie, the Lords by their letters to the Lord Deputie (being yet in England, but newly gone from London, and in his way towards Ireland), appointed that the ships of Bristol, which had transported one thousand two hundred foote from thence to Dublin, should there be staied, to the end they might transport a thousand men, which were to be sent from Dublin, to meete with three thousand more sent out of England, out of which the Garrison of Carickfergus was to be strengthened, and a new Garrison planted at Loughfoyle.

The Lord Mountjoy's letters to Sir Robert Sicill.

The Lord Mountjoy lying at Westchester for a passage into Ireland, and there receiving notice, that the imprisoned Earle of Essex had signed a submission to the Queene, whereupon her Majestie began to be inclined to shew him mercy, directed his letters thence the eighteenth of Februarie to Sir Robert Sicill Secretarie of State, therein avowing, that as his love made him interessed in that noble Earles fortunes, so hee would thankefully acknowledge from him such favour, as he should be pleased to shew that distressed Earle, withall protesting, that he would alwaies be a free man, and slave to no mans humour; but as he in this Irish imployment expected all favourable seconds from him (according to his noble promise, whereupon his hopes chiefely relied), so he would ever be honest and thankefull towards him in all occasions. And upon these termes all exchange of good offices passed betweene this Lord Deputie and Master Secretarie, till the fatall death of that noble Earle of Essex hereafter to bee mentioned, and the Lord Deputies participation of that ruine, made him change his stile, and never to cease, till hee had confirmed a neere friendship betweene himselfe and the Secretary, at least as intire, as greatnesse admits, as hereafter shall bee shewed.

A new Lord President of Mounster.

The twentie sixe of Februarie, the Lord Deputie landed in Ireland, and there received the sword, and within few dayes, by warrant out of England, he granted her Majesties letters Pattents to Sir George Carew, to bee Lord President of Mounster, which place had layen void some few moneths, from the death of Sir Thomas Norreys. The 27 he received advertisement from the Earle of Ormond, Generall of the English forces till his comming over, that Tyrone was in the West part of Mounster, having about him not only his owne forces, but those of the Rebels of that Province, which were so great, as he had not hitherto power to oppose them: but now having gathered all the Queenes forces he could make, purposed the next morning to set forwards towards him. The fifth of March his Lordship received advertisement from other parts, that Tyrone could not escape in his returne to the North, but either over the River Shanon, which passage the Earles of Thomond and Clanrickard might easily stop, or by the Westward borders of the Pale, where if his Lordship would draw his forces to Athboye, Mullingar, Ballymore, and Athlone, it was not possible for him to escape them. That Tyrone had thus engaged himselfe, presuming on the corruption of the State, and little expecting his Lordships so sudden comming over, so as if his Lordship forgave him this fault, he was not like to catch him againe in the like, neither could any thing but want of intelligence, make his Lordship faile in stopping the returne of Tyrone, and his forces into the North. Advising his Lordship to be wary in crediting intelligences, which were commonly false, and made of purpose, and to expect, that besides the knowne enemy, and a confused warre, he should finde a broken State, a dangerous Counsell, and false hearted subjects. The eight of March the Earle of Ormond sent advertisement, that Tyrone purposed to passe the River Shanon. That he had written to the Earle of Thomond to draw towards him, that they might oppose his passage, but that his Lordship could not performe his order, by reason that the Mayor of Leymricke would not afford him carriage for his victuals. That Tyrone in scattered Troopes and a cowardly manner, hastened his returne, and that present day had marched foure and twenty miles, without any stay. That Sir Warham Sent Leger, and Sir Henry Power, joint Commissioners for governing of Mounster, with the forces under their charge, had met neere Corke with Hugh Mac Gwier, chiefe Lord of Fermanagh (in the North) and that in the incounter Sir Warham Sent Leger, and the said Mac Guire were killed. That his Lordship had burned all the Townes where the Traytors might find reliefe, and that they used the same

Advertisements of the rebels.

[II. i. 55.]

The Earle of Ormond's Advertisement.

course towards her Majesties Subjects. The same day the Lord Deputy received further advertisement from Mounster, that Tyrone was compassed in by the Earle of Ormond, on the one side, and the Earle of Thomond on the other, and by the Commissioners forces on the third side, (who ruled the Province after the death of Sir Thomas Norreys, untill a Lord President should be chosen, for he that was newly sent over, was yet at Dublyn); that the Mayor of Lymbricke had commandement to lay ships and boates, to hinder his passage by that Haven, as likewise the Mayor of Galway to interrupt his passage by sea, and the Earle of Clanrickard, to stop his passage by land through Connaght. So as howsoever he were five thousand strong in able men, besides many of baser sort, yet he being far from any second of Ulster men, in whom the chiefe strength of the Rebellion consisted, and no way able to returne thither, his utter confusion was confidently hoped. But these were onely Irish ostentations of service, which seldome use to take effect, and many times are not truly intended, as the sequell will shew.

Advertisement from Mounster.

And lest the Lord Deputy should expect faithfull dealing of the English Irish Subject in the other kind of service, by supplying the Army of necessaries, the nobilitie & Gentrie of the very English Pale, the same day exhibited a petition to his Lordship, to prevent the opinion of disloialtie, upon refusal of such supplies, by pretending of disabillitie upon the great spoyles, which aswell the rebels, as the English souldiers had made upon all the inhabitants.

The Lord Deputie had written a former letter to Master Secretarie, in excuse of not reducing the Armie from foureteene thousand foote to twelve thousand, according to the new Establishment, aswell because the same was to begin the first of Februarie, which his Lordship could not effect, since he arrived not in Ireland untill the twentie sixe of the same moneth, as also because the Army was presently farre divided, the greater part thereof being with the Earle of Ormond, and for that, whensoever they returned, the discharged Companies must presently bee reduced into some other, or else so many men and Armes should bee meerely lost, as the Lords Justices had lately found by experience, when determining to cast a Company of one hundred and fiftie, being by Pole a hundred, of the oldest and best souldiers, with purpose next day to deliver them to other Captaines, upon the divulging thereof, onely three of the whole Company with their Armes could be found, to be so transmitted.

To this letter formerly written, and perswading that the two thousand might still be continued in pay, his Lordship received the following answere from her Majestie; dated the fifteenth of March.

Elizabeth Regina.

[II. i. 56.]

Letter from Her Majestie.

ALthough we have upon your earnest request (in whose affection and duty we doe repose trust and confidence) yeelded to the continuance of fourteene thousand foot for some small time, both because we conceive, that according to your reasons, it will give good assurance to the Plantation of Loughfoyle, and the reduction of Lemster, and prevent the present terror, which this proud attempt of Tyrones, to passe over all the Kingdome, hath stricken into the hearts of all our Subjects, and would increase, if we should presently have abated our numbers: yet must we let you know, that we doe expect at your hands, and doe determine, that assoone as the present bruites are passed, you shall diminish the same by little and little hereafter, according to our first determination: for we have had too good proofe of that governement, as not to know and discerne, that all the mischiefes of our service, have growne most by lacke of discretion and order, by vaine journies, whilst better opportunities have beene lost, by undiscreet carriages of all secret purposes, by placing Captaines of small merit or experience, and which is above all, by nourishing the Irish, who are snakes in our bosomes, whilst we hold them, and when they are out, doe convert upon our selves, the experience and strength they have gotten by our making them to be Souldiers. And therefore you shall understand now, that although we have beene content to grace some such as are of noble houses, and such others as have drawne blood on the Rebels, with charge of Companies, yet we find it now growne to a common opinion, that it is as good to be a Rebell as a Subject: for Rebels find and feele it, that they shall be hired (even with whole companies in our pay) onely to forbeare doing harme, and not for having done any such service, as may make them irreconciliable. And further we see, that others that are in pay in their owne Countrey, are so farre from doing service on their neighbours, that are out, as when they tarry in for a shew, they are the chiefest meanes under hand, to helpe the rebels with such powder and munition, as (to our no small charge) we put into their hands, to be used against them. In this point therefore, we command you henceforth to bee considerate, and not to be induced to put such in pay, as spend our treasure onely to their owne advantage, upon this supposition or bragge of theirs, that they must runne to the enemies if they be not entertained: for when we consider the effects that are derived from our charges, to have so many foote and horse of the Irish entertained, onely to save their owne Cowes and Countries, we are of opinion, so they went not with our Armes to the Rebels, that it were better service for us, to save our treasure, then to pay for their bodies, seeing they that live by the warre better then they should doe in peace, intend nothing lesse then our service. And therefore we command you, not onely to raise no more, when these shall be decaied, but to keepe them unsupplied that are already, and as they waste to Casse their bands: for we can never allow of this entertainement of them. Whilst you are forced to keep the 2000. men for our service, you may keepe the Captaines uncassed, but not give any warrant to them to supply their Companies with any more Irish. We doe also require you, that you doe seeke by all meanes possible, where the Irish are entertained, to use their service as farre from their owne Countries as may be; wherein we pray you especially to take care in the Province of Connaght, where there are so many Irish bands together, and rather to draw some of them to serve else where, and send English in their stead. This shal serve for the present, to answere your dispatch, wherein we doe write to you, (whom we know to love our Commandements) more directly in this point of our desire to have our charge abated, then we doe to you and the Counsell together, because we would have them apprehend, (seeing you thinke such an opinion would be good), that our Army shall not be so soone abated, as we hope you will; wherein notwithstanding we doe referre things to your discretion, whom we will trust with the charge of 2000. men, seeing we have committed to you our whole Kingdome, &c.

[II. i. 57.] *The Lord Deputy's second dispatch to Master Secretary.*

His Lordship in a second dispatch to Master Secretary, had written, that Tyrone having passed through the Pale into Mounster with some one thousand five hundred horse and foote, of such sort as so many of the Queenes worst men were able to encounter them, was now in Mounster with an Army of 4 thousand in reputation, and was there attended by the Queenes Army of three thousand foote, and three hundred horse, commaunded by the Earle of Ormond; so as onely the dregges of the Queenes Army were now neere him; out of which notwithstanding, he hoped to bee able to draw one thousand five hundred foote, and three hundred horse, and therewith to make head against Tyrone at his returne: but in regard the Plantation of Loughfoyle and Ballyshannon were presently commanded him, whether Sir Henrie Dockwra was to ship three thousand out of England, and another thousand were to be shipped from Dublin: these one thousand being part of the men he was to draw against Tyrone, he durst not leade them farre from the Sea, and so might perhaps be forced to loose good occasion of service, whereas if these things had been left to his discretion, hee would have deferred the Plantation of Ballishannon to a time of more safety, and with these one thousand men and their munition to bee sent thither, would now attend Tyrone in his passage with so great advantage, as he was not likely to finde hereafter, and if he escaped, would presently have put himselfe in the head of the Earle of Ormonds Troopes, to prosecute him into the North, and would further have advised Sir Henrie Dockwra in his passage from Chester to Loughfoyle, to descend at Carickfergus, and thence to take five hundred old souldiers, leaving so many new in their roome.

The Queenes gratious answere.

To this dispatch his Lordship received the Queenes gratious answere, by a letter dated the sixteenth of this moneth, wherein allowing his beginnings, and approving his reasons: the forbearing presently to plant Ballishannon, and the ordering of Lochfoyle Plantation, and the disposing of Garrisons aptly (for the defence of such as in that case offered to returne to due obedience), were all freely left to his Lordships discretion, with promise to make good construction of his actions, being confident that they had no other object, but loyall service.

The Lord Deputie having drawne as many together as hee could about Mullingar, to lye for Tyrone in his returne out of Mounster, received advertisement the fifteenth of this present, that Tyrone hearing of his preparations to meete him, had left a thousand Connaght rogues to assist Desmond, and some eight hundred men with Richard Butler, and having made Captaine Tirrell chiefe commander of all the Lemster Rebels, was stolne out of Mounster with sixe hundred in his company, and had passed the Enney, and so escaped into the North.

Tyrone stolne out of Mounster.

Whereupon the Lord Deputie the same day writ to the Earle of Ormond, to send backe from Mounster, the forces hee had drawne thither out of Lemster, and with all sent him her Majesties letters, importing thankes for the service hee had done, and her desire that hee would still hold the place of Lieutenant of the Armie. In the acceptance whereof, the Lord Deputie professed, that hee should esteeme himselfe much honoured, and would be ready, after putting off the person which now was imposed on him, with much contentment to be commaunded by his Lordship.

The same time the Lord Deputie Advertised Master Secretarie, that his intelligence had been so bad (not onely in false reports of Tyrones purposes, but also in the *False reports.* relation of the Forces he had with him to bee farre greater then indeede they were, by which intelligence of false hearted subjects to discourage the Queenes Forces, the Rebels used to prevaile more then by fighting, and now hoped to discourage him at his first comming, from any present attempt against Tyrones returne), as in one and the same day hee first heard together of Tyrones looking back out of Mounster, comming into Leymster, and passing over the Enney, and the next day being assured of his escape, hee then received the first intelligence (the former letters of the eight of March being not till then delivered) that ever came to his hands from the Earle of Ormond concerning Tyrone, who in this returne had gone further in three dayes, then at his setting forth in [II. i. 58.] thirteene, having in one day marched twenty seven miles, so speedily, as he could not overtake any of his troopes with the Queenes forces, though he marched after him twentie miles in foure houres; adding his purpose to make present head towards the North, without which diversion of the rebels, the Garrison to be planted at Loughfoyle was like to runne a dangerous fortune. And withall sending some of Tyrones Mandates, by which hee summoned the subjects of Mounster to appeare before him, and to joyne with him, of which I have thought good, for the strangenesse of the forme, to insert this one following.

[Oneale

Tyrone's Mandate.

ONeale commendeth him unto you Morish Fitz Thomas, O Neale requesteth you in Gods name to take part with him, and fight for your conscience and right; and in so doing, Oneale will spend to see you righted in all your affaires, and will helpe you: And if you come not at Oneale betwixt this and to morrow at twelve of the clocke, and take his part, Oneale is not beholding to you, and will doe to the uttermost of his power to overthrow you, if you come not to him at furthest by Satturday noone. From Knocke Dumayne in Calrie, the fourth of February 1599.

Oneale requesteth you to come speake with him, and doth give you his word that you shall receive no harme, neither in comming nor going from him, whether you be friend or not, and bring with you to Oneale Gerat Fitz-gerald.

Subscribed O Neale.

The Earle of Clanrickard.

The seventh of March the Lord Deputy was advertised, that Tyrone returned to Dungannon his House the fifteenth day, and brought with him out of Mounster foure pledges of Desmonds faith unto him. That the Earle of Clanrickard had sworne, so soon as the Lord of Dunkellyn his eldest sonne returned out of England, to take no longer day then May next, to joyne with Tyrone, and enter into action, (so the Irish terme rebellion): and that Tyrone had called the Lords of the North together, to consult about the opposition to be made against the intended plantation of the English Garrisons at Loughfoyle.

The Earle of Essex.

The twentieth of March Master Secretary wrote to the Lord Deputy, that the Earle of Essex, hitherto restrained in the Lord Keepers House, had found the Grace with her Majesty, to be sent to his owne house in London, yet with a keeper; for Sir Richard Barkley, had the guard of him, with the keyes of the water-gate and street doore, and the Earle had the freedome of the whole House, with a dozen servants to attend him, who might freely go in and out at pleasure, and the Countesse of

Essex had liberty to come thither to him. And the Lord Deputy still continued frequently to solicite the Secretaries favour to this noble Earle, many times inlarging himselfe so farre, as to justifie the Earles faithfull endeavours in the maine point of the late Irish service, about which he was most questioned. Insomuch as seeing the Earles actions in Ireland to be narrowly sifted, he wrote not long after to the Secretary, expressely avowing; That if the Earle of Essex had brought with him a farre greater Army, the estate of the yeere being as then it was, and he comming at that time of the yeere when he did, yet during his aboade there, (which was from March to September), there could no other consequence have justly beene expected in that so short time; but that the Rebels moved with the countenance and terrour of the Army, should generally (or for the most part) have sought her Majesties mercy, and making their submission, have beene received upon pledges to continue subjects, or else to have sought to have ruined them by planting strong garrisons, which in most places must have beene done by an Army, and they being in severall places, and many circumstances besides required thereunto, the effecting thereof would have taken up as much time as he spent here. And though the terrour of the Army did not worke the first effect, being in the choyce of the enemy, untill by the second course they might be constrained, that the fault was in their disposition, and not in the Earles endeavours or power. And though the garrisons were not accordingly planted, that as well the shortnes of the time, as the Counsels to which the Earle was tied at that time, might justly cleere him of that default.

The Lord Deputy justifies the Earle of Essex.

[Chap. II.

[II. i. 59.]

Chap. II.

Of the Lord Deputies particular proceedings in the prosecution of the Rebels in the yeere 1600.

The List of the Army.

He twenty foure of March, being the last day of the former yeere, the Lord Deputy signed the following List of the Army, to bee a direction to the Treasurer at warres, for the payment thereof, from the first of Aprill in the yeere 1600, so forward.

Generall Officers for the Army.

Generall Officers.

The Earle of Ormond Lord Lieutenant of the Army per diem three pound.

Sir Oliver Lambert Sergeant Major per diem twentie shillings.

George Beverley Controller of the victuals per diem ten shillings.

Five Commissaries of the victuals, whereof one per diem eight shillings, the rest sixe shillings a peece.

Twelve Colonels at ten shillings a peece per diem.

Earle of Thomond.	Sir Matthew Morgan.
Lord Audley.	Sir Christop. St. Laurence.
Lord Dunkellin.	Sir Charles Willmot.
Sir Henry Dockwra.	Sir John Bolles.
Sir Henry Poore.	Sir Arthur Savage.
Sir Charles Percy.	Sir Richard Moryson.

A Provost Marshal of Ballishannon, and another of Loughfoyle, each at foure shillings per diem.

Companies of Horse.

Companies of Horse.

The Lord Deputie, one hundred, at eighteene pence a peece per diem. The Earle of Ormond fiftie, at twelve pence. The Earle of Southampton one hundred, halfe at eighteene pence, and halfe at fifteene pence. The Earle of Kildare fiftie at twelve pence. The Earle of Clanrikard fiftie, at twelve pence. The Lord of Dunsany fiftie, at twelve pence. The Lord President of Mounster fiftie, at eighteene pence. Sir Garret Moore twentie five, at twelve pence. Sir Christopher Sant Laurence twentie five, at twelve pence.

The Lord Dunkellin	25
Sir Henrie Harington	26
Sir William Warren	25
Sir Samuel Bagnal	50
Sir Edward Herbert	12
Sir Oliver Lambert	25
Captaine Wayman Provost Martiall of Connaght	12
Captaine Richard Greame	50
Captaine Thomas Gifford	25
Captaine Fleming	25
Captaine Taffe	25

all 12 pence per diem.

Sir Richard Wingfield Marshall 50, whereof 20 at eighteene pence, and thirtie at twelve pence per diem.

Captaine Thomas White 50 }
Sir Anthony Cooke 50 } at fifteene pence per diem.

Sir Henrie Davers 100 at eighteene pence. Sir Henrie Dockwra 50, halfe at eighteene pence, halfe at twelve pence. Sir Grif. Markam 100, halfe at fifteene pence, halfe twelve pence.

Totall of Horse 1200.

Companies of Foot.

Companies of Foot.

To be sent from Dublin to Loughfoyle in Ulster.

Sir Henry Dockwra Governor of Loughfoyle, and Colonel of the Army	200
Sir Matthew Morgan Colonel	150
Sir John Chamberlaine	150
Captaine Errington	100
Captaine Heath	150
Captaine Badbye	150
Captaine Lister	100

To be sent out of England to the same place. [II. i 60.]

Sir John Bolles one of the Colonels of the Army	150
Captaine Vaughan	150
Captaine Thomas Coche	100
Captaine Dutton	100

Companies of Foot.

Captaine Ellis Flud	150	Captaine Hales	100
Captaine Ralph Bingley	150	Captaine Alford	100
Captaine Basset	100	Captaine Pinner	100
Captaine Oram	100	Captaine Orrel	150
Captaine Lionel Guest	150	Captaine Sidney	100
Captaine Leigh	100	Captaine Windsor	100
Captaine H. Clare	150	Captaine Sidley	100
Sir John Pooley	150	Captaine Digges	100
Captaine Masterson	100	Captaine Brooke	100
Captaine Stafford	100	Captaine Rand	100
Captaine Atkinson	100	Captaine Pluncket	100

Totall of Loughfoyle Garrison devided into three Regiments under the Governour Sir Henrie Dockwra, and the two Colonels above named, Sir Matthew Morgan, and Sir John Bolles, 4000.

Carickfergus Garrison. Foote.

Sir Arthur Chichester Governour	200	Captaine Egerton	100
Sir Fulk Conway	150	Captaine Norton	100
Captaine Laurence Esmond	150	Foote	700

Foote at the Newrie.

Sir Samuel Bagnol	200	At Carlingford Capt. Ferdinando Freckelton	100
Captaine Blanye	150	Foote	450.

Foote in the Province of Connaght.

Sir Arthur Savage Governour	200	Sir Robert Lovel	150
The Earle of Thomond	200	Sir Tibet Dillon	100
The Earle of Clanrickard	100	Captaine Thomas Bourgh	100
The Lord Dunkellin, the Earles eldest sonne	200	Captaine Tibet Nelong	100
Sir Thomas Burgh his younger sonne	150	Captaine Hugh Mostian	100
		Foote	1400.

Foote in the Province of Mounster.

Companies of Foot.

Sir George Carew Lord President	200	Captaine Roger Harvy	150
The Lord Audley	200	Captaine Thomas Spencer	150
Sir Henrie Poore	200	Captaine Flower	100
Sir Charles Willmot	150	Captaine Sheffeld	100
Sir George Cary Treasurer at warres	100	Captaine George Kingsmell	100
Sir Richard Percy	150	Captaine Garret Dillon	100
Sir Francis Barkely	100	Captaine Hugh Oreilly	100
Sir Edward Fitzgarret	100	Captaine William Poore	100
Sir John Barkley	200	Captaine Saxy	100
Sir Gerald Harvy	150	Captaine Bostock	100
Sir John Dowdal	100	Captaine George Blount	100
Sir Richard Masterson	100	Foote 2950.	

Foote in the Province of Leymster.

[II. i. 61.]

The Lord Deputies Guard	200	Sir Garret More	100
The Earle of Southampton	200	Sir Francis Rushe	150
		Sir Henrie Follyot	150
		Sir William Warren	100
The Earle of Ormond	200	Sir Thomas Loftus	100
The Earle of Kildare	150	Sir Oliver Saint Johns	150
The Lord of Dunsany	150	Sir Charles Ocarrol	100
The Lord Delvin	150	Sir Henrie Davers	200
Sir George Bourcher	100	Sir James Fitzpeirse	150
Sir Richard Wingfeild	150	Sir Francis Stafford	200
Sir Christoper Sant Laurence	200	Sir Henrie Harington	100
		Capt. Thomas Williams	150
Sir Charles Percy	200	Capt. Roe	100
Sir Oliver Lambert	200	Capt. Toby Cafeild	150
Sir Richard Moryson	200	Capt. Josias Bodley	150
Sir Thomas Wingfeild	150	Capt. Francis Shane	100
Sir Henrie Warren	100	Foote 4500.	

The totall of the Foote 14000.

[A List

The Army to prosecute Tyrone.

A list of such as the Lord Deputy could draw into the field to prosecute Tyrone, all consisting of the companies lying in Lemster, and those of the Newrie and Carlingford.

Horse.

The Lord Deputy 100. Sir Henry Davers 100. Sir Samuel Bagnol 50. The Lord Dunsany 50. Sir Garret More 25. Horse 325.

Foote.

The Lord Deputy 200. The Earle of Southampton 200. Sir Francis Stafford 200. Sir Samuel Bagnol 200. Sir Richard Moryson 200. Sir Henry Davers 200. Sir Charles Percy 200. Sir Oliver Lambert 200. Sir William Warren 100. Sir Oliver Saint Johns 150. Sir Henrie Follyot 150. The Lord of Dunsany 150. Sir Garret More 100. Sir Thomas Wingfeild 150. Captaine Edward Blanye 150. Captaine Josias Bodley 150. Captaine Ferdinand Freckelton 100. Captaine Toby Cafeild 150. Captaine Francis Roe 100. Captaine Thomas Williams 150. Foote 3200.

	Foote.	Horse.
Out of these taken to guard places til the returne of the Army	810	20
Dead payes allowed in each hundred of foote 9, and in each fiftie horse 4	288	26
Totall	1098	46

	Foot.	Horse.
Deduct this 1098 out of the Foote, and 46 out of the Horse, and so remaines for the Lord Deputies Armie in field	2102	279

Out of this a further allowance (though uncertaine) must be deducted for sick and deficient men not mentioned formerly.

Observe that many Gunners, Canoniers, Armorers, and Clerks of the Ordinance, some at foure s. some at two s.

per diem, and an Inginere at ten s. per diem. That some sixteene Surgians, the chiefe at five l. the other dispersed in Provinces and Garrisons at thirty or forty s. a peece the weeke, and that the Lord Deputies Doctor of Physicke at five l. the weeke, and his chiefe Chaplaine at the same rate, and some ten other Preachers dispersed, at thirty or forty s. the weeke: each are all paid by the defalcation of one pay in each company of foot, and likewise of certaine sutes of apparell due to the same companies. And that the Commissaries of the Musters (raised from five to twenty) at three s. 4 d. a piece per diem, are paied out of the Checques which themselves raise, and one of them following the Army in field in each Province, the rest are distributed to be resident in particular garrisons.

Having made distribution of the Forces for the present: It remaines I should discend to the briefe narration of the Lord Deputies particular Counsels, and actions against the Rebels. About the beginning of Aprill, it was determined in counsell by the Lord Deputy and the generall assent of the Counsellers, that the Ilander Scots should be hired to serve against James Mac Sorley. That Agnus pretending right to his Countrey, was the fittest for that purpose, and upon his refusall, Mac Alaine was thought fittest to be entertained for this service. That the number of Scots should be 1500. or 2000. at most. That they should not land till the end of August, and remaine in pay as occasion should serve, their pay being to each man a Cow for a moneth, or for the default of Cattell, sixe d. by the day. And that they should land betweene the Band and Oldenfleet, except they thought some other place fitter. Two Inhabitants of Caricfergus were appointed to treat with these Scots, and they were to have the L. Deputies Letters to the Earle of Argile, and to the Queenes Agent in Scotland, for the furtherance of this businesse. But this Councell tooke no effect, by reason the course was disliked in England. In the same Councell it was propounded, how the Army should be

The Ilander Scots.

[II. i. 62.]

The imployment of the Army.

imployed till the Lord Deputies going into the field, which in all probability could not be for some two moneths after. And it was resolved to prosecute the Rebels at one instant, both on the borders in the North, and in Lemster. For the North borders 650. foot, and 100. horse, were to lie in garrison in Dundalke, 700. foot, and 50. horse at Ardee, 400. foot and 50. horse at Kelles, 1000. foot and 50. horse at the Newry, and a hundred foot at Carlingford. If Tyrone drew not to a head; it was concluded these garrisons were to infest the Fewes, Ferny, Ohanlons Countrey, Mac Gennis his Countrey, and other parts of Monaghan, and the Cavan. If Tyrone drew to a head, then it was concluded, his owne troopes were like to spoile these Countries, and our men sent to Loughfoyle should plant themselves with more ease, & shortly be able to spoile both Tyrone and Odonnels Country. For Lemster a thousand foot, and a hundred horse, were to draw into Ophalia, to build up the Togher, to victuall the Fort of Phillipstone, and to spoile the Connors, Macgoghegans, Omoloyes, and Mac Coghlins. This done, it was concluded, these forces should passe into Leex, there to attend direction, or if that passage were difficult, then to returne the way they went, and by the way to send for further direction. And to further the last prosecution, the O Carrols were commanded at the same time to invade the Omoloyes, and the Lord of Delvin, and Sir Francis Shane were to meet, and joyne with the Lord Dunkellin in Mac Coghlins Countrey, and there to invade the neighbour Rebels.

Few loyall subjects in Ireland.

The third of Aprill the Lord Deputy advertised Master Secretary, that the Queene had few Subjects in Ireland of any sort, who had not either some kinde of intelligence with Tyrone, or had not framed their hearts that way, whereof the whole Pale made sufficient overture, by a petition lately delivered, and by their contestation at the Counsell Table. That the old Earle of Clanrickard, at Tyrones going into Mounster, had taken day with him till May next, to declare himselfe on that party: But that the Lord of Dunkellin his eldest sonne, hated by his younger brother, whom the father esteemed much above him, gave him great confidence of his firme alleagiance, who suspecting his fathers disposition that way, had taken occasion by repairing to Dublin, and after going for England, to put himselfe as a gage and bridle to his fathers proceedings. Concluding, that he the Lord Deputy had taken order for securing the Castle of Athlone, but that all his hope of keeping the Province of Connaght in obedience, was in the Lord of Dunkellins honesty. Neither was the Lord Deputy deceived in this worthy Lord, who as during his fathers life, so from his death, (happening within few moneths), to the end of the warre, served the Queene as nobly, valiantly, and faithfully as any nobleman or gentleman in the army.

The Lord of Dunkellin.

The Lord Deputy explaned the danger of the Irish Commanders and Companies, yet for the time shewed the remedy to be more dangerous then the disease, protesting that her Majesty could not take a more unprofitable way to satisfie the Irish sutors, then by giving them Companies. His Lordship further advertised Master Secretary, that upon Tyrones retiring out of Mounster into the North, in manner of a fearefull flight, he the Lord Deputy had drawne from the Earle of Ormond such Companies as were not appointed for Mounster, and upon their arrivall to Athye had sent Sir Richard Moryson, to take possession of the governement of Leax, and Sir Oliver Lambert, to leade and bring backe the forces sent with victuals to relieve the Fort, called Mariabourg (of Queene Mary) scituate in Leax, (otherwise called the Queenes County) which Fort being before in extreame distresse, now he had supplied for three moneths. That he had imployed Brimingham, (who had about that time submitted himselfe to the Queenes mercy), to put in some Cowes into the Fort of Ophaly. That he purposed to prosecute the Rebels in Lemster with one thousand foote and a hundred horse, and to lodge the rest in garrisons upon the North, so as on the sudden he might divert Tyrone from resisting

The danger of Irish Commanders.

our present plantation at Loughfoyle. That hee would presently send a thousand old souldiers from Dublyn to Loughfoyle, and likewise with them such as were to lie in garrison at Ballishannon, under the command of Sir
[II i. 63.] Matthew Morgan, but that, for some difficulties, they could not yet be setled there, yet lying at Loughfoyle in the meane time, might doe service, and alwaies be ready to be sent thither. That Tyrones confederates were discouraged at his fearefull retreat into the North, which could not have beene greater, if he had beene broken with an Army. For after an unreasonable dayes march, hearing of the Lord Deputies drawing towards him, within one houre of his sitting downe, he did presently rise againe at seven a clocke in the night, and being assaulted by some of our scattered bands, still marched, leaving to the sword as many of his men as were ingaged, and leaving or leesing all his carriages, so as now almost every day the heads of some rebels or others were sent him, and many services were of late done, as the recovery of a prey by the garrison at the Naas, with the killing of many Rebels, and the defeat of one hundred and forty Rebels by Sir Francis Shane, whereof forty five were killed, and of them some foureteene with his owne hand. And the Rebels of Lemster daily made meanes to be received to mercy. Onely the Townes were the stores of the Rebels, and stood so saucily upon their priviledges, as a sharpe rod and strong hand were requisite to amend them. For which cause his Lordship advised, that the Castle of Lymerik might be repaired, to bridle that Town, which seemed of more importance, then any other City of that Kingdome whatsoever. That the dispairing rebels were by Tirones cunning raised to some hopes, by two ships lately come into the North out of Spaine, which brought the rebels some munition, and either assurance of great and present succours, or Tyrone at least so used their comming to his purpose, as the rebels beleeved such assurance was given. Besides, many Priests came in those ships, of which one termed himselfe the Popes Legat,

Tyrone's Confederates discouraged.

The Townes the stores of the Rebels.

and Leger Ambassadour for the King of Spaine, and Archbishop of Dublin, giving out that he was content to suffer death, if he preached not in Dublyn before Michaelmas day. Whereupon the Rebels beganne to avow themselves the King of Spaines subjects, and onely the expectation of Loughfoyle garrison, together with the doubt of these succours, kept the very Pale from the boldnes to professe the same. Lastly, his Lordship vehemently complained, that her Majesty by absolute command disposed of charges in that Kingdome, so as he could neither pleasure his owne friends, nor reward her Majesties best servants; yea, that having already given the governement of Leax to Sir Richard Moryson, (a friend whom he confessed especially to love, and whom he would undertake to be as worthy in his profession, as any of his time, or any the Queene had in that Kingdome), now by the Lords Letters signifying her Majesties pleasure, he was forced to his friends and his owne disgrace, to conferre the place on another: and in conclusion, besought her Majesty, in such recommendations to leave them somewhat to his choice, promising to execute them, or else to yeeld great reason to the contrary.

The Popes Legat for the King of Spaine.

The sixth of Aprill the Lord Deputy advertised Master Secretary, that the Earle of Ormond was gone from Dublyn to his Country, having made great complements of affection to her Majesties service, yet it was apparant that either he was growne weaker in judgement, or worse affected to the Queenes service, then was imagined in England, affirming of certainty that in the last cessation he had thrice at least spoken very long with Tyrone, and at his last being in Mounster, had once heard from him. And in generall, that the subjects were no better servants to her Majesty then the rebels, with whom they daily practised, and would give no assistance with bodies or goods to her Majesties service, yea, would (no doubt) quit their allegiance whensoever they might doe it with safety. That every rogue asked a Company, and if he had one, then sought a Regiment, but that (God blessing

The Earl of Ormond.

her Majesties Army) he hoped shortly to give law to their irregular humours.

Affaires of Mounster.

The Province of Mounster (as I formerly said) was much confirmed in rebellion by the Earle of Tyrone his last journey into those parts, where he strengthened James Fitz-thomas, (who by the Northerne rebels sent thither from Tyrone, was exalted to be Earle of Desmond in the yeere 1598. and was by a nicke-name called the Suggon Earle), he combined with Florence mac Carty, (called by the Irish, Mac Carty more, a name greatly followed there) and in like sort with most of the great men of those parts, incouraging those whom he found willing to persist, [II. i. 64.] taking pledges of those he suspected to be wavering, and burning and spoyling those few, who did absolutely refuse to joyne with him, as the Lord Barry with some others. And at this time another accident seeming of great consequence, did much erect the hearts of the Rebels, and dismay the subjects of those parts, which I will briefely set downe.

Sir George Carew Lord President of Mounster.

Sir George Carew having newly received letters Pattents to bee Lord President of Mounster, and resolving presently to repaire to his charge, departed from Dublin on his journy thitherward the seventh of Aprill, and upon the ninth came to Kilkenny with the Earle of Thomond in his company, and one hundred horse to attend him, where the Earle of Ormond told them he had appointed to parley with some Rebels of those parts, wherof Owny Mac Rory was the chiefe, and desired them to accompany him. The tenth of Aprill they rode out of Kilkenny with some twentie Horse of the Earle of Ormonds followers, and some few others mounted upon hacknies, his Lordship refusing to have the Lord Presidents Horse to guard him. So they rode eight long miles to the place of meeting: and the Earle of Ormond left his Company of two hundred Foot two mile short of that place. The Rebell Owny came out of the Woods with five hundred men well Armed, and leaving his shot, and the grosse of his troope some Calievers shot distant from the Earle, came up to him with some choise pikes. After an hower spent, & nothing concluded, the Lord President moved the Earle to returne, but he would first speake with the Jesuit Archer, and the Rebels calling him, his Lordship reproved Archer, and called him traytor. In the meane time the grosse of the Rebels had crept over the shrubs, and compassed round the Earle and his companie, which the Lord President disliking, prayed the Earle to returne: but as he turned about his hackney, the Rebels tooke him prisoner, and Owny Mac Rory laid hands on the Lord President, but the Earle of Thomond rushing upon him with his horse, made him leave his hold, and they both escaped by the swiftnesse and strength of their horses from the pushes of many pikes, wherewith the Earle of Thomond was slightly hurt in the backe. This treacherie was said to be plotted by Owny and Archer, and very few others, for if more had knowne it, many thought that the Earle had such spies, and was so feared among the Rebels, as his Lordship would have had notice thereof either for feare or love. But there wanted not others, who thought the Earle was willingly surprised. Howsoever it were, the Rebels did him no hurt in his person, onely one of the Earles men was slaine, five were hurt, and fourteene taken prisoners. The Lord President with the one hundred horse attending him, and sixe hundred foote, which he sent for out of Mounster, kept the unsetled humours of those parts from present tumult, where the Earles true followers wanting their head, and the ill affected now standing in no awe of his power, were all at liberty. The Countesse of Ormond was much afflicted with her husbands misfortune, and with feare of her own and her daughters estate. For divers pretended to be heires to the Earle; as Sir Edward Butler his brother, and in respect his bloud was attainted, Sir Walter Butler the Earles Nephew, and for other reasons the Vicount Mount-Garret. And each of these was likely to seeke to have the Earles sole daughter in their hands, besides that these controversies bred distracted humours among

The Lord President taken prisoner and rescued.

Sir George Bourcher.

the Gentlemen and others of those parts. The Lord Deputie hearing hereof, presently dispatched Sir George Bourcher to command in chiefe, and Sir Christop. Saint Laurence to assist him, in guarding the Countesse, her daughter, and the Earles houses, with the forces appointed by the Lord Deputie for that service, namely,

The Earles Company of foote 200. The foote Company of Sir Christopher Saint Laurence 200. The Earles troope of horse 50. Horse of Saint Laurence 25. Sir George Bourchers horse 10.

Yet the Lord Deputie conceived the Earles surprise to bee an evill more spetious then materiall, seeing no reason, why the Counsels of the warre should stagger upon his wel or ill doing For wheras some were of opinion, that he was willingly taken, and would declare himselfe for Tyrone, his Lordship resolved, that if he continued faithfull, his Countries might easily be defended, if otherwise, as easily wasted, since after the Garrisons should be once planted at Loughfoyle, and, those parts on the backe of
[II. i. 65.] Tyrone, hee should bee able to spare forces for any such service. And whereas many thought the newes would much amaze the Court of England, his Lordship on the contrary (since neither the Lord President nor himselfe deserved any imputation for this event, the parley being contrived without the Lord Presidents privity, and both contrived and executed, without making himselfe acquainted therewith) conceived, it would make the Army both better, and more carefully seconded out of England. And whereas it was thought, that this accident would erect the rogues spirits, which before began to bee dejected, and so hinder the submission of many, his Lordship knowing that they would never be faithfull to the State, till they could not subsist against it, was of opinion, that till they were brought into greater extremities, it would prove better, that they should stand out, then come in.

His Lordship the fifteenth of Aprill advertised Master Secretarie of this accident, and how he had sent forces to strengthen those parts, and had taken speciall care for the safetie of the Earles daughter and heire, and being loth suddenly to give his opinion herein, onely professed to thinke it strange, that one so full of regard to himselfe in all his proceedings, should be so easily overtaken. Then his Lordship gave confidence, that if the Butlers declared themselves for Tyrone, as soone as Loughfoyle Garrison was planted at his backe, his Lordship doubted not to be able to meete the Lord President in Kilkenny, and with their joynt forces, to subdue the Rebels, and set those parts in obedience.

Forces to strengthen Mounster.

At this time the Fort of Phillipstown in Ophaley (otherwise called the Kings County) was to be victualed, and Ony Mac Rory with the O Mores in Leax, together with the O Connors in Ophaly, bragged that the Queenes forces should not be able to victuall it. Now by the emulation of one of our chiefe Commanders, against another preferred before him, and strengthened by the Court factions of England, the said Commander had set out some weake Companies for this service, to be led by the other, as in preheminence of his place, but a neere friend to the Lord Deputie, conceiving how much this first actions successe might adde reputation, or give a blemish, both to his Lordship and the Army, gave notice thereof, so as his Lordship offering the same Commander the leading of those Companies, he refusing to goe with them, manifested the suspected emulation. Whereupon his Lordship caused foureteene strong Companies to be allotted, and gave the command of them in chiefe to Sir Oliver Lambert, who conducted the victuals, and led the men with such judgement and valour, as being strongly fought with at the comming off, and especially at the going on, yet they performed the service with great losse and discouragement to those proud Rebels, and the fifteenth of Aprill his Lordship advertised Master Secretary of this good service.

The Fort of Phillipstown victualled.

The thirtieth of Aprill the Earle of Ormond sent to the Lord Deputie from the Woods the conditions Ony Mac

Rory demaunded under his owne hand for his liberty, which till then he could not get, because Ony staied for Tyrones and his confederats advice, adding a postscript of his Lordships owne hand; that the letter was brought to him ready written, neither was he allowed any man of his owne to write for him. The insolent demaunds were these: First, that her Majesties forces should bee removed from Leax, and the Garrisons delivered to Oney Mac Roryes hands. Secondly, that pledges should be delivered him for caution, that no garisons shuld ever be planted there, which done, Ony and his followers would submit themselves. Thirdly, if pledges were not given, then the Garrisons also in Ophaly should be removed, and every man left to shift for himselfe. The postscript required, that upon such pledges delivered, a generall protection for sixe weeks should be sent to Onye Mac Rorye, and all his friends in Lemster, whereupon answere should be returned, who desired the benefit thereof, but during the said time of the protection, no forces of her Majesties should bee sent against their confederates in Ulster and the North. The 5 of May the L. Deputie drew into the North parts, to make Tyrone look towards him, & so to give better facility to our men to settle themselves in garrison at Loughfoyle. But before his departure from Dublin, for the better governing & defending the Pale, his L^p. did by commission leave Sir H. Poore to commaund in all martiall affaires, and some of the Counsell to governe Civill matters during his absence. And staying some few daies at Tredagh, for the Companies which had victualed Phillipston, and for the Garrisons of Kels and Ardee, as also for victuals, he marched to Dundalke, whence taking that Garrison also with him, he passed the pace of the Moyry on Whitsunday morning, and so came to the Newry, where hee understood, that according to his opinion, Tyrone turning his forces from Loughfoyle, was come in great haste to Dungannon, had razed the old Fort of Blackwater, burned Armagh, and had drawne his men into the strong fastnes of Lough-

Owny Mac Rory's insolent demaunds.

The Lord Deputie draws into the North parts.

[II. i. 66.]

es, and some of the
during his absence
h, for the Compani
d for the Garrisus
als, he marched to
n also with him, &
hitsunday morning
ee understood, tha
ing his forces from
o Dungannon, had
and Armagh, and

lurken, where
trenches, and
His Lordship
on the 16 of
in the way
100 horse.
inquired after
and Sir Oliver
the Army, and
Sergeant Major
Lordship earely
Captaine Edward
secure their
who marched from
to the Faghard,
no danger. There
in two squadrons
passed to Dund
Lord Deputy
further, that his L
would meete him
at the causey
pace hath the name
having with him,
of Sir Oliver Lamb
50 horse of volun
where hee comm
mentioned to
then his Lordship
the second squadron
Companies of Sir O
Captaine Blany
towards the Fower
with Woods, in the
the Moyrye.
same, they discove
Wood, whereupon
passe over the

lurken, where with great industrie the rebels had made trenches, and fortified the place some three miles in length. His Lordship to the former end advancing towards him, on the 16 of May, drew out of the Newrie, and incamped in the way towards Armagh with 1500 foote, and some 200 horse. And there having notice, that the rebels inquired after the time when the Earle of Southampton and Sir Oliver Lambert Sergeant Major were to come to the Army, and with all hearing, that the said Earle and Sergeant Major were that day arrived at Dundalke. His Lordship earely in the morning on the 17 of May, sent Captaine Edward Blany with 500 foot and 50 horse, to secure their passage through the pace of the Moyrye, who marched from the Campe, and so through the Moyrye to the Faghard, from which hill to Dundalke, there was no danger. There he made a stand, and leaving his foot in two squadrons of 250 each, himselfe with the horse passed to Dundalke, and told the Earle of the forces the Lord Deputy had sent to conduct him, assuring him further, that his Lordship with the rest of the Army would meete him by two of the clock in the afternoone, at the causey beyond the pace, from which the whole pace hath the name of the Moyrye. Hereupon the Earle having with him, besides this convoy, the foot Companies of Sir Oliver Lambert and Sir Henry Follyot, and some 50 horse of voluntary Gentlemen, marched to the Faghard where hee commanded one of the two squadrons above mentioned to march on, and after that the carriages; then his Lordship with the horse followed, after whom the second squadron marched, and last of all the two foot Companies of Sir Oliver Lambert, and Sir Henry Follyot, Captaine Blany commanding the vanguard, advanced towards the Foure-mile-water, being a Forde all invironed with Woods, in the middest of this dangerous pace called the Moyrye. And comming within halfe a mile of the same, they discovered the rebels on both sides in the Wood, whereupon the Earle directed the Vanguard to passe over the water, and to make good the rising of

The fight at the Moyry.

the hill beyond it. When these came within a Musket shot, they perceived two hundred foote of the enemie lodged beyond the water, in the most advantagious places. Then Captaine Blany divided his men into three Maniples, sending 60 on the right hand under Captaine Henrie Atherton, and as many on the left hand under Captaine Williams his Lieutenant, and keeping the rest in the middest with himselfe. And so by the Sergeant Majors directions, they gave the charge. In the meane time the Lord Deputy being on the hill beyond the pace, had sent his Vanguard consisting of two Regements, the one under Sir Charles Percy, and the other under Sir Richard Moryson (two Colonels of the Army), to advance towards the pace. And at this instant, when Captaine Blany gave on upon the Rebels, the said Lord Deputies vanguard appeared on the left side, within two musket shot. After some vollyes on either side, the Rebels on the right hand, and those right before Captaine Blany quitted those places, and retired through the woods to the Earle of Southamptons Reare, so as Captaine Blany passing the water, made a stand there, as he was appointed to doe, till the carriage and horse should be passed. And now the Lord Deputies Vanguard being come to the passage of the said water, maintained a resolute skermish with the Rebels on the left hand, and altogether secured the Earles troopes on that side. The rebels thus beaten on both sides, left some one hundred shot to skirmish with the Lord Deputies vanguard, and all retired to the Earle of Southamptons reare, and came desperatly on our men, both with horse and foot. But Sir Henry Follyot made a very good stand, and Sir Oliver Lambert, fearing lest our men should be distressed, the more to incourage them, tooke his colours in his owne hand and together with some 30 of the Earle of Southamptons Vangards best men, sent back to the Rere, hastened towards the Assailants, to second the Earle, who at that time with some 6 horse did charge the assailing Rebels, and beate them a musket shot back, still pursuing them, til they

The rebels beaten.

[II. i. 67.]

having spent their powder, and throwne their staves, darts, and innumerable stones, recovered the place, where Tyrone stood himselfe with some 220 horse and 200 foote in sight (besides a far greater number hid in the woods), which never came unto this fight. When our men had thus gained much ground, the Earle commaunded them to march towards the Army, and presently Sir Richard Wingfeild the Marshal of the army of Ireland came to them, with order from the L. Dep. that since the repulsed rebels were not like to give any second charge, they should continue their march, following his L[ps]. troopes directly to the Newry. In this conflict 2 of our men were slaine, Capt. Atherton and Mast. Cheut were shot, and some few hurt with swords and such weapons. On the rebels side there were in all 1200 foot thus advantagiously lodged, and 220 horse, and Tirone himself confessed, that ten of his men died with overtravelling in this hasty march, besides such as were killed, whose number could not certainely be learned. The 21 of May, his Lp. was advertised from Sir Arthur Chichester, Governour of Carickfergus, that the English sent to plant at Loughfoyle were safely landed with small resistance, and had taken Newcastle belonging to Sir John Odogherty, whose country they had spoiled & wasted, and that some of them sent forth upon a draught, had taken good store of cowes, and killed some of Odonnels people, and that they were now busie in fortifying about the Derrie, so as many of that country Southward did passe their cowes and moveables into Scotland, depending specially upon the hopes of Spanish succours. That Brian Mac Art a rebel bordering on Carickfergus, had left his fastnes of Kilultagh, and now lay on the borders of Lecale, where he purposed to assaile him, the rather because he had sent 200 men to assist Tyrone: that divers Gentlemen and others did daily flie from the rebels, and resort unto him with their goods, to the number of 1200 cowes, and more would come, but that he doubted their faithfulnes. That to free himself of the imputation to keepe

Newcastle taken.

James Mac Surley an enemy, till he had revenged on him his brothers death, he had imployed Colonell Egerton to invite that rebell to submission, but received onely temporising answeres; whereupon according to his Lps. directions, hee had written and sent a messenger of purpose, to the Lord of Clantyer an Ilander Scot, to stirre him up against James Mac Surley, wrongfully possessing his rightfull inheritance in those parts of Ireland, offering to joyne the Queenes forces under his commaund, to those powers he should bring, for recoverie of this his right, so as he would after yeeld due tribute and obedience to her Majesty: but that upon the King of Scots late Proclamation, that al bearing Armes should be ready to attend the King on the 17 of July next following, in prosecution of the Ilander Scots (as was given out), refusing to pay tribute, he feared that this Lord would bee diverted from imbracing this busines, howsoever advantageous to him. That he had received Con Mac Neale, the son of Neale Mac Brian, and his horsemen, into her Majesties pay, and would shortly waste his fathers Country, whence Brian Mac Art and some 400 Bonnaghtes (or hired souldiers) were maintained and fed. Finally, that he thought fit to rebuild Olderfleete, and leave some in Ward there, because the Haven was commodious to succour weather-beaten ships, going to supplie the Garrison of Loughfoyle with necessaries.

The King of Scots' Proclamation.

Letter from the Lords in England.

The 26 of May, the Lord Deputie received a letter from the Lords in England, with full answere to his late dispatches. For the Earle of Ormonds detension, they signified her Majesties griefe to be the greater, because any attempt made for his recoverie was like to prove his ruine, and that her Majestie had written to the Countesse, to send the Earles young daughter and heire into England. For Sir Arthur Oneales demaunds, upon his comming in to serve her Majesty, in the first point concerning religion, her Majesty bare with it, because she took it to proceede of his ignorance, not of presumption, only wishing the L. Dep. to let him see, that her Majesty pursued none in those parts for religion, and so to satisfie him, but in no wise by any contract or condition. Next for his and others suits for land, and for entertainements, because such overtures were like daily to be made, by such as submitted themselves, and protraction of sending to and fro, might lose many opportunities. First, touching the sutes for land, her Majesties directions in particular cases following, should be a rule to the Lord Deputie for his graunts of that kind. And first for Sir Arthur Oneales demaunding Tyrones estate, that could not be granted him, by reason Tyrone, upon pretence of an old inquisition, had extended the limits of his Countrie, and incroched far into the South and East. But her Majesty was pleased to give him Tyrones principall seates, reserving places for forts, and lands to maintaine them, and reserving all dependancy of the Vriaghtes (or neighbour Lords), also reserving lands in Tyrone to reward the services of such Gentlemen as should serve under Sir Arthur in these warres, which they should onely hold of her Majestie by letters Patents. For the rest Sir Arthur Oneale to be chiefe in Tyrone, as well in superioritie, as in revenue. Touching Neale Garves demaunds for O Donnels estate, her Majesties pleasure was to reserve some Portes and Castles, and some lands to reward the services of that Countries Gentlemen, intending that these, and more specially the Mac Swynes, should depend onely upon her Majestie, and have right to those lands by her letters Patents. Touching Mac Guires Country, her Majestie directed like reservations of land, for Fortes and rewards of services, and generally in all grantes charged to reserve her Majesties ancient rights. Secondly, touching suitors for entertainements in pay, her Majesties pleasure was signified to allow one thousand pound a moneth, so long as the Lord Deputy and the Counsel there should thinke fit, to be imployed that way, according to the Lord Deputies discretion. But their Lordships advised warily to observe, and know, such as offered submission, because it had alwaies been the Arch-traitors

[II. i. 68.]

Sir Arthur Oneales demaunds.

Suitors for entertainements in pay.

practise, to let slip such as he could not defend, that they might save their goods, and live upon her Majestie, without any intent to doe her service. Lastly, whereas the Lord of Dunkellin by his letters, in regard of some restrictions, whereby hee was disabled to serve her Majestie as he desired, had made offer to resigne the governement he had in the Province of Connaght. And forasmuch as the Queene was alwaies unwilling to imploy any great Lord in his owne Countrie, yet finding him placed in that governement by the Earle of Essex, had still continued him there, only out of her speciall favor to him. And for that of late some insolencies had bin offered to Companies of the English, by the old Earle of Clanricards soldiers in her Majesties pay. Their Lordships signified, that the Queenes pleasure was, to accept the Lord of Dunkellins resignation, in the fairest maner, and with all carefull tendering of his honour, advising the Lord Deputie to invite him to accompany his Lordship, and serve in the Army under him. And Sir Arthur Savage then a Colonel of the Army, and lying with his Company at Athlone, was appointed provisionall Governour of the Province of Connaght, except the Lord Deputie knew some sufficient cause to the contrary. The Lord Deputy having attained his end of drawing the Army into the North, by the safe landing and setling of Loughfoyle Garrison, in the farthest North of Ireland, on Tyrones backe. His Lordship the twentie eight of May hearing that Tyrone had drawne backe his men two miles further into the fastnesse, and being informed that the Pace of the Moyrye, by reason of much wet lately fallen, and the Rebels breaking of the causey, was hard to passe, returned by Carlingford pace to Dundalke, and so to Dublin, where he understood that the Rebels had in his absence burned the Pale, though he left for defence of it 2000 foot and 175 horse in Lemster, but the damage was not answerable to the clamour; for many private men have in England sustained greater losse by casuall fire in time of peace, then the whole Pale had done by the

Sir Arthur Savage appointed governour of the Province of Connaght.

The Pale burnt.

enemies burning in warre, and many private men in England have in one yeere lost more cattel by a rot, then the Pale lost by this spoyling of the rebels, of which they lamentably complained. Besides that indeede this burning and spoyling of the very Pale, did further the greatest end of finishing the warres, no way so likely to be brought to an end, as by a generall famine.

The hearing of the Earle of Essex his cause.

Give me leave to digresse a little, to one of the fatall periods of Robert the noble Earle of Essex his tragedy, (and the last but one, which was his death) whereof the following relation was sent into Ireland. The fifth of June there assembled at Yorkehouse in London, about the hearing of my Lord of Essex his cause, eighteene Commissioners, viz. my Lord of Canterburie, Lord Keeper, Lord Treasurer, Lord Admirall, Lords of Wor- [II. i. 69.] cester, Shrewsbury, Cumberland, Huntington, Darby, & Zouch, Mast. Comptroller, Master Secretarie, Sir Jhon Fortescu, Lord Popham Chiefe Justice, Lord Anderson Chiefe Justice of the common Pleas, Lord Perian Chiefe Baron of the Exchequer: Justices, Gaudy and Walmesley. They sate from eight of the clock in the morning, till very neere nine at night, all at a long table in chaires. At the Earles comming in, none of the Commissioners stirred cap, or gave any signe of curtesie. He kneeled at the upper end of the Table, and a good while without a cushion. At length my Lord of Canterbury moved my Lord Treasurer, and they joyntly my Lord Keeper and Lord Admirall, that sat over against them, then was he permitted a cushion, yet still was suffered to kneele, till the Queenes Sergeants speech was ended, when by the consent of the Lords, he was permitted to stand up, and after upon my Lord of Canterburies motion, to have a stoole.

The manner of proceeding was this. My Lord Keeper first delivered the cause of the assembly, and then willed the Queenes Counsaile at Law, viz. Sergeant, Attorney, Solicitor, and Master Bacon to informe against him. The Sergeant began, and his speech was not long, onely a

The Sergeant's speech.

preface as it were to the accusations. The summe of it was, to declare the Queenes Princely care and provision for the warres of Ireland, and also her gratious dealing with the Earle before he went, in discharging ten thousand pound of his debts, and giving him almost so much more, to buy him horses, and provide himself, and especially in her proceedings in this cause, when as after so great occasion of offence, as, the consumption of a royall Army, fruitlesse wasting thirty hundred thousand d. treasure, contempt, and disobedience to her expresse commandement, she notwithstanding was content to be so mercifull towards him, as not to proceede against him in any of her Courts of Justice, but only in this private sort, by way of mercy and favour.

Master Attorney's speech.

After him the Attorney began, whose speech contained the body and substance of the accusation, it was very sharp, & stinging, for besides the many faults of contempt and disobedience, wherewith hee charged him, he did also shrewdly inferre a dangerous disposition and purpose, which was by many rhetoricall amplifications, agravated to the full; he divided his speech into three parts, Quomodo ingressus, Quomodo progressus, Quomodo regressus; In the ingresse, hee observed how large a Commission he stood upon, such a one as never any man had the like before, namely, that he might have authoritie to pardon all Traytors of himselfe, yea, to pardon treason committed against her Majesties owne person, and that he might mannage the warres by himself, without being tied to the advice of the Counsell of Ireland, which clause hee said was granted, that he might at first proceede in the Northerne journy, which the Counsell of Ireland (whose lands and livings lay in the South), might perhaps hinder, and labor to divert him, to the safeguard of themselves. In the other two parts of his speech were contained five speciall crimes, wherwith the Earle was charged, viz His making the Earle of Southampton Generall of the Horse. 2. His going to Lemster and Mounster, when he should have gone to Ulster. 3. His

The charge against the Earle.

making so many Knights. 4. His conference with
Tyrone. 5. His returne out of Ireland, contrary to her
Majesties command. These all saving the fourth, were
recited by the Lords in their censures, as the crimes for
which he was censured by them. The first was amplified, 1.
for that he did it contrary to her Majesties mind, plainely
signified unto him in England, that hee increased that
offence, by continuing him in that office stil, when her
Majesty by letters had expressely commanded him to
displace him; and thirdly, for that he wrote a very bold
presumptuous letter to her Majesty, in excuse of that
offence, which letter was afterwards read. The second 2.
point of his Southerne journy was agravated, in that it
was made contrary to her Majesties advised resolution,
agreed upon by her Counsel, and approved by her martial
men, as the only means to reduce Ireland, and contrary to
the Earles own project, yea, & that without the advice
of the Counsel of Ireland also, as appeared by a letter of
theirs under their hands, though now the Earle pretended
their advice for his own excuse, wherupon followed the
harrowing out, and the weakning of the royallest Army
that ever went out of England, the wasting of that huge
expence, and the overthrow of the whole action. The [II. i. 70.]
third point, viz. the making of Knights, was urged to 3.
have beene contrary to her Majesties expresse commandement, a question being once made, whether he should
have that authoritie or no, because he had abused it
before, yet the same being at the last granted, with this
limitation given him in charge, that he should make but
few, and those men of good ability, whereas he made
to the number of threescore, and those some of his meniall
servants, yea & that in a most unseasonable time, when
things were at the worst, which should have been done
upon victorie and triumph onely. The fourth point, 4.
namely, his conference with the Rebell, was agravated,
in that it was an equall and secret conference, dishonourable to her Majestie, for him that sustained her royall
person, to conferre in equall sort with the basest and vilest

traytor that ever lived, a bush Kerne, and base sonne of a Blacksmith; suspicious also, in that it was private and secret, no man suffered to approch, but especially no English man; the end of the conference most shamefull, that the wretched traytor should prescribe conditions to his Soveraigne; abominable and odious conditions, a publike tolleration of Idolatrous religion, pardon for himselfe and all the traytors in Ireland, and full restitution of lands and possessions to all the sort of them. It was added, that before this parley, a messenger went secretly from the Earles Campe to the traytor, viz. Captaine Thomas Leigh, if not sent by the Earle, at least by his connivency, at least by the connivencie of the Marshall,
5. whom the Earle did not punish. Lastly, the fifth point was urged to be intollerably presumptuous, contrary to her Majesties expresse commandement in writing, under the seale of her privy signet, charging him upon his dutie not to return until he heard further from her; that this his returne was also exceeding dangerous, in that he left the Army divided unto two divers men, the Earle of Ormond, and the Lord Chauncellor, men whom himselfe had excepted against, as unfit for such a trust, and that he so left this Army, as that if God his providence had not been the greater, the ruine and losse of the whole Kingdome had ensued thereupon. This was the summe of the accusation, every part interlaced with most sharpe and bitter rhetoricall amplifications, which I touch not, nor am fit to write, but the conclusion was (whereby a taste of the same may be had) that the ingresse was proud and ambitious, the progresse disobedient, and contemptuous, the regresse notorious and dangerous. Among other things the Lady Rich her letter to the Queene was pressed with very bitter and hard termes: my Lady Rich her letter he termed an insolent, saucy, malipert action. He proposed also in the end a president for the Earles punishment (saying, he was faine to seeke farre for one gentle enough): one William of Britten Earle of Richmond, who refusing to come home out of France upon

The conclusion.

the Kings letter, was adjudged to loose all his goods, lands, and chattels, and to indure perpetuall imprisonment. Master Attorney particularly said the following words, whereas the Earle in his letter exclameth, O tempora, O Mores (for so I thinke he construed these words of his, O hard destiny of mine, that I cannot serve the Queene and please her too)! let me also say with the Orator concerning him; Hæc Regina intelligit, hæc Senatus videt, hic tamen vivit. In the end of his speech, Now (saith he) nothing remaineth but that wee inquire quo animo, all this was done. Before my Lord went into Ireland, he vaunted and boasted, that hee would fight with none but the Traytor himselfe, he would pull him by the eares out of his den, hee would make the Earle tremble under him, &c. But when he came thither, then no such matter, hee goes another way, it appeareth plainely he meant nothing lesse then to fight with Tyrone. This was the effect of Master Attorneys part.

Master Sollicitor's speech.

Master Solliciter his speech followed, which contained the unhappy successe, which ensued in Ireland after the Earles departure, whereby appeared how little good the Earle had done, in that the Traitor was growne much more confident, more insolent, and stronger then ever he was before, as appeared principally by his declaration, which he hath given out since the Earles departure, vaunting that he is the upholder of the Catholike faith and Religion, that whereas it was given out by some that hee would follow the Earle of Essex into England, hee would perhaps shortly appeare in England little to Englands good: many things he added to that purpose.

[II. i. 71.]

Sir Francis Bacon.

After him Sir Francis Bacon concluded the accusation with a very eloquent speech. First by way of Preface, signifying, that he hoped both the Earle himselfe, and all that heard him, would consider, that the particular bond of duty, which he then did and ever would acknowledge to owe unto the Earle, was now to be sequestred, and laied aside. Then did he notably extoll her Majesties singular grace and mercy, whereof he said the Earle was a singular work, in that upon his humble sute, shee was content not to prosecute him in her Court of Justice the Starre-chamber, but according to his owne earnest desire, to remove that cup from him, (those he said were the Earles own words in his Letter), and now to suffer his cause to be heard. Inter privatos parietes, by way of mercy and favour onely, where no manner of disloyalty was laide to his charge, for (quoth he) if that had beene the question, this had not beene the place. Afterwards passing along most eloquently through the Earles journey into Ireland, hee came to charge him with two points not spoken of before. The first was a Letter written by the Earle unto my Lord Keeper, very boldly and presumptuously, in derogation to her Majesty, which letter he also said was published by the Earles own friends. The points of the letter which he stood upon, were these; No tempest to the passionate indignation of a Prince; as if her Majesty were devoid of reason, carried away with passion (the onely thing that joineth man and beast together): Her Majesties heart is obdurate, he would not say that the Earle meant to compare her absolutely to Pharaoh, but in this particular onely, which must needs be very odious. Cannot Princes erre: Cannot Subjects suffer wrong? as if her Majesty had lost her vertues of judgement, Justice, &c. Farre be it from me (quoth he) to attribute divine properties to mortal Princes, yet this I must truly say, that by the Common Law of England, a Prince can doe no wrong. The last point of that Letter, was a distinction of the duty a subject oweth to his Prince, that the duty of Allegiance, is the onely indissolueble duty, what then (quoth he) is the duty of gratitude? what the duty of obedience? &c. The second point of Master Bacons accusation was, that a certaine dangerous seditious Pamphlet, was of late put forth into print, concerning the first yeeres of the raigne of Henry the fourth, but indeed the end of Richard the second, and who thought fit to be Patron of that booke, but my Lord of Essex, who after the booke had beene out a weeke,

A Letter written by the Earle to the Lord Keeper.

A dangerous Pamphlet.

wrote a cold formall letter to my Lord of Canterbury, to call it in againe, knowing belike that forbidden things are most sought after: This was the effect of his speech. The spetiall points of the whole accusation were afterwards proved by the Earles owne Letters, by some of her Majesties Letters, and the Counsels, and by the letter of the Earle of Ormond and others of the Counsell of Ireland, openly red by the Clerke of the Counsell.

The Earle's speech.

The accusation ended, the Earle kneeling, beganne to speake for himselfe, in effect thus much. That ever since it pleased her gracious Majestie to remove that cup from him (which he acknowledged to have beene at his humble sute) and to change the course of proceeding against him, which was intended in the Starre-chamber; he laied aside all thought of justifying himselfe in any of his actions, and that therefore, he had now resolved with himselfe never to make any contestation with his Soveraigne: that he had made a divorce betwixt himselfe and the World, if God and his Soveraigne would give him leave to hold it; that the inward sorrow and afflictions which he had laied upon his soule privately, betwixt God and his conscience, for the great offence against her Majesty, was more then any outward crosse or affliction that could possibly befall him. That he would never excuse himselfe neither a toto nor a tanto, from whatsoever crimes of errour, negligence, or inconsiderate rashnes, which his youth, folly, or manifold infirmities might leade him into, onely he must ever professe a loyall faithfull unspotted heart, unfained affection and desire, ever to doe her Majesty the best service he could, which rather then he would lose, he would, if Christianity and Charity did permit, first teare his heart out of his breast, with his owne hands. But this alwaies preserved untouched, he was most willing to confesse and acknowledge whatsoever errours and faults it pleased her Majesty to impute unto him. The first part of his speech drew plenty of teares from the eyes of many of the hearers; for it was uttered [II. i. 72.] with great passion, and the words excellently ordered, and it might plainely appeare, that he had intended to speake no more for himselfe. But being touched (as it seemed) with the oversharpe speeches of his accusers, he humbly craved of their Lordships, that whereas he had perceived many rhetoricall inferences and insinuations given out by his accusers, which might argue a disloyall, malicious, wicked, and corrupt affection in him, they would give him leave, not in any sort to excuse himself, but only by way of explanation, to lay downe unto them those false guides, which had deceived him, and led him into all his errours, and so he entered into a kind of answering Master Atturnies speech, from point to point in order, alleaging, for the point of his large Commission for pardoning treason against her Majesties person, that it was a thing he had learned of Master Attourney himselfe, onely to meete with the rebels curiosity, which had an opinion, that all treason in Ireland, might be interpreted treason against her Majesties person, and therefore would trust no pardon without that clause. That in making the Earle of Southampton Generall of the Horse, the deceiveable guide which misled him, was an opinion that her Majesty might have beene satisfied with those reasons which moved him, as also with those reasons which he had alleaged in his letters, for continuance of him in the place, but that after he perceived her Majesties mind plainely in her second letter, he displaced him the next day: For his journey into Mounster, hee alleaged divers things, principally that the time of the yeere would not serve for an Ulster journey, and then the advice of the Counsel there, which he protested to alleage, not to excuse himselfe, but rather to accuse his owne errours, and the errours of the Counsellors in Ireland: and whereas some of them to excuse themselves, and charge him the deeper, had now written the contrary to the Counsell: he protested deepely that therein they had dealt most falsely, and it seemeth (saith he) that God his just revenge hath overtaken two of them already, the Earle of Ormond by blindnesse, and Sir Warham St. Leger, by violent death. For his making of Knights, he alleaged the necessity and straights he was driven unto, that being the onely way he had to retaine the voluntaries, the strength and pride of the Army; that he made but two of his servants, and those men of speciall desert and good ability: that he thought his service ought not to be any barre against them, for the receiving the reward of their deserts.

But before he had thus waded through halfe his answer, my Lord Keeper interrupted him, and told him, that this was not the course that was like to doe him good, that he beganne very well in submitting himselfe, unto her Majesties mercy and pardon, which he, with the rest of the Lords, were glad to heare; and no doubt but her Princely and Gracious nature was by that way most like to be inclined to him: that all extenuating of his offence, was but the extenuating of her Majesties mercy in pardoning: that he with all the rest of the Lords would cleere him of all suspition of disloyalty: and therefore he might doe well to spare the rest of his speech, and save time, and commit himselfe to her Majesties mercy. And when the Earle replied, that it might appeare by that hedge which he diligently put to all his answers, that he spake nothing but only to cleere himselfe from a malicious corrupt affection. My Lord Keeper told him againe, that if thereby he meant the crime of disloyalty, it was that which he needed not to feare, he was not charged with it, as the place & course taken against him might warrant; all that was now laied unto him, was contempt and disobedience. And if he intended to perswade them, that he had disobeyed indeed, but not with a purpose of disobeying, that were frivilous and absurd.

The Lord Treasurer.

Then my Lord Treasurer beganne to speake, and cleering the Earle from suspition of disloyalty, did very soundly controll divers of his other excuses.

Master Secretary.

After him Master Secretary, making a Preface why he spake before his turne, by reason of his place, tooke the matter in hand, and first notably cleering the Earle from all suspition of disloyalty, which he protested he did from

his conscience, and afterwards often iterated the same and preserved it unto him entire, he spake singularly for the justifying of her Majesties speciall care and wisdome for the warres in Ireland, in providing whatsoever could be
[II. i. 73.] demanded by the Earle for that service before his going out; with supplying him afterwards with whatsoever hee could aske, so it were possible to bee given him: in prescribing that course, which had it beene followed, was the onely way to have reduced that Realme, and which being forsaken, was the onely ruine and losse of that royall army.

And as for all those excuses which the Earle alleaged for himselfe, hee cleerely cut them off, shewing that his excuse of following the Counsell of Irelands advice, was nothing, his commission being so large, that he was not bound to follow them; and if he had beene, yet were they a Counsell at his command, he might force them to say what he list: his own letters which he alleaged, might be provisionary, written of purpose then to excuse him now. To be short, he greatly justified her Majesties wisdome, in managing that whole action, as much as lay in her, and laid the whole fault of the bad successe in Ireland, upon the Earles ominous journey (so he called it) into Mounster. And thus in the behalfe of her Majesty, he fully satisfied the Auditors. Master Secretary gave the Earle his right alwaies, and shewed more curtesie then any, yet saied he, the Earle in all his journey did nothing else but make (as it were) circles of errours, which were all bound up in the unhappy knot of his disobedient returne. Also he gave the Earle free liberty to interrupt him at any time in his speech.

The Earle contented.

But the Earle being contented with the opinion of loyalty so cleerely reserved unto him, was most willing to beare the whole burthen of all the rest of the accusation, and therefore never used any further reply; onely by reason of a question or two, that were moved by my Lord of Canterbury and my Lord Admirall, some little speech there was to and fro: My Lord of Canterburies question was concerning the conditions of yeelding unto Tyrone in tolleration of religion; the Earle heartily thanked him for moving that doubt, & then protested, that it was a thing mentioned in deed, but never yeelded unto by him, nor yet stood upon by the Traitor, to whom the Earle had said plainely, Hang thee up, thou carest for religion as much as my horse. Master Secretary also cleered the Earle in that respect, that he never yeelded to Tyrone in that foule condition, though by reason of Tyrones vaunting afterwards, it might have some shew of probability. By reason of my Lord Admirals question, the Earle spake somewhat of his returne, that he did it upon a false ground of hope, that her Majesty might pardon him, as shee did the Earle of Leicester in the like case, who returned out of the Low-Countries contrary to her Majesties expresse Letter. This I thought with my selfe, (quoth the Earle) if Leicester were pardoned, whose end was onely to save himselfe, why might not Essex be pardoned, whose end was to save a Kingdome. But Master Secretary replied, that upon his knowledge there never passed any letter from her Majesty, to forbid the Earle of Leicesters returne.

Judge Walmesley his speech.

Judge Walmesley his speech was more blunt then bitter, Prisoners at our barres (saith he) are more gracelesse, they will not confesse their faults. Again, he compared my Lord his comming home, and leaving the army there, to a shepheard that left his flocke to the keeping of his dogge.

The Earle's conclusion.

In conclusion the Earle protested, that all he sought for, was the opinion of a true and a loyall subject, which might appeare by the speech, wherewith he hedged in all his answeres, namely, that he intended onely to shew those false guides, which misled him, whether they were his owne errours, or the errours of his Counsellors, whom he followed, that he yeelded himselfe wholly to her Majesties mercy and favour, and was ready to offer up his poore carkasse unto her, he would not say to doe (for alasse he had no faculties), but to suffer whatsoever her Majesty should inflict upon him, and so requested them all, to make a just, honourable and favourable report of his disordered speeches, which had fallen from him in such sort, as his aking head and body weakened with sickenesse, would give him leave. This done, they proceeded to the censure. My Lord Keeper beganne with a good, powerfull, and eloquent speech.

My Lord Keeper's eloquent speech.

That by Justice and Clemency the Throne is established, as for mercy, her Majesty had reserved it to her selfe; but for the satisfying of her Justice, shee had appointed them to enquire into the cause. That they were to enquire onely of those faults of contempts and disobedience laid unto the Earle, and to censure him accordingly,
[II. i. 74.] and for her mercy, they had nothing to doe with it, onely God was to worke it in her Princely breast. In examining the Earles faults, he laid these for his grounds, that the two grounds and foundations of the Princes Scepter and Estate, are the reputation of a diligent and carefull providence for the preservation of her estate and Countries, and the obedience of her Subjects; and he that should take either of these from her, should take from her the Crowne and Scepter. For the first, he notably shewed at large, how her Majesty had deserved it in the whole course of the Irish warres; for obedience he shewed the nature of it, consisting in precisely following the streight line of the Princes commandement, and upon that straine he amplified to the uttermost all the Earles contempts and disobediences, that her Majesties great mercy might appeare the more cleerely. Among the rest, (for he went through them all in order) he answered thus to the pretence of Leicesters president for excuse of the Earles returne. In good things, the example is better then the imitation of another, he that doth wel of his owne head, doth best, and he that doth well by imitation, doth commendably in a lesse degree; but in bad things, the proportion is otherwise, the example being naught, the imitation is worse: Therefore if my Lord of Leicester did evill, in comming over contrary to the Queenes com-

mandement, my Lord of Essex did worse in imitating my Lord of Leicester, and is so much the more to be punished for it. In the end, he came to the censure, which was this. If quoth he this cause had beene heard in the Starre-chamber, my sentence must have beene so great a fine, as ever was set upon any mans head in that Court, and perpetuall imprisonment in that place which belongeth to a man of his quality, that is the Tower; but now that we are in another place, and in a course of favour, my censure is, that he is not to execute the office of a Counsellor, nor to hold himselfe for a Counsellor of Estate, nor to execute the office of Earle Marshall of England, nor of the Master of the Ordinance, and to returne to his owne house, there to continue a prisoner as before, till it shall please her Majesty to release both this and all the rest.

The censures of the rest.

After my Lord Keeper all the rest in order gave their censures, (amplifying her Majesties clemency and the Earles offences), according to the manner in the Starre-chamber; but all accorded to this censure, (for so they called it, and not a sentence), Master Secretary said, my censure is, that the Earle deserveth, &c. The greater part of the day was spent in the Lords censures, who were many of them very long, onely the noble men (not Counsellors) were short.

The Earle of Worcester.

The Earle of Worcester cited these two verses;

Silicet a Superis etiam fortuna luenda est,
Nec veniam, læso numine, casus habet.

Even for our fortune Gods may cast us downe,
Neither can chance excuse, if a God frowne.

The Earle of Cumberland.

The Earle of Cumberland said, if he thought that censure should stand, he would crave longer time, for it seemed unto him somewhat hard and heavy, intimating how easily a Generall Commander might incurre the like; but (quoth hee) in confidence of her Majesties mercy, I agree with the rest.

The Lord Zouch.

The Lord Zouch would give no other censure, but that

which he thought the Earle would lay upon himselfe, that was, that he would restraine himselfe from executing his Offices, &c. and keepe himselfe in his house, till her Majesty shall release all.

The Earle chearefull.

They all seemed by their speeches to conceive a sure hope of her Majesties releasing this censure, and the Earle was reasonably chearefull, onely his body seemed weake and distempered with sickenesse, and now and then he shewed most manifest tokens of sorrow for his offence to her Majesty, by teares in his eyes, (specially in the first part of his owne speech, and when my Lord Keeper spake).

Tyrone's letter to the Countess of Ormond.

Now I returne to the Irish affaires. Tyrone on the fifth of June wrote to the Countesse of Ormond, that he had written to Owny mac Rory, requesting him to take pledges for the Earle her husband, and so to inlarge him, conditionally, that he should sweare to doe henceforward no hurt or hinderance to any in action with him. And further, that the young Lady his mistresse, (meaning the
[II. i. 75.] Earles daughter and heire) should in no sort be taken for a pledge, especially because it was given out, that under that colour, he sought to marry her to his eldest sonne. Avowing lastly, that where it was said, that the Earle was treacherously surprised, (which could hardly have beene so proved, that Tyrone and his rebellious confederates should have beleeved it), he would in that case not onely take his favour from Owny, but procure the Earles inlargement without any condition, though by his release all Ireland should be destroied. To the same effect Tyrone writ to the Earle of Ormond, whose Letter he sauced with generall complaints against the Earle, for the rigorous prosecutions he had formerly made against him and his associates, but this letter being permitted to be sent to Dublyn, the said point could not be thought void of that cunning, wherein the writer excelled. A third Letter he wrote at the same time to Owny mac Rory, making Owny himselfe Judge, whether hee had treacherously taken the Earle or no, advising him to take

the best pledges he could, (the above named young Lady excepted); and for more security, to send them to be kept in Tyrone, if he concurred with him in opinion, that his so doing would be more safe, then if Owny himselfe should keepe them in those parts. These Letters he dated (forsooth) from his Campe neere the Newry, so gallant was the Gentleman, now the Lord Deputy was returned with his forces into the Pale, who otherwise never appeared in Campe, but hid himselfe and his in boggy woods, and like fortified passages.

The state of Connaght.

The eight of June the Lord Deputy wrote to Master Secretary concerning the state of Connaght, wherein nothing was surely the Queenes, but Athlone by a provident guard, and Galloway by their owne good disposition, wishing that the governement of that Province might be conferred on the Earle of Southampton, (to whom the Lord of Dunkellin would more willingly resigne, and might doe it with greater reputation to himselfe, in respect of the Earles greatnes), rather then upon Sir Arthur Savage, (who notwithstanding upon the Queenes pleasure againe signified, was shortly after made Governour of that Province). His Lordship protested that it was such a place, as he knew the Earle would not seeke, but onely himselfe desired this, because he knew the Earles aptnes and willingnes to doe the Queene service, if he might receive such a token of her favour, justly commending his valour and wisdome, as well in generall, as in the late particular service in the Moyry, when the Rere being left naked, he by a resolute charge with sixe horse, upon Tyrone in the head of 220. Horse, drove him back a musket shot, and so assuring the Rere, saved the honour of the Queenes Army. To which purpose, though not so amply, his Lordship also wrote to the Queene.

Counties over run by the Rebels.

At this time the County of Dublyn, on the South of the River Liffy, was in effect wholly overrunne by the Rebels, the County of Kildare was likewise possessed or wasted by them. The County of Meath was wasted, as also the County of West Meath, (excepting the Barrony of Delvin,) and the County of Louth: So that in the English Pale, the Townes having Garrisons, and the Lands from Drogheda (or Tredagh) to the Navan, and thence backe to Trym, and so to Dublyn, were onely inhabited, which were also like to grow waste, if they were further charged with the souldiers.

The Lord Deputy's orders to Sir Arthur Chichester.

The fifteenth of June the Lord Deputy wrote to Sir Arthur Chichester, Governour of Carickfergus, that he should not spare the subjects lately submitting, who protected the rebels goods; that he should receive no more, but such as would simply submit, and give good pledges, neither should give pay to any, except he knew their service would be very beneficiall to the Queene, that he should continue to treat with the Ilander Scots, till advice came out of England what course should be taken with them. That he should take in Shane Oneale, with promise of lands and entertainement, and promise, that for preyes hee should take of the Rebels, if the English assisted him, he should have a third part, and if he tooke them without the assistance of the English, he should have three parts of foure.

The Lord Deputy's letter to Master Secretary.

The nineteenth of June the Lord Deputy advertised Master Secretary, that he was more troubled to governe the friends, then to suppresse the enemies. That finding the Army a meere Chaos, he had given it forme. That finding it without spirit, he had given it life. That in all attempts, hee had preserved the whole body of it, and
[II i. 76.] every part from any blow, restored the reputation of it, and possessed it with a disposition to undertake, & a likelihood to effect great services. That he had omitted nothing, which might be performed by this Army, in this estate, during this time. That the assurance the Irish had received of succours from Spaine, was the onely fewell of the last blaze of this Rebellion: Therefore praying that, except Master Secretary had some certainety that Spaine would not at that time assist the Rebels, the Army might by all meanes be strengthened, which would

be necessary if such assistance were sent, and would make an end of the warres if none were sent. And howsoever that befell, yet for prevention of Munition and such supplies to be furnished to the Rebels from Spaine, advising that some few of the Queenes ships might lie on the West, and somewhat towards the North of Ireland: Adding that some little boats made both to row and to saile, would barre the Ilander Scots from supplying the Rebels with any munition: And that his Lordship to meet with the Earle of Ormond, (lately set free by Ony mac Rory, who had taken him Prisoner), that day tooke his journey towards Carlogh, where he hoped to sound the bottome of the conditions of his delivery, with the best course how to disintangle him, and by his conference, to make a shrewd guesse, how the Earle stood affected in these doubtfull times. His Lordship in his next Letters advertised into England, that he was not privy nor consenting to the giving of pledges at the Earle of Ormonds delivery; but since they were given, in regard of her Majesties extraordinary care for the Earles liberty, he did not shew any manifest dislike thereof; and now conceived the Earle did apprehend the indignity done to him by those base traitors, and therefore had such a spleene against them, as hee had joyned with him in divers plots, as well to recover the pledges (wherein the Earle protested to spare no money, if they were so to be redeemed; besides that he and their Fathers protested, that their danger should not hinder them from doing their uttermost service to the Queene), as also to worke his revenge upon the Rebels.

The Earle of Ormond set free.

At this time Tyrone attending the garrison at Loughfoyle, & Odonnel starting through Connaght into Thomond, and spoyling both Countries, Sir Samuel Bagnoll drew out of the Newry into Monaghan, where he tooke a prey, and killed sixe Commanders, and some sixty of the common rebels, onely three of his being slaine, and twenty hurt.

Sir Samuel Bagnoll.

The subjects of the Pale, (fearing belike to be complained on, for the small assistance they gave to the Queenes service), sent over the Lord of Howth, and Sir Patricke Barnewell, to make first complaint, (after the Irish manner) of the wrongs done them by the Army, never acquainting the Lord Deputy and Counsell therewith. And notwithstanding their former unwillingnes, to beare any charge for the Queenes service, now they were content, for these their Deputies expence in England, to cesse every plow land at three shillings.

Sir Oliver Lambert.

From the seventh of July to the twelfth, Sir Oliver Lambert with some troopes lay encamped at the Tougher in Ophalia, where he made a Causey, and built a Fort, and there left a Guard to keepe the passage alwaies open, for the victualling of Phillipstowne Fort, in which service the Earle of Southampton as a voluntary, by his presence and valour much encouraged our men. At this time many of the Rebels in Lemster, and the Northerne borders, made sute to the Lord Deputy to be received to mercy, with offer of large summes of money to the Lord Deputy for their pardons, but his Lordship refused their offer, till they had first done some service, and had drawne blood against some of their confederates. Thus much his Lordship advertised into England, the sixteenth of July, as likewise a good service presently done, and a great prey taken in the Fuse by Sir Richard Moryson the Governour of Dundalke.

The Lord Deputy's journey.

The same twelfth of July, his Lordship tooke his journey towards the borders of the North, upon hearing that Tyrone was drawne into those parts. There his Lordship intended to spoyle the corne, as likewise in all other parts, when it should be a little riper. Mac Mahowne, and Patricke mac Art Moyle, offered now to submit, but neither could be received, without the others head. But Oconnor Roe mac Guire, for good respects of service, was at the same time received to mercy. His Lordship hearing that Tyrone contained himselfe in his fastnes, and being required out of England to attempt
[II. i. 77.] something upon the Lemster Rebels, left the Northerne

borders strongly guarded against any invasion, and left order with the Counsell to hasten the generall hoasting, and make ready all provisions for a journey into the North, and leaving Dublyn the twelfth of August rode to the Nasse, and so marched to the Fort of Phillipstowne in Ophaly, with five hundred sixty foote and sixty horse, besides voluntaries in his company.

The Lord Deputy fights the rebels.

In the way into Leax his Lordship tooke a prey of two hundred Cowes, seven hundred garrons, and five hundred sheepe, besides great store of small cattell. The sixeteenth of August, his Lordship burning the Countrey and spoyling the corne, marched towards the passage, (one of the most dangerous in Ireland), where Sir Oliver Lambert with the forces he had was to meet him. Both of them fought all the way, and killed divers rebels, whereof the Lord Deputy left fifteene dead in the place, besides many hurt, they met together at noone. The seventeenth day the army marched towards a fastnes, where the rebels had stored great plenty of corne. At the entry there was a Foard, compassed in with woods, and a bogge betweene them, where the rebels let the vanguard of the horse passe; but his Lordship passing with a few gentlemen, and his owne servants before the vanguard of the foote, the rebels began the skirmish with him, and the foote wings being slowly sent out, they came close up to him, the traytor Tyrrell having appointed an hundred shot to wait on his Lordships person, with markes to know him. In this skirmish we killed thirty five rebels, and hurt seventy five on our part, two onely being killed, and a few slightly hurt, Captaine Masterson dangerously hurt in the knee, and his Lordship having a very good horse killed under him, and another killed under Master John Chidley a gentleman of his Lordships chamber: But the best service at that time done, was the killing of Owny mac Rory, a bloody and bold yong man, who lately had taken the Earle of Ormond prisoner, and had made great stirres in Mounster. He was the chiefe of the O Mores Sept

Owny mac Rory killed.

in Leax and by his death they were so discouraged, that they never after held up their heads. Also a bold bloody rebell Callogh mac Walter, was at the same time killed. Besides that his Lordships staying in Leax till the twenty three of August, did many other waies weaken them; for during that time, he fought almost every day with them, and as often did beate them. Our Captaines, and by their example (for it was otherwise painefull) the common souldiers, did cut downe with their swords all the Rebels corne, to the value of ten thousand pound and upward, the onely meanes by which they were to live, and to keepe their Bonaghts (or hired souldiers). It seemed incredible, that by so barbarous inhabitants, the ground should be so manured, the fields so orderly fenced, the Townes so frequently inhabited, and the high waies and paths so well beaten, as the Lord Deputy here found them. The reason whereof was, that the Queenes forces, during these warres, never till then came among them. The Lord Deputy in his returne the first day passed into another part of the Country with the foot alone; for the horse not able to passe were sent about, so as the rebels had the advantage they most desire, to fight with our foot, without assistance of horse: yet all the rebels of Lemster here gathered together, and fighting upon their naturall ground, had beene so beaten, as that they suffred our men to passe without a blow. That night eight heads were brought to the Lord Deputy, and with them one Lenagh a famous rebell, taken alive, who was presently hanged on the same tree, where he plotted all his villanies. Sir Oliver Lambert, with some troopes marched into Donnell Spagniahs Countrey, where he tooke 1000. Cowes, 500. Garons, great store of sheepe, and killed twenty rebels at the first entry, besides many killed in a fight, which the rebels after maintained all the day and part of the night. Sir Arthur Savage comming out of Connaght to meet the Lord Deputy, fought long with the Rebels, spoiled the Countrey, and tooke a great prey, but could not passe to his Lordship.

The rebels corne cut downe.

Lenagh, a famous rebell taken.

In the Lord Deputies returne out of Leax, Redmond, Keating, and the chiefe of the Septs of the Kellies and Lalors were received into her Majesties protection, upon condition to set at liberty the Earle of Ormonds pledges in their hands.

By this time his Lordship had received out of England gracious allowance of his former Northerne journey, with [II. i. 78.] her Majesties promise to reinforce the Army with two thousand foote, and two hundred horse, against the next journey into those parts, requiring him not to give any one man the commaund of both horse and foote; and whereas all Companies were of two hundred, or one hundred fiftie, advising to distribute some part into lesse numbers, that more Gentlemen might be satisfied with commaunds, with the onely increase of some chiefe officers pay, and that his Lordship would be sparing to give pasports for any to come into England, to trouble her Majestie with sutes, and most of all not to suffer able men to returne out of Ireland, as they daily did, with their Captaines pasportes. And to the end the Commaunders might not be idle, her Majestie required, that all services done by them, might be certified monethly into England. About this time the Earle of Southampton, leaving the warres of Ireland, sayled into England. This Summers service made it appeare, that journeys with a great Army did not so much good, as Garrisons lying upon the Rebels, which upon any sudden service, might easily bee drawne together in competent numbers, and in the meane time kept the Rebels at home, from seconding one another.

Reinforcements for the Army.

The Lord Deputy by his letters, during the foresaid journy, explained to the Lords in England, that he had been most carefull not to increase her Majesties charge in any thing, the want whereof would not have made the rest of her great expence to be unprofitable: and to the end the Commaunders might not be thought to lye idle, besides the good fortune that none of them had received any blow, hee particularly remembred many

The Lord Deputy's letters into England.

preyes taken, and services done, and for the chiefe Garrisons on the North borders, advertised, that Sir Arthur Chichester had layed all the Countrie waste within twenty miles of Carickfergus; that Sir Samuel Bagnol at the Newry had done the like; that Sir Richard Moryson at Dundalke had banished Turlough Mac Henry out of the Fuze into Monaghan, and yet the two last, with most part of their Garisons, had bin part of the Army in all former journies.

The Lord Deputy returns to Dublin.

The twentie sixe of August his Lordship returned from this journey of Leax to Dublin, and there received advertisement, that her Majestie could not refuse to heare the complaints of the Pale, by the Deputies formerly mentioned to bee sent over, though she had sharpely rebuked them, that they did not first complaine to the Lord Deputie, which they excused by experience, that like complaints in Ireland had ever been vaine. The chiefe complaints were these; that the forces that should lye upon the borders, neare the Rebels, were lodged upon them. That the fetching of one barrell of powder, was often made a sufficient reason to spoyle them, by a company of horse and foote sent to convoy it. That the Clarkeship of the Counsell was sold, and then executed by a Deputie, who for every small petition tooke great fees. That the spirituall livings were given to ignorant and idle persons, being the chiefe cause of this rebellion; scarce any Church standing for sixtie miles betweene Dublin and Athlone. That they were spoyled as much by the Army as Rebels, no souldier nor Captaine being punished, nor any order given for remedie taking effect. That private Captaines gave pasportes to run awaies, and her Majestie was deceived by false Musters, so as the forces were weake to end the warre, and they were spoyled as much as if the number were full, requiring that some Gentlemen of the Pale might be joyned with the Commissaries, in taking the musters of adjacent Garrisons. In the same letter her Majestie commaunded the Lord Deputy to signifie to Sir Arthur O Neale, that she

The complaints of the Pale.

purposed to create him Earle of Tyrone, and give him a portion of lands fit for an Earledome. And for Tyrone, that the Lord Deputy should proclaime him Traytor, with promise of two thousand pound to any should bring him alive, and one thousand pound to him that should bring his head to any of hir Majesties Fortes or Garrisons. Lastly, her Majesty gave letters of favour to the Deputies of the Pale, directed to the Lord Deputy, to whom the complaints were wholly referred, it being her Majesties pleasure, that only before him, and by him, they should be heard and redressed.

Tyrone proclaimed Traytor.

Yet because the Lord Deputie was many waies taxed in these complaints, hee did expostulate in his next letters to Master Secretarie, that hee should be taxed for those things, for which he expected approbation and thankes. The wisest Counsels (said he) are uncertaine, and the wisest men unperfect, and what shall I looke for, when out of my weakenesse (though free from wilfulnesse) I shall happen to commit any errour of consequence, seeing I am now charged with so many matters, and those nothing belonging to me. His Lordship added, that in his opinion, nothing had made the affaires of Ireland more unprosperous, then that the State used to heare every man against and before the chiefe Governour, so as hee was driven to let matters goe as they would, so as hee might save himselfe. Another discontented letter he wrote to the same effect, and to the same person, but therein explained other grievances, besides the former complaints. And whereas the Lords of the Counsell had taxed him, for being ruled by young counsell (wherby he understood his three most familiar friends to be meant, namely, Sir Henry Davers, Sir Richard Moryson, and Sir William Godolphin) he boldly answered, that besides the Counsellors of State, hee used the familiarity of none, which were not older then Alexander the great, when he conquered the World. Lastly, he protested to Master Secretarie, that he tooke him for his chiefest friend, and knew that he had more power to do him good or hurt,

[II. i. 79.]

The Lord Deputy expostulates to Master Secretarie.

then any other, yet as he would not dishonestly lose him, so he would not basely keepe him, beseeching him to use his power, in mediating licence unto him, that he might come over for a short time, to kisse the Queenes hand, for touching other favours concerning the publike, he would never acknowledge any particular obligation to him, or to any other, since hee made his demaunds as he thought best for the service, but the granting or denying thereof, concerned not him.

The Muster of the Army at Dundalke, before the sitting downe at the Faghard Hill.

The Muster of the Army at Dundalke.

Colonels of Regiments.		In Lyst.	By Muster.			Whereof Irishmen.	Swords wanting.	Sick & hurt lying at Dundalk.
Captaine Berey. 472.	The Lord Deputies Guard.	200	Targets	28				
			Pikes	32	120	01	00	16
			Shot	60				
	The Marshall Sir Rich. Wingfield.	150	Targets	4				
			Pikes	39	96	10	30	06
			Shot	53				
Under the Lord Deputie. 400.	The Sergeant Major Sir Oliver Lambert.	200	Targets	10				
			Pikes	46	108	08	05	05
			Shot	52				
	Capt. Handserd.	100	Targets	1				
			Pikes	28	79	20	10	06
			Shot	50				
	Capt. Fisher.	100	Targets	3				
			Pikes	21	69	05	20	11
			Shot	45				
Sir Christopher Saint Laurence. 367.	Sir Christopher Saint Laurence.	200	Targets	10				
			Pikes	61	141	113	14	12
			Shot	70				
	Sir Henry Follyot	150	Targets	6				
			Pikes	36	90	15	10	09
			Shot	48				
	Earle of Kildare.	150	Targets	6				
			Pikes	35	81	78	06	14
			Shot	40				
	Sir Fra: Shane.	100	Targets	00				
			Pikes	18	55	47	04	08
			Shot	37				

[II. i. 80.]

The Muster of the Army at Dundalke.

Colonels.		In Lyst.	By Muster.			Irish.	Swords wanting.	Sick & hurt.
Sir Charles Percy. 336.	Sir Charles Percy.	200	Targets Pikes Shot	10 54 85	149	28	30	04
	Captaine Williams.	150	Targets Pikes Shot	00 37 53	90	06	03	10
	Captaine Roe.	100	Targets Pikes Shot	4 25 30	59	08	05	01
	Capt. Staunton.	100	Targets Pikes Shot	00 18 20	38	00	00	10
Sir Richard Moryson. 473.	Sir Rich. Moryson.	200	Targets Pikes Shot	6 44 68	118	22	25	36
	Sir Hen. Davers.	200	Targets Pikes Shot	26 37 65	128	12	15	20
	Capt. Caufeild.	150	Targets Pikes Shot	07 32 55	94	10	10	28
	Capt. Constable.	100	Targets Pikes Shot	3 25 48	76	01	12	05
	Ca. Ravenscroft.	100	Targets Pikes Shot	3 24 30	57	01	23	06
Sir Thom. Bourk. 276.	Sir Thom. Bourk.	150	Targets Pikes Shot	06 25 54	85	82	26	14
	Iord Delvin.	150	Targets Pikes Shot	03 30 43	76	74	30	10
	Sir Henrie Harrington.	100	Targets Pikes Shot	03 20 17	40	37	08	12
	Sir Garret More.	100	Targets Pikes Shot	07 23 45	75	13	02	08

The Muster of the Army at Dundalke.

Colonels.		In Lyst.		By Muster.	Irish.	Swords wanting.	Sick & hurt.
Sir Oliver Saint Johns. 370.	Sir Oliver Saint Johns.	150	Targets 10 Pikes 33 Shot 52	95	24	15	05
	Sir. Thom. Wingfeild.	150	Targets 05 Pikes 29 Shot 68	102	25	20	13
	Capt. Billings.	100	Targets 03 Pikes 24 Shot 32	59	01	04	15
	Capt. Treavor.	100	Targets 06 Pikes 23 Shot 41	70	01	15	14
	The men of Dublin.	50	Targets 03 Pikes 15 Shot 26	44	40	00	01
Sir S. Bagnol. 346.	Sr. S. Bagnol with broken companies and his owne.	200	Targets 18 Pikes 24 Shot 158	200	20	30	00
	Capt. Esmond.	150	Targets 02 Pikes 28 Shot 52	82	15	10	14
	Capt. Freckleton.	100	Targets 03 Pikes 15 Shot 46	64	03	06	02
	Totall	4150	Totall	2640	702	388	315

[II i. 81.]

The greatest part of the Army have neither Armours nor Murrions, neither are here mentioned the sicke and hurt in other places besides Dundalke, nor yet the warders allowed out of some of these Companies.

The Lord Deputy at the hill of Faghard.

The fourteenth of September his Lordship began another journy into the North, and the fifteenth incamped at the hill of Faghard, three miles beyond Dundalke, and there his Lordship lay till the ninth of October, in such extremitie of weather, as would have hindred his passage, if the enemie had not withstood him, his Lordships tent being continually wet, and often blowne downe. Before his Lordship came, Tyrone with his uttermost strength had possessed the Moyry, being a strong fastnesse, as any the Rebels had, but his Lordship resolved to march over him, if hee stopped his way, and make him know, that his Kerne could not keepe the fortification against the Queenes forces. Many skirmishes fell out happily to us, and two severall dayes the Rebels were beaten out of their trenches with great losse, till at last, upon the eight of October, they left the passage cleere. Then after the army was a few daies refreshed at Dundalke, his Lordship marched the twenty one of October to the Newry, passing through the Moyry, where he caused all the rebels trenches to be laid flat to the ground, and the woods to be cut downe on both sides of the Pace. At the Newry for want of victuals, his Lordship staied till the second of November, when he set forward eight miles towards Armagh, and there incamped. The Rebels horse-men shewed themselves upon a hil; whereupon Sir Samuel Bagnols Regiment having the Reare, and being not yet come into the Campe, was directed to march towardes them, there being a bog between us and them, but the Rogues quickly drew to their fastnes. The next morning his Lordship rode some quarter of a mile from the Campe, and viewed a place where Sir John Norreys formerly intended to build a Fort, and liking his choice, set downe there with the Army to build the same. The place is a hill like a Promontory, all invironed with bogges, a River, and great store of wood. By it on the right hand over the River and a great bogge, was a little firme ground, and then another bogge, & over that a faire Countrey, with houses and much corne. His Lordship could by no meanes send over any horse, but foure miles about; wherefore he commanded a regiment of foote to advance to the first peece of firme ground, and from thence to send over the next bogge some few men, to bring in the Corne and Tymber of the houses, with directions to make their retreit to the grosse, if the enemies horses should fall downe that way. On the left hand and before was a bogge, over the bogge before a great wood, that continueth through all this fastnes, and over the bogge on the left hand a hill, where Tyrone all that day and most of the time that the Army lay there,

The Army marches to the Newry.

A Fort intended to be built.

did muster himselfe and his men. This day most of his horse and foote fell over, but farre about on the right hand, upon which, our straglers that went out retired to the firme ground, over the first bogge, and there beganne betweene our foote and theirs, a very good skirmish, till our men did beate them off, and brought with them great store of Corne and wood, and killed [II. i. 82.] divers of them. In the meane time, their scouts on the other side being somewhat busie with ours, Neal Oquin was taken prisoner, being the chiefe favourite unto Tyrone. *Neal Oquin taken prisoner.* The next day we beganne to worke, in the building of the Fort, and to impeach our worke, the rogues beganne to skirmish with us on both sides, which was excellently maintained by some few of our men, that we sent out: We saw many of them killed, and after understood they lost a great number, whereof many were horsemen, of the best sort, that had lighted to incourage their men to fight. They were then so well beaten, as they would never after offer to meddle with us, till our returne by Carlingford. The ninth of November the Fort being finished, his Lordship called it Mount Norreys, in honour of his Master, (so he tearmed him, under whom hee had served his apprentiship in the warres), and he left therein foure hundred foot, under the command of Captaine Edward Blaney, with six weekes provision of victuals.

The weather grew so extreame, as it blew downe all our Tents, and tore them in pieces, and killed many of our horses, so that the tenth day his Lordship putting all the Army in armes, with all the Drummes and Trumpets, and a great volly of shot, proclaimed Tyrones head, *Tyrones head proclaimed.* (with promise of 2000. pound to him that brought him alive, and 1000. pound to him that brought him dead), which was done in the face of his own army, and so his Lordship marched to the Newry. He had purposed to plant a garrison at Armagh 8. miles beyond Mount Norryes, but the rebels Cowes had eaten up all the grasse thereabouts, which should have fed our horses, and the time of the yeere with the weather, was now unseasonable for that purpose.

And whereas his Lordship was resolved to returne into the Pale by Carlingford, to discerne whether that way or the way of the Moyry were more safe, that the army might not runne so continuall hazards, this resolution was now confirmed by necessity, there being victuals at Carlingford, and none at the Newry or Dundalke. The twelfth of November his Lordship came with the army to the narrow water, whence he sent Sir Josias Bodley with three hundred choyce foot to possesse a peece of ground, and keepe the enemy from hindering our passage over the water, the streame whereof he found so exceeding swift, that it was like to be dangerous to venture our horses over. The first that tried was Doctor Latware, his Lordships Chaplaine, who only with his horse led by the boat side, and with some thirty foot, went over; but his Lordship perceived so great difficulty by his passage, that he passed the foot over as fast as might be, sent Sir Henry Folliot to possesse the pace of the Faddome, and made all the Horse and our Garrons to goe about that way. In the meane time wee might see the rebels forces draw over the mountaines towards the pace of Carlingford, and come close by our men that were first landed, yet they never offered any skermish. That night we encamped directly over the narrow water, betweene the pace of the faddome, and the pace of Carlingford, & having at midnight gotten over for our men some vittels, that came by water from Carlingford, his Lordship caused the same to be delivered before day, for the Army had fasted two daies, and after they had eaten but a little bisket, and cheese or butter, never men went on in a greater jollity. The thirteenth of November we were to rise very early, for otherwise we could not passe our carriages by the sea side, as we had determined, and by breake of day the Scoutmaster brought word that Tyrone with all his army was lodged in the pace, which is an exceeding thicke wood, at the foote of a great

Carlingford fight.

mountaine, reaching downe to the sea side, betweene which and the sea, there is in most places as much space as seven may march in ranke, but in some places lesse, and in some none at full water, but onely there is a narrow deepe high way through the wood.

Captaine Thomas Roper's forlorne hope.

Captaine Thomas Roper with the broken Companies sent out of the Pale, went on as a forlorne hope, and that day by course it fell out, that Captaine Benjamin Berry, with the Lord Deputies Regiment under his command, had the vanguard, Sir Christopher St Laurence, had the reare of the vanguard, Sir Richard Moryson had the vanguard of the Rere, and Sir Samuell Bagnoll the reare of the reare, so that we had but two bodies, a vanguard and a rere, thus subdivided. Captaine Trevor with as many as Captaine Roper had in the point, led a forlorne
[II. i. 83.] rere. Out of all the regiments his Lordship appointed three strong wings to goe on the right hand (for on the left hand was the Sea), commanded all by Captaines; the first by Captaine Billings, the second by Captaine Esmond, and the last by Captaine Constable.

The ground chosen by the rebels.

The ground the rebels chiefely chose to make good, was a little Plaine like a semi-circle, whereof the Sea made the Diameter, and a thicke Wood the Circumference. At the next corner to us, there ran into the Sea a River out of the wood, being a Foard of good advantage to the enemie. All along the circumference they had made divers trenches, even close up to both the corners, and at the furthest corner they had made a Barricado, reaching a good way into the Wood, and downe to the Sea. At the first they shewed themselves horse and foote upon this Plaine; but when his Lordship commanded ours to give on (which they performed presently and roundly), their horse drew off into the Woods, and their foote into their trenches, and never shot, till the Vanguard was drawne over the River, when from all partes they powred upon us great vollyes of shot; but presently Captaine Roper gave on the farthest trench on the right hand of the corner, Captaine Billings on the next with the wing hee led, and Captaine Berry with the rest of the Vanguard gave upon the farthest corner, where the Barricado reached from the Wood into the Sea. In some of them they made good resistance, and many of them lost their lives with the Pike and the Sword. But the last trench where they made greatest shew of opposition, they did soonest quit, though it were strongest for them, and to greatest purpose to arrest us: the reason his Lordship conceived to be, that in that place they were furthest from their retreat, and feared the forlorne Hope and Wing led by Captaine Billings might cut betweene them. When we had gained the trenches, the Vanguard made a stand, in the Rere of which, to countenance them (if there had been occasion), his Lordship stood with a troope of horse of voluntarie Gentlemen, and next to his Lordship (betweene the Van and next bodies of foote) Sir Henrie Davers and his Lordships troopes of horse. At this time they entertained skermish with all parts of our Army, but still falling towards the Rere, and at this time his Lordships Secretarie Master George Cranmer was killed, betweene Sir William Godolphin and Mast. Henrie Barkely, Master Ram his Lord[ps]. Chaplaines horse was killed, and a Gentleman of his Lordships chamber, called Master Done (that carried his cloake) shot through the leg. And I will not forget one accident, that might have proved of great consequence: During this stand, his Lordship roade up to a little hill in the edge of the Wood, underneath which our men were in skirmish with the rebels, beyond whom somewhat more then a musket shot off, on the side of a hil, by a few little houses, there stood in a troope some seven or eight horsemen on foote, with their horses by them, at whom his Lordship caused his footeman to shoot (who alwaies carried a long piece with him), who (as within two howers after it was told his Lordship by one that was at that time one of the number) killed the next man to Tyrone, on whose shoulder at that time he leaned. Sir Henrie Davers came unto his Lordship, and desired he might take twentie of

His Lordship's Secretarie killed.

his owne horse to fall into the Rere, because he saw all the enemies horse fall thitherward, and that the Irish horse onely that day had the Rere. His Lordship gave him leave, and withall sent young James Blount with 100 shot out of the Vanguard, Captaine Caufeild, and Captaine Constable with as many more out of Sir Richard Morysons Regiment, to reinforce the Rere, with whom the rogues continued a good skermish, almost for halfe an hower, untill their horse and foote comming on a little plaine, somewhat farre from the skirt of the Wood, Sir Hen. Davers charged home, & brake them, but in the beginning of the charge he was shot in the thigh. After this charge they presently drew off their foote by the Mountaines, and their horse by the strand over against the narrow water. In our Rere Captaine Richard Hansard and Captaine Trever were sore hurt, and Sir Garret Mores Ensigne and Hugh Hanlon killed, and in all wee lost not twenty, but above threescore were hurt. Of the enemie (as we heard then of certaine) there were fourescore killed outright, but within two daies after his Lordship understood by Maguire, that they lost two hundred. The Marshall and the Serjeant Major were alwaies in the Van or Rere, as in either place the fight grew hottest, and generally all the Commaunders and souldiers served with extraordinary forwardnes and alacrity. To conclude, by credible reports the Rebels lost in this journey above 800. and Tyrones reputation (who did all things by his reputation) was cleane overthrowne, so that from all places they began to seeke pardons or protections. On our part in the whole journey some two hundred were killed and dead of hurts, and some 400. were hurt, which shortly after recovered.

Fourescore of the enemie killed outright.

[II. i. 84.]

Give me leave to digresse a little to continue the journall of my travels, the writing whereof hath occasioned the relation of Irish affaires. When the Earle of Essex went Lord Lieftenant into Ireland, the Lord Mountjoy was first named to that place, whereupon by my brother Sir Richard Morysons inwardnes with him, I then obtained his Lordships promise to follow him into Ireland, in the place of his chiefe Secretary. But this imployment failing us both, I retired my selfe into Lincolneshire, where I lived till his Lordship was the last spring sent over Lord Deputy, and such was then my diffidence of vulgar reports, (for I had no other knowledge of his Lordships imployment), that I did not certainely beleeve the change of the Deputy, till his Lordship was ready to take his journey, which was besides extraordinarily hastened by the Queenes command, for the necessity of her affaires in that Kingdome: yet my letter swifter then my selfe came to his Lordships hands, before his going; and from him I received this honourable answere, that not knowing what was become of me, he had already received three Secretaries, yet wished me to follow him, for he would find out some fit and good imployment for me. The indisposition of my body by reason of an ague staied me some few moneths in that Countrey; but in July taking my journy for Ireland, I came to Cambridge, whereas yet I was one of the fellowes of Peter-house. The Master and Fellowes by speciall indulgence had continued unto mee my place, with leave to travell from the yeere 1589. to this present July, in the yeere 1600. At which time being modest further to importune so loving friends, and having the foresaid assurance of preferment in Ireland, I yeelded up my Fellowship, which in my former absence had yeelded me some twenty pound yeerely. And the society (to knit up their loving course towards me) gave mee aforehand the profit of my place for two yeeres to come: For which curtesie and for my education there, I must ever acknowledge a strict bond of love and service to each of them in particular, and to the whole body jointly. From thence I went to London, and so to Westchester; and whilest I staid there for a passage, I received another letter, by which I did gather that his Lordship purposed to imploy me in the writing of the History or Journall of Irish affaires. But it pleased God in his gracious providence,

Kindness of the Master and Fellowes of Peterhouse.

(which I may never leave unmentioned) to dispose better of me. For staying for a wind till the end of September, one of his Lordships three Secretaries, (either to avoide the trouble and danger of the warres, or for other reasons best knowne to him) came over, and told me that he had left his Lordships service. Thus with better hope of preferment, I crossed the seas in very tempestuous weather, (at our putting to sea the carkasse of a broken ship swimming by us, and at our entring the Port of Dublyn, another ship being cast away in crossing from one shoare to another, wherein a Bishop and his whole family were drowned). After few daies spent in Dublyn, I tooke my journey to Dundalke, on the Northerne borders, where my brother Sir Richard Moryson was then Governour, and there I lodged till the Lord Deputies returne with the Army. And the thirteenth of November, being the day of Carlingford fight above mentioned, whilest I walked in my brothers garden, I sensibly heard by reverberation of the wall, the sound of the vollies of shot in that skirmish, though the place were at least six miles distant. In this fight the Lord Deputy his chiefe Secretary George Cranmer (as is above mentioned) was killed, and his Lordship having now but onely one Secretary, did receive me the next day at Dundalke into Cranmers place.

Sir Richard Moryson, Governour.

Letter from the Lord Admirall.

I return to the Irish affaires. At Dundalk his Lordship received a letter from the Lord Admirall, signifying that hee had earnestly moved her Majesty to give him leave to come over for a short time, whose answere was, that there lived not any man that shee would be more glad to see then his Lordship: but that now he had
[II. i. 85.] begunne so worthily, and all things prospered under his worke, she would not give incouragement to the Rebels by his absence, whom his presence had so daunted.

The List of the Army, and the distribution of the same into Garrisons in the end of November.

The List of the Army and the Garrisons.

Twelve Colonels of the Armie.

The Earle of Thomond: Lord Dunkellin: Sir Henrie Dockwra: Sir Arthur Chichester: Sir Henrie Power: Sir Charles Percy: Sir Matthew Morgan: Sir Christopher Saint Laurence: Sir Charles Wilmot: Sir Arthur Savage: Sir Richard Moryson: Sir John Bolles.

Foote at Carickfergus.

Sir Arthur Chichester Governour, 150. Sir Foulk Conway, 150. Captaine Richard Croftes, 100. Captaine Charles Egerton, 100. Captaine Gregorie Norton, 100.

Horse.

Sir Arthur Chichester, 25. Captaine John Jephson 100.

Foote at Mount Norreys.

Captaine Edward Blaney Governour, 150. Sir Samuel Bagnol, 150. Captaine Henrie Athyerton, 150.

Horse at the Newry.

Sir Samuel Bagnol Governour, 50.

Foote.

Sir Oliver Saint Johns, 150. Sir Francis Stafford, 200. Captaine Josias Bodley, 150. Captaine Edward Trever, 100. Captaine Edward Fisher, 100. Captaine Ravenscroft, 100.

Foote at Carlingford.

Captaine Richard Hansard, 100.

Foote at Dundalke.

Sir Richard Moryson Governour, 150. Sir Henrie Davers, 150. Captaine Tobie Cafeild, 150. Captaine Ferdinand Freckleton, 100. Captaine Ralph Constable, 100.

The List of the Army and the Garrisons.

Horse.

Sir Henry Davers, 50.

Foote at Arde.

Sir Charles Percy, 150. Sir Garret More, 100. Captaine Thomas Mynne, 100. Captaine Thomas Williams, 150. Captaine Francis Roe, 100.

Horse.

Sir Henrie Davers, 50. Sir Garret More, 25.

Foote at Ballymore.

Sir Francis Shane, 100. Captaine Thomas Roper, 150. Captaine Rotheram, 100.

At Mullingar.

The Lord of Delvin, 150 Foote. Sir Christopher Saint Laurence, 25 Horse.

At the Navan.

Sir Thomas Maria Wingfeild, 150 Foote. The Lord Deputie, 100 Horse.

Foote at Drogheda.

Captaine Billings, 100. Captaine Linley, 100. Captaine Jefferey Dutton, 100. Captaine Morice, 100. Captaine Bentley, 100.

Foote at Trymme.

Sir Christopher Saint Laurence, 150. Sir Edward Harbert, 100. Captaine Yelverton, 100.

Foote at Kelles.

The Lord of Dunsany, 150. Captaine Hugh Orely, 100.

Horse.

Lord of Dunsany, 50.

Foot at Aboy, Clancary and the Castles of Ophalia.

Sir Henrie Folliot, 150. Captaine Lionel Guest, 150. Sir Henrie Warren, 100.

Foote in the Fort of the Dingon, and at the Nasse.

The List of the Army and the Garrisons.

Sir George Bourcher, 100. The Lord Dunkellin, 150. Sir Henrie Harrington, 100. Captaine Thomas Boyse, 100.

Horse at New-castle.

[II. i. 86.]

Captaine Daughtrey, 50. Sir Henrie Harrington, 25.

At Athey, Reban, and the borders of Leax.

Sir Henrie Poore, 150. Sir James Fitzpiers, 150. Master Marshel, 150. Captaine Philips, 100. Sir Thomas Loftus, 100 Foote.

The Marshall, 50 Horse.

Foote in the Forts, Sir Francis Rush, 150.

Foote in Occarrals Countrie, Captaine Mollrony Ocarrol, 100.

Foote and Horse in Kilkenny.

The Earle of Ormond Lieutenant of the Armie, 150. Captaine Marbery, 100 Foote. The Earle of Ormond, 50 Horse.

Foote and Horse in Kildare.

The Earle of Kildare, 150 Foote. The Earle of Kildare, 50 Horse.

Foote and Horse in the Countie of Waxford.

Sir Oliver Lambert, 150. Captaine John Masterson, 100. Captaine Esmond, 150 Foote. Sir Oliver Lambert, 25 Horse.

Foote at Dublin.

The Lord Deputies Guard, commanded by Captaine Berry 150.

Foote and Horse in Connaght.

Sir Arthur Savage Governour, 150. The Earle of Clanrickard, 150. Sir Thomas Bourk, 150. Sir Tibbot Dillon, 100. Captaine Clare, 150. Captaine Tibot Nelong, 100. Captaine Thomas Bourgh, 100 Foote. The Earle of Clanrickard, 50. The Lord Dunkellin, 25. The Marshall of the Province, 12 Horse.

The List of the Army and the Garrisons.

Horse in the Pale at the Captaines disposall neere themselves, or attending their persons.

Sir Edward Harbert, 12. Sir William Warren, 25. Sir John Barkley, 12. Captaine Rich. Greame, 50. Captaine Garret Fleming, 25. Captaine Pigot, 12. Captaine Darcy, 25.

At Loughfoyle a remote Garrison, under Sir Henrie Dockwra his command.

Sir Henrie Dockwra, 50. Sir John Bolles, 50 Horse. Foote under 25 Captaines, 2900.

In the Province of Mounster at the Lord Presidents disposall.

The Lord President, 50. Sir Anthony Cooke, 50. Captaine William Taaf, 25 Horse. Foot under 23 Captaines 2800.

Totall of Horse, 1198. Totall of Foote, 14150.

From Dundalke, the Lord Deputy, with his servants and voluntary horsemen, rode to Dublin the seventeenth of November. Within few dayes, upon Sir Arthur Savage his intreatie to goe for England, about his private affaires, his Lordship gave him license, and appointed Sir John Barkely to supplie his place of Provisionarie Governour of the Province of Connaght. At the same time his Lordship wrote into England for authoritie to passe unto certaine submitties their Countries, with reservation of her Majesties rights, and some other conditions for her profit and service, more particularly on the behalfe of Connor Roe Mac Guyre, who being put from the Chiefery of his Country by Tyrone, had quitted al his possessions and goods, to come to the Queenes service, when Tyrone had two of his sonnes for pledges, of which the elder lately escaping from the rebels, had likewise submitted himselfe, and they both had served valiantly in the late Northerne journey; so as the father had his horse killed under him, and the sonne killed

Sir John Barkely.

three rebels with his owne hand. And from thence both going into Fermanagh, had drawne many of that Country to follow them in the Queenes service, diverting all the Countrie from assisting Tyrone. Besides that in a late skirmish, they had taken Cormock, Tyrones brothers eldest sonne, a young man of the greatest hope in the North, whom the Rebels purposed to create Oneale after Tyrones death, for which respect he was a better pledge then any of Tyrones sons. This youth they had brought to the Lord Deputy, with great hazard to convoy him, and that when 3000. pound, and other ample conditions were offered them for his ransome. In the same moneth of November, many of the Northerne Rebels with great troops, (among them a Mounster man Piers Lacy of English race, a famous rebell), drew into the Brenny, meaning to passe to the Shannon side, and so into Mounster, after they had strengthened the broken rebels of the Pale with some assistance. But this their passage was so stopped, as it tooke no effect. The sixth of December his Lordship was advertised from an honourable friend in Court, that his late proceedings were mentioned by all men with much honour, and most of all by the Queene, who uttered to himselfe the most gracious and kind speeches of his Lordship, and the most extolling his valour and worthy parts, that ever he had heard her use of any.

Cormock, Tyrones brother's sonne taken.

[II. i. 87.]

Till this time, the rebels of the Mountaines neere Dublyn, called the Glinnes, gave allarums almost every night in the Suburbes of Dublyn. But the time when the insolency of some of them should bee chastened, was now come. The Obirnes having Phelim mac Feogh, the chiefe of their Sept, after the death of Feogh mac Hugh, (formerly mentioned) inhabited the Glinnes bordering on the plaines of Dublyn, extending some foure or five miles that way; and these being neerer then the O Tooles and other their confederates, were most insolent upon that City, and the Counsell there residing, when the Lord Deputy was farre off in any service with the horsemen.

The rebels neere Dublyn.

Now his Lordship was purposed to scourge them, and according to his singular secrecie, did so keepe his Counsell from divulging, and so cunningly masked his intent, as he came upon them, when they were most secure. It was confidently given out, that his Lordship meant presently to undertake some service against the O Mores of Leax, and Oconnors of Ophalia, and to that purpose meant to lie with his houshold at Monastreven, a great house kept by a Constable for the Queen: yea to make this project more beleeved, his Lordship sent Arras hangings, and many provisions to that house. And now the forces having beene refreshed, his Lordship the twenty two of December, being Monday, rode to the Nasse twelve miles distant from Dublyn, where the rendevous was appointed that day for the Lemster Garrisons, (for it was fit those bordering on the North, should be left strong.) On Wednesday his Lordship sent most of his houshold right forward to Monastreven thirteene miles distant; but himselfe with the rest of his servants and the forces, suddenly turned on the left hand into the Glinnes, and after a day and nights tedious march, over steepe mountaines covered with snow, he arrived on Thursday being Christmas day, at Phelim mac Feogh his house, so suddenly as his wife and eldest sonne were taken, and himselfe hardly escaped at a backe window, and naked, into the woods, where he kept a cold Christmas, while my Lord lived plentifully in his house, with such provisions as were made, for him and his Bonnaghs and kerne to keepe a merry Christmas. To vent his anger, he daily offered slight skirmishes upon advantage, but his heart was nothing eased therewith, being continually beaten. His Lordship with the Queenes Forces, lay in this Countrey till about the twentieth of January: In which time his troopes spoiled and ransacked the Countries of Rannelagh and Cashay, swept away the most part of their cattle and goods, burnt all their Corne, and almost all their Houses, leaving little or nothing to releeve them; and to finish the worke, his Lordship

The Lord Deputy's cunninge intent.

The rebels punished.

planted two strong Garrisons upon them, the one at Wicklo on the East side, (not able to come neerer, because a ship with our tooles and instruments was beaten backe by ill weather, and could not arrive in time); the other at Tullogh upon the west, so as they could not long hold from submitting or flying, being thus hedged in.

His Lordship at Monastreven.

This done, his Lordship came to Monastreven, with purpose to undertake the Mores and Connors. But having in few daies setled a correspondency for proceeding in that service, betweene our Forces in those parts, and the neighbouring septs of Odempsies, and some suspected subjects, of whose faith till then his Lordship stood not assured, and discerning the Mores to be weake in Leax, after the killing of their Chiefetaine Owny mac Rory, and the burning and spoiling in the Leax journey, so as they had not meanes to keepe their Bonnaghs, and hearing that the Oconnors were fled far from that part of Ophaly, so as neither of them could be found to make resistance to any reasonable strong Forces. His Lordship leaving [II. i. 88.] in these parts some few Companies to assist the subjects, rode from Monastreven the twentie nine of January to Abiconal, nine miles, passing by the ruined City of Kildare, now altogether disinhabited. The thirtieth we passed the Liffye, and came to Milhussy, one Master Hussyes Castle, eleven miles, passing by some pleasant Villages, and by Menouth, a faire house, belonging to the Earles of Kildare, now in the hands of the Countesse Mabell an old widdow. The thirty one we came to Trym, eight miles, champion ground. This is a pleasant *Trym.* towne for seate, if the inhabitants were sutable, through which the Boyne runnes, and it hath the ruines of a sumptuous Castle. This place his Lp. thought fittest for his present residence: for if Captaine Tirrel (now the chiefe rebel in Ophalia) should draw his force to the South of the Country, from hence his Lordship might easily fall back on him. If the rebels in the West desired to passe into Mounster (as they intended), then our forces were so disposed, as they could not escape without fighting with us upon disadvantage to them. And if neither fell out, then his Lordship purposed to plant a Garrison at the Cavan in the Brenny, and to settle our above mentioned Mac Guire in Fermanagh.

Neale Garve to have Tirconnel.

At this time his Lp desired to have authoritie out of England, to passe Tirconnel (the Countie of Odonel) to Neale Garve, reserving eight hundred Acres about Ballishannon, and the fishing of the Erne to her Majestie. And such was the opinion of the service his turbulent spirit could do the State, as he had the grant of three hundred foot, and one hundred horse in her Majesties pay, on condition he should bring the men serviceable, and maintaine them so, without further charge to her Majestie.

From Trym, lying in East-Meathe, his Lordship the eleventh of Februarie, passing by the Barron of Trimblestones house, rode to the Lord of Delvins house in West-Meath, eleven miles distant. The twelfth we passed ten miles further to Molingar, the Shire towne of West-Meath, compassed with bogges. Thence the fourteenth, wee went to Ballymore, Sir Frances Shanes house, ten long miles. The sixteenth to Sir Tibbot Dillons house, seven miles. Thence the seventeenth to Athlone, five miles, where the Governour of the Province of Connaght useth to lye in a strong Castle belonging to her Majestie, which being scituate in Connaght, is divided from the Towne by a River and a faire bridge of stone with eight arches, lying in West-Meath. And all this Countrie is Champion, whereof the greatest part lay waste. His Lordp returned back the eighteenth of February to Sir Tibbot Dillons house, and the nineteenth to Danoar twelve miles, being Brian Mac Gohagans Castle in West-Meath.

Captain Tirrels fastnesse.

While his Lordship lay in this Castle, he rode forth the twentieth of February, to view a strong hold, seated in a plaine, and in a little Iland, compassed with bogges and deepe ditches of running water, and thicke woods, in which fastnesse Captaine Tirrel, with some of the boldest Rebels then lay. At the first approch to the bogge, two shot of the Rebels came out, our horsemen standing on a hill, moved continually, but my selfe being a raw souldier, stood stil, and because I had a white horse, I gave the Rebels a faire marke, so as the first shot flew close by my head, and when I apprehending my danger, turned my horse, the second flew through my cloake, and light in my padde saddle, (which saved my life), and brused my thigh. Presently his Lordship sent Sir Christopher Saint Laurence, Captaine Winsor, Captaine Roper, and Captaine Rotheram, with wings of Foote into the Wood, to discover the fortified Iland. And on the other side sent Captaine Leg to the same purpose. While these skirmished with the rebels lying intrenched, Master Darcy riding by the skirt of the Wood, was shot in the neck. The two and twenty day his Lordship drew forth againe, and we carried hurdles and fagots to passe into the Iland, but the water carrying them away, and his Lordships Guard being not well seconded by the Irish, wee came off with losse, and Captaine Rotheram was shot.

A narrow escape.

Before I proceede, I must digresse a little to other matters. In this Journey (begun the twentie two of December) his Lordship received commandement to pardon all such in Mounster as should require it, and should be commended by the Lord President, with assurance that Spaine was so intangled with the warre of Savoy, as the Irish Rebels could at this time have small succour thence. His Lordship writ to Master Secretary to procure him leave to start over into England, to kisse the Queenes hands, and to conferre with him about the Irish service, professing that hee reputed him his honourable friend, and did much disdaine that humour in any subject (if any such were) which would thinke him tyed by any respect, from having his affection free to love him. In the beginning of Februarie, the Lord President of Mounster, excused himselfe to the Lord Deputy, that hee had made stay of some forces his Lordship had directed

Pardon for the rebels in Mounster.

[II. i. 89.]

to come from thence, because hee had intelligence that some Northerne Rebels were sent to invade Mounster. But his Lordship knowing that he had stopped their passage, and that they could not goe with any great numbers, if perchance they escaped, did againe require that these forces might be sent unto him. At this time, there was a plot for Tyrones head, the managing whereof was commended to Sir Richard Moryson Governour of Dundalke, whether Sir William Godolphin was sent with his troope of horse, to second this plot, which tooke not the wished effect; the undertaker Henry Oge Oneale failing in his courage, or in his faith.

A plot for Tyrone's head.

Now I will returne to his Lordships actions while hee lay at Maghogans Castle. The same two & twentieth of February, his Lord received a packet out of England, by which he understood that the Earle of Essex was committed to the Tower for treason, which much dismaied him and his neerest friends, and wrought strange alteration in him: For whereas before he stood upon termes of honour with the Secretary, now he fell flat to the ground, and insinuated himselfe into inward love, and to an absolute dependancy with the Secretary, so as for a time he estranged himselfe from two of his neerest friends, for the open declaration they had made of dependancy on the Earle of Essex; yet rather covering, then extinguishing his good affection to them. It is not credible that the influence of the Earles malignant star, should worke upon so poore a snake as my selfe, being almost a stranger to him yet my neerenesse in bloud to one of his Lordships above named friends, made it perhaps seeme to his Lordship improper, to use my service in such neerenesse, as his Lordship had promised and begun to doe. So as the next day he tooke his most secret papers out of my hand, yet giving them to no other, but keeping them in his owne cabinet: and this blow I never fully recovered while I staied in Ireland. In truth his Lordship had good cause to be wary in his words and actions, since by some confessions in England, himselfe was tainted with privity

The Earle of Essex committed to the Tower.

to the Earles practises, so that howsoever he continued still to importune leave to come over; yet no doubt he meant nothing lesse, but rather (if he had been sent for) was purposed with his said friends to saile into France, they having privately fitted themselves with money and necessaries thereunto. For howsoever his Lordship were not dangerously ingaged therein, yet hee was (as hee privately professed) fully resolved not to put his necke under the fyle of the Queenes Atturnies tongue. But his Lordships former service, and the necessity of his future imployment, together with his good successe, so strengthened him, as without great unthankefulnesse, and popular obloquy, he could not have beene questioned upon this weake ground.

Proclamation by the Lord Deputy.

The same twenty two of February, his Lordship in counsell resolved to proclaime, that all such as had any rebels goods, should discover them, or be guiltie of Treason: That none upon paine of death should parley with the rebels: that the Countrey should bring in victuals to the Campe, which no man (upon paine of death) should take from them without paying the price of the market. And thus purposing to force the rebels out of the fortified Iland, and then to plant a garrison at the Abbey neere adjoyning; and to charge the new submitted subjects to joyne with this garrison in the service, as also to take order for the safe victualing of the same when he should be gone, his Lordship resolved the next day to make another attempt against the Iland wherein Terril lay, preparing all things to second the same, and taking order to bring victualls to the Campe from all parts, and especially from Athlone by boates.

Terril's head proclaimed.

The twenty three of February, his Lordship drew forth to the Abbey, where hee had lodged foure hundred souldiers, there hee dined and proclaimed Terrils head at two thousand crownes, and after dinner drawing to the Iland, he divided the forces, sending part to put boates [II. i. 90.] into the water, and so to assaile the Iland, and causing the rest to be led into the Woods to fetch out the rebels corne, and to burne the houses, and such things for their reliefe, as they could not bring away. The twenty foure of February, being Shrove-tuesday, there fell a great snow, so that we were forced to lie still, and the next night the Rebels did steale away, leaving the Iland to his Lordship, where the next day wee found much corne, some Murrions and Peeces, eight Cowes, and some garrons.

The twenty six, his Lordship drew the forces beyond the Iland, into a pleasant valley, wherein was a ruined house of Sir Edward Herberts, and the ground was well plowed by the Rebels. Our men burnt houses and corne, and his Lordship gave an Angell to a Souldier to swim over the water, and burne the houses in another Iland. Then we came to a river, which divideth West Meath, and Ophaly; into which countrey his Lordship sent divers companies under Sir Christopher, Saint Laurence, to spoyle the same. The twenty seven, his Lordship rode six miles to Sir John Tirrels, a strong Castle, wee passed by the way Tirrels pace, compassed with bogges and hilly woods. This Knight was a subject, and here his Lordship rested the next day. The first of March his Lordship rode to Klonegave, the house of Sir Terrence O dempsey in Ophalia, being twelve miles; in the first part whereof wee passed a dangerous part of Tirrels fastnesse.

Letter from her Majesty.

Here his Lordship received a gracious Letter from her Majesty, whereby she made known unto him the Earle of Essex his death, & (to use her own words) professed, that in regard of his approved fidelity and love, it was some allevation of her griefe, to ejaculate the same to him. First, her Majesty required him to look wel in general, upon the dispositions of all his Captaines, whereof, some preferred by the Earle, might perhaps have hollow hearts towardes her service, for as shee was pleased to pardon those, who by his popular fashion and outward profession of his sincerity had beene seduced, and blindly led by him; so shee was carefull to sever the chaffe from the corne, and to deprive the malicious of meanes to prejudice her service. Secondly, whereas the Secretary in his Lordships name had moved her Majesty, that he might have warrant to come over; yet in regard the Spanish ships had not yet passed the narrow seas into Flaunders (whether surely they were sent, and nothing lesse then for Ireland, howsoever the Traytor made use of like rumors) her Majesty wished that hee would conceale this his desire for a time, with promise to call him home the next winter, and use his service neere her person.

Letters from the Lords in England.

The same time his Lordship received Letters from the Lords in England, giving allowance in her Majesties name, for the passing of Tirconnell to Neale Garve, upon the above mentioned conditions; yet advising that hereafter no Countrey should so absolutely bee passed, as all the inhabitants should depend upon one man, which would still kindle new flames of rebellion. By the same Letters his Lordship understood, that the supplies of money, victuals, and munitions, were ready according to his demands. And their Lordships advised the plantation of a garrison about Strangford, to prevent the assistance which the Scots gave to the Rebels. The third of March his Lordship rode ten miles to Bally Britton, Sir Henry Warrens house in Leax, which was kept for the Queene by a Constable and Warders. In the mid way we passed by Phillipstowne (otherwise called Dyngen) a strong Fort in Ophalia (otherwise called the Kings County) and that day his Lordship sent out many parties of souldiers into the woods, against Tirrell and the Oconnors, scatteredly lurking in those parts.

Directions to proclaime a new coine.

Here his Lordship received from the Lords, directions to descrie the silver mony, and to proclaime a new coine, three ounces fine; which base money was sent over, onely to impoverish the Rebels (as was pretended) who made warre against the Queene with her owne treasure; but in conclusion it was the undoing of all the Queenes servants there, for no man cared to lay it up, and all things were bought at excessive rates, after the exchange in England once failed. This exchange was proclaimed to be held at three Cities in England, and foure in Ireland; but by [II. i. 91.] reason that great summes were coyned by Rebels and strangers, and for other abuses of the same, as namely of the Merchants, who notwithstanding that the money was duly changed, did excessively raise all prices, this exchange soone failed, and our hearts therewith: for we served there in discomfort, and came home beggars, so that onely the Treasurers and Paymasters, (who were thereby infinitely inriched) had cause to blesse the Authors of this invention.

The Lord Deputy in Meath.

The fourth of March his Lordship rode five miles to Sir Edward Fitzgeralds house, scituate in Meath, in a pleasant and fruitfull Countrey. The fifth of March we rode ten miles to Moymeere, a very pleasant house, belonging to Sir James Dillon, and thence the next day two miles further to Trym. Sir Richard Moryson Governour of Dundalke, had lately advertised his Lordship, that Turlogh mac Henry, Tyrones brother, Captaine of the Fewes, had taken his oath to him, before a Priest and upon a Masse booke, that he would submit himselfe to her Majesties mercy, without any conditions at or before St Patricks day next following. And further had advertised that the Lord of Clancarvin humbly desired to be received to mercy with him. For better ratifying hereof, the said Sr Richard Moryson now brought the said Turlogh in person to his Lordship lying at Trim. The fifteenth of March his Lordship drew to Arbrachin, the Bishop of Meaths house, sixe miles distant, where his Lordship had appointed the adjoining garrisons to meete him the next day; and presently after their arrivall, his Lordship tooke horse towards evening, and thence we marched all night, being very darke, and in the morning suddenly fell into the Ferney, the possession whereof Ever mac Cooly, one of the Mac Mahowns then usurped; and there we burnt the houses and spoiled the goods of the Inhabitants, Sir Richard Moryson Governour of Dundalke, with that Garrison, and Sir Oliver Lambert with other troopes, and Captaine Thomas Williams with the

The Bishop of Meath.

forces of Ardee comming in divers wayes, & meeting his Lordship in that Countrey, with small or no resistance made by the rebels, to either party. The nineteenth we marched five miles to Ardee, the twentieth seven miles to Mellifant, Sir Edward Mores house, the twenty one two miles to Drogedagh, where his Lordship staied till the sixteenth of Aprill, and so returned to Dublyn. At Drogedagh his Lordship altered the list of the foot, the horse standing still as before.

The Disposall of the foot into garrisons the 23 of March, 1600.

The disposal of the foot into garrisons.

At the Newry under Sir Oliver St Johns 750. At Carlingford Captaine Hansard 100. At Mount Norreys under Sir Samuell Bagnoll 450. At Dundalke under Sr Richard Moryson 400. At Arde a refreshing but no standing garrison 350. At Luscanon 400. At Tullagh 350. At Wicklo 250. At the Navan 300. At the Nasse 100. In Westmeath 450. In Ophaly 200. In Leax 300. At Athy 100. At Monastreven 300.

In Connaght.

Sir John Barkely Deputy Governor 200. The Lord of Dunkellin now upon his fathers death Earle of Clanrickard 150. More under foure Captaines 500.

Foot in Galloway and Odoynes Countrey.

Three Captaines 400. Capt. Tho: Roper 150. At Reban 150. In Ocarrols Country 100. In Kildare 150. At Dublyn the Lord Deputies guard 200. At Carickfergus under Sir Arthur Chichester 550. Of new Companies 1150. being cast, and 50. made over to Loughfoyle Garrison, remained 800. Of Sr Charles Percies Company, 100 were made over to other Captaines, and 50 were added to Loughfoyle garrison. These Companies together with the foot in Mounster & at Loughfoyle, do make the new list of foot 13250.

Her Majesties charge in Ireland.

Her Majesties charge in Ireland from the first of Aprill in the beginning of the yeere 1600. to the last of March in the beginning of the yeere 1601.

Her Majesties allowances by establishment, and by her letters for increase amount to two hundred seventy sixe thousand nine hundred & foureteen li. nine s. foure d. ob. qu. demy.

[II. i. 92.] Hereof saved by the Lord Deputy his providence fifteene thousand two hundred sixty two l. sixe s. five d.

Saved also by Checks imposed on the Army, seventeene thousand twenty nine pound sixteene s. nine d. ob.

So her Majesties charge for the Army this yeere, besides munition and like extraordinaries, amounteth to two hundred thirty foure thousand six hundred twenty two li. five s. two d. qu. demy.

Mounster.

It remaines briefly to collect (out of the Lord Presidents letters to the Lord Deputy), the services done in Mounster the yeere 1600. now ended. About the sixteenth of Aprill, in the beginning of the yeere 1600. Sir George Carew Lord President of Mounster departing from Kilkenny, where hee had beene some daies detained by the Earle of Ormonds surprisall at a parley with the rebels, came to Waterford. And Thomas Fitz-James bastard sonne to James Fitzgerald late Lord of Decies, chiefe rebell in the County of Waterford fearing present prosecution, made sute to be received to her Majesties mercy, which the Lord President granted, aswell to draw from the titulary Earle of Desmond some part of his strength, as to open the passage betweene Waterford and Yoghall by land, formerly shut up, so as nothing could passe any way but by sea. The twenty three of Aprill at Dungarven his Lordship received advertisement that Florence mac Carty after many favours from the State, being wholly hispaniolised had great power in Carbry and Desmond, and according to his plot with Tyrone at his being there, was entered into open action, (so they terme rebellion). That Captaine Flower Sergeant Major of Mounster, had hereupon entered Carbry with 1200 foot, and 100 horse, burning and spoiling the same, and killing many rebels. That Florence had levied of the Provincials and Bonnaghs (so they call waged souldiers) 2000 foot, yet never attempted the English, till in their returne they came within five miles of Corke, where in a fastnesse the midway betweene Corke and Kinsale, they assailed the English, and were beaten by them, some 100. of the Rebels being slaine, in which conflict Captaine Flower had two horses slaine under him. The twenty foure the Lord President came to Corke, where he received the State of the Province by the relation of Sir Henry Pore sole Commissioner for Mounster, (since the killing of his partner Sir Warham St Leger by Mac Guire, likewise killed in the fight) and understood the rebels to be strong and masters of the field, supplied with all necessaries from the Townes through the perswasion of Priests, and the covetousnesse of the Townesmen. About this time Fitzgibbon called the White Knight, either ill used by Tyrone at his being in Mounster, or fearing prosecution, submitted himselfe to her Majesties mercy. Likewise Florence mac Carty by perswasion of friends, and upon safe conduct, came to the Lord President, and protested loialty to her Majesty, but refused to give his sonne for pledge, lest his waged souldiers should cast him out of his Countrey, till his Lordship threatned to lay aside all other service sharpely to prosecute him, whereupon he consented for his pledge, but required to have the County of Desmond given to him and his heires, with title of Mac Carty More, or Earle of Clancar, with like high demands, which being rejected, he desired leave to sue for these graces in England, with promise not to serve against her Majesties forces in the meane time, wherewith the Lord President was satisfied, having no other end for the present, then to make him stand neutrall, while the whole forces were imploied against the titulary Earle of Desmond, James

The Lord President at Corke.

Florence mac Carty.

Fitzthomas, called the Suggon Earle by nickename. Now one Dermod Oconnor, having no lands, yet by marriage with the daughter of the old Earle of Desmond and his great valour, had the leading of 1400. Bonnaghs. And because the Lord President hoped to ruine the rebels one by another; at this time by the wife of the said Dermod and other Agents his Lordship plotted with him, upon promise of great rewards to kill James the titulary Earle of Desmond: And in like sort, one John Nugent a rebell, upon promise of pardon and reward, did within few daies undertake to kill John the said Earles brother. About the beginning of May Redman Burke leading 500 Rebels, lost 120. of them while he adventured to take a prey in Oduiers Countrey, and being nourished by the Lord President, with hope to be Baron of Letrim, drew [II. i. 93.] his men out of Mounster into Ormond, with purpose to leade them into Connaght: And Tyrrell leader of the Northerne men, staied not long behind him, pretending discontent against Dermod Oconnor, but indeed fearing some plot against his head. It had beene long rumored that the Lord President would take the field the sixth of May, which made the rebels draw to a head and spend their victuals, so as after ten dayes they were forced to disperce themselves. The twentieth of May the Lord President tooke the field, and marching towards Lymbricke, setled Warders in some Castles to secure the passage thither from Kilmalloch. At Lymricke his Lordship understood that John Nugent above named, being ready (as he had undertaken) to kill John brother to the titulary Earle of Desmond, was by accident hindered from discharging his Pistoll, and being apprehended, was put to death; but as well John as the titulary Earle his brother, were so terrified herewith, as they durst never keep together, & thought themselves least secure in the head of their owne men from like practises. The Lord President marched into John Burkes Countrey, and spoyling the same, forced him to seeke her Majesties mercy on his knees, which at last he obtained, though with difficulty.

The Lord President takes the field.

His Lordship having gained here plenty of graine for the Army, sent five hundred foot into Omulrians Countrey, who spoiled the same, and killed many rebels. Then his Lordship returned to Limricke without any losse, and in the beginning of June divided the Army into garrisons not far distant, which his Lordship did though the time were fit for service, that he might attend the plot with Dermod Oconnor for killing the titulary Earle of Desmond, which could not well be done, except the rebels were dispersed, who would keepe together as long as the English Army was in the field. Besides, his Lordship upon their breaking, tooke advantage to settle a garrison at Asketon without any resistance. Dermod O Connor tooke the titulary Earle prisoner in the name of Oneale, pretending by a forged letter that he had plotted his death with the Lord President, & presently sent his wife for the money promised in reward, wishing the Lord President to draw his forces to Kilmalloch, where he would deliver him the prisoner, which his Lordship did accordingly the sixteenth of June, but the rebels having notice hereof, drew together foure thousand in number, stopped the passages, set the titulary Earle at liberty, and besieged Dermod O Connor in a Castle, till the Lord President marching thither the 29 of June, forced them to leave the siege. His Lordship kept the field, tooke the chiefe Castle of the Knight of the vally, wherein were slaine threescore warders, tooke other Castles, and did many good services, the rebels in great number lying neere him, but never offering to fight, by reason of the jelousies betweene them, whereupon 2500. Connaght men were sutors to his Lordship to returne home without impediment from his forces. At this time Oconnor Kerry yeelded his Castle to the Queene, and was received to mercy, and the Lord President at last granted a passe to the Rebels of Connaght, but the Lord Burke not knowing thereof, for a privat revenge, set upon them as they marched home, and slew threescore of them, besides many drowned. The sixteenth of July the Lord President

Plot to kill the Earle of Desmond.

Dermod O Connor besieged.

bestowed the Army in garrisons: The 23. of July his Lordship tooke the field againe, to releeve the men he had formerly sent into Kerry, and marching thither, took Lixnaw the chiefe house of the Lord Fitz Morrice, and many other Castles, for griefe whereof the said Lord died, yet leaving a sonne then as dangerous as himselfe. The Lord President returned to Cork about the eighteenth of August, leaving Sir Charles Wilmot Governour of Kerry, a valiant Gentleman, a chiefe Commander under him, and in the first ranke of those instruments he used in all services, who in short time brought most of the freeholders of Kerry to due subjection, and drove the titulary Desmond out of those parts. All the garrisons in time of harvest, gathered as much corne as they could, and destroied the rest, which made the rebels not able to subsist the yeere following. Sir George Thornton hearing that the titulary Earle of Desmond passed neere Kilmalloch sent the garrison out, and Captain Greame charging them with his troope of horse, killed 120. of them, in which conflict the English got 300. garons laden with baggage, 150 pikes and peeces with other weapons, and 40. horse, but the English had 16. horses killed in the fight. The titulary Earle of Desmond, could never after draw 100. men together, & was forced to flie into Tipperary with his brother John, Pierce Lacy an Arch-rebel, & the Knight of the Glin, whence his brother John

Sir Charles Wilmot Governour of Kerry.

[II. i. 94.] hasted into Ulster for reliefe from Tirone. And in the end of this Summer upon the departure of the Bonnaghs of Connaght and Ulster, & the good successe of the English, many of the Provincials submitted themselves, yet sent to Rome for dispensation of their so doing. About the middest of October James Fitzgerald (who had long been imprisoned in the Tower of London, being the next & true heire to the last Earle of Desmond, and released by the Queene with title of Earle by letters Pattents sent to the Lord President, and promise of a good proportion of land to support his dignity at the end of the warre, according to his deserts in her

James Fitzgerald released.

Majesties service, and in the meane time to live upon pay in the Army) landed at Yoghal, and the eighteenth day came to the Lord President at Mallogh, and was industrious in the Queenes service. Dermod O Connor being in Connaght, and hearing of the young Earle of Desmonds arrivall, upon promise of great services had the Lord Presidents protection to come unto him, but was set upon by Tybot ne long, his men defeated, he taken and hanged, whereupon Tibot having then a Company in her Majesties pay was cashered. Florence mac Carty having all this while practised underhand many things against the State, and putting still off his appearance by delatory excuses, at last in October by the desperatenesse of his estate was forced to submit, and obtained pardon upon pledges of his loyaltie. The titularie Earle of Desmond stealing backe into Mounster lived as a Wood-kerne, never having more then two or three in his Company.

Dermod O Connor taken and hanged.

In November, Sir Charles Wilmot took the last and only Castle the Lord Mac Morice had in Kerry, & his eldest sonne therin (betraied by a Priest for safetie of his life) and great provisions laid up in that Castle. In these two last moneths Sir Richard Percy lying in Garrison at Kinsale, twice passed into the Country, and tooke preyes of five hundred Cowes, killing many rebels. In December the Lord President had notice where the titulary Earle lurked, and sent men to surprise him: but he escaped in such haste, as hee left his shooes behind him. And now there was not a Castle in Mounster held for the rebels, nor any company of ten rebels together, though there wanted not loose vagabonds dispersed in all corners, so as his Lordship had leisure to looke into the Corporate Townes, being aiders, abetters, and procurers under hand of this rebellion, all the Queenes treasure being spent in them by the souldiers, and they underhand supplying the rebels with all necessaries, though at excessive rates. The rebels fled out of Mounster into Tiperarie and Ormond, had hitherto lived

The rebels in Mounster subdued.

there among the Bullers being subjects, without any disturbance, the rather for the Earle of Ormonds mourning for the death of his most worthy and vertuous Lady: but in January his Lordship sent some forces against them, who killed many, and forced the rest to flie, whereof some were drowned passing the waters then very high, and some chiefe rebels were taken and hanged at Kilkenny. About the end of January, the Lord President sent 1000 foote of the Mounster List, to be disposed by the Lord Deputie, as he had direction to doe. His Lordship to settle the Country the better, refused to renew any protections, so as all were forced to sue their pardons, and in two moneths space before the end of Februarie, upon his Lordships recommendation, more then foure thousand Mounster men had their pardons, granted by the Lord Deputie, and passed under the great Seale.

4000, pardons granted in Mounster.

Chap. I.

Of the Lord Deputies particular proceedings in the prosecution of the Rebels, and of the Spaniards invading Ireland, in the yeere 1601.

Hile the Lord Deputy lay at Drogheda (namely, from the one and twentie of March, till the sixteene of Aprill, upon which day he returned to Dublin), his Lordship assembled the Counsellers of State to attend him there. And upon the eight and twentie of March 1601, the Lord Deputie and Counsell wrote from Drogheda (vulgarly called Tredagh) their joynt letters to the Lords in England, whereby they advertised, that the Lord Deputie having spent the greatest part of Winter in the Irish Countries of Lemster, had by burning their Corne, consuming their cattel, and killing many of them, so scattered their maine strength, as certaine of the chiefe had since submitted to the Queenes mercy, and the rest were severed into small companies, and unlike to draw to any dangerous head; yea, Tirrel, in opinion the greatest among them (taken for Tyrones Lieutenant in Lemster), being forced out of his greatest fastnesse, now with a few base Kerne following him, was driven to wander in Woods and Boggs, seeking to escape into the North (as shortly after he did, notwithstanding that

Letters to the Lords in England.

certaine English Companies were left to hunt him in his walkes, and to stop his passage.) That his Lordship desirous to be at hand, to watch all opportunities of service upon the Northerne borders, had pierced into the Fearny, and that Sir Richard Moryson Governour of Dundalk with his Garrison had formerly wasted, and now passed through the Fewes, and met his Lordship there, so as both these Countries being spoiled, Ever Mac Cooly chiefe of the Fearny, and Turlogh Mac Henry, Captaine of the Fewes, had both been humble suters for her Majesties mercie, and were commanded to appeare shortly, and make their humble submissions: which course likewise the septs of the Brenny were like to take, for many of them chastised by the Army, and utterly discouraged, had alreadie divers times offered most humble submissions. That his Lordship hereupon had called the Counsellors to Tredagh, there to consider of the circumstances and conditions, to be observed in taking these submissions, as also to deliberate how the Army might be imployed most to vex Tyrone, til the Summer came on, at which time his Lordship purposed to dwell upon him, and put him to triall of his uttermost fortune. That it was resolved in Counsell to accept the submissions of the Chiefe of Fearny, and the Captaine of the Fewes, above named, as likewise of the septs of the Brennye (these three Countries being an hedge betweene the English Pale, and the North, and yeelding many commodities to passe into Tirone with her Majesties forces. That it was resolved to send Mac Guyer into Fermanagh with 200 men to helpe him for a time, against the rebel Mac Guyer (whom he and his sonne had already much impoverished), for hee was thought a fit instrument (in case he prevailed), as well to intangle Tyrone and infest Ororke, as to helpe the Plantation at Ballishannon, intended to be put in execution about June following, when forage could be had for horses.

The Counsellors called to Tredagh.

They further solicited by these letters for supplies of victuals, munition and mony, and that the victuals and munition should be addressed some part to Dublin and Tredagh, but the greatest part to Galloway, being intended for the forces to be planted at Ballishannon, and those to invade Tyrone that way; and the rest to Carlingford, intended for the forces to invade Tyrone by the way of the Newry, which invasion was purposed about the middest of June, when forrage might be had for the horse, and this they prayed, because the unshipping and reshipping of the victuals at Dublin, caused great expence of mony, and waste of the victuals. [II. ii. 96.]

The chiefes of the Fearny submit.

Tirlogh Mac Henry Captaine of the Fewes, and Ever Mac Cooly, of the Family of the mac Mahownes, chiefe of the Fearny, did about this time declare themselves to be subjects, and humbly made their submissions on their knees, signing certaine articles of subjection under their hands, and putting in pledges for performance thereof. And the said Ever in particular confessed in the Articles under his hand, that hee was not Lord, but Farmer of the Fearnye, binding himselfe to pay her Majestie his old rent. The one and thirty of March 1601, her Majestie signed the following Establishment. *An.* 1601.

Officers Generall.

The Establishment of the Army.

The Lord Deputy for his diet one hundred li. per mensem: a Band of Horse three li. foure s. per diem: fifty foot each at eight d. per diem: for allowance in lieu of cesse, ten li. per annum, besides his Companies of horse and foote in the Army. In all per diem twelve li. six s. sixe d. ob. qu. per annum, foure thousand foure hundred fortie foure li. seventeene s. one d. ob. qu.

The Lieutenant of the Army, three li. per diem; one thousand fourescore fifteene pound per annum.

The Treasurer at warres, thirtie five s. per diem; sixe hundred thirty eight li. fifteene shillings per annum.

The Marshall besides his thirty horse at twelve d. per diem without checque in the Army, five s. nine d. per diem; one hundred foure li. eighteene s. nine d. per annum.

The Establishment of the Army.

The Serjeant Major of the Army, twenty s. per diem; three hundred sixtie five li. per annum.

The Master of the Ordinance, twenty sixe s. eleven d. per diem; foure hundred ninetie one li. foure s. seven d. per annum.

Ministers of the Ordinance, twenty five s. two d. per diem; foure hundred fiftie nine li. five s. ten d. per annum.

Muster-master Generall, eleven s. sixe d. per diem; two hundred nine li. seventeene s. sixe d. per annum.

Comptroler of the victuals, ten s. per diem; one hundred eighty two li. ten s. per annum.

Five Commissaries of victuals, one at eight s., and foure, each at sixe s. per diem, thirtie two s. per diem; five hundred eightie foure li. per annum.

Fourteene Colonels, each at tenne s. per diem, seven li. per diem; two thousand five hundred fifty five li. per annum.

Scout-master, besides sixe horse, each at twelve d. per diem, part of the Army, sixe s. eight d. per diem; one hundred twenty one li. thirteene s. foure d. per annum.

Provost Marshall of the Army for himselfe and foure horsemen, foure s. three d. per diem, seventy seven li. eleven s. three d. per annum.

Officers Provinciall.

President of Mounster at one hundred thirty three li. sixe s. eight d. per annum; his diet and the Counsels at ten li. the weeke; his retinue of thirtie horse and twentie foote at thirty s. seven d. ob. per diem; three li. sixe s. sixe d. per diem; one thousand two hundred thirteene li. thirteene s. foure d. qu. per annum.

Provost Marshall in Mounster, fourteene s. per diem; two hundred fiftie five li. ten s. per annum.

The Commander of the forces in Connaght at ten s. per diem, with an increase of one hundred li. per annum; fifteene s. five d. ob. qu. per diem; two hundred eightie two li. ten s. per annum.

Provost Marshall in Connaght, besides twelve horsemen of the Army, five s. seven d. ob. per diem; one hundred two li. foureteene s. one d. ob. per annum. [II. ii. 97.] *The Establishment of the Army.*

Commander of the forces at Loughfoyle, besides his pay of ten s. per diem as Colonel, hath three s. foure d. per diem; sixty li. sixteene s. eight d. per annum.

Provost Marshall there, foure s. per diem; seventy three li. per annum.

Provost Marshall of Ballishannon, foure s. per diem; seventy three li. per annum.

Lieutenant of the Queenes County, sixe s. eight d. per diem; one hundred twentie one li. thirteene s. foure d. per annum.

Provost Marshall in Lemster for himselfe and sixe horsemen, five s. seven d. ob. per diem; one hundred two li. fourteene s. one d. ob. per annum.

Warders in Lemster per annum, one thousand three hundred ten li. nineteene s. two pence.

Warders in Ulster per annum, eight hundred twentie one li. five s.

Warders in Mounster per annum, five hundred forty two li. eighteene s. nine d.

Warders in Connaght per annum, two hundred li.

Twelve hundred horsemen distributed into foure and twenty Bands, the Captaine foure s., the Lieutenant two s. sixe pence, the Cornet two s. per diem, and three hundred horsemen, each at eighteene d. per diem, on condition they be English both horse and men, or else to have but twelve d. per diem. And 200 horsemen at fifteene d. per diem, and seven hundred horsemen at twelve d. per diem. Per annum twenty nine thousand two hundred seventie three li.

Fourteene thousand footmen, distributed into one hundred forty Bands, the Captaine foure s. Lieutenant two s. Ensigne eighteene d. the day, two Serjeants, a Drum, and a Surgion, each at twelve d. a piece per diem, & each souldier at eight d. per diem. Per annum one

The Establishment of the Army.

hundred ninety nine thousand seven hundred fifteene li. sixteene s. eight d.

Pensioners in the Muster-booke, per annum one thousand eight hundred nine li. fifteene s. ten d.

Pensioners by letters Patents per annum eight hundred seventy foure li. five s. nine pence, ob.

Thirteene Almesmen per annum eightie eight li. nineteene s. foure d. ob.

Officers of the Musters which are payable out of the checkes, namely one Muster-Master at sixe s. eight d. a Comptroller at ten s. and twenty Commissaries, each at three s. foure d. per diem. Per annum one thousand five hundred twenty li. sixteene s. eight d.

Extraordinarie allowance for Messengers, Espials, Post-barkes, rewards of services &c. per annum, sixe thousand li.

Totall of this Establishment per annum two hundred fifty five thousand seven hundred seventy three li. fourteene d. qu. denny.

Memorandum, that the dead paies allowed to the Captaines in each Company of horse or foote, are herein contained, but the charge of munition, of levying horse and foote for reinforcing the Army, with many like charges, are not herein contained.

Captaine Josias Bodley and Captaine Edward Blany.

The sixth of Aprill 1601, his Lordship received advertisement from Captaine Josias Bodley, at the Newry, that he, and Captaine Edward Blany, Governour of the Forte of Mount-Norreys, purposing to surprise Loghrorcan, could not carrie a boat, which they had provided to that purpose, but he carrying certaine fireworkes provided in case the boat should faile, went to the Fort, and joyning with Captaine Blany, marched towards that Iland, where they arrived by eight of the clocke in the morning, and leaving their forces behind a Wood, they both went together to discover the Iland; which done Captaine Bodley made readie thirtie arrowes with wildfier, and so they both fell downe with one hundred shot close to the water, where the shot playing incessantly upon the Iland, while the other delivered their arrowes, suddenly the houses fired, and burnt so vehemently, as the rebels lodging there, forsooke the Iland, and swumme to the further shoare. That after they saw all burnt to the ground, they fired a great house upon their side of the shoare, and killed there sixe Kerne, (gaining their Armes) besides Churles and Calliachs, and after the burning of other houses also, they brought away some Cowes and Sheepe, with other pillage; and they understood by a prisoner, that there were about thirty persons in the Iland, whereof onely eight swumme away, (of which foure were shot in the water), so as the rest either were killed or lay hurt in the Iland. Likewise they understood by the said prisoner, that great store of butter, corne, meale, and powder, was burnt and spoiled in the Iland, which all the rebels of that Countrey made their magasine. Further, that some forty kerne skirmished with them at places of advantage, in their retreat for two miles march: but howsoever the common opinion was, that the Rebels sustained great losse by this service, yet of the English onely two were slaine and seven hurt.

The rebels surprised.

[II. ii. 98.]

The seventh of Aprill Sir Henry Dockwra Governour of Loughfoyle wrote to his Lordship, that he had taken the submission of Hugh Boy, of whose service to her Majesty, he was confident to make manifold good uses, as well for the present setling Sir John Odogherties Countrey after his late death, as for revealing the Rebels secret counsels wel knowne to him. Among which, he confidently avowed that the King of Spaine had promised to invade Ireland this yeere, with six thousand men, & to land at some Towne in Munster, (swearing that three of the chief Cities had promised to receive them:) Adding that Florence Mac Carty had written to Odonnel, that he had submitted to the Queene onely upon necessity, and that upon the Spaniards comming hee would joyne with them. This Governour further advertised that Phelim Oge, chiefe of a contrary faction in Odogherties country, desired to make his humble submission to the Queenes mercy upon these conditions: to leave of the name of

Sir Henry Dockwra's letter to the Lord Deputy.

Odogherty, and obey any man, to whom her Majesty should give that Countrey. To pay all debts his men did owe to any subjects. To discharge his souldiers. To returne to the owners twelve hundred Beeves hee had cut for Odonnell. To make satisfaction for a Barke comming to the Liffer, which his people had taken and spoiled: And to yeeld up to him the Governor all the cattle should be found in his Countrey belonging to Odonnell. Adding, that Sir John Bolles in a journey made upon Ocane, had killed fifty of his people, had burned many houses and much corne. And that the garrison of the Liffer had spoiled Tirconnel, had slaine many, & had brought away two hundred Cowes, and great booties.

Submission of Sir Oghy Ohanlon.

The tenth of April Sir Oghy Ohanlon, a northerne Lord submitted himselfe on his knees to her Majesties mercy at Tredagh, and signed certaine Articles, for the performance whereof hee tooke his oath. And because these Articles (except there fell out some speciall reason to leave out some of them, and to adde others) were the same to which all submitties at this time were tied, I will once for all adde the briefe of them.

Articles of submission.

After his acknowledgement that Queene Elizabeth, by the Grace of God, Queene of England, France, and Ireland, &c. Is the true absolute and Soveraigne Lady of this realme of Ireland, and of every part, & of all the people thereof, with humble confession of his former disloyaltie, and of his penitency, and like profession that he had felt the waight of her Majesties power. This done, further to the example of all other offenders, he testified that hee made this his humble submission and protestation of his penitency, his future loyalty and indevour to redeeme his faults by his good services. Then he acknowledged under his hand, that now before the Lord Deputy and Counsell, he taketh a corporall and religious oath for all and severall Articles following; Namely, That he will ever continue a loyall subject. That for performance thereof, and of all the following

Articles, he will put in sufficient pledges. That hee doth renounce all manner of obedience to any forraine power or Potentate, depending only on the Queene his Soveraigne. That hee renounceth all Rebels, and will not aide them, but serve against them when he is commanded. That hee will to the uttermost of his power withstand and confound any disloyal subject, or forraine enemy attempting against the sacred person, or estate of her Majesty, or the quietnes of her faithfull subjects, more especially, against the Arch-traytor Tyrone, and the King of Spaine supporting him. That hee will come to the State whensoever hee is commanded, neither will upon wrongs seeke to right himselfe, but will seeke redresse by course of Law. That he will reveale all conspiracies [II. ii. 99.] of treason which hee shall heare. That he will sue out her Majesties pardon within certaine dayes, for him and his followers, and answer for their good behaviour. That hee will booke these followers within certaine dayes. That he will suffer all subjects safely to trade in his Countrey. That hee will extort no blacke Rents, or make other exactions on his people, but by due course of a subject. For sincere performance hereof, he testified that he had taken his corporall oath, upon his knees, before the Lord Deputy and Councell, (the same oath being solemnly ministred to him, and taken by him in the said assembly) and did againe vow the same upon his salvation, religiously professing, that if he should break those Articles or any of them, he would acknowledge himselfe not onely to be worthy of all infamy and extreame punishment; but ever after to bee most unworthy to beare the name of a Christian, or to injoy the society of men, to which, as hee had unfainedly sworne, so now in witnesse thereof, he did in this written forme of submission set to his hand, with addition of the day of the moneth, and of the yeere when this act was done by him.

Oath to be taken upon the knees.

The sixteenth of Aprill, the Governour of Loughfoyle by his letters intreated, that a pardon might be passed to Hugh Boy (which businesse the bearer had undertaken to solicite) and that Neale Garve, to whom the Queene had granted Odonnels Countrey, might be sent backe from Dublin, because the Irish were confident, that upon his arrivall all the people of Tirconnell would flocke unto him. Further advertising, that the garrison of the Liffer had burnt the New-towne, and killed twelve kerne and thirty eight of other people, and had brought backe some three hundred Cowes. And that the garrison of Donnegall, had burnt in Ocanes Countrey a great village, and many women, children, and Cowes, with the houses, and had killed some forty kerne and churles.

S. Georges feast kept at Dublin.

The three & twenty of Aprill, his Lordship kept S. Georges feast, at Dublin, with solemne pompe, the Captains bringing up his meat, & some of the Colonels attending on his person at Table. To which feast the Rebels were invited, whom his Lordship lately received to mercy, under her Majesties protection, till their pardons might be signed, namely Turlogh Mac Henry, Captain of the Fewes, Ever Mac Cooly, chiefe of the Fearney, Ohanlon a Lord of Ulster, Phelim Mac Feagh, chief of the Obyrnes, & Donnell Spaniagh, chiefe of the Cavanaghs in Lemster. These were entertained with plenty of wine, and all kindnesse, his Lordship assuring them, that as he had bin a scourge to them in rebellion, so he would now be a mediator for them to her Majesty, in their state of subjects, they standing firme and constant to their obedience. And no doubt, as there is a secret mystery of State in these solemne pomps; and as his Lordship therein, for his person and carriage, was most comely, and (if I may use the word) Majesticall; so the magnificence of this feast wrought in the hearts of those Rebels, and by their relation in the hearts of others after submitting, (both having first experienced the sharpenesse of the Queenes sword,) such an awfull respect to her Majesty, and such feare tempred with love to his Lordship, as much availed to containe them in due obedience.

The rebels awed.

From the end of March to the beginning of May, upon the Lord Presidents intercession by letters to the

Lord Deputy, many pardons were granted for life, land, and goods, to Chiefetaines of Countries, and Gentlemen in Mounster; namely, to Mac Carty Reough, Chieftain of Carbery, and two hundred & ten followers, as well men, as women and children: to Oswyllivan Beare, and some five hundred twenty eight followers, as also to Oswyllivan Brantry: to John Odoyre of Tiperary, and some one hundred fifty followers: to Fitz James Gerrald, with some three hundred seventy followers: and to Teig Mac Moreretagh Obrian, in the County of Lymrick, with some two hundred twenty one followers; and some others, which for brevity I omit. And it was concluded at the Councell Table, on the last of Aprill, that the two following provisoes, should bee inserted in all pardons, (and charge was accordingly given to the Queenes learned Counsell, and to the Officers, and to his Lordships Secretaries, whose hands al pardons passed, that the said Provisoes should be continually inserted) namely: First, in regard some notorious Rebels of the Pale might passe as followers to remote Lords, that the pardon be not available to any, but to the naturall inhabitants, tenants, and knowne followers of the Lord so pardoned. Secondly, in regard many Rebels taken, and to be judged according to the Law, might by oversight bee pardoned, proviso was to be entred, that no pardon should availe any, who were already in prison, or upon bayle.

Many pardons granted.

[II. ii. 100.]

The second of May, his Lordship wrote to the Lords in England, that Mounster was not only wel reduced, but began to taste the sweetnes of peace: that the like might be said of Lemster, except the Mores and Conners, who were scattered, & had sought, but could not obtain of him the Queens mercy. That the Northern borders of Ulster were assured, namely; Ohanlons Country, the Fewes, Clancarvill, the Ferney, most of the Galloglasses, and many of the Mac Mahownes, and that a garrison was planted in the Brenny, and the Queenes Mac Gwyer setled in Fermanagh. That Sir Henry Dockwra at Loughfoyle, and Sir Arthur Chichester at Carickefergus (commonly

The sweetnes of peace in Mounster and Lemster.

called Knockefergus) had made their neighbours sure to the State, and both had done her Majesty excellent service. That onely Connaght, most easily to be reduced, was most out of order. That for this reason hee thought fit to plant Ballishannon garrison through Connaght, which might be reduced with the very passing of the Army; and therefore had perswaded the Magazin of victuals at Galloway, specially since from those parts his Lordship might easily joine with the Lord-President, in case Spaine should invade Mounster. That in the meane time his Lordship would draw one thousand foot out of Mounster, to serve in Ulster, and for a time borrow thence five hundred Foot and fifty Horse for Connaght journey, the forces remaining being sufficient to guard Mounster, and greater then he had left in Lemster, in the peace whereof he might seeme to have more proper interest. But if Spaine should invade Mounster, then all the Army was to be drawne thither, and great supplies sent out of England, since the defection of the Irish was like to be great, even of those who yet had never declared any malice against the State: yet that his Lordship desired presently no supplies, in regard of her Majesties excessive charge, in levying and transporting them, trusting that by the Rebels forces diminished, occasion would be given to cast some of the Army, with which cast Companies the defects of the standing might be supplied, wherein his Lordship promised to proceed without preferring such, as even with their blood shed in his fight deserved advancement, or satisfying some worthy Commanders, (whose entertainement he had rather lessened) or pleasuring those, who might justly challenge preferment from him. Therefore praying, that her Majesty would not command him to bestow new Companies (as of late shee had done) upon such as of late had beene absent, and had onely served at the loosing of the Kingdome, so as they were least fit to be preferred before those who had hazarded their lives in regaining it: Adding, that he writ not this, to uphold any private dependency on himselfe, esteeming it

Connaght most out of order.

No supplies desired.

a great vanity so to doe, but onely to strengthen himselfe, so long and no longer then he should be imploied in her Majesties service. That in stead of new supplies, he desired leave to entertaine some of the Irish Submitties in pay, by them to consume the Rebels, and by the Rebels to diminish their number, since two things remained to settle the Kingdome. First the ridding Ireland of the Swordmen, (to which end the Irish affected some journey into the Low Countries or the Indies, which could not make them any whit more able Souldiers then now they were, nor adde to their knowledge of warre fit for Ireland, which they now had; but three parts of foure were like never to returne, if they were ingaged in such a voyage). Secondly, the making of the English owners fit to inhabit their lands, which was most difficult, in regard of their poverty, and of the great quantities of lands they possessed, since in particular of some gentlemen of Leax and Ophalia, each possessed as much land, as being well inhabited, would maintaine more men then all the Rebels of those Counties were in number.

Two things remaine to settle Ireland.

About the tenth of May his Lordship gave warrant to passe the pardon of Phelim mac Feogh Obyrn, of the Glinnes, with his followers, and likewise of Phelim mac Feogh O Toole of the Fartrey, with fifty six followers. And upon the humble submission of Rosse mac Mahowne, [II. ii. 101.] his Lordship granted him her Majesties protection, till he might sue out his pardon.

About this time his Lordship had advertisement from Sir Henry Dockwra Governour at Loughfoyle: That he had taken in Odogherties Countrey, and secured the passages into it, as well against Odonnell, as the false Inhabitants. That he having gathered the forces to spoile Hugh mac Hugh Duffes Countrey, the project was frustrated by an Irishman stealing from the Army, and given them intelligence hereof, so as they drove the prey farre off into remote parts. That Neale Garve with Cormocke O Neale, dispatched lately from Dublin, were arrived at Loughfoyle. That he the said Governour

Sir Henry Dockwra's advertisement.

deferring the prosecution of Ocane, because he had no Haven in his Countrey for the landing of Spaniards, nor could escape from the English forces, though Spaniards should land, the same time resolved to enter Hugh mac *Hugh Duffes Countrey.* Hugh Duffes Countrey, as more fit to receive forraigne forces, and to supply them with victuals or other necessaries. And to this end that he had assembled the forces to the Liffer. That Shane mac Manus Oge Odonnell, commanding certaine Ilands in the Sea, did there offer to submit, but upon such conditions as were unfit, yet the Irish extolling his valour, and intreating for him, and Neale Garve for the time being content to spare him of the men allowed him, fifty foot and twenty five horse, that he the Governour had further promised him, upon acceptable service, to procure him as many more men in her Majesties pay, whereupon he had taken his oath of obedience, and had secretly sent word to his people to spoyle Rory Odonnels Countrey; (who then had him in no suspition). This done, that he the Governour suddenly entered Hugh Duffes Countrey aforesaid, and spoyled the same, taking a prey of more then one thousand Cowes, with great numbers of Garrons, Sheepe, and Goates. That thence he marched into Fanaght, where Owen Oge mac Swinedoe, Lord of the Doe, met him on the borders, and delivering the chiefe pledges of his Countrey for his and their loyalty, tooke his oath of obedience to her Majestie. That hearing of Odonnels drawing into those parts, he thence retired with great part *Neale Garve's loyaltie.* of the forces, leaving Neale Garve with his Irish and some English Companies for his assistance, to spoyle and absolutely waste Fannaght, to whom Mac Swine Fannaght Lord of the Countrey, presently delivered pledges of his loyalty, taking his oath of obedience to her Majestie, at which time likewise Mac Swine Bone, and O Boyle, earnestly solicited the Governour to be received to mercy. That Neale Garve by the keeping of Tirconnell granted him at Dublyn for the time, till her Majesty might please to passe the same to him by Letters Pattents, and by great gifts he had there received, was puffed up with pride, desiring present possession of the Countrey, and calling the people his subjects, and saying to the Governours face, that he would punish, exact, cut, & hange them, as he list. But that he had calmed him with severe speeches, & with charge not to meddle with any man, or any part of the Countrey upon his alleagiance, since he had no right but from her Majesties bounty, not yet fully expressed, and that not soveraigne, but limitted, so as might best stand with the peoples good, who were not his but her Majesties subjects. That he found him to be in his nature proud, valiant, miserable, tyrannous, unmeasurably covetous, without any knowledge of God, or almost any civility, good to be used while he was satisfied, (which he could hardly bee, being like a Quince, requiring great cost ere it be good to eat), or whilst he was kept under (which was the fitter course to be held with him), yet that he thought him sure to the State, in regard of the pledges he had given, but much more, because he could no way better his estate by leaving the Queenes service, nor be secure of any word from Odonnell, whose brother he had killed. That Cormacke O Neale, being of late come from Dublyn, could hitherto have done no service, but that he was of reasonable esteeme among the people of his Countrey, and was of a mild honest disposition, willing to serve without grating beggery, or unreasonable demands, yet was Irish and little lesse barberous then the better sort of wood kern. That comming out of the woods without friend or kinseman, he could then give no pledges, but his wife and children were since come to him, and within the Governours power, besides that he seemed not to be inclined to trechery, neither could mend his estate by leaving the Queenes service, to which he came in voluntarily, without calling, forcing, or composition, and therein remained with his desires limitted, and to be contented with reason. That Hugh Boy, was subtill, wise, civil, a Papist, and aliened (but not deeply malicious) against Odonnels

Neale Garve's nature.

Cormacke O Neale.

[II ii. 102.]

Hugh Boy. person, yet firme in his allegiance, having come in with his Countrey, and delivered his chiefe pledges, offering any other to be delivered upon command; and having shewed the passages into his Countrey, and himselfe sollicited and furthered the fortifying thereof, daily giving sure and important intelligences, to the great furtherance of the service; besides that, all his wealth lay within the power of the Queenes forces. Lastly, that betweene these submitties were factions and heart-burnings, which discreetly measured, could not but advantage the service.

The fifteenth of May the Lord Deputy received (by the hands of Sir George Cary, Treasurer at warres) a *Proclamation of new monies.* Proclamation (signed by the Queene) to be published, for making the new standard of mixed monies to be onely currant in this Kingdome, all other coyns being to be brought in to the Treasurer. And likewise a letter from the Queene, requiring the Lord Deputy and Counsell to further the due execution of the contents of this Proclamation, and by some plausible graces, done in generall to the subject, (in the establishing an exchange of this coyne into sterling money of England, & taking away the impositions on sea coles transported into Ireland, and in particular to the Captaines of the Army, in allowing their dead paies in mony, after the rate of eight pence per diem, and some like favours), inviting all to swallow this bitter pill, which impoverished not only the Rebels, but her Majesties best servants in this Kingdome, onely inriching her Paymasters, sitting quietly at home, while others adventured daily their bloods in the service.

The twentieth of May the Lord Deputy and Counsell advertised the Lords in England, that they had given *300. Proclamations to be published.* order to print 300. of the Proclamations for the new coyne, to be published through all parts of Ireland at one time. That they had in Counsell agreed upon a generall hoasting for this yeere, to beginne the last of June following. And in the meane time, while that was preparing, that the Lord Deputy would draw the forces to Dundalke upon the Northerne borders, there to watch opportunities of service, and specially by his presence to animate the new submitties, to attempt some thing against the Arch-traytor Tyrone, and to put them in blood against him and his confederates. And that his Lordship towards the time of the said hoasting, purposed to returne to Dublyn, and to the end he might find there all things in readines for his intended prosecution of Tyrone in his owne Countrey, they besought their Lordships that victuals and munition might with all possible speed be sent thither out of England. The foresaid generall hoasting is a rising out of certaine foot and horse, found by the subject of the five English shires and the Irish Submitties, to assist the Queenes forces, and these, together with some of the English Companies, his Lordship used to lay in the Pale, for the defence thereof, at such time as the forces were to be drawne into Ulster.

The rising out of the Five English Shires.

The rising out of the five English Shires and the Irish Submitties. Vizt. Of the County of Dublyn. Besides sixteene Kearne.

	Horse.	Archers Horse.
In the Barrony of Balrothery.	nil.	26
In that of Cowlocke,	nil.	30
In that of Newcastle,	nil.	18
In that of Castleknocke.	nil.	11
In that of Rathdowne.	12	10

2. Of the County of Meath. Besides one hundred Kerne of the Pooles.

	Horse.	Archers Horse.
In the Barony of Dulicke.	nil.	32
In the Barony of Skrine,	24	30
In that of Ratothe.	nil.	13
In that of Dunboyne.	nil.	3
In that of Decy.	nil.	17
In that of Moyfewragh.	nil.	4
In that of Lane.	nil.	8

[II. ii. 103.]

The rising out of the Five English Shires.

	Horse.	Archers Horse.
In that of Navan.	nil.	48
In that of Kenlles, alias Kells.	16	6
In that of Slane.	6	11
In that of Fowere.	28	nil.
In that of Margallen.	7	1
Thirdly, Of the County of Westmeath.	60	2
Fourthly, Of the County of Kildare.		
In the Barrony of Sualt.	8	14
In that of the upper Naasse.	nil.	13
In that of the nether Naasse.	nil.	5
In that of Kelkullen.	8	2
In that of Narragh.	nil.	2
In that of Reban & Athy.	nil.	3
In that of Kilkey.	1	2
In that of Ophaly.	1	2
In that of Connall.	nil.	3
In that of Clane.	nil.	2
In that of Okethy.	nil.	5
In that of Carbery.	nil.	4
Fifthly, Of the County of Louth.		
In the Barony of Ferrard.	4	26
In that of Atherdy.	16	13
In the Townes of Lowth and of Dundalke.	16	6
Summa 207—374.	Totall both 581.	

The Irish Lords and their Captaines.

The rising out of the Irish Lords, and their Captaines.

The Obyrnes, over whom after the death of Sir Henry Harrington, his son Sir William Harrington, is Captaine by the late Queenes Letters Pattents, granted to his father and him, Horsemen 12. Kerne 24.

The Cavanaghs having then no Captaine over them. Horse 12. Kerne 30.

Other particular septs, besides those which were in rebellion. Horse 104. Kerne 307.

Totall, Horse 128. Kerne 361.

The project of disposing the Queenes forces for the following Summers service.

The disposing of the Queenes forces.

Out of Mounster we thought fit to be spared, and to be drawne into Connaght 1000 foot and 50 horse, (since there should still remaine in Mounster 1600 foot and 200 horse, for any occasion of service.) Foot 1000. Horse 50.

In Connaght were already (besides Tybot ne longes Company). Foot 1150 Horse 74.

These to be placed as followeth.

To keepe at Galloway and Athlone in Connaght, foot 350.

To leave at the Abbey of Boyle in Connaght under the command of the late Lord of Dunkellen, now Earle of Clanrickard. Foot 1000 Horse 62.

These to further the plantation of Balishannon.

To leave at the Annaly in Lemster side of the Shannon, under the command of Sir John Barkeley. Foot 800. Horse 12.

These fit to joine with the undermentioned forces of Westmeath, Kels, and the rest upon the Northerne borders, to stop the Ulster Rebels from comming into Lemster; or if they should passe them, then to joine with the forces of Ophaly, and the rest southward. Tybot ne long, (the payment of whose Company had long beene stopped) was to be kept in good tearmes. Oconnor Sligo to be threatned, that if he did not submit and declare himselfe against Odonnell before the planting of Ballishannon, he should have no hope of mercy. The forces at the Abby of Boyle were to infest Oconnor Sligo, and to keepe Ororke from joining with Odonnell. Those at the Annaly, to infest Ororke, besides the above mentioned,

The disposing of the Queenes forces. lying betweene any forces that might come out of the North into Lemster, and to follow them if they should escape, it being likely that about harvest time Tyrrell and the Oconnors will gather strength (if they possibly can) to returne and gather the Corne they sowed last yeere in Leax and Ophaly. And thus are disposed the above said Foot 2150. Horse 124.

[II ii. 104.] The Forces towards the South of Lemster to lie thus:

In Ophaly. The Earle of Kildare 150. Sir George Bourcher 100. Sir Edward Harbert 100. Capt. Carroll 100. Sir Henry Warren 100 Foot. In all 550. Earle of Kildare 25. Sir Edward Harbert 12. Horse. In all 37. In Leax. Sir Henry Power 150. Sir Francis Rushe 150. Sir Thomas Loftus 100 Foot. In all 400. Master Marshall 20. Captaine Pigot 12 Horse. In all 32. At Kilkenny. Earle of Ormond 150 Foot. Earle of Ormond 50 Horse.

The Forces towards the North of Lemster to lie thus:

In Westmeath. Lord of Delvin 150. Sir Francis Shane 100 Foot. In Kelles. Captaine Roper 150 Foot. Earle of Kildare 25. Sir Henry Harrington 25 Horse. At Liscannon in the Brenny. Lord of Dunsany 150. Captaine Esmond 150. Sir William Warren 100. Sir Henry Harrington 100. Foot 500. Lord of Dunsany 50 Horse. At Dundalke. Captaine Freckleton 100. Foot. In the Moyry. Captaine Hansard 100 Foote.

These of the North and the Garrisons at the Abby of Boyle, lie fit for correspondencie.

These of the South, together with the submitted Irish in Opprossery, and the Odemsies, Omolyes, and Mac Coghlins, lie fit for correspondency among themselves, as also with the garrison at the Annaly. Also all these of the South and North, lie aptly placed to answere one another upon occasion of service, and are in number, those of the South, Foot 1100. Horse 119. Those of the North, Foot 1100. Horse 100.

The disposing of the Queenes forces.

Both of the South and North. Foot 2200. Horse 219.

Totall, adding the forces abovesaid drawne out of Mounster, and those being in Connaght, (namely foot 2150. Horse 124.) Makes Foot 4350. Horse 343.

The Lord Deputies forces follow, wherewith he purposed to build a Fort at the Moyry, and put men into it to keepe that Pace: To plant a Garrison in Lecale of 500. foot and fifty horse. To give Sir Arthur Chichester the Governour of Knockefergus, two Companies for his better strength. To plant a garrison at Armagh, and another at the old fort of Blackewater, and a little loope sconce betweene them both. To see great store of hay made in time of the yeere at Armagh, and at Mount Norreis, for feeding of horses there in the winter following. To lie all the summer close upon Tyrone, destroying the new Corne, and spoyling the Countrey, and so to facilitate the planting of Balishannon, and perhaps to passe into Tyrones Countrey, the Garrisons of Knockefergus, Lecale, and Loughfoyle entering at the same time on al hands, and there ordered to meet him. And to draw towards winter to Athlone in Connaght.

The Lord Deputies said forces.

The Lord Deputy 200. The Marshall 150. Sir Oliver Lambert 150. Sir Christopher S[t] Laurence 150. Sir Fr. Stafford 200. Sir Oliver S[t] Johns 200. Sir Henry Folyot 150. Capt. Williams 150. Sir James Fitzpierce 150. Sir William Fortescue 100. Sir Garret Moore 100. Captaine Oreyly 100. Captaine Edward Blaney 150. Captaine Josias Bodley 150. Sir Henry Davers 150. Captaine Ghest 150. Captaine Roe 100. Capt. Masterson 100. Capt. Rotheram 150. Foot 2750. Lord Deputy 100. Sir Henry Davers 100. Sir Oliver Lambert 25. Sir Garret More 25. Sir Christ. S. Laurence 25. Captaine Darcy 25. Horse 300.

The disposing of the Queenes forces.

The Companies intended to be left in the garrison to be planted this summer at Lecaile.

Sir Richard Moryson the Governour 150. Captaine Cawfield 150. Captaine Trever 100. Captaine Constable 100. Foot 500. Sir Samuel Bagnol 50 horse.

The Garrison then being at Knockefergus.

Sir Arthur Chicester the Governour 200. Sir Foulke Conway 150. Captaine Egerton 100. Captaine Norton 100. Captaine Billings 100. Captaine Phillips 100. Foot 750.

Sir Arthur Chichester 25. Captaine John Jephson 100. Horse 125.

These two garrisons of Lecayle and Knockefergus, [II. ii. 105.] might meet upon all occasions, and so by the intended plantation of Lecayle, the garrison of Knockfergus was thought as much strengthened, as if those companies lay there.

Lying presently in garrison at the Newry, upon Ulster borders, Sir Samuell Bagnoll 150 foot. Sir Francis Stafford 50 horse.

Lying at the fort of Mount Norreys, Captaine Aderton 150 foot.

These two garrisons, and the two intended at Blackewater and Armagh, to be under one Governour, and to have correspondency as one garrison.

The garrisons at Loughfoyle to be drawne forth into the field.

At the Derry, in Lyst.

Sir Henry Dockwra the Governour 200. Captaine Digges 100. Captaine Willis 150. Captaine Lea 100. Captaine Oram 100. Captaine Brooks 100. Capt. Orrel 100. Foot 850. whereof to be drawne into the field 650.

At the Lyffer.

Captaine Coach 100. Captaine Morgan 150. Captaine Winsore 100. Captaine Dutton 100. Captaine Goare 150. Captaine Pinner 100. Capt. Rand 100. Foot 800. For the field 550.

The disposing of the Queenes forces.

At Dunalong.

Sir John Bolles 150. Captaine Floyd 150. Capt. Badby 150. Capt. Sidley 100. Capt. Basset 100. Foot 650. For the field 400.

At Kilmore, Captaine Alford 100. For the field 35. At Newtowne. Capt. Atkinson 100. For the field 40. At Romolyon, Capt. Bingley 150. At Culmerat, Captaine Vaughan 100. At the Cargan, Capt. Stafford 100. At Anny, Captaine Sidney 100. Foot 650. For the field 75.

Totall in List 3000. For the field 1675.

Thus at Loughfoyle with these English foote, and one hundred English horse, together with five hundred Irish foote, and one hundred Irish horse, and the helpe of the Submitties, especially of Neale Garve, and of Cormocke Oneale. It was thought that Sir Henry Dockewra might plant an intended garrison at Ballishannon, as by his owne offer he had projected in England, and besides keeping his owne, might also draw out sufficient forces to meete the Lord Deputy in the heart of Tyrone, if the project of planting Ballishannon could take such effect as was hoped. To the furtherance whereof, I did at this time, upon his Lordships command, devise a Cipher, to passe betweene his Lordship and the Governours of Loughfoyle, Knockefergus, and Lecaile, to the end, that if the rebels should light upon any their letters, contriving this meeting or other service, yet they might not be able to discover any their secret purpose, especially since they were so ignorant, as they could not attaine the deciphering of those Characters, or any like, though farre more easie: and this Cipher was presently sent to the above named Governours.

A Cipher devised.

His Lordship further resolved in Councel to write to the Lords in England, to have six thousand of the trained bands in readines, to be sent over presently upon the suspected invasion of forraigne powers, and to have a Magazin of victuals and munition at Limricke, aswell to answere the service in Mounster, if they should make

6000. *trained bands to be in readines.*

discent in those parts (being most likely) as to be drawne thence to Galloway, in case no such invasion were made, there to answere the prosecution of the Connaght rebels, intended the Winter following.

The Lord Deputy's journey to the North.

All things thus projected for the following prosecution of this warre, his Lordship on the two and twentieth of May, beganne his intended journey above mentioned, from Dublin, and the twenty three came to Tredagh, and the twenty five to Dundalke, where his Lordship lay, till the dispersed Companies could be drawne thither, and victuals brought. Here he composed all controversies betweene the late Submitties, and setled a correspondency betweene them, aswell to make them concurre in the defence one of another, as also in the defence of the Pale. Here his Lordship received the twenty eight of May, letters from the Lords in England, requiring that no Captain should supply his Company with Passe-volants at pleasure; but onely with such men as should bee sent out of England for supplies. That the Captaines refusing to shew their companies when they were required by the Commissaries of the Musters, should be checked two moneths pay. That such Pensioners should be checked as [II. ii. 106.] without speciall licence, should be absent from any service. And that speciall care should be had to punish and prevent such souldiers, as dismissed by their Captaines Passes, or running away from their colours, did duly returne into England.

Pardons to Mounster rebels.

The nine and twentieth of May, upon the intercession of the Lord President by his Letters, (according to the course held by directions out of England), the Lord Deputy granted his warrant for drawing of her Majesties pardon to Cnocher Omulrian, a Munster rebell, chiefe of his Sept (or name), and eighty three followers, aswell men as weomen and children of that sept. The second of June it was resolved in Councell, that letters should be written to the Lord President of Mounster, requiring him to draw the forces under him towards Lymricke, and in those parts to imploy them most part of the following summer, as well ready to attend the discent of any forraigne enemy, as fitly laid to give countenance to the prosecution of the rebels in Connaght, whether the said Lord President was to be further directed, to send a thousand foot and fifty horse, (according to the above mentioned project), to the end that the rebels being prosecuted in that Province, might have no leasure to joine with those of the North, for disturbing the planting of a garrison at Ballishannon, which Sir Henry Dockwra was to plant from the way of Loughfoyle. The fifth of June the Lord President advertised that warning had beene given to those of Mounster, for the sending of their men to the generall hoasting above mentioned, which the Lord Deputy had appointed to meet (according to the old custome) at the hill of Tarrogh, but that he feared the scarcity of victuals and want of furniture, would either hinder their full appearance, or make them of small use to the service. The sixth day upon the Lord Presidents letters, warrant was given for a charter of pardon without fine, to be granted to one hundred fifty one Inhabitants about Moghely in the County of Corke, as well men as weomen and children, for life, lands, and goods. And the like was granted to Oswillivan More of that Province with 481 followers.

The Lord Presidents advertisement.

The eighth of June being Monday, the Lord Deputy drew the forces out of Dundalke, and marched two miles to the hill of Fagher, neere the pace of the Moyry, where he encamped. And while he lay there, his Lordship caused a fort to be built in the said Pace, at the three mile water, not rising from thence till he had made this Fort defensible, so as leaving some warders in it, the workemen might in his absence finish the building. The thirteenth of June, in the Campe at the Fagher, his Lordship published the Proclamation of the new Coyne, all other monies having beene decried three daies before. And by his Lordships direction like Proclamations printed at Dublyn, & thence formerly sent to Loughfoyle & Knockfergus, & into the Provinces of Connaght & Mounster, were at the same time published together in all

The Lord Deputy at Fagher.

places. The foureteenth, in the same Campe, his Lordship and the Counsellors there, wrote the following letter to the Lords in England.

The Lord Deputy's letter to the Lords in England.

IT may please your most Honourable Lordships, perceiving by your Lordships Letters of the eighteenth of May, that the victuals expected to answere our purpose of planting Ballishannon by Connaght, could not arrive in such quantity nor time, as might inable us to proceed in that journey; and receiving some arguments of your Lordships inclination to Sir H. Dockwra his offer to plant that garrison from Loughfoyle, we grew into a new consultation, in what sort to make the warre this Summer. First, it was propounded with the Army to march by Lecaile and those parts into Colrane, the end whereof should have beene to have brought in subjection all the woodmen, and utterly taken from Tyrone all that part of Ulster between Colrane and Loughsidney to the Blackewater, from whence heretofore the Traitor hath gathered his greatest strength. The passages being not very dangerous, and we having the commodity of the Sea to supply us, we should have made the warre that way to great purpose, and with good conveniency, and perhaps might have fallen over the Banne into Tyrone, all other wayes being of extreame danger, to enter into that Countrey, except that one by Loughfoyle. The chiefe difficulty that did arise against this project, was the danger wherein we should leave all things behind us, if
[II. ii. 107.] the Spaniard should land, when we had carried the chiefe force of the Kingdome into the uttermost corner thereof: and the next was, that we being not able to leave any great guard for the Pale, should have left it naked to any attempt of Tyrone, and the new reclaimed rebels to the mercy of him, as the Pale to the mercy of both: But in the end we grew to this resolution. First, in the Interym, betweene this and the appointment of the generall hoasting, (by the which we should be supplied with carriages, and about which time we expect victuals

and munition out of England, of the first wherof we are more sparingly provided then may warrant the ingaging our selves into any great businesse, and of the second so utterly unfurnished, as wee scarce have powder to maintaine a good daies fight, nor tooles, nor other provisions to fortifie, which must be our chiefe worke, as we carry the rebels before us to dwell by them), we determine to assure the passage of the Moyry, then to plant a garrison at Lecaile, and to convay some more men to Sir Arthur Chichester Governour of Carickefergus, (who with that Garrison and those supplies, together with the advantage that our stirring in all other places will give him, may goe neere to work little lesse effect, then we with the whole Army should have done): and lastly, we purpose to lie with the forces as neere Tyrone as we can. After when victuals and munition should be arrived, (which we hope to receive by the last of June, being the time appointed for the generall hosting), we purpose (God willing) as neere as wee can to imploy her Majesties forces according to the inclosed project: (This project I have formerly set downe). With the particularities of Sir H. Dockewra his purpose to plant Ballishannon, (sent by Captaine Vaughan to your Lordships) we are not acquainted, onely Master Treasurer hath told us of such a proposition in generall. But wee doubt not, that withall he hath propounded to your Lordships for such meanes to accomplish his worke, as must be supplied from thence. For from us he can receive little other assistance, then our imploying the whole forces according to the inclosed project, which in every part is done as much as may be for his advantage, neither (which is worse) can we easily have any intelligence from him, or often heare one from another. But if we perceive that he shall find any impossibility to plant Ballishannon, wee thinke to advise him, with the whole grosse of his strength to fall into Tyrone, about such time as we shall be at Blackewater, whereby it may fall out, that we shall (with the helpe of God) meet at Dungannon, and utterly waste all the

Sir H. Dockwra to plant Ballishannon.

country of Tyrone, unto the which course if we be driven, we must resolve to make the warre this following winter in Connaght, (first leaving the Northern border in good strength), which we hope will reduce that Province, & ruine O Donnel; for if we keepe him out of Connaght, he cannot long subsist, and so we hope, for the continuall assurance of that Province, to plant the next yeere at Ballishannon with facilitie. But if the planting of so many Garisons doe seeme, by continuing the greatnesse of the Armie, to draw on too long her Majesties charge, wee doe first thinke, that to recover this Kingdome, and to preserve it from being hereafter chargeable, it will bee necessary, that Ballishannon, Loughfoyle, some Garrisons on the Ban, Lecayle, Mount Norreys, Armagh, Blackwater; and some other places, be continually kept, all which places may be ever victualed by Sea, or they being neare together, without any dangerous passage betweene them by land, may be victualed by Sea and land, without any further force then their owne. And if there be in every Fort some little Keepe (or Tower) of stone built, then as the warres decrease, or occasion shall serve, the places may bee guarded with a few men, and so continue bridles in peace, and fit places to put in more men to great purpose, when the rebellion shall at any time breake out. Neither neede these little Castles bee workes of any great charge, for they may be easily made such, as this people will hardly force them. To proceede in our project of this Summer service. The victuals alreadie contracted for, must arrive in due time, and your Lordships supply us with good quantities hereafter. For our onely way to ruine the rebels, must be to make all possible wast of the meanes for life, which done, if we be not supplied out of England, we shall aswell starve our selves as them; but especially where wee must make the warre, which is farre from the reliefe of any friend, and where nothing is to be gotten from the enemy, except it be by great chance, since what is in their Countries, they wil lightly either hide, or spoile, or convey to inaccessable

Towers of stone.

The onely way to ruine the rebels.

[II. ii. 108.]

Fastnesses. And because the greatest service here is to be done by long and sudden journies, which cannot be done without victuall, and no victuall but cheese well carried by the souldier, without garons (or carriage Jades) we must humbly desire your Lordships to send us some great quantities of cheese. In the provision whereof whatsoever inconveniences your Lordships shal find, we assure you they wil be ten times countervailed in the service. Lastly, because the Army is already weak of English, and this journy (without the extraordinary favor of God) must needs diminish them much, aswel by the sword as sicknes, we most humbly and earnestly desire your L^{ps}. assoone as conveniently may bee, to send us 1000 shot to Carlingford for supplies, that at our returne, we may both strengthen those English Companies, which we meane to leave behind us in the North, and such as wee carry with us for the Winter service. The time wil be exceeding fit for their arrivall; for besides the succour we may receive from them, if we grow very weake at our returne, they will come over well cloathed against the Winter, and may have time to rest, and to be seasoned, till Christmas, (till when in these warres it is the most unactive part of the yeere), and then may bee imployed till the end of May (which is the onely season to plague these rebels), and when the Summer is past (wherein those rogues revive and live like flies) then our Garrisons being well planted, and the Army strengthened with English, wee may begin to cast the Irish Companies, and to cleare the English Companies of them. For they must continue good subjects, or starve if they goe out, and have the Queenes sword hang over them, wheresoever they goe. In the meane time we thinke them necessarily entertained, for wee take so many men from the Rebels, and by them give unto our selves facilitie to plant the foundation of their owne ruine, and both with us and against us to wast them by themselves. For if wee should not entertaine them, they would lie upon some Countrie of the subject, and except it were defended by

1000. shot to strengthen the Army.

as many as themselves, they would waste and live upon it, so that in effect the very numbers entertained would grow all to one reckoning. And for a more particular instance of the benefit that ensueth the entertaining these Irish, we thinke we can give your Lordships an account of above one hundred that have this yeere been killed with the bullet, fighting on our side, who were formerly rebels (for of such wee speake) and questionlesse would have been so againe, if they had lived, and should have been put out of the Queenes pay. Wee humbly desire your Lordships to make a favourable construction both of our counsels, and the successes, since those grounds whereupon we doe now justly build our resolution, may by their alteration give us just cause to alter our course, and the want of such meanes, either in matter or time as we expect, may utterly hinder it. And that more especially, in case any forraine succours doe arrive. For then the whole frame of this our project is broken, and we must be presently relieved out of England, or else we with this Kingdome shall suffer much hazard. And because your Lordships in your last letters, gave us some light, that it might be, and leave to informe you, what likelihood wee could here receive, that it would be; wee have first the intelligence which we send your Lordships, with many other reports. Next we have a constant and of late an extraordinary conceived confidence in this people. And lastly we judge what a wise and a powerfull enemie will doe, by that which is best and easie for him to doe. So as wee have many reasons to thinke, that Spaine will send them helpes this yeere, and few to thinke otherwise, save that he hath so often deceived their expectations. For if the malice of Spaine continue to England, they have an easie and dangerous step thereto by Ireland; and if they doe not imbrace the occasion of this yeere, there is no doubt but the next will for ever loose it unto them. Now because it must please your Lordships to proportion our succours to the force we are likely to be offended with, and that from us you

100. former rebels killed fighting on the Queenes side.

Helpe expected from Spaine.

will expect our owne estates; it may please your Lordships to consider, that the power of this Kingdome consisteth of her Majesties English Army; of such Irish as are here in Companies by themselves, or in English Companies to serve as mercenaries, of the Nobilitie, Townes, and inbred people of this Nation, which live as subjects; and lastly of such meere Irish Lords and their people, as were lately reclaimed, or still remaine in [II. ii. 109.] rebellion. The English are few and farre dispersed, the Irish that serve with us exceeding mercenary, and therefore likely to follow their golden hopes of Spaine; the *Golden hopes of Spaine.* Nobilitie, Townes, and People, are of so obstinate a contrariety in Religion, that without question they are growne malicious to the Governement, and affect under the protection of the power of Spaine, to declare themselves: the Irish Lords with us, have the same motives as they against us, in their last necessitie to joyne with Spaine. And all these, especially the Townes, are more stirred on by this new coine (which though, if the aide of Spaine doe not arrive, may securely be established, yet if it doe, it will breede many dangerous inconveniences.) It may therefore please her Majestie, to have in a readinesse sixe thousand of the trained Bands of such Countries, serving best for transporting into Ireland, to be sent over into Mounster upon the first notice of any forraine power to be arrived there, and some part of her Navy in a readinesse, with a greater portion of munition *The Navie to be in a readinesse.* and artillerie for us, then otherwise this warre would require. We doe hope to give her Majestie a very good account of her Kingdome and of our selves, untill wee shall have cause to sue for more reliefe. And if it must needes fall out, that Spaine will have warre with England, we shall be glad that the warre of England may be made in Ireland, and that wee her poore servants shall have the happinesse to strike the first blowes for both her Royall Kingdoms, the which the eternall God preserve long unto her, and her unto them and us, &c.

The same fourteenth day, from the said Campe at the

Letter to Sir Henry Dockwra.

Fagher, his Lordship wrote to Sir Henrie Dockwra, Governour of Loughfoyle, first touching his Lordships purposes; That the generall hoasting being the last of June, his Lordship presumed within sixteene dayes after, to be provided of all meanes to put al the forces in action, according to their distribution (the project whereof he sent to him inclosed), and to bee himselfe as high as Armagh, with such a power, as Tyrone should have good reason to thinke, that he would doe somewhat more, and in the meane time he would (God willing) keepe the field as neere Tyrone, as his meanes would give him leave. So as his Lordship having planted at Armagh and Blackwater, hoped either by lying there to facilitate his planting of Ballishannon from Loughfoyle, or to breake into Tyrone, and meete him there. And if Tyrones Army should breake, as his Lordship expected, he thought to find no great difficulty herein, but otherwise held the passage to Dungannon not to be ventured that way. But touching the planting at Ballishannon, that Sir Henrie Dockwra should not build upon any supplies from his Lordship, of victuals, munition, or tooles: for artillery that he might use that he had at Loughfoyle, and either bring it back by water, or be after supplied thereof from Dublin. For munition, tooles, and like necessaries, that his Lordship could spare none, & if he could, yet had no speedy meanes to send them. For intelligence, that he had sent him a Cipher, which he might use safely in writing to his Lordship, not caring how the messengers sped, so the letters were not understood. That he had sent the like Cipher to Sir Arthur Chichester at Knockfergus, with whom he should have often intelligence, and might that way write most safely to his Lordship. That when he knew his owne meanes, and by his Lordships project, should find him in readinesse to answere his attempts, he should chuse his owne time for planting Balishannon, and as neere as he could, send his Lordship certaine notice of the time, and use all possible expedition. But if he could not plant there for any want or difficulty, that then hee should agree with Sir Arthur Chichester, that they might both at one time breake into Tyrone, where his Lordship, upon notice given him, would meete them, in which journey, besides all other effects of warre, they should burne all the dwellings, and destroy the corne on the ground, which might bee done by incamping upon it, and cutting it downe with swords, and other waies, holding it best they should spoile all the corne, except that which he could gather, wherein he should not regard the disswasion of the Irish Submitties in his Campe.

The same fourteenth day wee dislodged from the Fagher, and leaving the Moyry Fort defensible, with Warders to guard it, and the workemen, being to build a Tower or Keepe of stone, we marched eight miles, and incamped at Carickbane, a little beyond the Newrie. The fifteenth his Lordship rose, and marching some fifteene miles, incamped in Evagh the Countrie of Mac Gennis. The late Rebels neere Dundalke being all submitted, his Lordship had drawne Sir Richard Moryson with his Regiment from that Governement, purposing to place him in Lecayle, neerer to the enemie. And intending to march thither with the Army the next day, lest the rebels should have leasure to burne the Countrie, and carry away the prey, his Lordship sent Sir Richard Moryson this evening with sixe Companies of Foote, and one of Horse, to march all night into Lecayle, who comming suddenly on the rebels, tooke all the prey, and in taking of Downe Patrick, the Bishops seate, one of the Bradyes was taken, and his head cut off, the rest yeelding to mercy there, and in all adjoyning places. Here his Lordship was advertised from the Secretarie of Ireland, that the newes of the Spanish invasion this Summer was seconded from divers, comming from Cales. The sixteenth day his Lordship marched with the Army (through high Mountaines and Woods, and some dangerous paces) seven miles to the Blackstaffe river, neare a strong Castle, called Dundrom, lying on the North side of the Paces, where

The Moyry Fort.

[II. ii. 110.]

Downe Patrick taken.

the plaine Countrie opens into Lecayle, being an Iland compassed on the West side with this River, and on the three other sides with the sea, and two small armes thereof. This night his Lordship with some horse passed the Blackstaffe bridge, and rode three miles into Lecayle, to view the Countrie. In the way Phelim Mac Ever *Submitties.* submitted himself, and yeelded to the Queene his Castle of Dundrom. Also Mac Carty submitted himselfe, and drew his creaghts (or cattle, servants and goods) into Lecayle. His Lordship returned to the Camp, and the next day rode to Downe Patrick, and thence by Saint Patricks Well to Arglasse, being sixe miles, in which Towne two Castles yeelded to the Queene, and the Warders upon their lives saved, gave up their Armes. A third Castle there had been held for the Queene all the time of the rebellion, by one Jordane, never comming out of the same for three yeeres past, till now by his Lordships comming he was freed, and to him was given a reward from the Queene by Concordatum, besides his Lordships bounty of his private purse. After dinner his Lordship rode two miles to Russels Towne, and foure miles to the Campe at Blackstaffe. The eighteenth day Mac Rory, Captaine of Kilwarden adjoyning, was received *Sir Arthur Chichester.* to the Queenes mercy upon his submission. And Sir Arthur Chichester, Governor of Knockfergus, all this day expected, came in the evening, to whom his Lordship that night imparted his designes in the present service, and to the same effect sent a packet by him to Sir Henrie Dockwra, Governour of Loughfoyle; and to them both, as also to Sir Richard Moryson being to bee left Governour of Lecayle, his Lordship gave Proclamations to be published for establishing the above mentioned new coine. All this time Arthur Mac Gennis the chiefe of his name, & Edmond Boy Mac Gennis his Uncle, made meanes to be received to her Majesties mercy, but could not obtaine the favour, without first doing some service. This day his Lordship and the Counsell (following the Army) gave thirty pound by concordatum to Phelimy

Ever Mac Gennis for some special services; and Balinthor a strong Castle was taken by our men, with divers cowes and other goods, sixe of the Ward being killed, and the rest swimming away.

His Lordship having placed Sir Richard Moryson (with five hundred foote, and fifty horse under his command) to governe Lecayle (which had their residency at Downe), did march backe on the nineteenth day eleven mile, to five mile Church, neere the Newry, passing one pace exceeding strong by nature, and plashed with trees, which lay at the end of the Plaines of Lecaile, and entrance into the woody Mountaines. And before the entry of this pace, Sir Arthur Chichester having received two hundred Foote to strengthen his Garrison, returned backe to Knockfergus. The twentieth day his Lordship marched with his forces three miles to Carickbane, lying Northward of the Newrie.

Five mile church.

This day Sir Henrie Davers lying at Mount Norryes, advertised his Lordship, that Tyrone lying in a fastnes, and his men never venturing upon the Plaine, the souldiers left under his command there, could not in all this time get any occasion to fight with him, whereof they shewed great desire, onely the horse often shewing themselves upon the hilles, had kept him beyond Armagh, where he with his Creaghts lay, feeding some thousands [II. ii. 111.]
of Cowes. Whereupon because his Lordship desired to preserve the grasse neere Armagh for his horse troopes, as also to make store of hay there for the Winter following, He sent Sir William Godolphin with his Lord[ps]. troope of horse under his command, to second the forces at Mount Norreys, in attempting some service upon Tyrone, meaning to draw presently his whole forces thither. But in the meane time Sir Francis Staffords Lieutenant of his horse, sent by Sir Henrie Davers to spy the rebels proceedings, had passed to the view of Armagh, and found that Tyrone had sent backe all his cowes, upon the hearing of his Lordships returne out of Lecayle. For which cause, and upon notice that Tyrone had taken a dayes

Tyrone lies in a fastnes.

victuals for his men, as if he meant to attempt something, his Lordship recalled Sir William Godolphin with his troope. The one and twentieth day his Lordship lay still, in regard that, for difficultie of getting Garrons (that is, carriage Jades), or by some negligence, victuals were not (according to his former directions) put into Mount Norreys, to which place hee purposed to draw with his forces. This day three daies bread came to his Lordships forces, which in stead of other victuals lived upon beeves. And his Lordship writ to Sir Henrie Davers, that according to his daily use of late daies, hee should the next morning earely draw the forces of Mount Norreys towards Armagh, and should on the sudden possesse the Abbey there, and the Towne, whether his Lordship would also draw the Army presently for his second.

Scarcity of victuals.

The two and twentieth day, his Lordship having, by extraordinary pay above the Queenes price, gotten garrons, and carrying victuals with him for Mount Norryes, and for the Garrison he intended to plant at Armagh, marched sixe miles neere to Mount Norryes, where Sir Henrie Davers with that Garrison met him, having not been able, for some difficulties, to execute his Lordships former directions. From thence his Lordship (taking with him the said Garrison) marched forward seven miles, and that night incamped a little beyond Armagh, where some few rebels shewed themselves braggingly, but attempted nothing. His Lordship before his returne from Lecayle, was purposed to leave such forces at Mount Norryes, as might plant the Garrison at Armagh when they found opportunity: but lest they should have been hindred by a greater force, his Lordship rather then to returne towards the Pale (for the attending there of the generall Hoasting, where his Army should have spent the same victuals it now did) was resolved himselfe in person to plant it, imagining that Tyrone, not looking for him till the generall hoasting, would not have his whole forces with him, nor by that reason, and an opinion and feare that his Lordship intended to march further into Tyrone,

Bragging rebels.

would have any minde to follow his Lordship, or hinder his retreate when hee should have weakened his forces by that Plantation. Therefore the three and twentieth day his Lordship making a shew to draw from his campe beyond Armagh towards Blackewater, caused his forces to make a stand for his retreat, and so himselfe with his followers and servants rode more then a mile forward, to view the way to Blackewater Fort, and the place of the famous Blackewater defeat, under the Marshall Bagnols conduct, and having passed a pace without one shot made at his troope, he returned to his forces, and marching backe, he left a garrison of seven hundred fifty foote, and one hundred horse, at the Abbey of Armagh, under the command of Sir Henry Davers, and that night marched with the rest neere to Mount Norreys, where he encamped, having in this march from Armagh, viewed the Foard, where Generall Norries formerly was hurt, making a stand with his horse, to secure his foot distressed by Tyrones charge.

The Lord Deputy views the Blackewater.

The foure and twenty, his Lordship leaving at Mount Norries the foot and horse of that garrison, marched himselfe with 1250 foot, and 150 horse, sixe miles to Donanury, being two miles short of the Newry. This was a hill naturally and artificially of old fortified, where in regard of the weakenes of his forces he encamped, purposing there to attend and solicite the hastning, to send to him from the Pale, all the meanes hee expected to furnish him for his intended journy, to build the demolished Fort of Blackwater.

Donanury.

Here his Lordships Army was mustered, and was by Pole. [II. ii. 112.]

Captaines and Officers 87. Targets 112. Pykes 291. Muskets 125. Callivers 635. In all 1250.

Whereof besides Captaines and Officers, English 593. Irish the rest. Wanting Swords 191.

The six and twenty day, his Lordship sent victuals to the garrisons at Mount Norreis and at Armagh. The twenty nine day his Lordship received advertisement, that Sir H. Davers drawing out the garrison of Armagh into the fastnes, where Brian mac Art lay with his Cattle, had killed divers of his men, taken many horses from him, and spoiled much of his baggage, besides three hundred Cowes which he had taken from Mac Gennis. And the same day his Lordship received the examinations of certain Waterford Marriners, who testified, that being at the Groyne, they were pressed there to serve the King of Spaine, in a flye-boat of two hundred tun carrying bread to Lisbone; where there was an army of three thousand men to be shipped with victuals and munition for Ireland, and there heard that Tyrones Agent lay at Court, importuning aid to be sent him presently, being not able to subsist any longer without speedy aid. And that the examinates demanded if they were Pylots for the Irish Coast; and finding they should be imploied that way, had secretly got shipping to transport themselves into France, and so returned home.

Waterford marriners pressed for Spaine.

The thirtieth day Arthur Mac Gennis chiefe of the name, terrified by the plantation of the garrison in Lecaile, made humble sute for mercy, and obtained her Majesties protection for nine daies, conditionally that he should come the Satturday following, to submit himselfe in person to her Majesties mercy, and crave her gracious pardon at Dundalk, where his Lordship then purposed to be. And Rory Oge Mac Gennis, obtained the like protection for one moneth. The same day his Lordship upon the Lord President of Mounster his intercessory letters, granted warrant for her Majesties pardon, to be passed for two hundred seventy Artificers and Husbandmen of the County of Kerry. The first of July his Lordship had purposed to rise from Dunanurey, and to returne himselfe to Dundalke: but he staied that day, in respect the weather was very foule, and the rather to countenance the Convoy going with bisket up to Mount Norreis and Armagh.

Arthur Mac Gennis makes sute for mercy.

Hitherto his Lordship had kept the field, rather to make

Tyrone keepe his forces together, and so to weaken him, then for purpose of any other service of moment: but now hearing from Dublin, that the rising out for the generall hoasting, came slowly, and not onely victuals were not yet arrived there, but even the carriages and beeves for the Army, were like in great part to faile; the second day of July his Lordship dispersed his forces into the said garrisons fronting neerest upon the rebels, and so with his followers and servants rode to Dundalke, leading with him of his army onely three Companies of foot, and one troope of horse. The third day, Sir Francis Stafford Governour of the Newry, brought Arthur Mac Gennis to Dundalke, who made his submission to her Majesty, kneeling before the Lord Deputy & Counsell. Then he made certaine humble requests: First for his pardon which was granted: Secondly, for lands granted to his father by letters Pattents, which his Lordship promised to confirme, excepting only the Lands of Glasny Mac Gennis, on whom he should make no imposition. That he might take in such tenants as would come from the Rebels, acquainting the Governour of the Newry therewith before he received them, which was granted. Fourthly, that he might retaine and absolutely command all his old tenants, till Alhollandtide next, which was granted, excepting Glasny Mac Gennis. Fiftly, that he might enjoy the Corne he had sowed in Lecaile; which being sowed on other mens Lands, could not be granted, onely favourable respect to him was promised. Sixthly, that his people might be freed from all actions of privat wrongs in the warre, which was granted upon a fine of three hundred Cowes, presently to be delivered for the Army. The same time Patricke mac Mahowne, Nephew to the chiefe of that name, was upon like humble submission received to her Majesties mercy, with promise of his pardon.

Arthur Mac Gennis's humble requests.

[II. ii. 113.]

The fifth day the Lord President and Counsell of Mounster, by letters desired his Lordship, to recall his warrant of marshall Law, given to the Lord Bourke,

Warrant of marshall law recalled.

aswell because the Lords abused the same, to draw followers to them, and to revenge their private quarrels, as because the whole Province was peaceable, and willing to be governed by judiciall courses, and this warrant his Lordship presently recalled.

Letters from the Lords in England.

This day Sir Oliver S[t] Johns brought letters from the Lords in England, whereby her Majesty gave direction, that the Lord Deputy should publikely to all the Army, and privately to the chiefe Commanders, give thankes from her Majesty to them, for the zeale and duty they had shewed in her service, and signifie her gracious acceptance of their endeavours. The sixth day his Lordship staied at Dundalke, to hasten the supplies of the generall hoasting, which came in slowly, and to order the Irish forces of the same fitly for defence of the Pale. This day Captaine Thomas Roper, with his company of foot, according to his Lordships former directions, came from Kells, to serve in the army under his Lordship. And while his Lordship lay here, newes came from Armagh, that Sir Henry Davers had taken some chiefe horses from Tyrones campe, and had entred Mac Carty his Country, being one of the greatest fastnesses in Ireland, and brought from thence a great prey.

His Lordship finding that the rising out of the generall hoasting, would doe little good in the Army, and they being willing to undertake their owne defence, which at their owne perill his Lordship thought hee might best commit to their trust. The seventh of July his Lordship gave order, that the forces of the generall hoasting, for the Counties of Dublyn and Lowth, should lie at Lowth, under the command of the Lord of Lowth, and M[r] Garland of Killencoule. That those of Meath should lie at Kels, under the command of the Lord of Tremelstone, and M[r] Dillon his Deputy. That those of West-Meath should be commanded by the Lord of Delvin, and any Deputy his Lordship should chuse; so that his Lordship or his Deputy should alwaies in person be resident with them, and keepe them together ready to answere any

Orders for the generall hoasting.

service, upon paine of a fine and imprisonment, to such as should disobey. That those of Kildare, should under the Earle of Kildares command, lie at Athy, or else where, at his Lordships discretion: and that the Sheriffe of the shire command them under his Lordship.

The ninth day his Lordship marched from Dundalke towards the North, and gathering the forces to him out of the adjoining garrisons, encamped at Latenbur, beyond the Newry, where he lay still the tenth day, till the victuals was in readines to be carried to Armagh. The eleventh day his Lordship marched some foure miles, to an hill little beyond Mount Norreis, and that day his Lordship was advertised, that Sir Arthur Chichester had taken the sole Castle held in those parts of Knockfergus by Brian mac Art, namely, the Reagh, and that Sir Richard Moryson in Lecale, had taken in two Loughes (or Ilands in Lakes), being all the fastnesses (or places of strength) which the said Brian mac Art held there. The twelfth day the Army marched early in the morning to Armagh, and there resting some houres, marched againe after dinner a mile and a halfe beyond Armagh, and there upon an hill encamped.

Brian mac Art's fastnesses taken.

The thirteenth day of July, the Lord Deputy with the Army rose from the former Campe, and marched one mile and a halfe, to an hill on this side (namely the South-side) of Blackewater, where he made a stand, Tyrone and his horse and foot, shewing themselves out of a wood, beyond a Meadow on the other side of the River, and that with Trumpets and divers colours, (some wonne at the old defeat of the English in those parts), and with some Drummes, rather for a bragging ostentation then otherwise, since they fighting like theeves upon dangerous passages, used not to appeare in such warlike manner. And from the trenches kept by the Rebels on the other side of the water, some vollies of shot were powred upon us, which fell downe on every side dead on the ground, by reason of the distance betweene us, and did small or no hurt. We having a Rabinet & a Falcon,

Tyrone's bragging ostentation.

made from this hill, some shot at the rebels troope farre distant, whereupon their Puppits bravery suddenly vanished; and according to their wonted manner, they hidde themselves in the woods. Presently the Lord Deputy sent three hundred foote to another hill
[II ii. 114.] on this side of the River, adjoining to the old Fort lying beyond the water, and his Lordship rode to that hil, whom many voluntary Gentlemen with his servants followed. And in the way my selfe and some others lighted in a Valley to refresh our selves by walking, but found an enemies soile no place for recreation, for out of the Ditches & Furrowes many shot were made at us; whereupon we tooke our horses, one shot dangerously, yet (God be praised) without hurt passing betweene my legges, while one of my feete was in my stirrop, and so we retyred to the grosse, standing in more safetie. Towards evening, wee incamped upon the above mentioned hil, at which time wee saw farre off by a Wood side, Tyrone draw some horse over to our side of the water, either (as we imagined) to assayle Tirlogh Mac Henrie of the Fewes, lately submitted, and comming after us to attend the Lord Deputie in this service, or else to conferre with him and his companie: but assoone as Sir William Godolphin Commander of the Lord Deputies troope of horse, by his Lordships direction made towards Tyrone, he with his horse presently retired backe. That night we made Gabyons to enter the Rebels trenches, and sent the Rabinet and Falcon to be planted on the other hill, where our above mentioned three hundred foote lay. All the night the rebels out of the trenches shot at our men, while they were busie in working. But the fourteenth day very early at the dawning of the day, upon our first discharging of the said great pieces, charged with musket bullets, and after some three vollies of our smal shot, the rebels quitted their trenches, basely running into the Woods, and our three hundred men passing the River, under Captaine Thomas Williams his command, possessed the trenches, and the old ruined Fort, with the Plaine

An enemies soile no place for recreation.

Preparations for assault.

in which it lay, the Wood being almost musket shot distance, whether the rebels were fled, and had by night carried their hurt and slaine men. Presently the Lord Deputie sent one Regiment to lye beyond the Blackwater, upon a hill where his Lordship had made choice to build a new Fort. Upon view of the trenches made upon every Foard, his Lordship found they were strongly and artificially fortified, wondring much that either they should so laboriously fortifie them, if they meant not to defend them, or should so cowardly quit such strong places, and so suddenly, if they had former resolution to make them good. In gaining them wee had some twentie men hurt, and two slaine, and they had greater losse, especially in the going off, though we could not truly know it.

The rebels flee.

The fifteenth day his Lordship with a troope of horse, and foure hundred foote, drew towards Tyrones Wood, and viewed the paces in the sight of the rebels, who ran away with their cowes, onely at his Lordships retrait making some few shot at our men, but hurting not one man. In the evening, Captaine Trever, and Captaine Constable with their Companies came to the Campe, sent thither from Lecayle to strengthen the Army, according to his Lordships direction to Sir Richard Moryson, after the Countrie was all taken in, and Mac Gennis the greatest neighbor Rebel had submitted himselfe.

The 16 day the L. Deputy drew out a Regiment of Irish, commanded by Sir Christo. St. Laurence, and passing the Blackwater, marched to Benburb, the old house of Shane O Neale, lying on the left hand of our Campe, at the entrance of great woods. There our men made a stand, in a faire greene meadow, having our camp and the plaines behind them, & the wood on both sides, & before them. The rebels drew in great multitudes to these woods. Here we in the Campe, being our selves in safety, had the pleasure to have the ful view of an hot and long skirmish, our loose wings sometimes beating the rebels on all sides into the Woods, and sometimes being driven by them back to our Colours in the middest

Benburb.

of the meadow, (where assoone as our horse charged, the rebels presently ran backe) and this skirmish continuing with like varietie some three howers: for the Lord Deputie, as he saw the numbers of the rebels increase, so drew other Regiments out of the Campe, to second the fight. So that at last the Rebell had drawne all his men together, and we had none but the by-Guards left to save-guard the Campe, all the rest being drawne out. *Doctor Latwar mortally wounded.* Doctor Latwar the Lord Deputies Chaplaine, not content to see the fight with us in safetie, but (as he had formerly done) affecting some singularitie of forwardnesse, more then his place required, had passed into the meadow where our Colours stood, and there was mortally wounded [II. ii. 115.] with a bullet in the head, upon which hee died the next day. Of the English not one more was slaine, onely Captaine Thomas Williams his legge was broken, and two *The Irish losses.* other hurt, but of the Irish on our side twenty sixe were slaine, and seventy five were hurt. And those Irish being such as had been rebels, and were like upon the least discontent to turne rebels, and such as were kept in pay rather to keepe them from taking part with the rebels, then any service they could doe us, the death of those unpeaceable swordmen, though falling on our side, yet was rather gaine, then losse to the Commonwealth. *Tyrones Secretary killed.* Among the rebels, Tyrones Secretary, and one chiefe man of the Ohagans, and (as we credibly heard) farre more then two hundred Kerne were slaine. And lest the disparitie of losses often mentioned by me, should savour of a partiall pen, the Reader must know, that besides the fortune of the warre turned on our side, together with the courage of the rebels abated, and our men heartned by successes, we had plentie of powder, and sparing not to shoote at randome, might well kill many more of them, then they ill furnished of powder, and commanded to spare it, could kill of ours.

These two last dayes our Pioners had been busied in fortifying and building a new Fort at Blackwater, not farre distant from the old Fort, demolished by the rebels, and for some daies following, his Lordship specially intended the furtherance and finishing of this worke, so as many souldiers were extraordinarily hired to worke therein as Pyoners.

The nineteenth day his Lordship wrote to the Lords in England, that had not the Irish submitties for the new coyne (now currant over all) furnished the Army with beeves, it had been in great distresse, since the victuals of the new contract were not arrived, and that of the old store consisted principally of saltfish, whereof the souldier could not feede, especially in Summer, besides that by long keeping it was of ill condition, so as infection was feared in the Army, praying that in the next contracts, the soldier might be fed therewith onely one day in the weeke. That he had in his directions to Sir Henry Dockwra, given him choice, either with the countenance of his Lordships Army on this side Tyrone, to goe forward with planting Ballishannon, or concurring with the Governour of Knockfergus, to enter into Tyrone, where his Lordship upon notice would meete them; and in respect he since understood, that he wanted tooles for the Plantation, he thought the second project would rather be followed by him. That Tyrone lay with all his forces to hinder his Lordship from passing to Dungannon, which he most feared, and had no fastnesse but onely this to stop it, so as hee doubted not to breake in to meete Sir Henrie Dockwra, if he could once be assured of his resolution. Further, he besought their Lordships to give warrant for allowance to the Captaines for broken Armes, upon bringing the old, because upon the breaking of pieces, the souldiers were turned to serve with Pikes, and our shot diminished daily, and the Pikes were increased more then our use required, the Captaine excusing himselfe, that upon breaking of pieces, he was not able to provide other Armes then Pikes for his men. Likewise he advertised to their Lordships, that since the last dispatch, Sir Henrie Dockwra had taken in Newtowne, being some sixteene miles from Dungannon

Ill Food.

Allowance for broken Armes.

(Tyrones chiefe seate), on the North side, (as he the Lord Deputy had planted at Blackwater, being some fifteene miles from Dungannon, on the South side); and that Sir Henrie Dockwra had spoiled and burned the Countrie there about, and had taken some one thousand cowes, from the parts neere the Lough of Earne. That Sir John Barkley, Governour of the forces at the Anneley, had met with Tyrrels men, as they passed towards Ophaly, (for which purpose that Garrison was specially laied there), and had taken from them three hundred cowes, and killed some of them, and had stopped them from troubling that Countrie. And that he the Lord Deputy with the Army had destroied the rebels Corne about Armagh (whereof he found great abundance), and would destroy the rest, this course causing famine, being the onely sure way to reduce or root out the Rebels. Finally, praying their Lordships (as formerly) to send one thousand shot for supplies, the strengthening of the English being the next way to diminish her Majesties charge, since the Irish were kept in pay rather to prevent their fighting against us, then for confidence in their fighting for us.

Rebel defeats.

Supplies of shot desired.

[II. ii. 116.] The same nineteenth day of July, the Lord Deputy wrote to Sir Robert Cecill, her Majesties Secretary, that he found upon good consideration, that the Governement of Connaght was not in his disposall, and therefore being loth to exceede his Commission, he would onely assure him, that as it was requisite, a man of experience, and fit for the present service, should have that Governement, so he conceived none to be fitter then Sir Oliver Lambert, who had already deserved well in this service, and would (in his opinion) be able to doe her Majestie as good service, as any in that place, whom (if it might stand with her Majesties pleasure, to give him warrant), he was desirous to imploy in those parts, fearing it would be a great hinderance to his intended worke, if any should be put into that Governement, who might prove unfit, or unable to make that warre; In which respect, he having no other end but the advancement of her Majesties

Sir Oliver Lambert to be Governour of Connaght.

service, was bold to make it his humble suite, that Sir Oliver Lambert might bee placed in that Governement.

While the Army lay at Blackwater to build the new Fort, his Lordship on the twentieth of July, drew out two Regiments into the woods, aswell to view the paces, and provoke the rebels, as to fetch some houses thence, for the building of our Fort, and to cut a field of Corne lying on the skirt of the Woods; which was all performed; the rebels on the further side of the Blackwater, onely making a slight skirmish with our men, upon their retreit on this side the River. The two and twentieth day, wee cut all the Corne by the Bogge and Wood side, neere our Fort, except that which our men had power to reape. The three and twentieth day Captaine Thomas Williams with his Company, being left to governe the new Fort (who before the Blackwater defeat did valiantly defend the old Fort there, being after demolished by the rebels) his L^p. with the army dislodged, and at our rising, a Proclamation was made, that how soever Tyrone vaunted, that his Pardon was offered him, and he might have it at pleasure, her Majestie was not onely resolved never to receive him to mercy, but was pleased againe to renew her gratious offer, that whosoever brought him alive, should have 2000 li. and whosoever brought his head, should have 1000 li. for reward. Thence we marched two little miles to an hill South West-ward in Henrie Oges Countrie, where we incamped, and cut downe the Corne on everie side. The seven and twentieth day his Lordship leaving Sir Henrie Follyots Regiment to guard the Camp, drew out three Regiments, expecting that the Rebels would fight, who shewed themselves on an hill neere us, with all their horse and foote, and sounding of Trumpets, yet our men not onely cutting downe the corne close by them, but entring the Woods to cut Corne there, and burning many houses in the skirts of the woods, they were so patient, as after one volley of shot, they retired into the thickest Woods. The same day the Army dislodging, marched a mile or two more

Rebel's Corne cut.

The Lord Deputy's Proclamation.

The rebels patient.

Southward, where we cut down great abundance of Corne with our swords (according to our fashion), and here Shane Mac Donnel Groome, Tyrones Marshall (whose Corne this was) upon humble submission was received to her Majesties mercie, and came to his Lordship in person the same night at our setting downe in our last Campe, whether we returned. The eight and twentieth his Lordship leaving Sir Christopher Saint Laurence his Regiment to guard the Camp, drew out three Regiments both in the morning & evening, to countenance two convoies of victuals. This day his Lordship sent a dispatch to Sir Henrie Dockwra, about their concurring in the present services, and the like to Sir Arthur Chichester, to the same purpose. His Lordship staied the longer in these parts, to see the Forts wel victualed, and to cut downe the Corne, whereof he found great store.

Submission of Tyrone's Marshall.

The nine and twentieth day his Lordship was advertised, that Sir Henrie Poore had scattered and broken three hundred rebels in Leax, and had beggered them by divers preyes of cattell taken from them, and among them, being of the Sept of O Mores, had killed, burnt and hanged forty at least, and after had slaine in fights O Connor Mac Lyre, and most of his men, and hurt many of those which escaped.

Rebels broken in Leax.

And this day great store of victuals for the Forts came from the Newry with a convoy safely to the Campe. The thirtieth day his Lordship rose with the Armie, and marched Northward backe to the new Fort of Blackwater,
[II ii. 117.] and beyond it, in all some three miles, along the South side of the River, and there his Lordship incamped close upon the Bogges and the Fastnesses (or fortified passages) in the Wood. The same evening his Lordship drew some choice men out of every Regiment, and some troopes of horse, and with them rode to view the Countrie, and woody paces, more specially that pace which lay right before us Northward, where the neerest and best passage was to enter Tyrone, the Arch-traytors chiefe house Dungannon, being some tenne miles distant, to which,

after the passage of this pace and Blackwater, the plaine Countrie lay open, yet being in some parts boggy. Here Tyrones men lay intrenched on the other side of the River, in such trenches as he had made to impeach the building of our new Fort at Blackwater, and cowardly quitted them (as is above mentioned.) The Rebels bestowed some vollies of shot on his Lordships troopes, but they returned safely, having onely one man hurt. And here one of the three Trumpets in Tyrones pay, ran from him to our Campe.

The one and thirtieth day his Lordship drew out (as before) and that day and the first of August next following, cut downe the Wood, to cleare the said pace, lying betweene us and the said passage over Blackwater. And this day the rebels attempted to cut off a guard, which we had placed on a remote hill, to second the workemen cutting the Wood, but were by them and the workemen stoutly received, and by our seconds beaten backe.

An accident to the horses.

At the same time, by accident we had almost lost all our best horses: for at the Alarum given, the horses being frighted with the skirmish, and with divers horsemen hurrying out to answere the Alarum, broke their headstals, and ran backe to Armagh, and some of the best as farre as the Newry, whether our men following, did recover them all: but had the rebels horsemen followed them, no doubt they might have caught them, and defeated our men loosely following them, and so by this advantage have done us more mischiefe, then they could otherwise have done with their forces doubled.

The second of August his Lordship with the Army rose, and marched backe to Armagh, to the end he might shun all paces, and from thence have an open passage into Art Mac Barons Countrie. We marched sixe miles to Armagh, and three to Rawlaghtany, where while we incamped, Sir Henry Davers with three hundred foote, and fortie horse, was sent into a Fastnesse to burne some twentie faire timber houses; which he performed; and about the time to set the watch, hee returned towards

Rebels houses burned.

the Campe, and at his retreat all Tyrones Forces guarded with three hundred horse, skirmished with our men, but they seconded out of the Campe, came off orderly, the rebels following them to our very Campe, into which they powred a volley of shot, and by reason of the Fastnesses adjoyning, and night approaching, retired in safety.

The Earle of Ormond's success.

Here his Lordship was advertised, that the Earle of Ormond had executed in the borders of Kilkenny and Tiperary nine and twenty rebels, of which Tybot Leyragh Butler, and David Bourke, and Ulicke Bourke, were the chiefe, and that the Company under his Lordships command, had slaine eight and twentie, of which two principall men of the Omores, one Okelly, one Captaine Edmund Roe Bourke, and one Richard Bourke, sonne to Ulicke, were the chiefe.

The third of August we rose, and having marched three miles backe, we incamped betweene the paces and Armagh, a little beyond Armagh towards the North, to the end our messengers and our convoyes for victuals might more safely passe (which was the chiefe end of our returning), and that we might have better grasse for our horses, all the higher Country above, being eaten by the rebels Creaghs (or cattell); and al the way we marched the rebels in their fastnesses drew downe close by, and followed us all the way, being very strong. Here the Commissary tooke a view of the Army in field with his Lordship.

Regiments.

The Army in the Field.

First, of Sir Benjamin Berry his Lordships Lieutenant of his foote, in List 825, by pole present in the Campe 490. 2. Regiment of Sir Oliver Saint Johns, in List 875, by Pole 533. 3. Regiment of Sir Hen. Folliot, in List 500, by Pole 305. 4. Regiment of Sir Christopher Saint Laurence, in Lyst, 750, by Pole 400. Totall in List 2950, by Pole 1728.

[II ii. 118.] Herein are not contained either Officers present, or the sicke, or hurt, or upon other occasions absent. The fourth day some Companies were drawne out to cut the pace of Armagh, and the rebels being in sight, offered not to skirmish with them. But towards night they drew downe strong out of the woods, to an hill under which we lay encamped in a faire meadow. They came with cries and sound of Drummes and bagpipes, as if they would attempt the campe, and powred into it some two or three thousand shot, hurting onely two of our men. But his Lordship commanding that none in the Campe should stirre, had lodged in a trench some foure hundred shot, charging them not to shoot till the rebels approached neere. And after these our men had given them a volly in their teeth, they drew away, and we heard no more of their Drummes or Bagpipes, but onely mournefull cries; for many of their best men were slaine, and among the rest one horseman of great accompt, and one Pierce Lacy an Archrebell of Mounster. The next morning we found some dead bodies at the skirt of the wood, and three scattered peeces. Hence his Lordship sent direction to Sir John Barkeley, to bring with him to the Campe a regiment from the Annaly & Liscannon, because Tyrone was growne strong by the comming to him of his Mac Guire, and his Mac Mahownd, and of Cormocke mac Baron, (comming to him from the frontires of Loughfoyle). The fifth day his Lordship sent againe some shot, with Pyoners, to cut the pace close by the Rebels.

A skirmish.

Tyrone grown strong.

The sixth day his Lordship purposed to rise and meet our Convoy bringing victuals from the Newry: but being staied by ill weather, sent early some horse to stay the Convoy, till his Lordship drew downe towards those parts. This day his Lordship gave order to Master Treasurer, that proportions of new monies should be sent to all the Market Townes, to change the same for sterling, and that Proclamations should be made in them to decry the old sterling monies, and onely make the new to be currant. The seventh his Lordship rose to draw towards the Newry, and marching to Mount Norreis, encamped neere

Orders for the new monies.

the said Fort. The eight day his Lordship dispatched the Earle of Clanrickard into Connaght, to command the forces in those parts, having sent for Sir John Barkeley to come with a regiment to the Campe. Here his Lordship gave warrant for the passing of her Majesties pardon for land, life, and goods, to Arthur Mac Gennis, chiefe of his Sept, with some 170 followers.

Arthur Mac Gennis pardoned.

Here his Lordship received letters out of England from Mr Secretary, signifying that the Lord President had sent to her Majesty divers advertisements, that the Spaniards would presently land in some part of Mounster, from whence the Lord Deputy for necessity had lately drawne one thousand foot and fifty horse into Connaght. That her Majesty did well allow of his Lordships care in drawing those men to that service, and not leesing the present certainty for apprehension of the future, not so assured. That it was probable that the King of Spaine would doe something now at the upshot, and though it was not credible, that he would send ten or twelve thousand men into Ireland, yet since he had from February last begunne a foundation to provide forces for the Low-Countries or Ireland, as his affaires should require: and since the Low-Country Army was reinforced by land out of Italy, her Majesty thought he might with ease transport foure or five thousand men for Ireland, and was like to doe it, and so he might for the time turne the state of Ireland, would thinke them well bestowed, if he should leese them all at the yeeres end. That in this respect her Majesty had resolved to leavy five thousand men to be in readines, and to send two thousand of them presently for Mounster, to arrive there by the tenth of this moneth; so as if the Spaniards should land, the Lord President might be enabled to keepe the Provincials from revolt, till he the Lord Deputy might come thither, and more forces might be sent out of England; and if they should not invade Ireland, then his Lordship might keepe the one thousand he had drawne from Mounster, to finish the worke whereof he had laide

Advertisements of a Spanish landing in Mounster.

an happy foundation, heartily wishing that his Lordship might be the happy Instrument to save Ireland, to whom he professed himselfe tied in most constant and honest friendship, and praying his Lordship to esteeme these ready seconds, besides the publike duty to proceed much out of an extraordinary respect to his Lordship. That for bestowing of the Companies to be sent into Mounster, [II. ii. 119.] as he who was gone, (meaning as I thinke, the Earle of Essex), made too great a Monopoly in bestowing all such places himselfe, so now there was a great confusion, every Lord importuning to preferre his friend and follower; *Preferrements.* but that for his part, he sought no mans preferrement herein, but onely advised that those might be first respected, which came over with the Lord Deputies recommendations. That the Lord President had earnestly moved him, and in good sort challenged to have hopes in him for the procurement of some meanes to gratifie his followers; and had by other friends obtained of her Majesty, that some of those Companies might be sent over undisposed, and left to his disposall, to which he the Secretary had given second, rather then that the places should be bestowed in England, without any thankes either to the Lord Deputy or Lord President. Protesting that howsoever he loved the Lord President, he would not scant his due respect to his Lordship, wherein he thought to give him the least discontent. That he conceived the Spaniards would not make discent at Corcke, *Fit places for the Spaniards discent.* which Towne was not guardable when they had it. Nor yet at Lymricke, though fit by the scituation, because an enemy ingaged so farre into the Kingdome, could not hope for supplies, when her Majesty should take due resolution to oppose them. But rather judged Galloway a fit place for their discent, giving commodity to joine with the Northerne rebels, and seated in a Countrey all out in rebellion. Or else Waterford, in respect of the goodly River and the peoples affection to Spaine, advising that the Fort of Dungannon should carefully be furnished with a Commander, men, and necessaries. Lastly, that

News from the Low Countries.

Ostend was obstinately besieged by the Arch-Duke, with thirteene thousand foote, and sixty peeces of battery; and howsoever the States had left two thousand Dutch there, yet their Army being at Bercke, whence it would not be raised, the Town had beene carried within ten daies, if Sir Francis Vere had not throwne himselfe into it with one thousand sixe hundred English, to whom her Majesty sent one thousand men, and prepared to send 2000. more, to succour the place, because part of the Army in Italy was come downe to the Arch-Duke.

Sir Henrie Dockwra's want of match.

The ninth of August his Lordship & the Counsellors present in the Campe, writ to the Lords in England. That the Army had bin imployed in preparing her Majesties Forts, & fitting them for the winter war, & in the present spoyling of the rebels corne, (the only way to ruine them), hoping to keep the army in field til harvest were past; so that it being impossible to cut all their corne, our garrisons might have opportunity to gather the rest, and the rebels might be hindred from gathering any, except it were Tyrones corne neere Dungannon, whereunto the passage was so difficult, as his Lp. for so little thought not good to hazard al, especially since Sir Hen. Dockwra for want of Match (as he had written) could not meete his Lordship in Tyrone, according to their former project, whereof his Lordship notwithstanding professed himselfe nothing sorrie, in regard that meeting would have given the Arch-rebell power to fling the Dice againe for recoverie of their fortune, & that upon an unequall hazard, by setting his rest upon either of them apart, divided into three bodies, under the Lord Deputy, the said Sir Henrie Dockwra, and Sir Arthur Chichester, even with the whole force of his Northerne partakers, though his other friends further off were kept from aiding him, by the disposall of our other forces. That besides the spoyling of their corne, his Lordship by search had found an easie way to passe to Dungannon, which hitherto was never by any Guide made knowne to us, & had cut down a broad pace, through a thick Wood in two dayes labour, and so came to the River, where he purposed, as soone as might be, to build a Fort with a Bridge, there being from thence to Dungannon lesse then foure miles, all in a plaine; That this would cut the Arch-traytors throat: for howsoever the name of Oneale was so reverenced in the North, as none could bee induced to betray him upon the large reward set upon his head, yet when the hope of assistance from Spaine should be taken away, they seeing their Corne spoyled, and upon our expected supplies seeing us enter Tyrone, could not but see their apparant confusion. That howsoever this Summer few of their cowes had been taken (which worke is more proper to the Winter warre), yet they had been forced to feede them within their fastnesses, which they used to keepe for feeding them in Winter, so as they must either starve them by keeping them there in winter, or hazard the taking of them by our Garrisons, if they feede them abroad. That for the future service, they besought againe to be inabled, by the sending of one thousand shot out of England for supplies, and that the rather, because Tyrone was very strong, as appeared by a note delivered by Shane Mac Donnel Groome, who having been Tyrones Marshall, was received to mercy the seven and twenty of July, besides our experience of their strength, when few daies since they powred three thousand shot into our Campe, and could hardly be kept from forcing it. So as our army consisting only of one thousand seven hundred nintie eight by Pole, and more then halfe of them being Irish, the speedy sending of the supply was most necessarie. As also the sending of munition and victuals, without which all this labour would be lost, and the souldier forced, not onely to leave his Garrison, but to live idly in the Pale upon the subject. Lastly, that the Army (by Gods grace) had not had any disaster, but burning their houses in the very Woods, had still beaten the Rebels, few or no English being lost. Together with these letters were sent divers notes of victuals and munition remaining, and new stores to be

An easie way found to passe to Dungannon.

[II ii. 120.]

1000. *shot necessarie for supplies.*

sent over. And therewith was sent the above mentioned note of Tyrones forces, as followeth.

A note of Tyrone's forces.

A perfect note of such Captaines and Companies, as are under the command of the Traitor Tyrone, within Tyrone, not mentioning the Chiefetaines, as O Donnel, O Cane, Mac Gire, and the rest of the Ulster Lords, but onely such as attend him in his Countrie.

Horse.

Tyrone for his Guard, 100. His sonne Hugh Oneale, 100. His brother Cormock, 100. Art Mac Baron, 20. Phelim Ohanlons sonne, 10. Tirlogh Brasils sonnes, 50. Con, Tyrones base sonne, 20. In all 400.

His Guard of Foote.

Led by James Osheale a Lemster man, 200. Led by Jenkyn Fitz Simon of Lecayle, 200. In all 400.

Other Foote.

Hugh Mac Cawel, and two other Captaines under Cormock, Tyrones brother, 600. Con, sonne to Art Mac Baron, 100. Brian Mac Art, 200. Con, Tyrones base sonne, 100. Mac Can, 100. Owen O Can, 100. Donough Aferadogh Ohagan, 100. Owen Ohagan, 100. Donnel Oneale for Owen Evalle O Neale, 100. Three Brothers, Gillaspick Mac Owen, 100; Rory Mac Owen, 100; Randal Mac Owen, 100. Kedagh Mac Donnel, 100. Owen O Quin, 100. James O Hagan, 100. Phelym Oge O Neale, 60. Tirlogh Brasills sonnes, 200. Henry Wragton, 200. Henry Oge Mac Henrie Mac Shane, 100. Tirlogh Con Mac Barons sonne, 100. Art O hagan, sonne to Hugh, 100. Hugh Grome Ohagan and his Cosin, 100. Donnel Grome Mac Edmund, 100. Patrick Mac Phelim, 100. Gilleduff Mac Donnel, one of Connaght, 100. In all 3260. Totall of Horse and Foote, 4060.

All these (three hundred excepted) had meanes for themselves and their companies within Tyrone, and divers of them have great forces besides these, which they keepe in their owne Countries for defence thereof.

This present ninth of August the Lord Deputie wrote to Sir Robert Cecyll the Secretarie this following letter.

The Lord Deputy's letter to Sir Robert Cecyll.

SIr, I received your letter of the five and twentie of July, the fourth of this moneth, being in Campe neere the place where the Marshall Bagnol was slaine. The newes you received from the President of Mounster, of Spanish succours, I doe find no waies more confirmed, then by the assured confidence this people hath thereof, out of the which they are growne from the most humble begging of their peace, to exceeding pride, and the traytor himselfe so strong, as (beleeve me Sir) he hath many more fighting men in his Army, then we. And yet we doe [II. ii. 121.] not omit any thing of our purposes, but have since our comming to this Camp, made that a faire way to Blackwater, which the Marshall shunned, when he was overthrowne, and every day cut downe either his Woods or his Corne in his sight, onely with some slight skirmishes, in all which (God be thanked) we cannot say, we had any disaster hitherto, but in all he loseth some of his best men. I presume there could nothing be added to our Counsell of the distribution of her Majesties forces: but whether the fault hath been in the Commanders of the severall parties, or in some impediments which they pretend, I know not; but wee receive little assistance by any of them, and the whole brunt of the warre lieth upon us. But out of the present judgement wee make of this Countrie, wee have discovered, and directed Sir Arthur Chichester a course, which if we may inable him to go forward in, will, I hope, utterly banish Tyrone; and have found another way into his country, that if we can but build a Fort, and make a passage over the River, we shall make Dungannon a center, whether we may from all parts draw together all her Majesties forces, and (as I

A course to banish Tyrone.

presume) before this winters end, not leave a man in the Country of Tyrone. Whatsoever others have undertaken, I beseech you Sir to remember, that in all my dispatches, I have declared, that the uttermost you could looke from us in this Summers work, should be to plant such Garrisons as must take effect this next Winter, and that we should proceed slowly, & come short of our purpose, if we were not continually supplied with meanes, and in time, of victuals and al kind of munitions. If you have not been informed in due time of our wants, I must excuse my selfe, that being continually imploied in the active prosecution of as busie a warre as any is in the World, and most commonly farre from Dublin, where our Magazins are, I am driven in al the severall kindes of our meanes, to appoint of the Counsell Commissioners, whom I have desired in my absence to informe you of the estate of these things, and to solicite our wants, having directed the particular Ministers of every nature, to informe them of the remaines, and to deliver them (to bee sent over) estimates, of what wee should want. Onely in generall I have in all my dispatches protested, that without sufficient supplies of these things, wee should bee driven to sit still, and make all the rest of her Majesties charge unprofitable. Sir, I cannot from a quiet judgement make you a large and perfect discourse at this time of our affaires, for I am continually full of the present busines, and have so little rest, as sometimes these rogues will keepe us waking all night: but in short, I dare assure you, I see a faire way, to make Ulster one of the most quiet, assured, and profitable Provinces, if the Spaniard doe not come. If they doe, I cannot say what we shall first resolve on, till by the event we see their purpose; for to provide for all places, that carrie equall probabilitie of their undertaking, wee cannot, neither can I put my selfe into any part of Ireland with my chiefe strength, but I may happen to be as farre from their discent, as I shall bee where now I am, which maketh me the more loth to forgoe my hold in those

Planting of Garrisons.

The Spaniards.

parts, and yet for all occasions you must not imagine me to be now in the head of a great Army, but of some sixteene hundred fighting men, of whom there are not halfe English, and upon the newes of Spanish succours, I know few Irish that I can reckon ours. With this Army I must make my retreat, which I resolved to have left most part in Garrisons all this winter in these quarters; and in truth Sir, I cannot at this present thinke of a better counsel, then that we might goe on with the warre by these Garrisons against Tyrone, as wee were determined, whether the Spaniards come or no, and to make head against them, chiefely with meanes out of England. By this course they shall give each other little assistance, and if we doe but ruine and waste the traytors this Winter, it will bee impossible for the Spaniards to make this people live, by which course I presume it is in her Majesties power to give the King of Spaine a great blow, and to quit this Country of them for ever. If in the checkes, the Queene doe not finde the weakenesse of her Army, I disclaime from the fault; for without a wise honest Muster-master, of good reputation, to be still present in the Army, the Queene in that kinde wil never be well served, and upon those Officers that are, I doe continually call for their care in that matter. If according to our desire you had sent us one thousand supplies of shot to the Newrie, it had advanced the service [II. ii. 122.] more then I can expresse, but some you must needs send us, to be able to leave those garisons strong in winter. Most part of these troops I have here, are they that have stricken all the blowes for the recoverie of the Kingdome, and been in continuall action, and therefore you must not wonder if they be weake. If Sir Henrie Dockwra do not plant Ballishannon, I thinke it fit, that Sir Arthur Chichester had a thousand men of his List, whom I hope we would finde meanes to plant within foure or five miles of Dungannon, and by boats victuall them commodiously. I doe apprehend the consequence of that plantation to be great: but till I heare from you againe, I wil take no men from Loughfoyle, because I am loth to meddle much with that Garrison without direction: but I beseech you Sir by the next let me know your opinion.

The nomination of captaines.

I pray you Sir give me leave to take it unkindly of my L. President to informe you, that Sir Hen. Dockwra hath had greater favor in the nomination of Captaines then he; for he never placed but one, whom I displaced after. To have some left to his nomination, is more then I could obtaine, when the last supply came to me. But since it is the Queenes pleasure, I must beare this (and as I doe continually a great deale more) with patience. And though I am willing you should know I have a just feeling of these things, yet I beseech you Sir to beleeve, that my meaning is not to contest, or to impute the fault unto you, for (by God Sir) where I professe my love in the same kind I have done to you, they shall bee great matters that shall remove me, although they may (and I desire that I may let you know when they do) move me. I do only impute this to my misfortune, that I perceive arguments too many of her Majesties displeasure: but while for her owne sake she doth use my service, I will love whatsoever I suffer for her, and love the sentence, that I will force from the conscience of all, and the mouth of the just, that I have been, and will be, an honest, and no unprofitable servant unto her. I dare undertake, we have rid my Lord President of the most dangerous rebell of Mounster, and the most likely man to have renewed the rebellion; for that night I received your letters, the rogues did powre above three thousand shot into our Campe, at which time it was our good fortune to kill Peirce Lacie, and some other of their principall men. Wee are now praying for a good wind, for wee are at our last daies bread, if victuals come in time, we will not be idle. Sir, if I have recommended any into England, I am sure it was for no charge; for I know none that have gone from hence but there are many that continue here more worthy of preferment then they, therefore I pray Sir let them not be reckoned mine,

Peirce Lacie the most dangerous rebel of Mounster.

that there challenge any thing for me, but whatsoever shall please their Lordships, I must be contented withall, and it shall not much trouble mee, for I meane not to make the warres my occupation, and doe affect asmuch to have a great many followers, as to bee troubled with a kennel of hounds. But for the Queenes sake, I would gladly have her served by such, as I know to be honest men, and unhappy is that Generall, that must fight with weapons of other mens choosing. And so Sir, being ashamed that I have troubled you so long, I desire you to be assured, that no man shall love you more honestly and faithfully, then my selfe.

From the Campe neere Mount Norreys this ninth of August, 1601.

Yours Sir most assured to
doe you service
Mountjoy.

Touching the above mentioned distaste betweene the Lord Deputy and the Lord President of Mounster, his Lordship shortly after, wrote a letter to him, resenting himselfe in very high tearmes, of the wrong he conceived to be offered him, as followeth in his Lordships letter.

[II. ii. 123.]

Letter to the Lord President of Mounster.

MY Lord, as I have hitherto borne you as much affection, and as truely as ever I did professe it unto you, and I protest rejoyced in all your good successes as mine owne; so must you give me leave, since I presume I have so just cause, to challenge you of unkindnes & wrong, in writing into England, that in preferring your followers, Sir Henry Dockwra hath had more power from me then your selfe, and consequently to solicite the Queene to have the nomination of some Captaines in this Kingdome. For the first I could have wished you would have beene better advised, because upon my Honour he never, without my speciall warrant, did appoint but one, whom I after displaced; & I do not remember that ever since our comming over, I have denied

Letter to the Lord President of Mounster.

any thing, which you have recommended unto me, with the marke of your owne desire to obtaine it, and in your Province I have not given any place (as I thinke) but at your instance. For the other, I thinke it is the first example, that ever any under another Generall desired or obtained the like sute. And although I will not speake injuriously of your deserts, nor immodestly of mine owne, yet this disgrace cannot make me beleeve that I have deserved worse then any that have beene Generals before me: but since it is the Queenes pleasure, I must endure it, and you chuse a fit time to obtaine that, or any thing else against me. Yet I will concurre with you in the service, as long as it shall please her Majesty to imploy us here: but hereafter I doubt not but to give you satisfaction that I am not worthy of this wrong. The Counsel & my self, upon occasion of extraordinary consequence, sent for some of the Companies of Mounster out of Connaght, when we heard you were to be supplied with two thousand out of England, but we received from them a flat deniall to come, and the coppy of your letter to warrant them therein. If you have any authority from the Queene to countermand mine, you may very well justifie it, but it is more then you have vowed to me to have, when I (before my comming over) protested unto you, that if you had, I would rather serve the Queene in prison, then here. My Lord, these are great disgraces to me, and so conceived, and I thinke justly, by all that know it, which is and will be very shortly all Ireland. My alleagiance and owne honour are now ingaged with all my burthens, to goe on in this worke, otherwise no feare should make me suffer thus much; and what I doe, it is onely love doth move me unto it: for I know you are deere to one, whom I am bound to respect with extraordinary affection. And so my Lord I wish you well, and will omit nothing (while I am in this Kingdome) to give you the best contentment I can, and continue as,

Your assured friend,
Mountjoy.

The Lord President within few daies, not onely with a calme, noble, and wise, answere, pacified his Lordships anger; but also by many good Offices betweene his Lordship and Master Secretary, (with whom as a most inward friend hee had great power) so combined their new begunne love, as hee ingaged his Lordship in a great bond of thankefulnes to him.

The eleventh of August, his Lordship wrote to the Governour of the Newry, that to avoid the continuall trouble of Convoyes hereafter, he should presently send up as great provision of victuals to Armagh as possibly he could, while his Lordship lay in that part with the Army: For two daies after, by reason of much raine falling, and the expecting of these victuals, his Lordship lay still in the Campe neere Mount Norris. The thirteenth the victuals came, but not in such great proportion as was directed, because the victuler had failed to bake great part of his meale, and the Cowes expected from Dundalke, were not yet sent by the Submitties, according to their promise. The same day his Lordship rose, and incamped three miles short of Armagh. The foureteenth his Lordship rose with the Army, and put all the victuals he had received into the Abbey of Armagh and the Fort of Blackewater, and returned back to the same camping place. The fifteenth his Lordship drew backe to his former Campe, neere Mount Norreis, and sent out some Companies of Horse and Foote to the skirts of the wood neere the Fort, to guard those that cut wood for making of Carres, to transport more victuals to the said garrisons. The sixteenth his Lordship drew backe to Carickbane, neere the Newry, to hasten the provision of victuals, in as great quantity as might be, which was dispatched within few dayes. The twenty three his Lordship wrote the following letter to M[r] Secretary.

Provision of victuals to Armagh.

[II. ii. 124.]

SIr I did ever foresee, and have signified so much, that any forraine succours would cleane alter the State of this Kingdome, and the whole frame of our proceedings, and doe find that the assurance that these people doe now receive thereof, doth make them stand upon other termes then they were wont, and much divert our purposes, which we had conceived with good reason and great hope. *The state of the country.* Of any but the English we have small assurance, and of them the Army is exceeding weake. The Irish newly submitted, & their wavering faith hitherto we have used to great effect: for we have wasted them, and the rebels by them, but when we come to lay our Forces in remote garrisons, they flie the hardnes of that life, and doe againe betake themselves unto any head that is of power to spoile, and with the best paid and prevailing party they will ever be. I am certainely told by Sir John *Spaniards arrived at Sligo.* Barkely, that some Spaniards that arrived at Sligo (as they say to discover, and with assurance of the present comming of a great force,) doe there fortifie, and (as he hath been more particularly informed) not in a compasse only capeable of themselves, but in such sort as it will be able to lodge great numbers. This, (& my being prevented to follow my purposes in these parts as I would,) draweth me into the Pale, to advise of the best assurance for the maine, and yet not to quit my purposes in such sort in these parts; but if the Spaniards doe not come, I may againe look this way with my former desire, which was to beat the chiefe Traitor cleane out of his Countrey: for untill that be done, there will be ever left a fier, which upon all occasions will breake out more and more violently. When I have spoken with the rest of the Counsell, and considered more neerely the disposition of these inward parts, I will more largely relate unto you my opinion, neither will I now much trouble you with my owne estate, although not onely my selfe, but (I protest) the service doth feele the effect of a general conceived rumour of her Majesties displeasure to me. I am so neerely interessed therein; that I cannot speak much of that matter, without the prejudice of a private respect to my selfe: but onely this, I most humbly desire her Majestie for her owne sake to use me no longer here, then shee thinketh me fit to be trusted and graced; for without both, I shal but strive against the wind and tide, and be fit for nothing but my owne poore harbour, unto the which I most humbly desire to be speedily called with her gracious favour, since my owne conscience maketh me presume to desire so much, that best doth know with how untollerable labour of minde and body, I have and doe continually serve her. And so Sir I beseech God to send you as much contentment as I doe want. The 23 of August 1601.

Yours Sir to doe you service, Mountjoy.

The fortifying of the Spaniards at Sligo, vanished with the rumour, which was grounded upon some arriving, to bring the Rebels certaine newes of present succours, and presently returning. And the brute (or perhaps his Lordships jealousie) of her Majesties displeasure, arose from the confessions of some examined, about the rash attempts of the unfortunate Earle of Essex, who had accused the Lord Deputy to be privy to that project. His Lordship purposing to draw into the Pale (or parts neere Dublyn), left his forces in the North, (for those of Loughfoyle had not yet correspondency with these), in this following manner disposed.

The disposal of the forces.

At Carickefergus.

Sir Arthur Chichester Governour 200. Sir Foulke Conway 150. Captaine Billings 150. Captaine Phillips 150. Captaine Norton 100. Captaine Egerton 100. Foot 850.

Sir Arthur Chichester 25. Captaine John Jephson 100. Horse 125.

At Lecaile.

Sir Richard Moryson Governour 150. Captaine Toby Cawfield 150. Foot 300.

These following forces, when they should be drawne out, for convoy of victuals or otherwise, were to be com- [II. ii. 125.]

The disposal of the forces.

manded in chiefe by Sir Francis Stafford, and were thus disposed in severall garrisons.

At the Newry.

Sir Francis Stafford Governour 200. Captaine Josias Bodley 150. Sir William Warren 100. Foot 450. Sir Francis Stafford 50 Horse.

At Mount Norreis.

Captaine Edward Blaney Governour 150. Captaine Atherton 150. Sir Samuell Bagnoll 150. Captaine Rotheram 150. Foot 600. Sir Samuell Bagnoll 50 Horse.

At Armagh.

Sir Henry Davers Governour 150. Sir H. Follyot 150. Capt. Guest 150. Capt. Thomas Roper 150. Captaine Francis Roe 100. Capt. Trever 100. Foot 800. Sir Henry Davers 100. Captaine Darcy 25. Horse 125.

At Blackewater.

Captaine Williams Governour 150. Captaine Constable 100. Sir Garret Moore 100. Foot 350.

An Englishman sent in Bonds to the Lords in England.

The twenty foure of August, his Lordship leaving the field, rode backe to the Newry, from whence he sent one W. an Englishman in bonds to the Lords in England, for the reasons following. Sir Henry Davers after his elder brothers perishing in the late Earle of Essex his attempt, was desirous by active prosecution of the Rebels, to deserve her Majesties good opinion. And for this cause, as for that hee was enabled to doe great services, aswell by his noble vertues, as by the command he formerly and now had both of horse and foot; his Lordship in speciall love to him, being most willing to give him all opportunity to attaine this his desire, appointed him Governour of Armagh, advising him to be often stirring with the forces under his command, and to practise what possibly he could devise upon the person of the

Arch-traitor. To him this Englishman made offer to kill Tyrone, yet would not discover his plot for greater secrecy (as he pretended), neither would he presse him further, since he required no assistance; and so in the night he was suffered to goe by the watches, and passed to Tyrones Campe, whence he was imploied to the Ilander Scots, and comming to Sir Arthur Chichesters hands, was by him sent backe from Knockefergus to his Lordship at the Newry, where being examined what he had done in Tyrones Campe, he avowed that once he had drawne his sword to kill him, though under pretence of bragging what he would doe for his service, yet gave he no good accompt of his actions or purposes, but behaved himselfe in such sort, as his Lordship judged him franticke, though not the lesse fit for such a purpose. Now because hee had not performed that he undertooke, and gave an ill accompt of himselfe in this action; his Lordship, aswell for the discharge of Sir H. Davers, who imploied him, as of himselfe who consented thereunto, and advised Sir H. Davers so to doe, thought good to send him prisoner to the Lords, that he might be there examined, where by reason of his friends dwelling in London, they might be sufficiently informed of the mans quality.

The English-man's brag.

The five and twentieth, his Lordship and the Counsel there present, wrote from the Newry this following letter to the Lords in England.

IT may please your Lordships. Since our last letters we have for the most part imploied our selves in putting up as great quantity of victuals as we could to Armagh and the Blackewater, being loath to ingage our selves into any thing, which wee had further purposed, untill we should see the issue of this assured expectation of the Spaniards invasion, or till we might by some meanes better strengthen this Army. Of the first we have reason to be jealous, both by many arguments of assured confidence in this people of present succour, and by the arrivall of a Spanish ship, in which the Arch- [II. ii. 126.]

traytors agent is returned, with assurance that he left the Spanish forces ordained for his aide in a readinesse to set out. For the strengthening of our Armie wee had good reason to bee provident, considering the weakenesse thereof, and especially of the English, and finding by experience the rebels strength now, when he had none but the forces nourished in Tyrone to assist him. Wherefore hearing that Sir Henrie Dockwra had planted a Garrison at Dunnagall, and had left O Donnel possessed in a manner of nothing in Tirconnel, and that upon the late arivall of his munition, he intended to be active in those parts neere Loughfoyle, and understanding by Master Secretary, that about the twelfth of August there were two thousand men to be supplied for Mounster, we *Distribution of the Forces.* resolved to send for some of the Companies in Connaght of the Mounster Lyst, and to put the rest into Galloway and thereabouts, for the assurance of those parts, and upon the receiving of that addition to our strength, to have drawne to Monaghan, and spoiled the Corne of that Country, being of exceeding quantitie, or if we had seene reason, to have left a Garrison there, and to have inabled it to gather the most part of that Corne for their better provision, or otherwise to have continued the prosecution in these parts, until we should heare of the Spaniards landing, or by any assurance of their not comming, should be at liberty to proceede in our former purposes. But receiving answere from the Captaines of Mounster, that they had direction not to stirre from Connaght upon any other order whatsoever, then from the President of Mounster, in regard of the present expectation of Spaniards to land in those parts: and we thereby being not so well able to wade any further in our determinations for the North, & receiving some probable intelligence, that the place designed for the Spaniards landing was Sligo, wee resolved to leave the Northerne Garrisons very strong in foote and horse, and as well provided with meanes as we can, and to draw our selves with the rest of our force towards Connaght, appointing the rest of the Counsel to meete us in the way at Trym, to advise with us of the best course to establish the heart of the Pale, and to answere the present expectation of Spanish forces. And although by our suddaine leaving the North, we have ommitted some things which wee conceived to bee of great consequence to the service, yet if it shall please your Lordships to supply the foundations we have laid in those parts with one thousand shot, according to our former sute, and with store of victuals for the Garrisons in Winter, we hope you shall finde no small effect of our Summers labour. But seeing we are perswaded, that if any Spanish forces arrive, they wil land at Sligo, where they have a fit place to fortifie, to be relieved by sea, to unite themselves with all the Rebels force, and where they have a faire Countrie to possesse, with an easie way (by the rebels assistance) into Mounster, or the hart of the Pale, or especially to Loughfoyle, where we cannot, without great difficulty, affront them, having no magazins of victuals or munition at Athlone or Galloway, and where it is unpossible for us to provide our selves, or if we could, most difficult to carrie them by land, when we are so farre in the Countrie, and have no meanes for carriage. Therefore we most humbly desire your Lordships to send good store of victuals and munition to Galloway, and to Lymbrick, which howsoever our expectation fall out, will be most necessarie for the prosecution of Connaght, and that prosecution as necessarie this Winter, since O Donnel hath forsaken his owne Countrie, and betaken himselfe to live in that Province. But because we doe foresee it to be no ill Counsel for the Spaniards to land at Sligo, and think that Tyrone will presently urge them to cut off our Garrison at Loughfoyle, whether from thence they have a faire way, and secure from our opposition, and may imagine, that it will be no great difficulty for them with such royall provisions as they wil bring, to force those slender fortifications. We beseech your Lordships to send a large provision of victuals and munition to Carling-

Good store of victuals needed for Galloway and Lymbrick.

ford and Knockfergus; for we cannot by any other way then that relieve Loughfoyle if it be distressed. Neither can her Majestie hazard any losse in these great provisions, though we never use them; for all kinde of victuals may be issued in this Kingdome with great gaine, and especially Corne, which we chiefely desire; and for munition, it

[II ii. 127.] may be kept with providence as a store for all occasions. Thus howsoever it fall out, we shall be inabled to make

The warre to be prosecuted in the Winter.

such a prosecution this Winter in Connaght and the North, as in all reason will ende these warres, if the Spaniards come not, and will leave this Province of Ulster in farre greater subjection, then ever any of her Majesties Progenitors had it. And since wee apprehend, that Spaine may make in this Countrie a dangerous warre for England, we conceive that if not now, yet with his first abilitie, he will imbrace it, which makes us to have the greater desire (if it bee possible) to prevent his footing here for ever, and that (by Gods help) we hope to do before this next Summer, if we may be inabled this winter to ruine Tyrone and O Donnel. We have great neede

Neede of Northerne horses.

of one hundred Northerne horses, for our horses here grow weak, and ill, and if your Lordships please to afford us that number, we will so handle the matter, as it shall bee no increase of the Lyst. If the Spaniards come, we must have at the least three hundred, and if they be Northerne horses, and Northerne Riders, we assure our selves they will be much fitter for this service, then such as are usually sent hither, who come with purpose to get licence to returne, and yet are a greater charge to her Majesty. But for the one thousand foote wee desired by our former letters, we find their comming to be of that necessitie, as wee must bee most humble and earnest sutors to your Lordships to send them presently: for our Companies

The Soldiers weake.

are so exceeding weake, and now decay so fast, by the extremitie of the weather, as a much greater number will not supplie us, but that the checkes will bee as great as now they are, and they little be seene amongst us, which gives us cause to wish now, and humbly to move your

Lordships, to be pleased to send one thousand foote more soone after. The reports here are so uncertaine, as untill we meete the rest of the Counsell at Trym, we know not how the Pale stands affected, upon this assured confidence of the Spaniards comming, onely this we perceive, many of them are wavering, yet the Lords hereabouts, namely, Mac Gennis, Tirlogh Mac Henrie, Euer Mac Cooley, and O Hanlon, keepe with us, notwithstanding that Tyrone hath sent them word, that hereafter it will bee too late for them to make their peace with him, if they doe it not now upon this occasion, and they assure us, as much as men can doe, that they will not fall againe from their obedience, though thereby their state bee no better then horseboyes. But of this wee can give your Lordships no assurance, neither in them have wee any extraordinarie confidence. It may further please your Lordships to be advertised, that the Lord of Dunsany, having the command of a Fort in the Brenny, called Liscanon (where wee had placed certaine Irish Companies, as fittest to spoile and wast the Countrie thereabouts), did lately draw most of them into Mac Mahowns Countrie, for the taking of a prey, which they lighted on, (as is said) to the number of some sixteene hundred Cowes: but in their returne, being hardly laied unto, (as some of them say, with very great numbers, yet as we have heard by some that were present, not above sevenscore), they did not only lose their prey, but according to the manner of the Irish (who have no other kind of retreat) fell to a flat running away to the Fort, so as poore Captaine Esmond (who had the command of the Reare, and very valiantly with a few made good the place) was sore hurt, and afterwards taken prisoner, and forty or fiftie of our side slaine. We cannot learne that any English were among them, so as we account our losse to be no more then the taking of the Captaine, neither doe the Rebels bragge thereof, both because they scaped not free, loosing very neere as many men as wee did; and for that they knew they dealt but with their Countrimen, who (as

The Lord of Dunsany's mishap.

they doe) hold it no shame to runne, when they like not to fight, though wee meane to call some of ours to account thereof. And so we most humbly take leave.

Letters from the Lord President.

The eight and twentieth of August, his Lordship received two letters from the Lord President of Mounster; the first imported, that hearing that his Lordship had sent into Connaght for part of the Companies of the Mounster Lyst to come into the North, he prayed to bee excused, that hee had given contrary directions, upon feare of the Spaniards landing, & the knowledge of Tirrels purpose to come with the banished Mounster men, and aides of Northerne men out of Connaght, presently to disturbe the Province of Mounster, and signified, that now to manifest his precise obedience to his Lordships commands, hee had sent them directions to march towards
[II. ii. 128.] his Lordship upon sight of his letter, yet praying his Lordship to send some part of them into Munster, without which helpe he could neither keepe the field against Tirrel and the Provinciall fugitives at their first entrie, nor upon the Spaniards arrivall, give any impediment to their disposing of such Townes, as were recommended to his speciall care, and assuring his Lordship that the Spaniards had been seene at Sea, and that in his judgement and by vulgar report, it was likely they would make discent in some part of Mounster. Lastly, advertising that he had sent James the Suggon pretended Earle of Desmond, and Florence Mac Carty (the chiefe practiser with the Spaniards in those parts) into England. The second letter imported the Lord Presidents recommendation (which by established course was effectuall) to his Lordship, for the granting of her Majesties pardon for lands lives and goods, to five hundred fortie two inhabitants of Muskery, and other parts in the Countie of Corke, for which present warrant was accordingly given.

James the Suggon and Florence Mac Carty sent into England.

The nine and twentieth day his Lordship came to Trym, where the Counsellers comming from Dublin met him, according to appointment. Heere they consulted of the publike affaires, more particularly how that part of the Army within Lemster, might be employed to prosecute Tirrel, sent by Tyrone to disturbe that Province, and yet to be ready upon any sudden occasion to make head against the forraigne enemie. And the advertisements being daily multiplied, that the Spaniards were at Sea, it was concluded, that in regard these forces were not able to answer both, or either the ends aforesaid, great part of the Army in Ulster should be drawne downe, and both forces joyned, should assayle Tirrel, who came to insult over the subjects, and to draw them to rebellion, but especially the late Submitties, whom by many promises and threatnings he had tempted to a relapse, but prevailed not with them. And his Lordship resolved, by his presence to give a sharper edge to this service, till either hee should be called, to affront the Spaniards landing, or to draw backe into the North, if they landed not.

Advertisements of the Spaniards.

The third of September his Lordship and the Counsell here wrote unto the Lords in England, excusing that the extraordinary expences had farre passed the limited sum of sixe thousand pound yeerely, which was farre too little, for the transportation of victuals, carriage of munition, charges and imprests to victualers, rewards to messengers, and for speciall services, making of boats, and things of like necessitie, and the repairing of Castles, Houses, Bridges, Forts, and all buildings. In which last charge, they had not been able fitly to repaire Athlone Castle, the Key of Connaght, nor the Castles and Bridges of Carlogh and Laughlin, and the Forts of Phillipstowne and Maryburgh, being of great consequence, to curbe the Traytors, and assure the subjects, and the decay whereof would give the rebels free passage into many Countries, besides our dishonour to neglect those places, which the wisedome of former times with great policie planted; the great charge of repairing whereof, appeared by the transmitted certificats of Commissioners appointed to view these places. And for these reasons they besought her Majesties warrant, to leave this charge to their discretion for a time, without any limitation, promising not to

Athlone Castle the Key of Connaght.

inlarge the same in any thing, which might be spared, without apparant prejudice to her service, and giving their opinion, that in this time of the new coine, these places might be repaired with small charge. Likewise they desired to have great store of munition and victuals sent over, and that presently, to prevent the usuall contrarietie of winds after Michaelmas, and all the Winter season. Lastly, they desired to have the one thousand shot presently sent over, for which they had formerly written; the Army consisting in great part of Irish, which could not be kept to live in Garrison out of their owne Countrie. And they advertised the Lords, that divers of the horse at twelve pence per diem had quit their pay, being not able to live thereupon in those deare times.

This third of September likewise his Lordship received letters from her Majestie, giving warrant for the pay of two thousand men sent into Mounster, being above the Establishment. The same day his Lordship received letters from Sir Robert Cecyll Secretarie, that the Spaniards were discovered neere the Silly, and as hee thought they would land at Lymrick, being fortie five sayle, whereof seventeene were men of warre, whereof sixe were Gallions, the rest of one hundred, or one hundred and fifty tunnes burthen, and had in them sixe thousand souldiers, praying his Lordship to demand such supplies as he thought needfull, and upon the Spaniards landing, to name the places whether the supplies should be sent, and assuring his Lordship that the two thousand men for Mounster were already imbarked.

The Spaniards discovered.

[II. ii. 129.]

The same time his Lordship received letters from the Lords in England, importing her Majesties acceptance of his service, with her willingnesse and theirs to send him needefull supplies, ,praying him to demand them timely, because hee could hardly receive them from England in sixe weekes after the demand, the wind standing favourable. Likewise professing that it is the fault of the Commissioners and Commissaries for victuals, if there be any want thereof, since the proportions required by them were arrived in Ireland; as likewise that the souldier made not some part of provision for victuals by mony (especially in parts neere the sea, and like places, where victuals were to be bought), since by these great provisions of victuals in England with sterling mony, her Majesty lost the third part of the profit she hoped to make by the new standard of Ireland, & which might be made, if vittels were provided by the souldier in Ireland, having full pay in that mixed mony. Also advertising, that her Majestie had sent for Ireland twenty lasts of Powder, with all munitions in proportion necessary, halfe by land, and (for sparing of carriage) halfe by Sea, praying that care might be had in issuing thereof, since they were informed, that great wast thereof had been formerly made, by the Irish bands, converting the Powder to their private gaine, and by the whole army, under pretence of her Majesties remittall of Powder spent in service (which had been defalked out of the souldiers pay, but was after held an hard course, to punish them for their good deserts), now charging upon her Majestie all wilfull and fraudulent consumptions of Powder. Further signifying, that Sir Henrie Dockwra his failing in correspondency with his Lordship this Summer, for want of match, was distastfull to them, had he not made amends by surprizing of Donnegall, which would facilitate the planting of Ballishannon. That her Majesty referred the garrison of Loughfoyle wholly to his Lordships direction, and the transposing any part thereof to the inabling of Sir Arthur Chichester at Knockfergus, the charge of that garrison being exceeding burthensome to her Majesty, by reason that Coast in Winter is so subject to stormes, and for that it was supplied with all provisions out of England bought with sterling money, and small quantity of the Irish mixed monies could be there issued to any such purpose, in which regard her Majesty wished that the Irish in those parts (in whose service no profit was found) should either be cast, and pensions of mixed monies given to the chiefe Lords, or at least should receive no victuals

Powder and munitions for Ireland.

out of the stoare, but have their full pay in that standard, to provide therewith for their Companies. Touching the expected landing of the Spaniards, their Lordships being of opinion that they would presently land in Mounster, advertised his Lordship, that two thousand men were imbarked for that Province, and two thousand more should be readie within twentie daies at the Sea-side, to come where his Lordship should direct them. Touching the exception above mentioned which his Lordship had taken, that part of the Officers for the Companies sent into Mounster were left to the Lord Presidents disposall, and all the rest were bestowed in England, their Lordships professed, that as in all circumstances of honour and contentment, they desired to respect his Lordship, so they praied him to consider, that it stood with the reputation of a Counsel of State, to conferre some such imploiments, and keepe men of quality at Court, to be upon all occasions used in her Majesties service, wherein notwithstanding they had preferred few or none, who had not his Lordships letters of recommendations to that Board, and now referred them all to bee continued or cassed at his pleasure. Lastly, whereas their Lordships were informed, that some were apprehended in Ireland for coining of the new mixed monies, they signified her Majesties pleasure, that those men should be executed, the rather to prevent the great inconvenience might arise, in maintaining the exchange for such counterfet monies, and otherwise.

Coiners to be executed.

[II. ii. 130.] The fourth of September his Lordship wrote from Trym to Sir Robert Cecyll the following letter.

SIR at my comming into these parts, I found them not so distempered as I was borne in hand I should, so as I make no doubt at all, but if the Spaniards doe not come, I shall be able to give her Majesty a good accompt of my charge here; and I am not out of hope, but rather of opinion, since they have staied so long, that they will not come this Winter, though I desire not to leade you into that conceit, nor omit not my selfe to provide for the worst may happen: and therefore have sent Master Marshall towards Leax, with almost a thousand foot and some horse, both to be neere the Lord President of Mounster, for what may fall out that way, and to prosecute Tyrrell in the meane while, who with some two hundred Rogues is gotten thither, and with the remaine of the Moores, Connors, and their followers, whom I could not cut off the last yeere, are altogether drawne to be above foure hundred. For Connaght, I have appointed Sir Oliver Lambert, with as many Companies as I can spare him, untill I may understand her Majesties further pleasure, because I know him to be very active, and find a necessity to imploy some forces that way, so long as the brute of the Spaniards comming doth continue; especially now, that Odonnell doth make his residence in that Province about Sligo, and might otherwise doe what hee list without impeachment. For my selfe, I thinke it fittest to stay hereabouts a while, for from hence I may aptly draw towards Mounster or Connaght as need requires, or fall backe towards the North, so soone as we can gather any certainty of the Spaniards not comming. And if we may be supplied with the 1000 shot, so earnestly desired by our former letters, (and without which, our foundation will be in a manner overthrowne), to strengthen the English Companies here, (I assure you) growne exceeding weak, (otherwise I would not put her Majesty to that charge); I make no doubt but we shall be able to doe her Majesty that service there this Winter, (those shot being landed at Carlingford or the Newry, with the victuals, munition, and other meanes desired), that the Spaniards shall not from thenceforth be able to get footing, to doe us any great annoyance, especially if it would please you to procure, for an addition to the rest two hundred shot to be sent for the supplying of Sir Arthur Chichester at Carickefergus: for from that place we have discovered such an entrance into the heart of Tyrone, as in all likelihood will soon ruine that

Connaght.

Arch-Traytor, if Sir Arthur may be enabled with meanes, as from me he shall not want what I can yeeld him. I have here inclosed sent a note, that you may see how the garrisons are planted North-wards, and who it is that commands in each of them, in the absence only of Sir Francis Stafford, for he hath the chiefe command over them, as the best meane to make them joine upon all occasions of the service.

2000. men arrived in Ireland.

The ninth of September his Lordship received advertisement from the Lord President, that the two thousand men embarked in England for Mounster, were arrived, part in Corkharbour, part at Waterford, of which companies some were left by the Lords of her Majesties Counsell, in their directions to his disposall, but he left them to his Lordships pleasure, knowing the duety he ought to his Generall. And whereas the Lords of the Counsell, in the same letters gave directions that the foot Companies of the Lord President and Earle of Thomond, being each 150, should be increased each to two hundred, the Lord President avowed that it was obtained by the said Earle, joyning him for countenance of the sute, altogether without his privity, which he praied his Lordship to beleeve: for since his Lordship had promised that favour to him upon the first occasion, he protested that he never had any thought to make so needlesse a request in England. Therewith hee sent his Lordship the list of the said Companies newly arrived, being one thousand foure hundred under foureteen Captaines named in England, one hundred for the increase of the Lord Presidents and Earle of Thomonds foot Companies, and five hundred which hee the Lord President, by vertue of the Lords letters, (the Lord Deputy pleasing to give his admission) assigned to five Captaines, being in all two thousand foot.

His Lordship having disposed the forces as is above [II ii. 131.] mentioned, and written from Trym to the Lord President, desiring him to meet him upon the borders of Lemster, meaning Kilkenny, as the fittest place for that meeting, tooke his journey thitherward, and arriving at Kilkenny the thirteenth of September, the same night received advertisement from the Lord President, that the Spaniards were met at Sea, bearing for Ireland, and therein (as he was informed) for Mounster, so that he craved pardon that hee came not to meete his Lordship, whose pleasure hee conceived to bee, that in this case hee should not be absent from those parts, where the enemies discent was expected; and he further prayed his Lordship so to fashion his affaires in Lemster and the North, as the forces he meant to bring might be in readinesse; withall protesting, that he staied only for a second direction, which if he received, he would come without delay to his Lordship.

The Spaniards met at Sea.

The next day his Lordship wrote the following letter to Sir Robert Cecyll her Majesties Secretarie.

SIr, having left the Northerne borders as well guarded, as in providence I could, the command wherof I left to Sir Joh. Barkeley, and having sent Sir Oliver Lambert into Connaght to settle those parts, & Sir Rich. Wingfeild the Marshal into Leax, to prosecute Tirrel with his adherence, I wrote to the President of Mounster to meete me about Kilkenny, if hee conveniently might, with a desire to establish a full correspondencie for the resistance of forraine forces, if they should arrive, or otherwise for making the warres in all parts this Winter, the rather because I know not how (for the present) Galloway, and consequently Asherawe (if it be planted) might be supplied of munition and some other provisions, but out of, and by Mounster: & further my being in those parts seeming to me of no small purpose, to devide the Birnes and Cavenaghs from holding intelligence, or joining with Tyrrel, & to nourish the overture I have lately entertained from O.M.S. the chiefe of the Moores, to bring me Tirrel alive or dead, which he desires should passe as a secret between only me, himself, and Omoloy, to whom he hath already given a pledge to performe it. Now that I

Sir Joh. Barkeley Commander in the North.

might not disinable any of the forces, I am come to Kilkenny onely accompanied with some threescore horse, without any one Commander or Captaine of the Army, having left them all with commandement to be resident on their charge. Onely when I came neere Master Marshall, I sent to conferre with him, being before accompanied with none of the Counsell, but onely Sir Robert Gardner chiefe Justice. As I entred into Kilkenny, I received intelligence from the Lord President of the Spaniards being at Sea, and returned his messenger, desiring him not to stirre from his charge, but to advertise me often of occurrents. My selfe purpose to returne presently to Carlogh (whether under the colour to prosecute Tirrel, I will draw as many of the forces, as I can, to imploy them in the meane time, and to be ready to answere such occasions as shall fall out in Mounster) that being (as things stand) the place best to give direction to all parts, and to assure the most dangerous. Now Sir, what I should desire to advise from hence, on so great a sudden, as I thinke it fit to make this dispatch, and in so great a matter, I am not very confident, but propound to your much better judgement what I thinke first and fittest to be thought of. That it may please the Lords to send over the two thousand men by their last letters signified to me to be at Chester, with all expedition, one thousand of them to Carlingford, the other to Dublin. These I intend to thrust into other companies, to make them full (if I can) to a man, whereby the Queene shall be served with all their bodies, and yet her Lyst no way increased, nor other charge but transportation. I desire so many at the least may be sent to Carlingford, because I am confident that it is the best counsell, whether the Spaniards land or no, to strengthen that part of the Armie, which will be able to assure the Pale that way, and to ruine the Northerne Rebels, in such sort, that it shall not be in the power of forraine force to make them live, and if the worst happen, they be therby inabled to come off to us, if we send for them, where now they cannot except

The Lord Deputy's purposes.

we fetch them. In generall, for such a warre you must send great Magazins of munition and victuals, and when you resolve how many men you will send, or have sent, the proportion will bee easily cast up by such Ministers as you have there in those kinds. The best place for the greatest quantity will be Dublin; for from thence we may finde meanes to transport what other places shall have neede of, except the warre be in Connaght, for then onely from Lymrick and Galloway all our provisions must come, and in Connaght I chiefly expect the Spaniards first discent, yet there with most difficulty can front them with any warre before Galloway, or Athlone (from Lymricke) be throughly supplied with provisions. If forraigne force doe not arrive, these provisions will not be lost; for this Winter Odonnell must be forced out of Connaght, or else he will get there what he hath lost in Tyrconnell, and so, this Winter we must doe our endevour to doe the like in Ulster, to ruine Tyrone, which is a worke of no small difficulty, but of so great consequence, that I am perswaded it would not onely turne the professions of this people, but even their hearts to her Majesties obedience, for such as love Tyrone, will quit their affections, when the hope of his fortune failes, and such as doe not, their dependancy on him will fall, when their feare of his greatnes shall be taken away: for beleeve me Sir, I observe in most (if I be not much deceived) of the Irish reclaimed Lords, great desire to continue Subjects, if they might once see apparance of defence, though perchance not so much out of their honest dispositions, as the smart they yet feele of a bitter prosecution. If you heare that forraigne powers in any great numbers are arrived, you must resolve to send at the least 200 Horse out of England, and two thousand men more well armed, for you must beleeve Sir, that then it will not be the warre of Ireland, but the warre of England made in Ireland. If we beat them, both Kingdomes will be quiet, if not, even the best in more danger then I hope ever to live to see. If you provide us more men when

Great Magazins of munition required.

[II. ii. 132.]

Odonnell to be forced out of Connaght.

wee send you word that the Spaniards are landed, wee will write whether we desire they should be sent. Howsoever, I presume her Majesty shall not repent the putting over so many men hither; for we hope to ease the charge in the shortnesse of the worke: If this aide arrive not here, and if any forraigne force arrive in England, (the which we gather by some intelligence may be), then if you send hither new men to assure places fit to bee kept, we may bring you over old souldiers & Captaines, two or three thousand; which I wil undertake shal strike as good blowes as ten thousand ordinary men. I have made some of the subjects lately reclaimed, and in these times suspected, put themselves in blood already, since my comming hither; for even now I heare my Lord Mountgarrets sonnes have killed some of the Clancheeres, and some of Tyrrels followers, since I contested with their Father, about somewhat I had heard suspicious of them. Sir I will againe advertise you of our affaires here very shortly, and desire you now to pardon my hast. From Kilkenny this foureteenth of September 1601.

Your most assured friend to
doe you service,
Mountjoy.

His Lordship returned from Kilkenny to Carlogh, where he disposed the forces to answere the service in those parts of Lemster. Thence he wrote to the Lord President to meet him some time at Kilkenny, if possibly he could: And within few daies hearing that the Lord President having left Sir Charles Wilmot with the forces at Corke, was on his journey towards him, his Lordship parted from Carlogh, and the nineteenth of September met him at Laughlin, whence they rode together to Kilkenny.

Before I proceed further, I will briefly adde the affaires

Mounster. of Mounster till this time, collected out of the Lord Presidents letters. The setling of peace in the yeere 1600. was interrupted by the allarum of a Spanish invasion generally given in the beginning of this yeere

1601. And in the moneth of Aprill the Mounster Rebels which fledde the last yeere into Connaght and Ulster, attempted againe to returne into Mounster, having beene strengthened by Tyrone; but the Lord President sent Captaine Flower with one thousand foote to the confines, and these forces of Mounster on the one side, and Sir John Barkeley with the Connaght Forces on the other side, so persued them, as the same moneth they were forced to breake and returne into Ulster. Florence mac [II. ii. 133.] Carty notwithstanding his protection, had procured the sending of the said Rebels out of the North, and besides many rebellious practices, about this time laded a Barke with hides, which should bring him munition from forraigne parts. The Lord President ceased not to lay continuall plots to apprehend the titulary Earle of Desmond, & having often driven him out of his lurking dennes, (in which service the Lord Barry having a Company in her Majesties pay, did noble endevours,) at last the Lord President understanding that he lurked in the white Knights Countrey, his Lordship did so exasperate him with feare of his owne danger, as in the moneth of May he tooke him prisoner and brought him to Corke, where hee was condemed for treason, to intitle the Queene in his lands, and for a time kept prisoner there.

The titulary Earle of Desmond taken prisoner.

In the moneth of June the Lord President received this gracious letter from the Queene, written with her owne hand.

Letter from the Queene.

MY faithfull George. If ever more service of worth were performed in shorter space then you have done, we are deceived among many eye witnesses: we have received the fruit thereof, and bid you faithfully credit, that what so wit, courage, or care may do, we truly find, they have all been throughly acted in all your charge. And for the same beleeve, that it shall neither be unremembred, nor unrewarded, and in meane while beleeve, my helpe nor prayers shall never faile you.

Your Soveraigne that best
regards you, E. R.

The Lord President's Advertisements.

In the beginning of July the Lord President advertised the Lord Deputy, that according to his directions hee would presently send into Connaght 1000 foot and fifty horse of the Mounster list, though upon good and fresh intelligences, the arrivall of Spaniards was daily expected in that Province, and the forces remaining with him, were not sufficient to guard Kinsale, Waterford, Yoghall, Killmalloch, Lymricke, and Cork, (the last whereof according to his Lordships directions, he would have care specially to strengthen). That he had given the chiefe leader of the said forces Sir Fran. Barkely direction to returne to him upon his letter, if her Majesties service in his opinion should require it, praying the Lord Deputy to allow of this direction, since hee meant not to recall them, but upon sudden revolt of the Provincials or arrivall of Spaniards. That the Prisoner usurping the title of Earle of Desmond, and many other evidences made manifest, that the rebels of Ulster, and especially the Spaniards, did most relie upon the helpe of the said prisoner, & Florence mac Carty, which Florence though protected had assured them of his best aide, and had prevailed in a Councell held in Ulster, that the Spaniards should land at or neere Cork. And that hereupon he the Lord President had apprehended Florence, and sent him together with the said Earle Prisoner into England, where they were safe in the Tower, which being in time knowne to the Spaniards, might perhaps divert their invasion of Ireland. And no doubt the laying hand on these two Archrebels, much advanced her Majesties service in the following invasion, whereby the Lord President deservedly wonne great reputation. Thus much I have briefly noted to the time above mentioned, when the Lord Deputy wrote to the Lord President to meet him on the confines of Mounster.

Florence mac Carty sent Prisoner into England.

The landing of the Spaniards.

They meeting (as I said) at Laughlin, rode together to Kilkenny, where the twenty day of September they sate in Counsell with the Earle of Ormond, and the rest of the Counsel with purpose, so soone as they had resolved of the meetest course for the present service, to returne to their severall places of charge. But the same day newes came by post, (for Postes were newly established for the same purpose) that a Spanish Fleet was discovered neere the old head of Kinsale, whereupon they determined to stay there all the next day, to have more certain advertisement therof. The three & twentith day another Post came from Sir Charles Willmot, advertising the Spanish Fleete to be come into the harbour of Kinsale, and it was agreed in Counsell, that the Lord President should returne to Corke, and the Lord Deputy for countenancing of the service in Mounster, should draw to Clommell, and gather such forces as hee could presently, to draw to Kinsale, nothing doubting but that this forwardnesse (howsoever otherwise the Army, neither for numbers of men, nor sufficiency of provision, was fit to undertake such a taske) would both cover their many defects from being spied by the Country, and for a while, at the least stop the currant of that generall defection of the Irish, which was vehemently feared. This was resolved in Counsell, after the Lord President had given them comfort to find victuals and munition at Corke: for at first they were not so much troubled to draw the forces thither, as suddenly to bring victuals and munition thither for them. But when they understood, that his Lordship had fed the souldiers all Summer by cesse, and preserved her Majesties store of victuals which they thought to be wasted, they were exceeding joyfull of this newes, and not without just desert, highly commended the Lord Presidents provident wisdome, in the said most important service to the State.

The Spanish Fleete in the harbour of Kinsale.

[II. ii. 134.]

The same day they wrote these letters to the Lords in England.

IT may please your Lordship: The Spanish Fleete so long expected by the Rebels here, is now in the harbour of Kinsale or Corke, as it may appeare unto your Lordships for a certainty, by the copies of these inclosed

Letters to the Lords in England.

letters, from Sir Charles Wilmott, and the Major of Corke, which is as much newes as we have yet received, so as we can not judge, whether this be the whole Fleete set out of Spaine, or whether part thereof is comming after to them, or bound for any other harbour, onely we have some reason to thinke (the weather falling out of late exceeding stormy and tempestious) that all the ships could very hardly keepe together, and the report was, the whole number were at least seventie. We are now to be earnest sutors to your Lordships, to supply us with all things needefull for so weighty an action, and so speedily as possibly it may be. The two thousand foote already (as we conceive) at Chester, we now desire may presently be sent to Waterford (and neither to Carlingford nor Dublin, as I the Deputie thought fittest in my last dispatch, when I meant to have used them in the North), two thousand more at the least had neede come soone after unto Corke, if it be not invested before their comming, but if it bee, their landing must then be at Waterford or Yoghall, and with them three hundred horse will be as few, as we conceive wee have reason to demand, and therefore expect both the one and the other so soone as may be, also munition and victuall must be sent for ten thousand men, to come likewise to Waterford (unlesse your Lordships heare from us to the contrary), for if in those two kinds we be not royally supplied, men and mony will serve us to little purpose, with all which we recommend to your Lordships consideration, whether it were not fit to send some part of her Majesties Navy to lie upon this coast, aswel to assure the passage by Sea, as to attempt something upon the Spanish shipping. Thus having briefly set downe our requests, as sparingly as we may do, the danger considered, we think it not impertinent to acquaint your Lordships with the cause of our meeting here, and purposes. We thought fit upon the expectation of these forraine forces, before we held it of any certaintie, to conferre with the Lord President of Mounster, and to consult upon the generall disposall

Requests for supplies.

of the forces of this Kingdome, how to make the warre upon their arrivall, which we could hardly doe, without being thorowly informed by him, of the state of that Province, and what meanes of victuall, munition, and other provisions we should finde there, if we should draw the army thither, or from thence were driven to make the warre in Connaght, where wee found it would bee of exceeding great difficulty, unlesse wee might have good helpes out of Mounster. For this purpose meeting at this place upon Munday the one and twentieth of this present, the next day while wee were in consultation, came the first of these letters from the Maior of Corke, assuring us of the discovery of the Fleete neere the old head of Kinsale, but whether friends or enemies he then knew not, but that being made certaine by the rest of the letters that came since, we presently grew to this resolution, that the President should returne with all speede possible, though before hee left the Province, hee tooke order to the uttermost that could bee done in providence, aswell to settle the same, as to defend all places likeliest to be invaded; and we concluded, that I the Deputy should draw forward, as farre as Clommell, to be neere the chiefest brunt of the warre, and upon the present apprehension of all things there, to give directions to the rest of the Kingdome, and yet to omit no occasions against the invasion, whilest the Marshal drew up as many of the forces to me, as he can with best conveniency and expedition. For since the two thousand supposed to be at Chester, came not to Carlingford and Dublyn, in time to supply the Companies Northward, that they might have gone on with their prosecution, we have now resolved to leave no more in those parts, then are sufficient to keepe the garrison places, because wee hold it to bee to no purpose, untill her Majesty send hither greater forces, though we are still of opinion, it were the best course to proceed there, if her Majesty would be pleased to enable us, for otherwise it cannot be looked for, but that we shal go backward greatly in

[II. ii. 135.] *Dispositions of the Forces.*

this busines. Thus being confident your L^ps^. will be carefull of us, we take this to be sufficient uppon this sudden, since what is any way necessary or fit for us, is to your Lordships in your wisdome and experience best knowne, and so we doe most humbly take leave, with this assurance, that we will leave nothing unperformed, that may give true testimony to the World, that we value our duty to our most gracious Soveraigne, and tender the preservation of this her Kingdome, committed to our charge (as we know we ought) before our lives and livings, and doubt not but to give her Majesty a very good account of all our doings. From Kilkenny this three and twenty of September, 1601.

Your Lordships most humbly to command, &c.
signed by the Lord Deputy and Councell.

The foure and twentith day, his Lordship wrote this following letter to Master Secretary.

SIR I did ever thinke, that if any forraigne force should arrive, it would be doubtfull for me to lay my finger on any sound part of all this Kingdome, which if our supplies had come in time, to have left the Northerne garrisons strong, we might in some good sort have provided for, but now my resolution is this, to bend my selfe as suddenly as I can against these forraigne forces. If wee beat them, let it not trouble you, though you heare all Ireland doth revolt, for (by the grace of God) you shall have them all returne presently with halters about their neckes: if we doe not, all providence bestowed on any other place is vaine. Till I know more particularly in how many places they have made their discent, I cannot write much; but for the present I apprehend a world of difficulties, with as much comfort as ever poore man did, because I have now a faire occasion to shew how prodigall I will be of my life, in any adventure that I shall finde to be for the service of my deere Mistresse, unto whom I am confident God hath given me life to doe acceptable service, which when I have done, I will sing

The Lord Deputy's resolution.

Nunc dimittis. This day I expect to receive light and further ground to write more at large, and being now ready with the President to take Horse, whose fortune & mine shall now be one, I leave you to Gods continuall blessings, in hast. Kilkenny the foure and twenty of September 1601.

Master Marshall dispatched into the Pale.

The same day Master Marshall was dispatched into the Pale, to draw the Companies thereabouts towards Mounster, and to procure from the Councell at Dublyn all things necessary for that businesse. Sir Henry Davers was sent for the Companies about Armagh, and Sir John Barkeley had direction to bring other Companies that were laid about the Navan. And the L. Deputy the same night rode to Kiltenan, a Castle and dwelling of the Lord of Dunboyne, being a great daies journey, where he was assured that the Spaniards were landed and entered into Kinsale. The five and twenty his Lordship rode to Clommell, where Sir Nicholas Walsh, one of the Councell, came to him, and there it was resolved, his Lordship should goe on to Corke, and so to proceed as there should be cause. The six and twentieth his Lord[p]. rode to Glonowre, the Lord Roches Castle. The seven and twentieth his Lordship rode from Glonowre to Corke, accompanied with the Lord President, Sir Robert Gardener, and Sir Nicholas Walsh, Counsellors.

[II. ii. 136.]

The Spaniards commanded by Don Jean de l' Aguyla.

The eight and twenty day his Lordship was advertised by a Scot comming from Lisbone, that the Spaniards sent to Kinsale, were sixe thousand in number, commanded by Don Jean de l' Aguyla, who had beene generall in Britaine, that one thousand of them scattered by tempest, were since arrived at Baltemore. That they were directed to Kinsale, with promise of great succours by the pretended Earle of Desmond, lately taken and sent into England, and by Florence mac Carty, whom the Lord President upon suspition had lately taken, and in like sort sent prisoner into England. That the Spaniards gave out, that assoone as they could have horses from Tyrone, and other Irish rebels, in which hope they had brought foure hundred, (or as after was credibly advertised 1600 saddles), they would keepe the field, and therefore would not fortifie at Kinsale, and that upon the revolt of this Countrey, the King of Spaine meant from these parts to invade England.

1600. saddles brought by the Spaniards.

Whereupon the same eight and twenty day the Lord Deputy resolved in Counsell, that letters should bee written into England, that it was given out, the Spaniards in Mounster were sixe thousand, and that of certaine they were five thousand commanded by Don Jean del' Aguila, whereof three thousand were arrived in Kinsale, and the Vice-Admirall Siriago, (for Don Diego de Brastino, was Admirall of the Fleet), with foure other ships scattered by tempest, were arrived at Baltemore. That no Irish of account repaired to them, excepting some dependants of Florence mac Carty, (of whose imprisonment the Spaniards had not heard before their landing), who was the perswader of their comming to that Port. That to keepe Rebels from joining with them, it behoved us presently to keepe the field. That it was requisite to send some of the Queenes ships, who might prevent their supplies, and give safety to our supplies, both out of England and from Coast to Coast, and might bring us to Corke Artillery for battery, with munition and victuals. Likewise to write presently for three hundred Northerne horse, and for the two thousand foot at Chester, and two thousand more. To write for sixe peeces of battery, the biggest to be Demy Cannon for the field, with carriages and bullets. To certifie the Lords that Artillery could not be brought from Dublyn, because the Irish ships had not masts and tackle strong enough to take them in and out, (besides that, Easterly and Northerly winds onely serving to bring them, were rare at this season of the yeere;) and that the greatest Peeces in Mounster lay unmounted on the ground. And lastly, to write for powder for five thousand shot, and for sixe Peeces of Battery, (which must be some sixty last), and for fifty tunne of lead, with like quantity of match, and five thousand Pyoners tooles.

Queenes ships desired.

Cannon for the field.

Peeces of Battery.

The same day his Lordship was by letters advertised, that a Frier in a Souldiers habit, was dispatched from Kinsale the foure & twenty of September, and passed through Clommell, naming himselfe James Flemming, and from thence went to Waterford, where hee aboad few dayes, and named himselfe Richard Galloway. That he had Buls from the Pope, with large indulgences to those, who should aide the Spaniards, (sent by the Catholike King to give the Irish liberty from the English tyranny, and the exercise of the true olde Apostolike Roman Religion), and had authority to excommunicate those that should by letters, by plots, or in person joyne with her Majesty, (whom the Pope had excommunicated, and thereby absolved all her Subjects from their oath of alleagiance). That every generall Vicar in each Diocesse, had charge to keep this secret till the Lord Deputy was passed to Corke, when he assured them, his Lordship should either in a generall defection not be able to understand these proceedings, or hearing thereof should be so imploied, as he should have no leisure to prevent them. That he gave out, the Spaniards at Kinsale were 10000, besides 2000 dispersed by tempest, which were landed at Baltimore, having treasure, munition, and victuals for two yeers. And that Tyrone would presently come up to assist them at Kinsale, and to furnish them with horses, which they onely expected from him, and had brought saddles and furniture for them. Lastly, advice therein was given to his Lordship to write to the corporate Townes and chiefe Lords, not to beleeve these fabulous reports, but to take advice (not given out for feare of their defection, but onely for their good) to continue loyall subjects.

Buls from the Pope.

Spanish lies.

The nine and twentieth his Lordship with the Lord President and the above named Counsellors, tooke some horse for guard, and rode to view the Towne and harbour of Kinsaile, and the Spaniards Fleete, that upon that view, they might resolve of the fittest place for our Campe to sit downe by them. They [II. ii. 137.]

found the Spaniards possessed of the Towne, and the greatest part of their shipping to have put to Sea for Spaine, (for of thirty foure ships arriving there, only twelve now remained in the Harbour, some of the other being lately put out, and then seene under sayle), so as they saw there was no more to be done, till our forces should be arrived out of the North and Lemster, and we inabled from England to keepe our selves from breaking, after we should take the field.

Letters to the Lords in England.

The first of October his Lordship and the Counsell here, wrote to the Lords in England, according to the project resolved on the eight and twentieth of September. Further beseeching their Lordships to pardon their earnest writing for munition and victuals, though great proportions of them were already sent, and that in respect the magazines formerly appointed for the best, when the place of the Spaniards discent was unknowne, were so farre divided, as we could not without great difficulties make use of them in these parts, and at this time, when for the present the Spaniard was Master of the Sea, and the Queenes forces being drawne towards Kinsaile, the rebels might easily intercept them by land, but especially for that great use might be made of those provisions in the very places where now they were, if Tirone come into Mounster with his forces, as no doubt he would, namely, the magazin at Lymricke would serve excellently for the prosecution formerly intended, and after to be made in Connaght, though by sea or land they could not be brought to Corke, without great difficulties and dangers. Adding that for the present, the Lord Deputie was forced to draw most of the forces of the North into Mounster, leaving onely the Fortes guarded, and so the Pale was not able to defend it selfe against Tyrone, whereas he hoped to have been enabled both to continue the prosecution in the North, and also to besiege the Spaniards at one and the same time, whereof yet hee did not altogether despaire, so as their Lordships would speedily furnish such things, as were earnestly desired by them

Onely the Fortes guarded in the North.

for the good of the service, being confidently of opinion, that the only way to make a speedy end of the rebellion, and as quicke a dispatch of the Spaniards out of Ireland, was to make the warre roundly both in the North, and in Mounster at one time. Also advertising that the Spaniards (as they for certaine heard) brought with them not onely sixteene hundred Saddles, upon the Rebels promise of horse, but also great store of Armes for the common people, upon hope they had given them of their generall revolt; and humbly praying their Lordships, that in regard our greatest strength and advantage consisted in our horses, they would cause a thousand quarters of Oates to be speedily sent for Corke, without which store, our horses were like to starve within a short time, and in case they approved the prosecution in the North to bee continued without intermission, then they would bee pleased to send the like quantitie of Oates to be kept in store at Carlingford. Lastly, praying their Lordships to send hether a Master-Gunner, with sixe Canoniers.

Oates wanted for the horses.

The second of October, his Lordship wrote this following letter to Master Secretarie.

The Lord Deputy's letter to Master Secretarie.

SIr I doe thinke we shall finde these forces out of Spaine to be above foure thousand, aboundantly provided with Munition, Artillery, and Armes (besides their own use) to arme the Countrie people, great store of treasure, and of all victuals but flesh. All the Chiefes that are in rebellion, and all the loose sword-men, will presently take their parts. The Lords that we have reclaimed, if we doe not defend them from Tirone, must and will returne unto him. Upon the first good countenance the Spanish army shall make, I feare me, many will declare themselves for them, but upon the first blow we shall receive (from the which I hope God will preserve us), I doubt there would fall out a generall revolt. The Commander of the Spanish Army is one of the greatest Souldiers the King of Spaine hath, the Captaines under him are most ancient men, their Bands, some out of Italy, some from the

[II. ii. 138.]

The Spaniards good Souldiers.

Terceraes, and few Bisonioes. They are specially well armed, all their shot (as I heard) muskets, they have brought sixteene hundred saddles, and Armes for horsemen, of light shot, whereof they make account to be provided in Ireland, and so may they be, as well as in any part of Christendome, and likewise to have horses for their saddles, but therein I thinke they will be deceived. There are not yet come unto us any other forces, but such as onely I found in this Province. Upon the arrivall of the first troopes (which I looke for howerly) we shall send you word of some good blowes that will passe betweene us, for I meane to dwell close by them (by the grace of God) to put them to it. Sir, the King of Spaine hath now begun to invade her Majesties Kingdomes, if only to put Ireland in generall commotion, he hath chosen the worst place, if to doe that, and to lay a sudden foundation for the warre of England, the best: if he hath beene deceived in any expectation here, the State of Spaine must now make good the errour, and doubtlesse is ingaged to supplie all defects. The commodity that is offered unto her Majesty is, that shee may sooner prevent then Spaine provide: Now as her Majesties faithfull workeman, I am bold to propound in my own taske, that it may please her to send presently good part of her royall Fleete, and with them such provisions for battery as we did write for, and at the least so many horse and foote as by our letter we have sued for, with victuals and munitions in aboundance for them. It will be fit that this Winter there be a sharpe warre made in Ulster, which will keepe the Spaniard from any important succour, and ruine for ever the Traitors, if the warre be well followed. If it be made by the severall Governours, the effect will not be so great: if you will have it performed thorowly, you must make one Governour of all Ulster, and the fittest man that can bee chosen in England or Ireland is Sir Arthur Chichester. If you resolve on that course, from him you must continually receive his demands, onely of the three hundred horse

The Lord Deputy's desire.

wee did write for, it were good he had sent him out of the North one hundred. For foot, if you send him out of England to supply the Companies at Loughfoyle and Knockefergus, above our proportion, it will be much better: for Armagh and those parts shall receive from us. This course I hope will soone make an end of the warre in Ireland, of Spaine in Ireland, and perchance of Spaine for a long time with England. I doubt not but you will conceive this action to bee of no lesse importance then it is. What goodly Havens are in these parts for shipping, how many fighting men of the Irish may be from hence by the King of Spaine carried for an invasion of England; (the want of which two kinds hath beene his chiefe impediment hitherto) you well know. Beleeve Sir, out of my experience here, if the King of Spaine should prevaile in Ireland, he may carry above ten thousand men from hence, that joined with his Army, will be of more use for the invasion of England, then any that can be chosen out of any part of Christendome. And now Sir, that you know (as I hope) the worst, I cannot dissemble how confident I am, to beate these Spanish Dons, as well as ever I did our Irish Macks and Oes, and to make a perfect conclusion of the warre of Ireland as soone, as if this interruption had never happened, if wee have Gods blessing and the Queenes, and those ordinary meanes without the which none but infinite powers can worke. I beseech the eternall God preserve her Majesty and her Kingdomes, and send me the happinesse to kisse her royall hands, with the conscience of having done her the service I desire. And so Sir I doe wish you all happinesse, and will be ever

10000. *Irish to invade England.*

Yours Sir most assured to doe
you service, Mountjoy.

From Corke the 2 of
October 1601.

The same day his Lordship wrote another letter to Master Secretary as followeth.

Letter to Master Secretary.

SIR here are divers worthy men very fit to have charge, who have followed the wars here as voluntaries to their very great expence, & look now by my meanes to have command upon the comming over of the next Companies, [II. ii. 139.] if you send more then serve only for supplies. I have no meanes to keep them from going thither, to use the helpe of their friends and get them Companies there, but by promising them any thing that I can doe for them here, for by that course I conceive I ease you of that trouble, which their importunate sutes would breede you, and hold them here ready for any service upon the sudden, thinking it no pollicy at this time to spare any, that may give furtherance to the great worke we have in hand. If it will please you to doe me that favour, to procure that the Companies to come over, may be appointed Captaines of my nomination, I shall be able to satisfie those Gentlemens expectations, who I am perswaded will be fitter for this imployment then any that can be sent from thence, and they finding their advancement here, where they are to be tied to their taske, will (in my judgement) endeavour to deserve the best, being in the eye of him that was the meanes thereof, which for the service sake chiefly I affect, though I can be content Sir to acknowledge unto you, that I would gladly have the World see, that I am no lesse graced in my imployments then my Predecessours have beene; for this people doe not little observe it, and at this present especially I hold it a matter of that consequence, as without it, I shall be the lesse able to weeld this great businesse, with that successe that otherwise I am hopefull of: We have not here any of the Queenes Pinnisses, whereof at this time there is great want. At my comming out of the North, although the Rebels in generall did give out, that they were out of hope of forraigne succours this yeere, (I thinke in policy, and to make us slow to call for supplies), yet Tyrlogh mac Henry did assure me upon his life, that the Spaniards would come, and further told me that one Bathe Agent for Tyrone in Spaine, and since returned to him, was sent into Scotland, whence he was presently to returne: Whereupon I delivered a description of the man to Captaine Button, and willed him to lie upon the Coasts to apprehend him, assuring my selfe that I should have wrested out of him the certainty of all things. Since that time I have heard nothing of that Captaine, nor of the Queenes Pinnis under his command. I pray you Sir let us have some of the Queenes shippes with expedition, for without them we shall not be able to convay any thing upon this Coast from place to place, and the waies by land will be dangerous. So Sir I wish you all happinesse.

The third of October, his Lordship and the Counsell here wrote to the Lords in England this following letter.

Letter to the Lords in England.

IT may please your Lordships. Having seriously considered of the great worke we have now in hand, wee observe that besides the forraigne enemy the Spaniard with whom wee are first to deale, and the knowne Traitors and Rebels already in armes, there are two other sorts of people here, which if wee doe not carefully provide for, they will soone adheare unto the rest, and make their party so strong, as in judgement wee cannot see how we shall be well able to encounter it, unlesse by good providence it be prevented, which is the marke we aime at. The one of these two sorts is the subject, who hath lands and goods to take to, for whom wee must provide defence, else with his livelyhood wee are sure to loose him, and therefore wee will omit nothing that our meanes will stretch to, that may preserve, cherish, and content him. The other sort are such as have no living, nor any thing that will afford them maintenance, and yet hitherto have not shewed themselves disloyall, though all of them bee Swordmen, and many Gentlemen by discent, and are able to draw after them many followers. To this sort wee heare for certaine, the Spaniards make offer of great entertainement, and if wee should not in some sort doe the like, wee cannot in reason looke but they must and will fall to their partie. Wee have therefore out of this necessitie resolved, to take as many of them into her Majesties intertainement, as wee have any hope will truly sticke unto us, being confident that wee shall make good use of them against the Spaniard; for wee meane thorowly to put them to it, though if wee should faile in our expectation, and finde them cold or slacke in serving with us, yet will it bee a great counten-[II ii. 140.] ance to the service to shew the persons of so many men on our side, where otherwise they would have been against us: and of this we can assure your Lordships, that when they have served our turne against the Spaniards, untill wee have freed our selves of them, we can without danger ease her Majestie of that charge, and wil no longer hold them in entertainement. In the meane time they shall spend little of the Queenes victuall, but being paid of the new coine, provide for themselves, which may bee with lesse oppression to the Countrie, then if in that sort they were not entertained, for then they would spoile all, and put out such as otherwise will continue in subjection. Of this course of ours, we humbly desire your Lordships approbation (though wee will be very sparing to entertaine more then shall be necessary) and warrant to Master Treasurer to make them paiment, and hold us we beseech you excused for resolving it, before we acquainted your Lordships therewithall, seeing we were enforced thereunto by necessitie for the service sake (since many of them were active, and would otherwise have served the enemie), and wee could not sooner write unto your Lordships of it, and even so, &c.

Companies drawne to Corke.

The same day Sir Benjamin Berry came to Corke with his Lordships Guard which he commanded, and with some other Companies (for till this time his Lordship had no part of the Army with him, but only the Bands of the Mounster Lyst.) The ninth day the Companies came to Corke, which Sir Richard Wingfield the Marshall had drawne out of the Pale, and Sir John Barkeley Serjeant Major had drawne from the frontiers of Lemster and

Connaght. The tenth day being Saturday, the Companies came to Corke, which Sir Henrie Davers had drawne from Armagh and the Northerne Garrisons. And this day Sir Richard Wingfield Marshall, and Sir John Barkeley Serjeant Major, were sent with some horse and foote, to view and chuse a fit ground neere Kinsale, where our Army might sit downe to besiege the Towne. The next day some horse and foote were sent out to keepe the Irish from selling victuals to the Spaniards. The twelfth two French men ran from the Spaniards to us, who confessed that three thousand Spaniards landed at the first in Kinsale, beside sixe hundred since arrived in a great ship scattered from them by a tempest.

An advertisement of the Spaniards.

This day one advertised his Lordship, that under pretence of favouring the Spaniards discent, he had spoken with their General; who inquired whether the L. Deputie in person came to view Kinsale, and with what numbers, to which he answered, that he was there in person with foure hundred foote lodged not farre off out of sight, and foure troopes of horse. That he asked what souldiers the Lord Deputy had, to which he answered some eight thousand, besides the daily arrivall of others of the Army in Lemster and the North: what souldiers were new, and what weapons they had, and what artillery the Lord Deputy had, to which hee answered with addition to our strength. He said that the Generall presumed by the contrary winds, that they in England heard not of his arrivall, and though hee told him the English Fleete was at Plymoth, he seemed not to beleeve it, and made countenance, that they should have enough to doe, to defend the English coast from invasion, and much insisted upon the copper money the Queene sent, with purpose to make the Irish her slaves: but promised gold and silver from his Master. That he inquired of Tyrone and Odonnel, seeming to distaste their being so farre off, and the way to them being dangerous, and his owne want of horses, and therefore prayed this Gentleman to certifie Tirrell and the Lord of Leytrim, that hee expected

Tyrone with horses and beeves, which hee praied them to supply in the meane time, both sending him notice before they came, adding that himselfe had Bread, Rice, Pease, and Wine for eighteene moneths, and store of treasure. And that he inquired much after the strength of Corke, and the Queenes new Fort there. Lastly, he advertised, that the ships returned were foureteene (of them six the Kings owne of one thousand tun the least, in which was the Admirall Generall, Saint Iago, and the great Admirall of Castill, Don Diego de Bruxero.) That the twelve remaining were smaller, and embarged (or arested) to serve the King, whereof some were Irish. That the ships at Baltemore had 700 men. That by his view, these were 3000 in Kinsale royally provided of all provisions for war, having many saddles for horses; and that upon Tyrones expected comming, they intended to take the field.

Ships returned to Spain.

[II. ii. 141.]

The thirteenth it was resolved we should presently take the field, though wee had not as yet any provisions fit for that purpose, but that day and the two dayes following we could not stirre from Corke, by reason of extreame raine and foule weather. Neither artillery, munition nor victuals were yet come from Dublin, yet it was thought fitter thus unprovided to take the field, then by discovery of our wants to give the Irish opportunitie and courage to joyne with the Spaniard.

END OF VOLUME II.

19 07
UNIVERSITY·PRESS
ROBERT·MACLEHOSE·&·Cº
JAMES·J·MACLEHOSE·&·Cº
GLASGOW

Lightning Source UK Ltd.
Milton Keynes UK
UKHW011335100219
336964UK00010B/814/P

9 781331 280583